MIL

GLORY VI

JUSTICE *OF* *AFFLICTION*

A novel about the earth's last days.

WENDIE L. EDWARDS

Cover and book design

Ronn Raymond © 2007

Published by Seventh Seal Publishing, Inc.

Cedar Hills, Utah

This is a work of fiction. The characters, names, incidents, places, and dialogue are products of the author's imagination, and are to be construed theoretical.

Library of Congress Catalog Card Number: 2007906082

ISBN-10: 0-9712228-7-8

ISBN-13: 978-0-9712228-7-8

First Printing 2007

First Edition

Printed in the United States of America

INDEBTEDNESS

I am deeply indebted to a great team of readers and editors that have joined my writing projects. It is through them that this work is allowed to progress as it is. Kathryn, Rosanna, David, Grace, Courtney, Melynda, Bonnie, Amy, Ric, Jerry, and Kate. All of you are gifted and bless my life! Thank you from the bottom of my heart!!! XOXO

FOLLOW THE PROPHET

I have been asked the question, "Why isn't the Prophet a central character in your books?" This is a very good question. I often refer to the living prophet as well as past prophets in the endnotes as well as in the dialogue with utmost respect. I hope all can recognize that the characters in the book strive to follow the Prophet as well as the Lord, Jesus Christ.

We are told that in the last days, the Spirit will be poured out upon all flesh and our sons and daughters will prophesy and our young men shall see visions as the old men shall dream dreams. Even all God's servants, both men and women, we are told in Acts 2 and Joel 2, will prophesy, and this because we will become an intensely spiritual people, all seeking the face of the Lord. But even in these times, I know we will seek out the words of the prophet and be led by God's chosen vessel.

My challenge in writing this series is that I don't know the words the Prophet will speak to us in the future, nor do I want to be so presumptuous to guess the mind of the Lord. What I can and do is stay one level removed and expound upon the scriptures and the prophetic statements already given in a bounteous amount, and do it through the eyes and hearts of simple people like you and I.

Because the Lord is the same yesterday, today, and forever, the value of the words within these books comes not from what I can conjure up, but how I can relate the words of God to those who read. By using the scriptures as a backbone, I can explore the future safely, knowing all the knowledge presented has been revealed by our Creator and feeling confident in its application.

I love the Prophet and he is central to my beliefs. In the days to come I know that he will lead us in the ways we need to go, giving light in days of darkness. May we seek and treasure all the words that come out of his mouth!

The Millennial Glory Series

Hidden Light, Millennial Glory I

A strange plague breaks out among a rebellious segment of society. The sickness is related to a mysterious man who claims that he is the resurrected Savior of the world. His intent is to hide the light of the truth as he stands in its stead. His words are hypnotic. His message is deadly. Corrynne Rogers is an Intensive Care nurse who cares for the dying. Through her hospital association she uncovers a destructive plan to implant computer chips under the skin in any who worship the false Christ in an effort to control them. Some followers are killed by a flesh-eating bacteria as they turn away from the religious leader. Eventually, Corrynne exposes the deadly plan but not in time to protect one of her own from the lethal chip. The Zulu countdown has begun. Fire is prophesied to rain from heaven to punish those who refuse to accept the false Christ. But will it? Time will tell.

Wars of Light, Millennial Glory II

Bo, the father of the Rogers family, learns that he and his eldest son, Braun, share a gift of dreams and are able to see mysterious things that often tell of the future. Through his dreams Bo realizes that two of his children will soon fall prey to the mysterious Antichrist that is growing in power. Bo is painfully admonished by the Spirit not to interfere but to allow his children to face the evil man alone in fulfillment of agreements they made before their life on earth. How can he do this? Through his trials he learns that an unseen war comprising all of God's children, both good and evil, continues in the world from when it began in heaven. Bo comes to understand that there are greater powers than his own in charge of his life. He is expected to exercise true faith in God's power and not to lean on his own understanding. Can he be brave enough to sit back and trust in Heavenly Father's promises to save his children? It's a request almost too hard to bear.

Apocalypse, the Unveiling, Millennial Glory III

Chaos hits Utah as a large earthquake rips the land apart. The Rogers family must escape its fury. It's their struggle to see God's wisdom in the trial of the Saints. Dane Rogers lies in a coma induced by the deadly bacteria unleashed in his hand by the chip. In his deep sleep he is introduced to the Spirit World and the reality of God's existence is unveiled. In the world of light he learns of the eternal nature of God, the importance of the plan of salvation, and preparations of the world by both the living and the dead for the Second Coming of Christ. He also learns that this life is only a moment in time but it is in that moment that we define ourselves and our futures. Through the Rogers family's difficulties they become stronger, realizing their true blessings on earth lie in each other.

The Ascension, Millennial Glory IV

Braun, the eldest son of the Rogers family, is directed by the Spirit to fulfill an internship as an aide to the Secretary General of the United Nations. Through his dreams and visions of beasts and monsters he is able to act as Daniel of old to Secretary Klump to warn him of things to come. Together they uncover an ancient secret design as it unfolds. The man who is one of the richest on the earth plots to take control of the world through manipulating its leaders. Braun feels a great responsibility to stop his ascension to total and complete power, but what can he, a lowly aide, do? Conrad, the second oldest in the Rogers family, is on a mission in Israel. At first, he has limited success among the Jews, but as time moves on, the Spirit of truth rests heavily upon him. He's able to be instrumental in the conversion of a group of Rabbis who in turn bring other Jews to the church in droves as they begin to believe in Christ.

Hanging by a Thread, Millennial Glory V

Braun Rogers travels to America and takes a position at the White House in an effort to warn the President of the danger that awaits the nation. He finds the country in political disarray as the constitution hangs by a thread. Through his visions, he sees the outcome of the present chaos as it spirals toward destruction. The country must return to the values that inspired its beginnings if it hopes to be protected from the secret combinations that are designing its downfall. Brea Rogers, the eldest sister of the family, discovers that she is trapped in an unholy web of deceit as she unravels the truth about her husband, Matt, and his family. The facts are too horrible to believe and too deadly to ignore. She must make some difficult decisions to protect her unborn children. Just what will that do to her love for Matt and the marriage they share? Elder Conrad Rogers becomes a hostage in the country of Israel but his burden is made light through participating in prophecy. The long awaited Jewish temple rises. The Jews know their Messiah is coming. Do you?

Justice of Affliction, Millennial Glory VI

Braun is protectively catapulted to the deadliest, northernmost region of the world to hide from the mastermind behind America's destruction. At the same time, Dane, now a soldier in the National Police, is caught on the East Coast of America. The nation begins a melt-down that has been carefully planned and executed by that same mastermind and his secret, international associates. Dane must use all his resources and knowledge if he's going to avoid the violent and hungry mobs that rampage over the land. His goal is to make it home alive! Brea is condemned to a life of loneliness in her last term of pregnancy as Matt divorces her to appease his father. Young Carea is ripped from the ones she loves and taken to the prison camps in response to violence. She is targeted as a high-risk to the nation's security because of the chip that remains in her forehead. Bo's heart is ripped from his chest in mourning as Corrynne tries to comfort him. His family is falling apart! Did God forget them? Is he forsaking them? Life is full of affliction! Where is their justice?

IT IS THE END OF DAYS AND ALL IS IN COMMOTION!

AN AUTHOR'S NOTE TO YOU

"It is the duty of nations, as well as of men, to owe their dependence upon the overruling power of God. We have been the recipients of the choicest blessings of heaven. We have been preserved, these many years, in peace and prosperity. We have grown in numbers, wealth and power as no other nation has ever grown; but we have forgotten God! We have forgotten the gracious hand which preserved us in peace and multiplied and enriched and strengthened us; and we have vainly imagined in the deceitfulness of our hearts, that all these blessings were produced by some superior wisdom and virtue of our own" (President Lincoln, "Thanksgiving Proclamation," March 30, 1863).

Dear Reader,

Feelings within me burn with bright flame. I think I see for the first time the miracle of the Constitution. I think I see the miracle of those that came before us who were inspired to sacrifice everything as a loyal parent would for the future of their children. I think I see the love of God shining through the clouds in columns of golden power to bless us with freedoms to live life according to our conscience. I think I finally see how long it took me to understand all of my many blessings and I'm afraid to admit it, but as I look back at the dark clouds of ignorance I'm ashamed that it took me this long to see what blessings were constantly held out to me!

I love my opportunities. I love the second chance the Lord has given me. How great is his patience and his love! How great his understanding of my flaws and his prodding me to learn what I should have always known. Swellings, tears, emotions of thanksgiving—how do I keep these feelings alive?

"I'm proud to be an American where at least I know I'm free…."

I testify that we, as a righteous people, will uphold the standard given to us. *We will be successful!* The Constitution will continue through us! There is no doubt about that future. Though dark times will come, our faith will continue as bright as the morning sun. As we prepare, our confidence will wax strong and we shall inherit glory in the Eternal Heavens above!

Thank you dear Father!

Sincerely,

Wendie Edwards

CHARACTERS

ROGERS FAMILY

Bo Andrew Rogers	46	Father
Corrynne Rochelle Rogers	43	Mother
Braun Joseph Rogers	22	First Son
Conrad Ryan Rogers	21	Second Son
Brea Nicole Rogers	20	First Daughter
Dane Russell Rogers	19	Third Son
Carea Lorrell Rogers	17	Second Daughter
Jax William Rogers	12	Fourth Son
Ry Benjamin Rogers	10	Fifth Son
Rocwell Joshua Rogers	8	Sixth Son
Striynna Chandelle Rogers	18 mo.	Third Daughter First Twin
Strykker Adam Rogers	18 mo.	Seventh Son Second Twin

TABLE OF CONTENTS

CHAPTER ONE

FISHERS OF MEN

"Verily I say unto you, There be some standing here, which shall not taste of death, till they see the Son of man coming in his kingdom" (Matthew 16:28).

00:03:14, 06:30:22, Zulu
Tuesday, September 16th

Missionary Work Through Service

Yamal Peninsula, Russia
7:30 p.m.

Elder John Zebedee and his companion walked across the flat, frozen, grassy fields of the Yamal Peninsula. It was cold as the September weather pressed upon them. Along the Arctic Kara Sea the snow had come but had not stayed. What was left lay in patches on the clay and silt of the flat land. But by the look of the clouds that hung low above them, that wouldn't last long. The snow was coming and it would fall until spring, but that wouldn't stop them.

The Elder scanned the bright horizon despite the evening hours. Because of their extreme northern location, Darkness wouldn't come for a while yet.

Six conical tents were off in the distance. The people of this Yamal tribe weren't born of the water, but they were believers in Num, and very friendly. He knew they wouldn't hesitate to invite strangers into their tent if he asked them. That way, he could both continue to prepare the hearts of these locals, and teach the Americans tribal ways. Time was growing short.

As Elder Zebedee and his companion walked, some children ran by, happily playing with their Siberian Husky puppy.

The Elder smiled and waved.

One little boy, probably about five, stopped, smiled, and then waved back.

"Is that your reindeer?" asked Elder Zebedee in Nenets, pointing at a single stray that wandered around the tents.

The little boy nodded. "He eats food from our tent."

"Is he alone?"

"He lost his mommy," said the little boy, and then he took off again, frolicking with his pet.

Elder Zebedee spoke to his companion, "Those that are coming could use a reindeer for transportation. These people might let them have a stray."

The companion nodded and then said simply, "I agree."

"Then we're set?"

"Yes," said Elder Zebedee's companion nodding again. "I'll gather the brethren to bring the man and the woman here."

"Good," replied John. "I'll warn these good people to prepare for the visitors."

"Good," repeated his companion. Then with a bowed head, he vanished.[1]

Elder Zebedee continued towards the tents. He was in the mood for some good old-fashioned teaching in the manner of the ancient ways. It had been a while since he had taught. Normally, the young men of the tribes did the missionary work from the camps, but this time around, he would do it. The end of his long mission was coming and soon he would be reunited with his friends of old. It was a good day.

The Beloved

Somewhere in the sky
An unknown time

The engine hum was constant. Braun's body vibrated with it as his mind awakened just enough to realize that he was being transported—somewhere…to where, he didn't care. All that he had been commanded to do was finished. His task was complete. He had delivered his message and whatever happened to him now was in God's hands.

Braun sensed the comforting presence of the Spirit near. He surrendered to it, wanting the peace it could bring him. Soon, he was enfolded in a delicious light that fed his yearnings as he lapsed into a dream.

In his sleeping vision, Braun was shown twelve white-robed beings. He knew without explanation that these were witnesses of Christ[2] the faithful of his early apostles.[3] With warmth beginning in his heart, a new power filled him with energy. He wasn't one who could feel the personality of others, but suddenly he was looking into the apostles' souls with new senses. These were good men. He felt their eternal desires for good, their great bravery, and the strength of their spirits. Braun could sense even now in the eternal realms, their willingness to walk both in the past and in the future on any path towards fulfilling all righteousness.

Another being appeared amidst the first twelve whose glory was even greater than all of them put together. A tingling sensation spread over Braun as he realized that this was Jesus Christ, the Savior of the world! Braun spiritually reached out to him. He wanted to know the Lord. Would he be able to sense him too? Braun was happy when he realized, yes, he could!

The Savior bore the same magnificent characteristics as his apostles, only his desires, willingness, and godly attributes were a thousand times more brilliant. Christ was like the sun, and the apostles were the heat and energy that emanated from the sun. They were extensions of him, unified with him and the will of the Father.[4]

"Unified with the will of the Father…." That was an interesting thought. What would it take to be unified with the will of the Father and inherit such an honored place next to Christ as his apostles enjoyed?

As if he had audibly asked the questions, Braun was shown the heavy burdens that each apostle had been asked to bear in life. He saw how they were hung, beaten, treated disrespectfully, and tortured in defense of the truth. It was painful to witness, but in watching, Braun understood the meaning of martyrdom.[5] They had each given up everything for the gospel: money, prestige, honor, family, their mortal future—and their life.[6] Each of these apostles, except for one, had died, just like Christ, in the name of the eternal freedom of man.[7] They had paid the ultimate price asked of them.[8] The thing that made this vision all the more poignant was that Braun knew Jesus had forewarned his apostles that they would suffer and die in his name,[9] just as he would have to suffer and die for mankind.[10] They had served Christ with foreknowledge of the price they would have to pay. Could he have done that? He didn't know. How hard an apostle's life on the earth must have been![11] His thoughts turned to thankfulness for his own life. He had been so blessed!

Braun slowly considered these lessons. He wasn't in a hurry. After all, wasn't he in a place where time didn't exist? He had all the time in—heaven? Where was he? Was he in heaven? *Had he died?*

Died….

The word hung in his mind until it didn't mean anything anymore. It wasn't important. What was death? It was nothing compared to *eternal life*! …Then it struck him! *Death—didn't matter! It was insignificant!* What really mattered were all the moments leading *up* to death. It was the faith exhibited by every soul during their life, blinded by mortality and hoping for an afterlife, which made *all the difference*.[12]

Braun smiled. Now he understood. Fear stops men. Fear makes men weak. Christ and his servants were strong because *they weren't afraid*! They weren't afraid of the powers of men, or the weakness of the flesh. They weren't even afraid of death. They understood that death was only a door to walk through to the rest of their lives! That was the *key*! Knowledge of the truth gave them the strength to face their challenges with great bravery! They were able to endure torture, loss, and defeat without losing heart because they had a vision of what was beyond it.[13] In death all of them had proven their love for their master. All of them were able to transcend mortality and, through Christ, they were able to take their lives again at the side of their Lord in eternal victory, never to be harmed again![14] It was in suffering that these men earned justice, for it was in affliction that they gained their great positions and honor.[15] Wow…Braun was amazed. *One could receive justice in affliction*…suffering for good wasn't for nothing! It mattered! It made a difference!

Braun looked at his Savior, still absorbing his new understanding when he noticed his Lord was holding out a hand to one particular young and kind-looking apostle to his right. Braun perceived that this young man was the only one that hadn't been a martyr. But still, he had been given the same position next to Christ as the others. Braun felt the young man's heart and knew why. There had been nothing he had been asked to do that he refused.[16] He loved his Savior and served him with every fiber of his being. He too had been through great affliction.

The apostle, who couldn't have been older than twenty-four, stepped forward, as if to greet him. Braun was honored. To what did he owe this great opportunity? He held out his hand to shake the apostle's, but before he could, he was swept to another place.

There was a body of water and smoke in the air. Braun was sitting by a fire at night, among mortal men. They were all listening to a man who looked like a teacher while they ate a meal of fish and bread.

The smell of the roasted fish made the air delicious as the men hungrily picked at their dinners. Bare fish bones were strewn at the foot of the fire, telling of just how many fish had been caught that day by the now empty nets that lay in a pile near the shore.

Braun wondered, as he searched his surroundings, where in time had he been taken? By the absence of technology, the tattered robes of the men, their full beards and their sandals, he could tell it was most likely in the past. But…Braun considered how he was feeling inside. Curiously, he was still feeling the characteristics of the men beside him. They were the same as in the previous realm: strength, righteousness, loyalty…. Could it be that he was still among Christ and his apostles?

Braun focused on the man who was speaking. Was this the Savior? Instantly he knew it was. Although Jesus' body didn't glow with light, he had the same mannerisms of the being he had seen moments before…Braun's mind stopped. He couldn't think anymore because what he saw sent a sickening, overwhelming feeling into his gut.

On the Savior's hands and wrists Braun couldn't help but stare at his gaping, ugly wounds.[17] They would peek out as Christ's robe shifted on his arms when he gestured with his hands.

The sight of the cruel wounds was—*shocking*! Braun had learned about Christ's death and resurrection his whole life, but to see the nail prints himself—no, prints was not the right word. They were nail rips, punctures, *holes* made from large pieces of metal and a pounding hammer at the merciless hands of a Roman soldier. It was just…all so—so—*wrong*. Upon the body of Christ, the wounds were *irreverent—and unjustly ugly*![18]

Braun's emotions were getting out of control. He took a deep breath and shook the anger from his mind. He couldn't be angry right now. He knew his dreams would end if he didn't keep his emotions in check. He needed to maintain an attitude of reverent attentiveness if he wanted to see this vision to its end.[19] Braun wouldn't look at the wounds anymore.

Of course, intellectually he knew how the puncture marks were placed on Jesus' hands and wrists, but Braun found that that didn't change how he felt when he witnessed them himself. Despite these thoughts, he now understood that he was seeing Christ after his death. This was his resurrected body, tempered to look like a mortal man's.[20]

In his mind, Braun reviewed his knowledge. Because Christ had the wounds in his hands, this meeting was occurring after the crucifixion. With that clue Braun knew exactly where he was in time. He was sitting at the Lord's feet during the forty days he taught his disciples at the Sea of Tiberias. This setting by the sea made sense now.

There was a young man to the right of Jesus with a pleasant Jewish look. He couldn't have been older than twenty-four—wait! Braun recognized him! He was the apostle that had been introduced to him just a few moments before. He remembered his look…and his heart.

Braun watched the young man at Christ's side. He was the one person in the group that wasn't fidgeting in any way. As everyone else was chewing or licking their fingers, this man was watching the Savior, taking in every word as if it were his last. He had a longing in his eyes, a hunger for knowledge. Braun knew that look because he had seen it in the mirror after his own dreams or in times of personal mental agony. He had it most often when he was searching for some bit of knowledge that seemed impossible to find. Was this man in mental agony too? Braun began to watch and study the man. Who was he? He hadn't been told his name.

As if hearing Braun's thoughts and those of the man beside him, Christ turned to his young apostle. He studied him momentarily and then with a look of perfect understanding mixed with satisfaction, Jesus asked, "John, my beloved, what desirest thou?"

Braun felt like snapping his fingers. He should have guessed this was John. This was the author of the book that had been haunting his dreams and yet revealing the knowledge that had changed the course of his life…. Braun had to quell his rapid thoughts to catch what Christ would say next.

Jesus continued in a gentle baritone, "For if you shall ask what you will, it shall be granted unto you."[21]

Braun's breath caught in his throat. Whatever John requested, Christ would bestow upon him! What confidence the Lord must have had in him! Braun was filled with admiration. He wished the Lord had that kind of confidence in him too!

John's expression turned from longing to joy in a moment. He paused as he seemed to weigh his words. Then with a hint of apprehension and a look of apology for unspoken weaknesses, he smiled tentatively saying, "Lord—give unto me…." His request faltered as sweat broke out on his brow. Looking intently at the Lord, he lingered as if to receive permission to continue.

The Savior gave a confirming nod and patted John's hand which was clenched into a fist on his right knee.

Then with energy John's words tumbled out unrestrained. *"Lord! Give me power over death, that I may live and bring souls unto thee!"*[22]

Christ looked down at the sand on the ground and then at the fire as he nodded slowly with knowing resolve in his face.

Many of the men that watched the Lord had gasped at John's request. Braun knew they thought John was asking the impossible! How could such a request be answered?

No one made a sound as they waited for Christ to respond.

With a smile breaking forth on the Savior's face he patted John's right fist again and said, "Because thou desirest this…" He brought up one hand as if pointing into the horizon and said, "Thou shalt tarry until I come in my glory. Therefore more blessed are ye, for ye shall never taste of death; but ye shall live to behold all the doings of the Father unto the children of men, even until all things shall be fulfilled according to the will of the Father, when I shall come in my glory with the powers of heaven."[23]

There were both confirming and surprised statements around the circle as the men whispered their astonishment at Christ's answer. No one looked as surprised as the man who sat at Christ's left, opposite of John. Braun assumed this man was Peter. It seemed the same question played in everyone's minds: Would that mean that Christ's return would be within John's lifetime, or did that mean John would live until Christ came at the end of the world?

But the Lord did not finish there, he continued, "And thou shalt prophesy before nations, kindreds, tongues and people."[24]

Peter leaned forward to catch the Savior's eye. Then he asked the question, "Lord, what shall this man do?"

Jesus looked at Peter. With gentleness he said, "Remember when I told you that there were some standing among you, which should not taste of death till they saw the kingdom of God?"[25]

Peter nodded. "Thou sayest that before we went upon the mount of transfiguration."

"I have given John what he requested. He will tarry till I come."

Peter looked confused. To Braun he looked as if he was toying with the idea of whether or not he should have asked the same blessing.

"What is that to thee?" asked the Savior, his eyes fixed on Peter.

Peter stared back for a moment. Then it seemed he dismissed his question. Nodding in acceptance, he sat back.

"Follow thou me," said Christ to Peter.

Peter nodded again with a thoughtful look in his eye as he studied his fellow apostle, John. "Let it be said then among the brethren, that this disciple should not die."[26]

There was a hushing of noises in Braun's mind as the vision was swept from him. It was over. He had seen the things he was supposed to see but questions still burned in his mind. What was the grand purpose of the vision? What was he supposed to obtain from it? He hadn't been able to ask any questions.... Braun's mind continued to work as he processed all that he had seen. If John could not die, then that would mean he was still on the earth right now, in his time. What an intriguing thought. So then, where was he? What was he doing? Why hadn't anyone seen him? Or—maybe he had been seen, but no one recognized him. The questions just kept coming without answers.

There wouldn't be any answers now as Braun's mind returned to the present. He was exhausted. The dream had sapped his strength and now he needed to rest. Sleep was good.

The buzz of engines and the never-ending feeling of turbulent flying overtook him once again.

Notes to "Fishers of Men"

Missionary Work Through Service

[1] This companion who can vanish is one of the three Nephites. His body is in a translated state and is serving a mission until Christ comes again in his glory, just like John (3 Nephi 28:7). His name is never mentioned in the text, because, for some reason, the names of the three Nephites were not to be known to us (3 Nephi 28:25). In the Doctrine & Covenants, we learn that John is among the lost tribes, preparing them to return (D&C 77:14). In Third Nephi, we learn that the three Nephites will minister among the lost tribes also (3 Nephi 28:29), thus it is this author's choice to place them with John in performing the massive work of preparation for the ten lost tribe's return.

As discussed in previous books, the reason John and the three Nephites can vanish into thin air is not one of fantasy or science fiction, but of scripture. In Third Nephi, we learn that translated bodies can not only be impervious to injury, pain, and suffering (3 Nephi 28:38) but they are like angels and can tele-transport from place to place by merely "praying unto the Father in the name of Jesus" (3 Nephi 28:30). This topic will be more completely covered in subsequent books.

The Beloved

[2] "To these chosen twelve, the call to follow Christ meant to forsake all and to physically accompany the Lord in his ministry. Their call was a privileged one. They walked and talked with the Son of God daily. They knew the Lord intimately and feasted upon his word with humble and receptive hearts. They loved him, and Jesus called them his friends (See John 15:14, 15.)" (Howard W. Hunter, "An Apostle's Witness of Christ," *Ensign*, Jan 1984, 69).

[3] "The word 'Apostle' is derived from a Greek word meaning 'one sent forth.' Such an appointment requires a divine commission and priesthood authority. This office relates to the special responsibilities to take the gospel to all the peoples of the earth and their unique commission to assist in the overseership of the Church" (Edward J. Brandt, "'And He Gave Some, Apostles' (Eph. 4:11)," *Ensign*, July 1999, 14).

[4] "So we, being many, are one body in Christ, and every one members one of another" (Romans 5:12).

[5] "Eventually, with the known exception of John the Beloved, Peter and his fellow Apostles were martyred" (M. Russell Ballard, "Restored Truth," *Ensign*, Nov 1994, 65).

[6] "'He who is not able to abide the law of a celestial kingdom cannot abide a celestial glory' (D&C 88:22). The law of sacrifice is a celestial law; so also is the law of consecration. Thus to gain that celestial reward which we so devoutly desire, we must be able to live these two laws. Sacrifice and consecration are inseparably intertwined. The law of consecration is that we consecrate our time, our talents, and our money and property to the cause of the Church: such are to be available to the extent they are needed to further the Lord's interests on earth. The law of sacrifice is that we are willing to sacrifice all that we have for the truth's sake—our character and reputation; our honor and applause; our good name among men; our houses, lands, and families: all things, even our very lives if need be. Joseph Smith said, 'A religion that does not require the sacrifice of all things never has power sufficient to produce the faith necessary [to lead] unto life and salvation' (*Lectures on Faith*, p. 58)" (Bruce R. McConkie, "Obedience, Consecration, and Sacrifice," *Ensign*, May 1975, 50).

[7] "But now, as then, there are other classes—men who love their own ease; who will not endure these privations; who will not go through that which the Apostles had to meet and, of course, though they may be worthy people in many respects, they cannot hope to attain unto the same glory as these did who made such immense sacrifices for the truth. Therefore, there is, as Paul says, one glory of the sun, or the celestial glory. Who shall attain unto that? Those who keep the law that pertains to that glory; those who do everything that is commanded them of God; those who are willing to endure everything for His sake and to do that which He requires at their hands. There have been, no doubt, millions of people on the earth who have had this willingness. They will attain, we are told, unto the celestial glory. Where God and Christ are they will dwell. They are promised crowns, thrones, exaltation. Everything that heart can desire, or that will add to the glory of a human or an immortal soul, will be given unto this class. Jesus is the great exemplar of that class. He himself came here on earth. He forsook His throne and His glory; He left his father's presence, and was willing to come down here and suffer as he did suffer. In the short space of time that he labored upon earth He suffered everything that a human soul could suffer; and after having endured such agony that he sweat great drops of blood, He was crowned with thorns, and then was crucified, thus pointing out the path for all his followers to take, giving them the example. Now, those who would reign with Christ, those who would have the glory that Christ has attained unto, must be equally willing to endure all things for the sake of the Gospel that He has revealed. These are the sons of God, the daughters of God, who will attain unto this great exaltation in the presence of the Lamb" (George Q. Cannon, "Foreordination and Predestination", as quoted by Brian H. Stuy, *Collected Discourses*, April 27th, 1890, 5 Vol., p. 2).

[8] "A martyr is one who gives his life rather than forsake Christ, the gospel, or his righteous beliefs or principles.…Where a testament is there must be the death of the testator (Heb. 9: 16–17). Many were slain because they testified of these things (3 Ne. 10:15)" (*Guide to the scriptures*, "Martyr, Martyrdom," www.lds.org).

According to accepted Christian tradition, all the apostles, except for John the Beloved and Judas who died at his own hand, were martyred in the name of Christ. The deaths suffered are as follows:

James, the brother of John, was beheaded. Philip was crucified. Matthew was killed by a halberd, which is an axe-like spear. James, the brother of Christ, was beaten after being crucified and stoned. Matthias, the apostle that replaced Judas, was stoned and beheaded. Andrew was crucified. Mark was beaten to death. Peter was crucified upside-down. Paul was beheaded. Jude was crucified. Bartholomew was crucified. Thomas was killed by a spear.

Luke was hanged. Simon was crucified. Tradition has it that John the beloved was boiled in oil but miraculously escaped and then was sent to the island of Patmos. One may read more information about the death of the apostles at: http://en.wikipedia.org/wiki/Christian_martyrs.

[9] "But before all these, they shall lay their hands on you, and persecute you, delivering you up to the synagogues, and into prisons, being brought before kings and rulers for my name's sake. And it shall turn to you for a testimony. Settle it therefore in your hearts, not to meditate before what ye shall answer: For I will give you a mouth and wisdom, which all your adversaries shall not be able to gainsay nor resist. And ye shall be betrayed both by parents, and brethren, and kinsfolks, and friends; and some of you shall they cause to be put to death. And ye shall be hated of all men for my name's sake. But there shall not an hair of your head perish. In your patience possess ye your souls" (Luke 21:12–19).

[10] "Yea, even so he shall be led, crucified, and slain, the flesh becoming subject even unto death, the will of the Son being swallowed up in the will of the Father" (Mosiah 15:7).

[11] "Men and women who keep the commandments of God in their fullness; who labor continually, as many have done, to carry out the principles of truth; who are willing to suffer martyrdom for the sake of the truth, as the Apostles did in the days of Jesus; men and women who have died by hundreds and by thousands, in various ages of the world, for the truth—these will undoubtedly receive a greater glory than those who have never made such sacrifices. There are people who have not stamina to stand up to suffer for the truth, and who are not willing to endure the persecutions that follow the practice of truth. They weaken before the opposition that is brought to bear against them. They love popularity, they love a good name, they love the good things of this life, and they are willing to trust the future to itself. They go in for the enjoyment of the present day, of the present hour, and are willing, as they say, to risk the future. But there are others who look above and beyond this; who love the truth better than they love worldly ease, or comfort, or riches, or good name, like our Lord and Savior and His Apostles. They went through life enduring every conceivable hardship and privation, and at last had their lives taken from them. Why was this? Because they knew that God had in store for them a wonderful reward, a great glory. As Jesus said, in response to a question of one of the Apostles: 'Ye which have followed me, in the regeneration when the Son of Man shall sit in the throne of his glory, ye also shall sit upon twelve thrones, judging the twelve tribes of Israel.' They believed the words of Jesus. They believed that Jesus would give them thrones, that they would be rulers in the Kingdom of God....And they looked forward with perfect confidence to the fulfillment of that promise. Therefore they endured these privations" (George Q. Cannon, "Foreordination and Predestination," April 27th, 1890, Brian H. Stuy, *Collected Discourses*, 5 vols. p. 2).

[12] "Life on earth is of limited duration. There comes a time for all of us when the spirit and the body are separated in death. But because of the resurrection of Jesus Christ, we will all be resurrected, regardless of whether we have accomplished good or evil in this life. Immortality is the gift to every mortal child of our Father in Heaven. Death must be viewed as a portal to a new and better life. Through the glorious resurrection, body and spirit will be reunited. We will have a perfect, immortal body of flesh and bones that will never be subjected to pain or death. But the glory we attain to in the next life will depend on our performance in this life. Only through the gift of the Atonement and our obedience to the gospel can we return and live with God once again" (L. Tom Perry, "The Plan of Salvation," *Ensign*, Nov 2006, pgs. 69–72).

[13] "They then would want that more sure word of prophecy, that they were sealed in the heavens and had the promise of eternal life in that kingdom of God. Then, having this promise sealed unto them, it was an anchor to the soul, sure and steadfast. Though the thunders might roll and lightnings flash, and earthquakes bellow, and war gather thick around, yet this hope and knowledge would support the soul in every hour of trial, trouble and tribulation" (Joseph Smith, *Teachings of the Prophet Joseph Smith*, p. 298).

[14] These are the words, given through John, that Christ had for his apostles who died for his name:

"These are they which came out of great tribulation, and have washed their robes, and made them white in the blood of the lamb. Therefore are they before the throne of God, and serve him day and night in his temple: and he that sitteth on the throne shall dwell among them. They shall hunger no more, neither thirst any more; neither shall the sun light on them, nor any heat. For the Lamb which is in the midst of the throne shall feed them, and shall lead them unto living fountains of waters: and God shall wipe away all tears from their eyes" (Revelation 7:14–17).

[15] "When it costs us but little to give, the treasure laid up in heaven is a small one. The widow's mite, given in sacrifice, weighs more heavily in the eternal scales than the bulging granaries of the rich man" (Bruce R. McConkie, "Obedience, Consecration, and Sacrifice," *Ensign*, May 1975, p. 50).

[16] "...To gain celestial salvation we must be *able* to live these laws to the full if we are called upon to do so. Implicit in this is the reality that we must in fact live them to the extent we are called upon so to do.

"How, for instance, can we establish our ability to live the full law of consecration if we do not in fact pay an honest tithing? Or how can we prove our willingness to sacrifice all things, if need be, if we do not make the small sacrifices of time and toil, or of money and means, that we are now asked to make?" (Bruce R. McConkie, "Obedience, Consecration, and Sacrifice," *Ensign*, May 1975, p. 50).

[17] According to Dr. Richard Lloyd Anderson, a professor of history and ancient scripture at Brigham Young University, historical documents, compared to scriptural accounts and the analysis of ancient skeletal remains, paints a picture of the crucifixion.

"Recently unearthed skeletal remains of Jehohanan, a person crucified in Jesus' day, raise questions on what is really known about ancient crucifixion. The four gospels relate Jesus' execution with marked terseness; ancient readers were familiar with the grim procedures of death on the cross." The cruel torture of crucifixion was initiated by arrest and then the prisoner being "first scourged and then crucified" (*Jewish War,* Vol. 2, p. 306).

"The gospels are explicit regarding the Lord's being 'fixed to the cross' (the literal meaning of 'crucifixion')....The first archaeological example of crucifixion gives evidence of the practice of piercing the feet....Dr. N. Haas, professor of anatomy, commented in detail on the skeletal remains of Jehohanan, which bare certain marks of crucifixion. The most impressive evidence was a seven-inch spike piercing the remains of Jehohanan's two heel bones, with a piece of olive wood at its point. To date most scholars have accepted Dr. Haas' belief that the victim was transfixed to a cross at his heels. This evidence, contemporary with Jesus, suggests that feet were pierced in Palestinian crucifixions....This recent find has two other major dimensions, the first bearing on the question of where the nails were placed in the hands. Could there be additional nails? ...Dr. Haas observed that Jehohanan's right radius (the upper arm bone as the arms outstretch) had both a surface cut and a distinct wearing, which he reasoned was the initial slice of the nail and the later wearing action from the victim's writhing on the cross. This "scratch" on the bone was positioned between the two lower arm bones at a structurally more solid location to fix a nail. This evidence, coupled with a strict reading of the New Testament, indicates that both hand and wrist could have been pierced" (Richard Lloyd Anderson, "The Ancient Practice of Crucifixion," *Ensign*, July 1975, pgs. 32–33).

[18] The question arose: Why Christ, being perfected in resurrection, still maintains the marks of his crucifixion? The answers discovered to that question delivered multifaceted answers.

Identification: Despite Christ's own prediction of his death and resurrection three days later, his own apostles, those that had been taught at his feet daily for years, did not believe Mary

Magdalene, nor Mary the mother of James' report that an angel had appeared to them and told them that Christ had risen (Mathew 28:1–8, Mark 16:1–7, Luke 24:1–10, John 20:1–2), believing the women's words were "idle tales and believed them not" (Luke 24:11). Christ appeared to two disciples walking to Emmaus who recounted the strange stories of the women when they discovered it was he, Jesus, the resurrected Savior who was walking with them (Luke 24:25–30). They rushed to tell the disciples but it tells us in Mark 16:13 that again, the apostles "neither believed they them". Suddenly Christ appeared in the room with all the disciples and frightened the men. They initially thought he was a ghost. Christ offered for them to feel his body, look at the prints in his hands and feet and put their hands in his side, but still, "yet they believed not for joy" (Luke 24:36–44). It wasn't until he ate food that they realized Christ not only had an outward form, but internal organs too. If it be this difficult for those who were close to Christ and were taught of him to believe in his resurrection, this might give an indication why Christ needs to have identifying marks when he appears to people on earth.

Will Christ's body always bear these marks? From the words of Joseph Fielding Smith, he says, "It can hardly be accepted as a fact that these wounds have remained in his hands, side and feet all through the centuries from the time of his crucifixion and will remain until his Second Coming. But they will appear to the Jews as a witness against their fathers and their stubbornness in following the teachings of their fathers. After their weeping and mourning they shall be cleansed" (*Doctrines of Salvation*, p. 292).

Will our bodies display the marks of our death as Christ's did? This question found a surprising answer. See Elder Talmage's comment on Christ and his resurrection: "The resurrection of Jesus Christ was absolutely literal. He took up that body from the tomb as it had been laid down, for it had been predicted that he should not see corruption. The body bore all the marks of the crucifiers. So shall the resurrection of everyone be literal in this sense" (James E. Talmage, *Conference Report,* April 1928, Third Day—Morning Meeting, p. 95).

Joseph F. Smith gives us a similar statement, saying, "The body will come forth as it is laid to rest, for there is no growth in the grave" (Gospel Doctrine, p. 566). Then concerning wounds: "Even to the wounds in the flesh. Not that a person will always be marred by scars, wounds, deformities, defects of infirmities, for these will be removed in their course, in their proper time, according to the merciful providence of God" (*Gospel Doctrine,* p. 30).

To study further, Joseph Fielding Smith clarifies what Elder Talmage and Joseph F. Smith may be referring to. He says, "Bodies will come up, of course, as they were laid down, but will be restored to their proper, perfect frame immediately....Infants and children do not grow in the grave, but when they come forth, they will come forth with the same body and in the same size in which the body was when it was laid away. After the resurrection the body will grow until it has reached the full stature of manhood or womanhood. He did not intend to teach that the adult who loses a leg will come forth without that leg until it can be grafted on after the resurrection. Rather his body will come forth complete in every part. Deformities and like will be corrected, if not immediately at the time of the uniting of the spirit and body, so soon thereafter that it will make no difference. We may be sure that every man will receive his body in its perfect frame in the resurrection" (*Doctrines of Salvation*, pgs. 292, 294).

[19] "Inspiration comes more easily in peaceful settings. Such words as quiet, still, peaceable, Comforter abound in the scriptures: 'Be *still*, and know that I am God.' (Ps. 46:10; italics added.) And the promise, 'You shall receive my Spirit, the Holy Ghost, even the Comforter, which shall teach you the peaceable things of the kingdom' (D&C 36:2)" (Boyd K. Packer, "Reverence Invites Revelation," *Ensign*, Nov 1991, 21).

[20] Immortal bodies have the ability to appear in full glory or without glory as mortal men. We see this ability in the scriptures. When Christ appeared to two disciples walking to Emmaus, he looked like a normal man, so much that the witnesses did not recognize him as Christ. (See

Luke 24.) When Christ appeared to Joseph Smith, he and God the Father were arrayed in glory, "whose glory defy all description" (JS-H 1:17).

[21] See D&C 7:1.

[22] See D&C 7:2.

[23] 3 Nephi 28:5–7. This was a statement made to the three Nephites who were translated as John, but the statement applies to John as well.

[24] See D&C 7:3.

[25] See Luke 9:27.

[26] See John 21:23.

CHAPTER TWO

LIGHTS AND CONFUSION

"And there shall be signs in the sun, and in the moon, and in the stars; and upon the earth distress of nations, with perplexity; the sea and the waves roaring" (Luke 21:25).

00:03:13, 20:26:54, Zulu
Wednesday, September 17th

Return to Eden

Siberia, Russia
5:34 a.m.

Whispers.

Voices overhead. The words meshed together in an incomprehensible gurgle of language. It was as if Braun was listening under water.

"Braun…"

Of all the words he heard, Braun only understood one of them. It was his name. It echoed in his mind then, as if there weren't another word spoken. He found he couldn't think adequately. It had grown too cold. Now he never wanted to awaken.

"Braun…Braun? Get up, Braun! I need you to *get up*!"

Someone shook his shoulder vigorously. Braun's mind woke to slight awareness again. Someone was calling him, prodding him. He opened an eye. It was painful. All he could see was a blinding brightness that reached in every direction. He closed his eyes again where there was peace. Quiet and peace.

"Braun! Wake up! *You have to wake up!*"

Suddenly a harsh cold blast hit his face. Was that snow? *"What the…"* Braun opened his eyes and sat up angrily. *"Who did that?"* he asked as gruff as he could manage in his weak state. His reaction was the same as if a brother had just snuck up and pelted him when he was sleeping.

"I did," said a girl's voice from behind.

Braun turned around to see the most beautiful sight he could ever have hoped for. *"Ch—Chenille?"* he gasped in a forced whisper, feeling like the air had just been knocked out of him.

Chenille smiled. She didn't need to answer.

Braun struggled to get up but he was too weak. All of his muscles felt like putty. He couldn't make them respond.

Chenille stood and said, "Take it easy, Braun."

But Braun continued to thrash about, finally managing to get to his feet for a moment. "What's wrong with me?" he mumbled as he stumbled back to his knees.

Chenille caught Braun to stabilize him. "It's just the residual effects of the gas. You'll be fine in a while."

Braun tried again to stand. "What gas?"

"Matt gave you a gas to put you to sleep…"

"Who's Matt?" asked Braun looking at Chenille, using all his energy to figure out what she was saying.

"Matt, Brea's husband. Remember?"

Braun tried to remember but his thoughts were so foggy. "No, I don't remember."

Chenille put Braun's arm over her shoulder to support his weight. "That's OK. It will all come back to you soon. Now let's get to the snowmobile. Walk with me. It's up here a ways."

Braun looked down at the snow that lay all around. It was hard and frozen under his feet. He looked down at himself. He was wearing a long fur coat that reached to his shins and thick snow boots. "Who dressed me?" he asked.

Chenille was breathing hard under the weight of Braun's unsteady step. "You dressed you. I only put your coat, mask, hat, gloves, and boots on," she said in a strained voice. "You would have frozen to death in seconds if I hadn't."

Braun looked over at Chenille. He could smell her hair as it draped over her fur-covered shoulder near his face. She was beyond all descriptions of beauty. He wondered if he was still dreaming. Could she really be here?

"Where did *you* come from?" he asked lazily.

Chenille looked at Braun briefly and said, "I'll tell you everything later, when you'll remember what I say. You're still groggy from the gas so just be quiet and help me out here."

"Kiss me and I'll be quiet," said Braun with a sly smile as he turned a goofy look at her.

Chenille looked at Braun and laughed abruptly. "You're funny when you're drugged."

"I'm serious," said Braun trying to keep up with her. "I didn't kiss you enough when you were with me at the UN."

Chenille laughed again. "Kiss me enough?" she asked. "You didn't kiss me at *all*."

Braun tried to remember his time at the UN. "I didn't?" he said surprised. "That was *stupid*!" he responded. "Why was I so stupid?"

"But that's OK. Who cares? That's not what matters," said Chenille. "What matters is that we get out of the open and into a shelter before tonight. We have a long way to go before that can happen."

"I can build a snow shelter," said Braun as Chenille unwrapped his arm from her shoulder, leaving him struggling to keep his balance.

Chenille brushed snow from an object that Braun hadn't noticed was there even though they were standing only two feet away.

"I know you can," responded Chenille in a patient voice as she bent down to pull on the borders of a white tarp. "You're quite resourceful when you're in your right mind." With a tug, it came loose and revealed a two-person snowmobile.

"Where'd you find that?" asked Braun amazed.

"Remember, I told you a snowmobile was over here?"

Braun shook his head. He really didn't.

"Well, here it is. Get on, Braun," said Chenille as she stepped up on the machine and swung her leg across the seat. Next she pulled a small hand-held computer-like thing from her coat pocket and looked out to the horizon.

Braun lifted his heavy legs as he took the last two steps unsupported on the snow. Each step was still difficult. Weakly he climbed on behind Chenille. "Why do you get to drive?" he asked enviously as Chenille still studied the screen on the computer.

"Because I'm not under the influence of drugs. I'm your designated driver," she said with a serious voice as she looked up to the horizon.

"Is that a GPS?" asked Braun looking over Chenille's shoulder at her global positioning digital device.

"Yes."

"Do you know where we're going?" asked Braun.

"Generally," she said as she slipped the object back into her pocket and started the machine. "Hang on, Braun," she said as she revved the engine and then engaged the clutch. The machine bolted forward with surprising force.

Braun grabbed Chenille's waist suddenly, almost losing his seating but recovering enough to rebalance himself.

"We'll be riding all day. Might as well relax," yelled Chenille over the sound of the engine.

Braun readjusted his grip around Chenille's waist. He had to shake his head to decide if he was dreaming this snowmobile ride or if he was truly sitting behind Chenille. He took in what his senses were telling him. It was cold. He felt the vibration of the snowmobile under him and the force of the ride. He concentrated on his arms. Yes, his arms were indeed around what seemed to be Chenille. It was her voice and her looks and her—scent. Braun breathed deep. He could smell shampoo residue from the hair flowing from under her hat. It was a wonderful coconut smell. Yes, he was awake and this was Chenille...but how? His mind was a blank. How did he get here? What was happening?

Braun felt Chenille's body relax as she sat back into his chest. This changed his thoughts. Suddenly he couldn't think of anything else but her. Yes, this was reality. Who cared where he was? Who cared what was happening? He had Chenille and that's all that mattered.

"Let Eden begin," Braun whispered to himself. For all he knew, he had entered a brand new world.

Short Circuits[1]

U.S. Space Station
Independent of time zones

"Do you see that, Parker?"

"Yeah. Woohoo!" hooted the astronaut named Parker. He was watching the wall-sized computer screen intently as it displayed mountainous energy readings. "That's a big one. I knew there were going to be solar flares[2] firing at us soon because of all the sun spots we've been monitoring,[3] but look at the energy of that bugger! It has to be an X80 at least!"[4]

"It's going to get wicked up here,"[5] commented Carter.

"That's an understatement! With the size of that emission, we're not only headed for a solar storm[6] but quite a doozy of a magnetic storm too.[7] Oh yeah, it's going to get rough!"

"That flare is coming at us fast! We need to batten down the hatches!" added Carter as he reached behind to check on some readings that were printing. "About time something exciting happened up here," he said smiling, hiding his worry.

"What? Eating Frosted Flakes in your underwear every day at work not bonus enough for you?" asked Parker sarcastically.

Carter frowned as he quickly wrote in a log book. "Hey, I don't eat Frosted Flakes every day—and I never walk around in my underwear." It was a stupid argument but it was a good distraction from what he was really thinking.

"What do you call those things you wear then?" asked Parker with a smirk.

Carter could tell from Parker's looks that he was feeling the same apprehension, but he continued the joking. "I call them 'work-out pants'," he said, acting a little miffed. "Everyone but you would know that."

"So when do you work out?" chided Parker as he typed something on the computer.

"Hey, what do you mean? I push the buttons in here just as well or better than you. The amount of computer mathematical calculations I do can be exhausting," said Carter as he closed the log book and put the pencil behind his ear.

"Ahh," said Parker with a nod as he studied two of his side-by-side screens. "You just keep enabling your bad habits and rationalizing. I'll look all the better to the bosses."

"If you live that long," said Carter as he spun around to study more computer screens. The statement was meant to be a joke, but after he said it, he cringed as he realized it wasn't. There was too much risk in their jobs to kid about death.

Parker didn't say anything.

Changing the subject and hoping to erase his last comment, Carter asked, "What do you think's going to happen down there with all this solar wind since the earth's magnetic field has been weakening like it has for the last 300 years?"[8] He fiddled and then flicked a sticky knob.

"Down there? Power outages, glitches in computers,"[9] said Parker with a look of contemplation. "But it's not down there I'm worried about, it's up here."

"I know. Sorry about that comment. It was…"

Parker didn't wait for Carter to finish. "No, you're right. We're going to get hit in five minutes by a cloud of radiation forty times the size of that solar flare. It's traveling a million miles an hour! It's going to go through us like we're not even here, touching every molecule of this station and every atom of our DNA. We may not live a long life."[10]

"Ahhhkkkkkk!" said Carter as he dramatically grabbed his neck, over-exaggerating the moment, trying to lighten the mood. He was very uncomfortable with serious topics. "How do we get our money back? We're too young to die."

"Chances are, we won't die, we'll just get cancer,"[11] said Parker in a flat voice, resisting Carter's attempts at humor again.

"That's the same thing."

"Buck up. It's the price you pay for science," said Parker as he put an earpiece in. "Didn't you know that when you signed on? We're one step above guinea pig."

"Well, I was willing to sacrifice my body back then because space seemed so adventurous," said Carter, getting up to retrieve another sheet from the printer.

"What do you mean? Isn't our job here adventurous?"

"Do I look like I'm having an adventure? This is nothing like Star Trek. I haven't seen one beautiful alien yet," said Carter as he sat back down.

"Yes, well the extra radiation might help you grow a sixth finger," offered Parker.

"What would I do with a sixth finger?" asked Carter with a confused look on his face.

"It might put an extra *snap* in your day," said Parker sarcastically with a snap of his own fingers.

"Ha, ha—funny."

"It might help you with your typing," offered Parker.

Carter shook his head. "Whatever," he said, still trying to act like there was nothing wrong. "I'm turning off our computer systems. We'll just free-float for a little while. Can't have any energy zapping our motherboards.[12] I'll notify Houston."

"Good thinking. See? You do have a good thought once in a while," said Parker as he sat leaned back in his chair and interlocked his fingers behind his neck.

"It's the Frosted Flakes," said Carter, laughing. "It's brain food."

"You keep thinking that when you're fat," said Parker. "Hurry and shut the computers down now. That solar flare is only seconds away."

"When I'm fat? I'm already fat," continued Carter. "Fat and happy."

"Now see? You've made me hungry," said Parker as he watched Carter type in the connection validation for communication with NASA.

"Houston, we've got a solar flare in progress," said Carter. "It'll hit Earth in approximately twenty seconds. We'll be off-line. Will connect when it's over. Powering down."

"Copy that. You'll be powering down," answered NASA. "Talk to you soon."

Parker hit the master electricity switch for the station and the lights and all the computers went black.

Seattle, Washington
8:30 p.m.

"Troy! Hurry! Look at the sky."

"What's up?" asked Troy, his mouth full of a turkey hoagie. He came to the porch and looked into the sky.

"What are those lights?"

Troy swallowed and said, "That's the Aurora Borealis."

"Are you sure?"

"Yes, I'm sure." Troy took another bite.

"I thought you could only see that in places like Alaska," said Melynda.

"Normally, that's true," said Troy, again with a full mouth, nodding.

"Well, whatever it is, it's gorgeous! Look at it!" said Melynda with amazement as she pulled her thick brown hair behind her shoulders.

"Oh, yeah," Troy said as he swallowed. "All those colors mean that there's been a spike in solar activity."[13]

"Yesterday, you said this would happen. How did you know?" Melynda asked watching the sky. "You're an accountant for heaven sakes, not a meteorologist."

"I have many talents."

Melynda nodded. "I know that but…"

Troy pointed in the sky with the hand holding the hoagie. "It's been about eleven years since the last storm." Then he took another bite of his sandwich. With a full mouth he managed to say, "It's about time."[14]

"Where did you learn about this stuff?"

"On the Internet."

Looking back at her husband standing behind her, Melynda said, "Hmmmm, I should look that stuff up. I'd like to learn about the sky." Returning her gaze at the aurora activity she said, "Look at those colors go! They're so brilliant! I didn't even know these kind of colors existed naturally," said Melynda. "I should call Corrynne and see if she and Bo can see them too."

"I'm sure they can. These lights should almost reach the equator tonight. But you can call your sister tomorrow. Just be with me tonight," said Troy swallowing again.

Melynda looked at her husband. He was serious and she was flattered. She smiled and looked back at the sky. "Doesn't it look like armies battling? Or maybe fire-breathing dragons?"

"You've got an active imagination," said Troy as he finished up the last bite of his sandwich.

"But doesn't it?"

"Yeah, I guess so," Troy said, chewing. "I always thought the aurora looked like ghosts flying around."

Melynda laughed and looked up at Troy. "I can see that. So, tell me what causes those lights?" asked Melynda changing her focus back to the sky.

Troy pointed at the waving, streaming colors and said, "As I understand it, those colors are actually energized electrons and protons that have come from the sun and are interacting with the magnetic field of the earth. The energy is flowing past us like a river."[15]

"I see," said Melynda as she put her arm around Troy's thick bicep. "It's gorgeous."

"But even though I know what makes an aurora work, I still look into the sky and think about God. He not only created the world, he made it beautiful."

"I like how you think, Troy," said Melynda looking up at her husband. "Even if you talk with your mouth full."

"What? I talk with my mouth full?" asked Troy, forcing a surprised look.

"Yes, you do," said Melynda, standing on her tip-toes to kiss him on the lips. "Mmmm," said Melynda, licking her lips. "Honey mustard and mayo dessert."

"Come here you," said Troy with a smile as he took Melynda in his arms. "I'll give you honey mustard. Hurry and shut the front door so the kids can't find us!"

Melynda laughed as she allowed herself to be wrapped in Troy's arms.

Troy leaned down and kissed his wife long and hard under the brilliant northern lights.

Las Vegas, Nevada
8:35 p.m.

"Ted! Look outside!" Julie's voice was pierced with worry. "Something's happening in the sky! I think we're being attacked! There must be a bomb going off somewhere! Pack the car!"

"Pack the car? Why?"

"I think we need to go to Utah. Las Vegas is getting too dangerous."

"And do what?"

"Stay with Bo, Corrynne, and the kids."

"No, no, Julie," Ted said as he caught her by the shoulders near the large kitchen windows. "We don't need to go to Utah. Our son has enough to worry about right now without us showing up on their doorstep. We're going to stay right where we are because gas is too expensive to waste like that and there's no bomb…." But then he saw a huge light in the sky. "***Whoa!*** *What in the heck was that?*"

"See? I told you," said Julie with a look of satisfaction. "Those lights aren't normal. I bet there's some fires somewhere and the light's reflecting off the clouds."

Ted squinted and took a step toward the windows. "What clouds, Julie? There aren't any clouds. It's a clear night."

Julie joined Ted and squinted too. "I'm sure there are some. We just can't see them."

"Are your glasses dirty?" asked Ted.

"No," said Julie, taking off her bifocals and looking at them. "Maybe you should put your glasses on to see better," suggested Julie as she breathed on her own lenses and cleaned them anyway with her blouse. Just in case.

"I don't use my glasses to see far away, Julie. And even if I needed glasses, I would know that fire doesn't put green lights in the sky."

Julie folded her arms and watched the sky for a few moments, then with a sigh she said, "OK, maybe there aren't any clouds, but—there's something strange going on here."

Ted patted his wife gently on the back and said, "Oh, stop being so jumpy. I'm sure it's nothing. Let's turn on the news. Maybe we'll see what's happening."

"That's a good idea," said Julie as she moved to her remote and pushed the power button.

The television came to life. "Eight minutes ago the sun released a solar flare the size of Mount Everest…"

"See here, Ted," said Julie pointing her perfectly manicured finger at the screen. "They're talking about it here!"

"The energy is now interacting with our atmosphere, delighting our city with a treat that most people at our latitude have never seen. What you are watching is an aurora, normally only seen at the farthest north and south ends of the earth, but because the magnetic field of the earth is at its lowest strength in a couple thousand years, those in our city can enjoy the sights as they bask in the warm Vegas breezes."

"See, Julie?" said Ted folding his arms. "There's nothing to worry about. It's just lights in the sky. There aren't any fires."

"Shhh, I want to hear this," said Julie briskly.

"Now, because of the strangeness of this experience, there are thousands of callers jamming up the phones. Do not be alarmed, repeat, do not be alarmed. We at KAXI assure all of you that all the satellites are functioning appropriately and not exploding in fire, raining down on earth; nothing as dramatic as that. So, just sit back and enjoy. Our meteorologist has notified us that we should be seeing more of this in the future…."

Suddenly the television and all the lights in the house turned off.

"…Ted?" called Julie, reaching her arm out to find her husband.

"What, Julie?"

"The electricity is off."

"I know Julie. I'm standing in the same room you are."

"Where?"

"Just a few feet from you. Take three steps toward my voice and you'll find me."

Julie did as her husband instructed and found him. She took his arm firmly in hers. "Do you think a breaker has blown?"

"Maybe. Do you know where the flashlights are?"

"When John's kids were over yesterday, they played with them. Who knows where they are now."

"Great, Julie. You can't let our grandkids do that. Now we're going to have to figure things out in the dark," said Ted. "Have a seat on the couch. I'll go check the breaker. Careful, don't fall."

"I won't," said Julie as she carefully felt her way to the seat of the couch. "You be careful and don't step on Molly," she called back.

"Molly will get out of the way," said Ted.

"She's too old," said Julie, as she sat on the couch with her hands clasped together and looked around in the dark. "She might not move fast enough."

"Hey, Julie," called Ted as there was the sound of rolling metal.

"What happened?"

"Nothing, I just kicked Molly's water bowl."

"Don't slip and break your hip!"

"Thanks, Julie. Ahh, could you look outside, see if the neighbors have electricity."

"OK," said Julie as she carefully felt her way to the windows. Just beyond them she could see that no one had electricity. "The whole neighborhood is dark. The only lights outside are the ones in the sky."

"Hmmm," said Ted.

"What's wrong?"

"I wonder if those lights have anything to do with this power outage."

"Can that happen?"

"Sure. When there are surges of electricity, it can wipe out the circuits that control the energy."

"So how long do you think we'll be in the dark?"

"Probably till morning," said Ted coming closer. "The best thing we can do is not to worry, go to bed, and let the electric company do their work."

Julie stood from the couch and walked around it to join her husband. "Since we can't find our flashlights that might be a good idea," she agreed.

"Take my hand. I'll help you down the hall," said Ted.

Julie did as Ted suggested and they moved carefully down the hall together.

"Don't worry. It's just a power outage," said Ted. "Now let's get some rest. Things will be back to normal when we wake up."

"I hope you're right," said Julie as they rounded the corner to their bedroom.

Electric Generation Complex
Manhattan, New York
10:47 p.m.

"We have a problem."

"What?"

"Manhattan's out."

"Which part?"

"All of it."

"All of it? You've got to be kidding."

"It's no joke. Look for yourself."

"What are we going to do?"

"I guess, get to work."

"I knew those electric loads were too much for the system. According to this display, we have a weak spot in the power grid. The 100-ton static capacitor at the Manhattan sub-station has tripped and gone off-line."

"We've got to get out there and fix that. There's going to be loss of regulation with huge power swings and a reduction of power generation in the network. I hope another power capacitor doesn't fail in the meantime."

"Too late, now another one has failed in the same station."

"Another one?" The comptroller rolled his chair over to the next computer screen to see for himself.

"Now two more in the next station over."

"Two?"

"Now five."

The comptroller shook his head. "Oh, New York is not going to be happy in the morning. In 59 seconds the whole northeast part of the region has lost electricity. Good thing it isn't winter."

"No, but it's fall. It's still not toasty in New York."

"True. Let's get to work."

"Got ya. I'll get the keys."

"I'll get my chips. It's going to be a long night."

White House
Washington, D.C.
10:55 p.m.

The computer screen flickered as the lights flashed. Grace looked around the Oval Office as the electricity threatened to fail.

"No, no, don't do this! I'm not finished." Then when she looked at her computer screen again, the document she had been working on was full of jumbled words and odd symbols.

She frowned and hit the enter button, and then another and another button, but the computer didn't respond to her repeated poking. It was frozen. She hard-booted the machine, but worried about her document. She hadn't saved for a while.

As the computer came back to life, Grace crossed her fingers. "Come on, come on. Don't do this to me now. It's not a good time." She couldn't afford the time to do a rewrite. She was running out of time. Soon, it would be morning.

The computer's face lit up and luckily, her document had been auto-saved. Relief filled Grace as she prepared to send it to the Senate and the House. She needed to get this document out before everyone woke up. In the morning, she knew her term would be over. MD had destroyed her politically. This document would explain why within 24 hours money would be missing from banks all over the nation. It was a call to unite to fight the international powers that threatened to eat America for lunch, but inside she knew it was too little too late. To be honest, she didn't know what she was going to do next. It was a very lonely moment.

She attempted to connect to the Internet to send a mass e-mail, but a message came up telling her that her wireless system was down.

"What's going on now?" she asked the air as she pushed the button to connect her to her maintenance night personnel. She was met with a busy signal.

"That's strange," she said as she tried again. Again it was busy.

Frustrated, she stood from her desk and walked to the door and poked her head out into the hall outside the Oval Office. There wasn't anyone in the halls. It was late. What did she expect?

Again, the lights flickered, only this time, they went out.

Grace stood in the pitch black, waiting for the lights to come back on. An eerie feeling came over her as she stood in the doorway of her office. It was disturbing that she couldn't assure her own safety. If the lights were out, did that mean the security systems were out too?

Once again she tried to use her cell phone. She'd call security this time. For a third time, she was met with a busy signal.

"Ohhhh," she said in frustration as she flipped her phone closed. Quickly she retreated back into her office and closed and locked her door. Then, trying to be brave, she proceeded to all the windows to make sure they were locked. Feeling with her hand, she was able to tell that the locks were in place.

Next, Grace walked into her quarters, right off the Oval Office and locked the door behind her. Methodically, she checked all the windows in the room. It comforted her that all of them were locked here, too.

Suddenly, the lights came on again.

"Finally!" she whispered in relief. But now she was too tired to fight her computer. Grace was emotionally drained. She was sure there would be havoc in the morning. She'd send the e-mail then. It was time for bed.

Quickly, she shed her clothes, turned off the light, and crawled into her high pedestal bed, rationalizing that she had brushed her teeth earlier. Burying herself underneath her covers she curled up in a ball around her pillows. All she wanted to do was make the world disappear. Maybe she'd wake up in the morning and things would be different.

Grace knew she was fooling herself, but it was OK. Whatever she had to do…she'd deal with it in the morning.

With a yawn, the President fell into a welcome sleep.

Notes to "Lights and Confusion"

Short Circuits

[1] Much attention has been given to global warming in our day, which may or may not be a scientific fact. John Christy, the director of Earth System Science Center and critic of severe warming predictions, was quoted saying forecasting the future "gets messy quickly." He goes on: "'The Earth system has more unknowns than we are generally willing to acknowledge,' he told CNN via e-mail. 'It is very difficult for [scientists] to say, 'I don't have a clue.'...Our pronouncements often express more confidence than is warranted given the level of ignorance in which we presently operate."

"A minority of scientists reject what they call 'alarmist' global warming on scientific grounds. They raise three major objections, which most researchers agree remain troublesome. [a] Natural climate variability is not well understood and may be greater than once thought. [b] Computer models are oversimplifications that cannot simulate the complexities of the real climate. [c] Temperature extrapolations of the past are not precise enough to make dire conclusions about 'normal' warming. Richard Lindzen, a respected meteorologist from the Massachusetts Institute of Technology, says in light of these uncertainties, pronouncements about climate change are both self-serving and unscientific. 'Scientists make meaningless or ambiguous statements. Advocates and media translate statements into alarmist declarations. Politicians respond to alarm by feeding scientists more money,' said Lindzen at a scientific conference this January. He added that the accepted evidence is 'entirely consistent with there being virtually no problem at all' (Michael Coren, "The Science Debate Behind Climate Change" *CNN.com*, February 6, 2006, http://www.cnn.com/2005/TECH/science/04/08/earth.science/index.html).

In researching the scriptures to understand the possible causes of the plagues of the last days, the sun is mentioned more than one time in more than one place in the scriptures as being hotter than expected as in this scripture: "And men were scorched with great heat, and blasphemed the name of God, which hath power over these plagues: and they repented not to give him glory" (Revelation 16:9). This heat is different than the heat that eventually will cause the elements to melt as the earth is burned, for men will not be able to withstand that heat to blaspheme God.

Since global warming, even if a valid theory, wouldn't affect the earth as the above scripture describes for hundreds of years, and we being at the end of the sixth seal and beginning of the seventh seal, logically the earth must heat up by a quicker natural process than the effects of man on the environment. In researching possible causes of increased heat of the sun on the earth, some interesting things were discovered.

It is a fact, a less known and certainly less publicized fact, that the earth's magnetic field is weakening and has been for the last 300 years. The magnetic field is the very mechanism that protects the earth from bursts of radiation from the sun. Not only that, the sun is actually heating up. We are heading for the biggest solar maxima ever recorded in approximately 2010-2012 according to NASA. A hotter sun and a weakening magnetic field would translate into a warmer atmosphere, as would the increased radiation from the sun to a depleted ozone layer. These documented, not theorized, changes in the earth's extraterrestrial environment are real, and soon we'll be experiencing its effects. It is upon this premise this text is written.

[2] "A solar flare is a violent explosion in the sun's atmosphere with an energy equivalent to a billion megatons, traveling normally at about 1 million km per hour (about 0.05% the speed of light), though sometimes much faster" ("Solar Flare," *Wikipedia*, http://en.wikipedia.org/wiki/Solar_flare).

[3] "Most flares occur *around* sunspots, where intense magnetic fields emerge from the sun's surface into the corona. The energy efficiency associated with solar flares may take several hours or even days to build up, but most flares take only a matter of minutes to release their energy" ("Solar Flare," *Wikipedia*, http://en.wikipedia.org/wiki/Solar_flare).

[4] "Solar flares are classified as A, B, C, M, or X according to the peak flux (in watts per square meter, W/m2) of 100 to 800 picometer X-rays near Earth, as measured on the Geostationary Operational Environmental Satellite (GOES). Two of the largest GOES flares were the X20 events (2 mW/m2) recorded on August 16 1989 and April 2, 2001. However, these events were outshone by a flare on November 4, 2003 that was the most powerful X-ray flare ever recorded. This flare was originally classified as X28 (2.8 mW/m2). However, the GOES detectors were saturated at the peak of the flare, and it is now thought that the flare was between X40 (4.0 mW/m2) and X45 (4.5 mW/m2), based on the influence of the event on the earth's atmosphere" ("Solar Flare," *Wikipedia*, http://en.wikipedia.org/wiki/Solar_flare).

[5] "Space weather is nasty. The winds that blow through the galaxy are winds of radiation, some of the most harmful from distant exploding stars. But there is another source which is much nearer, which is our sun. The sun itself is a thermonuclear furnace and this flings off huge amounts of dangerous material in very large explosions. In some cases, [the explosion] is about the same mass as Mount Everest actually coming towards us. Every few hours the sun ejects billions of tons of electrically charged particles, the solar wind. Often the Earth lies directly in the path of this onslaught" ("Magnetic Storm," *Nova*, (transcript), http://www.pbs.org/wgbh/nova/transcripts/3016_magnetic.html).

[6] "...Researchers announced that a storm is coming—the most intense solar maximum in fifty years. The prediction comes from a team led by Mausumi Dikpati of the National Center for Atmospheric Research (NCAR). 'The next sunspot cycle will be 30% to 50% stronger than the previous one,' she says. If correct, the years ahead could produce a burst of solar activity second only to the historic Solar Max of 1958. ...Dikpati's forecast puts Solar Max at 2012. Hathaway believes it will arrive sooner, in 2010 or 2011. (Dr. Tony Phillips, "Solar Storm Warning," *Science@NASA*, March 3, 2006, http://science.nasa.gov/headlines/y2006/10mar_stormwarning.htm?list862664).

[7] "A geomagnetic storm is a temporary disturbance of the Earth's magnetosphere. Associated with solar coronal mass ejections (CME), coronal holes, or solar flares, a geomagnetic storm is caused by a solar wind shock wave which typically strikes the Earth's magnetic field 24 to 36 hours after the event. This only happens if the shock wave travels in a direction toward Earth. The solar wind pressure on the magnetosphere will increase or decrease depending on the Sun's activity. These solar wind pressure changes modify the electric currents in the ionosphere. Magnetic storms usually last 24 to 48 hours, but some may last for many days" ("Geomagnetic storm," *Wikipedia*, http://en.wikipedia.org/wiki/Geomagnetic_storm).

[8] "The rate of change is higher over the last 300 years than it has been for any time in the past 5,000 years. It's going from a strong field down to a weak field, and it's doing so very quickly" (John Shaw of University of Liverpool as quoted by "Magnetic Storm," *NOVA*, http://www.pbs.org/wgbh/nova/magnetic/about.html).

"If the trend continues, [the Earth's magnetic field weakening] the field may collapse altogether and then reverse. Compasses would point south instead of north. ...Earth's geodynamo creates a magnetic field that shields most of the habited parts of our planet from charged particles that come mostly from the sun. The field deflects the speeding particles toward Earth's Poles. Without our planet's magnetic field, Earth would be subjected to more cosmic radiation" (John Roach, "The Earth's Magnetic Field is Fading," *National Geographical News*, September 9, 2004, http://news.nationalgeographic.com/news/2004/09/0909_040909_earthmagfield.html).

[9] "Without our planet's magnetic field, Earth would be subjected to more cosmic radiation. The increase could knock out power grids, scramble the communications systems on spacecraft, temporarily widen atmospheric ozone holes, and generate more aurora activity. A number of Earth's creatures, including some birds, turtles, and bees, rely on Earth's magnetic field to navigate" (John Roach, "The Earth's Magnetic Field is Fading," National Geographical News, September 9, 2004, http://news.nationalgeographic.com/news/2004/09/0909_040909_earthmagfield.html).

[10] "Solar flares release a cascade of high energy particles known as a proton storm. Protons can pass through the human body, doing biochemical damage" ("Solar Flare," *Wikipedia*, http://en.wikipedia.org/wiki/Solar_flare).

[11] "The penetration of high-energy particles into living cells can cause chromosome damage, cancer, and a host of other health problems. Large doses can be fatal immediately. Solar protons with energies greater than 30 Megaelectronvolts(MeV) are particularly hazardous. In October 1989, the Sun produced enough energetic particles that an astronaut on the Moon, wearing only a space suit and caught out in the brunt of the storm, would probably have died; the expected dose would be about 7000 rem. (Astronauts who had time to gain safety in a shelter beneath moon soil would have absorbed only slight amounts of radiation.) The astronauts on the Mir station were subjected to daily doses of about twice the yearly dose on the ground, and during the solar storm at the end of 1989 they absorbed their full-year radiation dose limit in just a few hours" ("Geomagnetic storm," *Wikipedia*, http://en.wikipedia.org/wiki/Geomagnetic_storm).

[12] The computer is very fragile when it comes to extra energy in the air. Even common static electricity can destroy a computer component. See the following:

"The microprocessor is the component of the personal computer that does the actual processing of data. A microprocessor is a central processing unit (CPU) that fits on one microchip. It is the "brain" of the computer.... The microprocessor integrated circuit package holds a silicon chip that contains millions of transistors and other components fabricated into the silicon. Because the transistors on the chip are very tiny, even a small zap of high voltage current (such as from static electricity) can destroy a chip" (Thomas E. Beach, PH. D.,

"Computer Concepts and Terminology; Processors," *University of New Mexico—Los Alamos*, http://www.la.unm.edu/~beach/terms/processors.html).

[13] On November 11, 2004, a coronal mass ejection, which is a "spike in solar activity" caused tremendous auroras that could be seen all over America. See the following article:

"A spot on the sun is bursting with large flares and tremendous coronal mass ejections, sending charged solar particles to Earth. The waves of particles descending on the planet are responsible for the aurora displays that have been visible as far south as the Carolinas. Aurora forecasters at the Geophysical Institute (University of Alaska Fairbanks) predict maximum aurora activity until Friday, Nov. 12, and possibly into the weekend. The aurora should be visible in regions far south of the Arctic, including most of the United States, if clear skies cooperate" ("Solar Disturbances Spike Aurora Activity," *Technology Research and Development of Alaska*, http://trendalaska.org/?q=node/187).

[14] "Every 11 years solar activity reaches a fever pitch: Solar flares erupt near sunspots on a daily basis. Coronal mass ejections, billion-ton clouds of magnetized gas, fly away from the Sun and buffet the planets. Even the Sun's awesome magnetic field—as large as the solar system itself—grows unstable and flips. It's a turbulent time called Solar Max" (Dr. Tony Phillips, "The Resurgent Sun," *Science @ NASA*, http://science.nasa.gov/headlines/y2002/18jan_solarback.htm).

[15] "Auroras are luminous, deeply mysterious curtains of light that often grace dark skies near the North and South poles. They occur when a space weather event energizes the magnetic force field shielding our planet, churning up electrons and protons and causing them to smash into the mix of gases in the upper atmosphere. The result is a bright glow that can last anywhere from a few seconds to a few hours" (Lexi Krock, "Gallery of Auroras," *Nova*, http://www.pbs.org/wgbh/nova/magnetic/aurora.html).

CHAPTER THREE

FALL FROM GRACE

"Yea, they shall not be beaten down by the storm at the last day; yea, neither shall they be harrowed up by the whirlwinds; but when the storm cometh they shall be gathered together in their place, that the storm cannot penetrate to them; yea, neither shall they be driven with fierce winds whithersoever the enemy listeth to carry them" (Alma 26:6).

00:03:13, 12:50:35, Zulu
Wednesday, September 17th

Traumatic News

Washington, D.C.
6:10 a.m.

From the helicopter pad at the White House, the rotating electromagnetic engines of Air Force One purred quietly as President MacEntire strapped herself into her oversized window seat. A successful liftoff in the early morning hours by the new shuttle-like airplane occurred from a standstill. Amidst a turbulent and rapid ascent, her environment changed quickly.

"I would like to speak to the Vice President," she said aloud. Microphones in the ceiling picked up her request.

"Connecting," said the Air Force One's automated computer voice.

Against the pull of multiplied gravity, the president lifted her hands to her face to discretely blow her nose. Then with effort she reached out to pull down a mirror that was tucked in the wall. Her eyes were puffy from a morning of crying and relatively no sleep. She was grateful she could just hide away for a while. Who would have thought, with all the mechanisms of control at her fingertips, things would end up so upside down and backwards?

The memory of Braun's warnings about America's destruction if it didn't turn back to God came rushing back to her mind. She nodded in acceptance. He was right. Destruction was at the doors. Obviously God wasn't going to save them this time.

"Vice President Krantz here," came a familiar voice, breaking Grace out of her thoughts.

"Krantz. Good. I'm glad I could talk to you. Did you receive my e-mail this morning?"

"No, not yet. My Internet is down."

"Mine was too, earlier," said Grace becoming suspicious. "And that was strange. I never have problems…"

"Grace, everyone's Internet was down."

"Why?"

"There've been blackouts all over America. New York has been especially affected. They still don't have electricity. Don't you watch the news?"

Grace was irritated by the question. "No, Krantz, not before breakfast I don't. Just tell me what's going on." She secretly worried about an electromagnetic pulse from an atomic weapon detonated in the airspace above America. MD had all but threatened an attack the day before.

"There's been a massive solar flare from the sun. We're supposed to expect problems with electricity and technology off and on for the next couple days. After that, the solar winds should calm down and things should go back to normal."

"Ahh," said Grace nodding and feeling relieved. She was sure her staff would have updated her if she had gone to breakfast as per her normal routine. "OK. At least it's not something that can't be handled."

"No…and I'm assuming we've got bigger problems to discuss."

"Right. Then you've heard," said Grace, nodding even though he couldn't see her.

"Not really. I just know you're nowhere to be found. I assume you're in the shuttle. Has something happened?"

Grace blew out her cheeks and blinked hard. Then emphatically she said, "Yes."

"So we're in emergency mode."

"Yes."

"Clue me in."

"I plan to disappear for a couple days up here until things calm down on the ground. I expect our lives will be in jeopardy of assassination within a matter of hours."

"What are you talking about? Is it really that bad?"

"Oh yes," said Grace nodding her head.

"So tell me."

"I suggest you disappear somewhere too. We can conduct any business via satellite."

"That might be difficult. Some of the satellites are down. I understand radio waves aren't behaving right now with all the extra energy in the air."

"Well, we'll have to do our best," said Grace. "Anyway, even if we can't communicate, just run with the ball according to the State of Emergency Protocol. Read my e-mail to review your responsibilities."

"Was it encrypted?"

"Of course."

"Good."

"Why?" asked Grace.

"Because if things are as bad as you are leading me to believe, we'll need all our communications to be encrypted."

"Absolutely."

"So, tell me what's going on, Grace."

Grace put a hand to her forehead and then dropped it. "Are you sitting down?"

"Yes."

"Yesterday morning I was escorted *in to* and *out of* Matthew Daimler's office at the IMF in New York."

"Why? What'd that man want with you?"

The President grimaced. "The International Monetary Fund called in all their loans yesterday."

"What does that mean?"

Still grimacing she said, "That means that all the banks in America will be drained dry to pay America's debt to the IMF sometime soon."

"What? Wait... What are you talking about?" asked the Vice President, shocked.

"That means that every savings account, every checking account, and every retirement account will be emptied."

"What?"

"Yes. I checked last night to see if MD was telling the truth and according to the Federal Reserve, he was. I was hoping it was just another threat."

"So you're saying—*there's no money*." The Vice President's voice sounded strangled.

President MacEntire shook her head, even though Krantz couldn't see her. "No money."

"Anywhere?"

"Not in the banks. We still have the gold in Lauderdale and Knox and whatever's in the American people's pocket but other than that, America's broke."

"...How? I haven't heard anything about it."

"That's because it hasn't happened yet. Maybe with the electrical problems and computer glitches the transfer will be delayed. In my book, that's a small blessing."

There was a pause and then Krantz asked, "So how did this happen?"

President MacEntire sneered allowing herself a little angry indulgence. *"How do you think? MD reached his power-hungry, fat-fingered hands into the cookie jar and took every last crumb."*

"Can he do that?"

Grace shrugged in response to her own powerlessness. With raised eyebrows she said, "No. Not technically. He's supposed to notify us and we're supposed to scramble funds together so we don't lose face with the rest of the world. But, because of his majority ownership of stock in the member banks that own the Federal Reserve[3] and his connections there on the various boards of trustees, he by-passed me and every other federal position of authority and took the funds without our knowledge."

"And the banks let him do that?"

"He's their boss. What choice did they have?"

"Can't you fire the Board of Governors for that?"

"Sure, but what's the point? The deed has been done. It wouldn't change anything."

"Isn't there some organization over MD that we could go to for retribution?"

"No. MD is the god of money on this planet. He's the IMF. He owns the majority of the stocks, thus controlling the Federal Reserve member banks. Because of that, he has all the power.[4] No nation in the world will go up against MD if they expect some sort of future goodwill, especially after what happened today. We're on our own."

"What about Great Britain? Couldn't they help us out?" asked the Vice President.

"They're in a stranglehold, too. It won't be long until they join us in ultimate submission," said Grace with sarcasm. "MD will make sure of that."

"So...." There was quiet for a long period of time. Then there was a heavy breath and the Vice President started again, "So, what happens next?"

"We know what happens next, Krantz," said the President in a monotone. She was running on automatic, way beyond emotion.

"We do?"

"Yes, a very similar thing happened in Argentina in 2001."

"Oh, yes, the IMF refused to give Argentina money for some reason. Ahhh...let me remember. The whole place was a mess."

"Right," said President MacEntire. "The IMF refused to give Argentina more loans to float their economy. Argentina had to pay previous interest before receiving any more."

"I remember now."

"In an effort to make good on their responsibilities, the country closed down the banks and used the people's money to pay their interest payments. Caps were placed on all bank accounts so the people couldn't get to their deposits."

"That was in poor form."

"Of course it was," said Grace. "It was the worst political thing a country could do to its people."

"So how is that situation like ours?" asked the Vice President. "We're not doing that."

"Krantz, it doesn't matter who took the money, the issue is that soon the money will be gone and we're going to be blamed for it. Our people will think we took their money. They'll act the same way the Argentinean people did, if not worse."

"So what happened in Argentina? Refresh my memory."

"The country went hungry and mass hysteria, chaos, and lawlessness erupted."

"Ohhh. That doesn't sound good. That can ruin a good day."

"The President was run out of office, leading to five presidents over a two week period," continued Grace. "The whole country was put into a 'State of Siege,' suspending the Argentinean's constitutional rights so the government could stop the violence but still, stores were looted, buildings were set on fire, banks were rushed, and people died. It was very ugly."[5]

"Doesn't sound optimal, does it?"

"No, Krantz, it doesn't. I'm sick about this. We're heading off a cliff and there aren't any brakes."

"What are we going to do? Have you looked at our options?"

"All morning. I've been staring at computer screens till I couldn't see straight. I've been talking to key people that I thought maybe could pull some strings and stop MD's money snatch, but no luck. The deed's as good as done and we're sunk."

"So what's going to happen?"

"Well," President MacEntire took a breath. "We're going to do all that we can do. We'll call all our troops home, declare Martial Law,[6] and try to maintain—slash—restore peace."

"Martial Law? The people aren't going to like to hear that. It might cause more rioting."

"We'll call it a 'State of Emergency' then. Oh well, let's be honest, it's the same thing. FEMA[7] has its marching orders just like you do. Luckily the Internet worked long enough today for me to send my go-ahead to them, as well as my explanations and apologies to Congress."

"I got ya. What authority do we need to put this in order?"

"We've got it already. I've instituted Executive orders[8] numbers 10995 through 11000,[9] and a few others. I've also enacted a few of my own."

"What are they?"

"Weapons control and people control. We need to take away all the weapons and round up the volatile groups that might prey on people during this time."

"Are we ready for this?"

"It doesn't matter. What other choice do we have?"

"Hmmm," said Vice President Krantz.

"...Krantz?" President MacEntire asked after an uncomfortable pause.

"Yes?"

"I need you behind me on these things," said Grace, her voice as strong as she could muster.

"I'm behind you."

"Good. Thank you," said the President as she laid her head on the wall and watched out the window. "We have to act as quickly as possible *before* things get out of control."

"Umm, I have a question, if you don't mind," said the Vice President.

"What?"

"If all the money is gone, how are we going to pay our troops and feed the country?"

The President lifted her head off the wall and brushed some lint off her skirt. "Well. We do have what's left of the gold in the Federal Reserve. I believe it's about sixty billion. We've been tapping into it to pay interest on those *stupid* loans so it's a third what it should have been but it's better than nothing."

"So we'll issue gold certificates?"

"Yes. Those will get us by for a little while. It will at least help us establish some peace."

"OK. Sounds like it might work. We'll need to get those into circulation fast."

"Sure. Promise everyone a tenth of what they had in the bank. The banks will hand them out for us."

"A tenth?"

"That's all we can afford, Krantz. Sixty billion is a far cry from the six hundred that was taken."

"I see." The Vice President sounded unsure.

"It won't solve all the problems but there's no other plan. We'll hold back twenty billion to feed the hungry, because there's going to be a lot of them. America is out of work."

"Alright."

There was another long silence. President MacEntire shook her head as she reviewed her conversation with MD in her mind.

"Grace?"

"Yes, Krantz?"

"You won't be giving up your office and leaving me in the lurch, will you?"

Grace looked back into the mirror. She paused and then said, "I haven't made up my mind, to be honest with you."

Krantz laughed nervously and said, "*No, no, no, no*, Grace. Now, you can't. That wouldn't be kosher in my book."

Grace was slightly amused. There was genuine fear in Krantz's voice. "I didn't know you were Jewish."

"You know what I mean."

The President considered her options, which were growing fewer by the second. "Oh Krantz, who really cares any more? No one cares who runs this country. I could be a monkey organ grinder and it wouldn't make a difference."

"Yes, it would. It would make a difference to me and everyone else who's close to you."

"Yeah, yeah, yeah." Grace shook her head. "You know what, Krantz?"

"What?"

"Soon there won't be an America to worry about."

"Don't you think that's being a little dramatic?"

"No, I don't."

"Why?"

"MD assured me he was planning on buying up all the land in America. Do you know what that means?"

"No, what?"

"We're going to be assimilated."

"What kind of word is that? *Assimilated?*" Krantz was getting angry.

"The right kind. We're going to become a part of the collective. Resistance is futile."

"Why are you making jokes?"

Grace smirked and then shook her head. What else could she do? She tried to speak, but found she couldn't answer. She was beginning to become emotional again. A desire to disappear was growing within her. All she wanted to do was walk away. She'd do it after the TV cameras went dead, but she didn't tell Krantz her thoughts. She had to seem positive and in control. This was not the time to seem overwhelmed.

President MacEntire took a deep breath, cleared her throat, and said, "I suggest you put the things in motion outlined by the e-mail and then go into hiding. Anyone who even looks like a politician will be a huge target to anyone who has a chip on their shoulder and you and I both know that will be everyone in America once they learn their hard-earned money is gone."

"OK…." There was a big sigh and then silence.

"Krantz?"

There wasn't an answer. It seemed she had been disconnected. "Get Krantz back on the line for me."

"Right away, Madam President," said the automated voice.

As Grace waited to be reconnected she fiddled with her wedding ring. Could this really be the end? She had been in shock before, but now that she had talked to Krantz, all of it was beginning to sink in. What would she do? How would she stay safe? Could she return to the White House….

"Hello?" It was Krantz's voice again.

"Oh, good, Krantz. I'm glad I got you again. We lost the connection."

"I know. We might lose it again because of the power surges. Let's hurry."

"I sensed you had a question for me. What was it?" asked the President.

"Yeah, ummm, so how much time do you think we have?"

"I have no idea. The money's been taken. It's gone. Like I said, as soon as it registers on the computers across America, that's it."

"OK," said Krantz. He too was beginning to sound emotional. "Got it....Well. God bless you, Grace."

"You too, Krantz. You too," said the President, her lip quivering and another tear falling down her cheek. It was good the conversation was over. "I'll be in touch." But she didn't know if that was true or not. Would phones work tomorrow? Actually it didn't really matter. Even if they did work it would only be a short time until no one could pay their bills. Without federal money the phone companies would go out of business. There was a click and Krantz was gone. She wondered if she would ever see him again. She wondered if anything would ever be normal for her again.

Snow Storm

Siberia, Russia
9:30 p.m.

Despite the masks, the frozen night air ripped Braun's lungs as he tried to breathe. He had to purse his lips to warm the air enough to begin to inhale. But now it was beginning to snow and by the looks of the black sky, it was going to snow hard.

The snowmobile came to a stop on the lee side of a short fir tree covered in white. Chenille had selected the side opposite the wind to shelter the machine from becoming buried under the falling blanket of snow.

When the hum of the snowmobile ceased, the howl of the wind took over. It was so loud that communication between the two was impossible. Without words, both Chenille and Braun dismounted. Chenille pushed a button on the back of the machine to open the seat and grabbed a small pack hidden inside. Next they dove for the tree branches. An immediate shelter was needed if they were going to survive this storm and the tree would provide it.

With gloved hands and quick movements, Chenille and Braun dug into the soft new snow until they hit the hard re-frozen layer fastened around the branches, holding them as if in icy suspended animation.

Braun looked up from digging. He was worried. It seemed there was no way to get under the branches to get away from the cold. He moved parallel to the place he had just uncovered as Chenille moved in the other direction. To Braun's dismay he found the ice continued to be impenetrable from days of melting and refreezing. He continued around the whole tree, hoping there would be a break somewhere. Finally after coming back to his starting point, he stood up and stamped on the sheet of ice surrounding one large branch with all his weight, but he was only rewarded with a dull thud-like feeling in his feet. What were they going to do? He attempted to look for another tree, even if it was a ways off, but the heavy snow created a complete white-out.

Braun stood up and looked around. Where was Chenille? "Chenille?" he called.

He listened. All he heard was the howling wind.

"Chenille!" he yelled again, his hands cupped around his mouth. He began to circle the tree again. She had to be around here somewhere! When he had circled the tree once again and didn't even see her footprints, he yelled a third time, *"Chenille!"* When, again, she failed to respond, Braun had a frightening thought. What if somehow she had fallen unconscious from the cold? She had been fighting the brunt of the wind when they were on the snowmobile. Maybe she was colder than he was! What if she was being buried in the snow and dying of hypothermia right at this moment? *He had just found her! He couldn't let her die!*

With a great surge of energy Braun began to yell Chenille's name and dig in the surrounding snow. He had to find her! He'd warm her up with his own body temperature. He'd build them a shelter! His mind was wild with fear as the thought of being left alone out in this wilderness, not knowing what had happened or where he was or how he was going to survive. The horror of it all was enough to kill him!

Suddenly, Chenille was there as if she had appeared out of thin air! "Braun!" she yelled in the raging wind. "What are you doing?"

Braun ripped off his goggles to look at her. Now, was he imagining her? He took heavy steps through the mounting snow until he could take hold of Chenille with both hands. "You're real!" he said with genuine tears freezing on his face.

"Of course I'm real!" she said into his ear, with a confused look. "What's going on?"

Braun yelled, "I thought you had been buried in the snow! I couldn't find you!"

Chenille smiled slightly and said with effort, "I didn't get buried in the snow. I found a way under the branches."

Braun's heart was still beating rapidly and his emotions were uncontrollable. He tried to calm himself, but the fright had been so poignant and so terrifying that he almost had to keep crying just to purge it from him. He shook his head as he tried tc get ahold of himself. He couldn't afford anymore crying, his eyelids were freezing together. What kind of man was he to cry so easily? Maybe it was a side effect of the drugs he had been given. Yes, that had to be it.

"Come on! Let's get out of this snow!" Chenille yelled as she took Braun's hand.

Gratefully, Braun followed. He would follow this woman to the ends of the earth. He would never leave her side.

Chenille moved to the opposite side of the tree where the wind was the worst. She brushed the snow from a section and pulled apart two thin half-dead branches where obviously she had broken them off. The wood bowed enough to allow her to wiggle in between them and Braun followed with difficulty since he was significantly larger. Inside the branches there was just enough light to see that there was a break in the ice near the inside of the tree that began on his side but became larger on the other side of the tree trunk. Chenille squatted down and crawled around the trunk under the other branches, and then slipped through the icy hole.

Braun waited until she was completely under and then called, "Is there enough room down there for me? Right here is OK for me if there isn't," said Braun, wanting to sacrifice for Chenille if it meant her increased comfort. "I could make a bed right here," he said as he tested the ice beneath him by hitting it gently with his fist.

A light illuminated the area below Braun and burst through the hole that Chenille had disappeared into.

"There's lots of room down here," said Chenille, her voice echoing. "This tree is huge, you just can't tell because it's covered with snow. There's a cave down here that, I would guess from the branches, has been forming for a while. It goes all the way around the trunk. Hurry down here!" called Chenille.

Braun crawled a little farther and then stuck his legs through the hole. He attempted to slide down like Chenille had but his large coat stopped him. He was just too wide. He tried to chip away the thinner ice that held him fast, and with a couple of quick punches, it gave way, widening the opening just enough for him to pass.

"Use the branches like stairs, Braun," said Chenille from below.

Braun reached blindly with his feet to find the branches.

"There's a branch to your right," called Chenille.

With some searching, Braun found the branch and eased his weight through the hole. Reaching around with his left foot, he found another one nearby and continued his descent. Within half a minute he was standing in a room of ice. It resembled an inverted tee-pee with the large area up around the bows of trees that were held fast in the snow and ice and the narrow area around the base of the tree.

"Isn't this place perfect?" asked Chenille who was holding up a yellow neon light stick. "Look, there's an opening for air above and the tree branches protect us from the snow."

Braun nodded. It was perfect. It was better than anything he could have built himself. "How did you know this was down here?" asked Braun.

"I didn't know, I just assumed."

"Good assumption."

"Thanks," said Chenille pushing her hood off her head.

Braun noticed her hair shimmered in the light. It made him want to pull her close to him. It had been so long since he had seen her and now that he wasn't drugged anymore, he was realizing how blessed he was to have a second chance.

Chenille smiled at him and then turned around and began rummaging in her pack. "Might as well set up camp."

Braun moved close and said, "What do you have there?"

"Just a survival pack until we can find a place to stay," she said as she pulled something out. "Would you like some beef jerky? I'm sure you're hungry."

Braun accepted the hard leathery meat. "I love beef jerky. Thanks."

Then Chenille headed for the tree trunk with an aluminum mess tin in her hand.

"Where are you going?" asked Braun.

"I'm going up to fill this cup outside so we can have some water."

"Good idea." Braun looked at the pack. "I'm sure you have matches. Do you want me to collect some of those dead branches up there and start a fire?"

Chenille looked back with one hand on a branch and nodded. "If you think that hole up there is large enough to let the smoke out."

Braun started looking around. "I think I could figure something out."

Chenille nodded once. "OK, that's your job. You're in charge of the fire."

"Good," said Braun as Chenille began to climb out. "Ahh, Chenille?"

"Yes?" said Chenille as she peeked down from the hole at the top.

Braun hesitated. He wanted to tell her he loved her, ask her to marry him, and tell her that he couldn't live without her but it was all too soon. Instead he swallowed and said, "...It's good to be with you again."

"You too, Braun," said Chenille with a half-shy smile. Then she quickly disappeared.

Braun took a deep breath. He needed to slow down and get his thoughts and desires under control. He knew that if he moved too fast he might scare Chenille away forever and that was the last thing he wanted to do. This was the most wonderful opportunity ever given to him and he didn't want to botch things up. Now that his faculties had returned he could think clearer. He needed to plan to woo Chenille because although she was here with him, she wasn't his...yet. He had to be careful and patient. He had to allow her to lead the relationship if there was going to be one. Braun winced at his painful thoughts. *There had to be a relationship!* After all, the Lord had shown him that at one time she was meant to be his wife. He was sure she still was. The Lord would help him. All he had to do was be led by the Spirit and it would be fine.[10]

Braun took another look around the ice cave. He had many questions about why he was here but the first order of business had to be survival. The rest would come.

Notes to "Fall From Grace"

Traumatic News

[1] The purpose of this section is to demonstrate the fragility of our economic and governmental systems. Although the United States seems strong, at any moment all of that could change. The scenario presented in this text is a fictional extrapolation to help all those that read it, see that the need to become prepared is ***immediate.*** Financial and governmental ruin has been prophesied in abundance by the early leaders of the church and it will happen quickly.

"I ask myself the question, 'Can the American nation escape?' The answer comes, 'No.' Its destruction, as well as the destruction of the world is sure; just as sure as the Lord cut off and destroyed the two great and prosperous nations that once inhabited the continent of North and South America, because of their wickedness, so will he them destroy, and sooner or later they will reap the fruits of their own wicked acts, and be numbered among the past....There are changes awaiting us, they are even nigh at our very doors, and I know it by the visions of heaven; I know it by the administrations of angels, and I know it by the inspiration of heaven, that is given to all men who seek the Lord; and the hand of God will not stay these things. We have no time to lose" (Wilford Woodruff, *Journal of Discourses*, August 1, 1880, Vol. 21, p. 301).

[2] There are elements in our government that have unbridled power, much different than the Founding Fathers desired for our country. The Federal Reserve Banks and Executive Orders are a couple of examples of the unchecked power, not supported, nor voted for by the people. Despite the non-democratic powers that struggle to control the country, America will not be controlled. Those at the helm will fall. See the following quotes:

"...He will speedily fulfill the prophecy in relation to the overthrow of the nations, and their destruction. We shall be obliged to have a government to preserve ourselves in unity and peace; for they, through being wasted away, will not have power to govern" (Orson Pratt, *Deseret Evening News*, October 2, 1875, Vol. 8, no. 265).

"Freedom is the natural condition of the human race, in which the Almighty intended men to live. Those who fight the purposes of the Almighty will not succeed. They always have been, they always will be, beaten" (Abraham Lincoln, quoted by Lucius E. Chittenden, *Recollections of President Lincoln and his Administration*, p. 76).

It has been prophesied that behind the face of American democracy, there will be an organized network of power that will attempt to enslave the people, leading to the downfall of our great nation: "Wherefore, O ye gentiles, it is wisdom in God that these things should be shown unto you, that thereby ye may repent of your sins, and suffer not that these murderous combinations shall get above you, which are built up to get power and gain—and the work, yea, even the work of destruction come upon you, yea, even the sword of the justice of the Eternal God shall fall upon you, to your overthrow and destruction if ye shall suffer these things to be. Wherefore, the Lord commandeth you, when ye shall see these things come among you that ye shall awake to a sense of your awful situation....For it cometh to pass that whoso buildeth it up seeketh to overthrow the freedom of all lands, nations, and countries; and it bringeth to pass the destruction of all people, for it is built up by the devil, who is the father of all lies...." (Ether 8:22-25).

John Taylor, at the time of his life, disclosed that these combinations were present even then and gaining strength in our nation: "Already combinations are being entered into which are very ominous for the future prosperity, welfare, and happiness of this great republic. The volcanic fires of disordered and anarchical elements are beginning to manifest themselves and exhibit the internal forces that are at work among the turbulent and unthinking masses of the people" (John Taylor, *Journal of Discourses*, April 9, 1882, Vol. 23, p. 62).

Woodrow Wilson, a President of our nation, disclosed their presence at his time also: "Some of the biggest men in the United States in the field of commerce and manufacture are afraid of something. They know that there is a power somewhere, so organized, so subtle, so watchful, so interlocked, so complete, so pervasive that they had better not speak above their breath when they speak in condemnation of it" (*The New Freedom, A Call For the Emancipation of the Generous Energies of a People*).

[3] In researching the Federal Reserve, initially, it was surprising to this author how true the rhetoric surrounding it, was. The point of contention has been; what powers controlled the Federal Reserve and its choices? Was it true that Federal Reserve was not governed by our constitution? Did a private, "for profit" corporation with selfish interests, run it? And if it did, who had the power to stop those powers from exploitation of the American People? After asking these questions and finding the startling answers, it makes one wonder; how could it be possible that we the people are not in control of our financial freedoms that weave the daily fabric of our lives? See the following general domain quotes:

"The financial system [of America] has been turned over to the Federal Reserve Board. That Board administers the finance system by authority of a purely profiteering group. The system is private, conducted for the sole purpose of obtaining the greatest possible profits from the use of other people's money" (Charles A. Lindbergh Sr., 1923).

"The Federal Reserve Banks are not federal instrumentalities..." (Lewis vs. United States, 9th Circuit 1992).

"The regional Federal Reserve banks are not government agencies....but are independent, privately owned and locally controlled corporations." (Lewis vs. United States, 680 F. 2d 1239 9th Circuit 1982).

The Federal Reserve Act (ch. 6, 38 Stat. 251, enacted December 23, 1913, 12 U.S.C. ch.3) was an act of Congress that created the Federal Reserve System, the central banking system of the United States of America, which was signed by President Woodrow Wilson. After his term of presidency he had words of remorse for putting so much power into the hands of private corporations/bankers:

"A great industrial nation is controlled by its system of credit. Our system of credit is privately concentrated. The growth of the nation, therefore, and all our activities are in the hands of a few men who, even if their action be honest and intended for the public interest, are necessarily concentrated upon the great undertakings in which their own money is involved and who necessarily, by very reason of their own limitations, chill and check and destroy genuine economic freedom....We have restricted credit, we have restricted opportunity, we have controlled development, and we have come to be one of the worst ruled, one of the most completely controlled and dominated, governments in the civilized world—no longer a government by free opinion, no longer a government by conviction and the vote of the majority, but a government by the opinion and the duress of small groups of dominant men" (The New Freedom, A Call For the Emancipation of the Generous Energies of a People, excerpts from Chaps 8, 9. "Woodrow Wilson," *Wikiquote*, http://en.wikiquote.org/wiki/Woodrow_Wilson#The_New_Freedom_.281913.29)

[4] It seems the Federal Reserve does hold unbridled power in the United States and can direct economic affairs as it sees fit. See the following quotes:

"How powerful is our 'central bank?' The Federal Reserve controls our money supply and interest rates, and thereby manipulates the entire economy—creating inflation or deflation, recession or boom, and sending the stock market up or down at whim. The Federal Reserve is so powerful that Congressman Wright Patman, Chairman of the House Banking Committee, maintains: 'In the United States today we have in effect two governments....We have the duly constituted government....Then we have an independent, uncontrolled and uncoordinated government in the Federal Reserve System, operating the money powers which are reserved to Congress by the Constitution' Neither Presidents, Congressmen nor Secretaries of the Treasury direct the Federal Reserve. In the matters of money, the Federal Reserve directs them! The uncontrolled power of the 'fed' was admitted by Secretary of the Treasury, David M. Kennedy in an interview for the May 5, 1960 issue of the U.S. News & World Report: 'Q. Do you approve of the latest credit-tightening moves? A. It's not my job to approve or disapprove. It is the action of the Federal Reserve'" (Gary Allen, *None Dare Call It Conspiracy*, p. 51).

[5] The Argentinean failure is a fact. See "Argentina in a State of Seige After Deadly Riots" at: http://archives.cnn.com/2001/WORLD/americas/12/19/argentina.riots/index.html for details of the Argentina economic collapse and their interaction with the IMF.

[6] "Martial law is the system of rules that takes effect when the military takes control of the normal administration of justice. Usually martial law reduces some of the personal rights ordinarily granted to the citizen, limits the length of the trial processes, and prescribes more severe penalties than ordinary law. In many states martial law prescribes the death penalty for certain crimes, even if ordinary law does not contain that crime or punishment in its system" ("Martial Law," *Wikipedia*, http://en.wikipedia.org/wiki/Martial_law).

[7] "The Federal Emergency Management Agency, or FEMA, is an agency of the United States Department of Homeland Security (DHS) within the Emergency Preparedness and Response Directorate. FEMA's purpose is to coordinate the response to a disaster which has occurred in the United States" ("FEMA," *Wikipedia*, http://en.wikipedia.org/wiki/FEMA).

[8] An Executive Order is a law written by the President of the United States without going through the process set aside by the Constitution to create laws. This eliminates the people and Congress as well as their ability to accept or reject the laws that govern them. See the following excerpt from the encyclopedia:

"An executive order in the United States of America is an edict issued by the President of the United States, the head of the executive branch of the United States Government....Until the early 1900s, executive orders went mostly unannounced and undocumented, seen only by the agencies to which they were directed. However, the United States Department of State instituted a numbering system for executive orders in the early 1900s, starting retroactively with what may be the most famous of executive orders, President Abraham Lincoln's 1862 Emancipation Proclamation. Today, only National Security Directives are kept from the public. Critics have accused Presidents of abusing executive orders, of using them to make laws without Congressional approval, and of moving existing laws away from their original mandates" ("Executive order," *Wikipedia*, http://en.wikipedia.org/wiki/Executive_order).

[9] The following are short descriptions of Executive Orders that the president can enact without the approval of Congress pertaining to states of emergency in the United States. Essentially, at that point, the President becomes a dictator without any other entity to balance powers. Although meant for times of emergency, it has been purposed by many circles that potentially, emergencies could and have been created for the purpose of obtaining more power over the country and eliminating liberties of the people.

Executive Order 10990 allows the government to control modes of transportation and control of highways and seaports.

Executive Order 10995 allows the government to control the communication media.

Executive Order 10997 allows the government to control electrical power, gas, petroleum, fuels, and minerals.

Executive Order 10998 allows the government to control all food resources and farms.

Executive Order 11000 allows the government to organize civilians into a labor force.

Executive Order 11001 allows the government to control health, education, and welfare functions.

Executive Order 11002 assigns the Postmaster General to register all people in the United States.

Executive Order 11003 allows the government to control airports and aircraft, commercial and otherwise.

Executive Order 11004 allows the Housing and Finance Authority to relocate people, even whole communities, build new housing, and decide which areas are to be abandoned.

Executive Order 11005 allows the government to control railroads, waterways, and public storage facilities.

Executive Order 11051 specifies that the Office of Emergency Planning can enact all Executive Orders during times of increased international strife and economic crises.

Executive Order 11310 grants authority to the Department of Justice to enforce the Executive Orders, to establish judicial and legislative arm, to control all aliens from other countries, and to operate penal and correctional institutions.

Executive Order 11921 allows the FEMA to control production and distribution, of energy sources, wages, salaries, credit and the flow of money. It also provides that when a state of emergency is declared by the President, Congress cannot review the action for six months.

Executive Order 12148 was an executive order to reorganize FEMA and to combine it with other agencies that previously were linked to emergency management and civil defense.

Executive Order Number 12656 is another EO that combines many others that came before it. Essentially, this EO combines all the power of the president to manage all the elements of the government in one EO.

Snow Storm

[10] "Live to fulfill your family dream. The longing of the human heart for this fullness is a source of great power, even—especially—on those cloudy days, or years, when your dreams seem impossible. Your longing to belong forever to a loving family comes from God, and He has promised its fulfillment to the faithful: 'For he satisfieth the longing soul, and filleth the hungry soul with goodness' (Ps. 107:9). You can live happily ever after, for the Lord God has spoken it. I have seen the mountain of the Lord's love. I know His promise is sure" (Bruce C. Hafen, "Happy Endings," *New Era*, Oct 1999, p. 44).

CHAPTER FOUR

THE UNRAVELING

"Fret not thyself because of evildoers, neither be thou envious against the workers of iniquity. For they shall soon be cut down like the grass, and wither as the green herb" (Psalms 37:1-2).

00:03:13, 03:53:11, Zulu
Wednesday, September 17th

Hot Tea

Siberia, Russia
10:07 p.m.

Braun picked up a stick he had retrieved from among the dead under-branches of the tree. He jammed it into the ceiling of the ice cave, picking at the ice and loosening the snow. He was attempting to tunnel through to the outside. After some effort, he found he couldn't reach any higher so he began to carve steps in the side of the wall to give him a boost.

"What are you doing?" asked Chenille from behind.

Braun turned and said, "I'm digging another hole in the roof."

"Why? Aren't we trying to keep the snow out?" asked Chenille with a puzzled look.

"Yes, but if we're going to build a fire to keep warm, we need another opening in this cave to create better air exchange. With two holes, the smoke will be drawn out of here."

Chenille looked back at the main entrance opening above them and then to the hole that Braun was digging. "I guess I have to trust you. ...Is there anything I can do to help? I've gathered sticks for a fire but I can see we aren't ready for that yet."

Braun looked around the ice cave. "Yes. Grab another thick piece of wood and start digging. We'll need three levels in here: the highest level for the fire, a middle level for us, and the lowest level for the cold air to settle in."

"Settle?"

"Yes, hot air rises and cold air falls. The fire on the highest level nearest the ventilation will encourage the hot air to take the smoke out. We'll be safe from the fire and smoke if we are below the fire but warmer if we are not at the lowest point in the cave."

Chenille nodded as she looked around the cave. It looked like she was hiding a smile. "Hmmm, that makes sense."

"Good," said Braun feeling a touch of satisfaction. "Just don't break a sweat," he added. "Sweat freezes and will make your clothes inefficient. We need to stay dry."

"Got ya," said Chenille as she sorted through the sticks on the sloping floor of the cave, looking for a strong one to dig with. "Braun?"

"Huh?" answered Braun looking back.

"How do you know all these things?"

Braun turned back to the wall, continuing to dig and said, "Snow camping. Scouts—you know. It was a mandatory thing in my house."

"Ahhh," said Chenille nodding. "Did you become an Eagle Scout?"

"Yep," replied Braun. "With some prodding," he added.

"Well, it's paying off now," said Chenille as she set into a digging rhythm.

"I guess so," said Braun, finishing a step. "Can I ask you a question?"

"Of course."

Braun hesitated and then asked, "Where have you been?"

Chenille stopped digging for a moment and looked up. "What do you mean?"

"I haven't seen you for a while and then suddenly, *poof*! You're here."

"You know where I've been," said Chenille, returning to her job. "I was right where I told you I'd be."

"So, you've been working at the EU? With President Lityny?"

"Yes," answered Chenille, pushing loose snow to the side.

"How's that been going?" Braun asked over his shoulder as he pulled a chunk of ice from the wall.

"Frankly, it's been a pain."

"Why?" Braun was surprised and looked back briefly. "I thought that was your dream."

"No..." started Chenille, but she didn't finish.

Braun waited for her to finish, but when she didn't, he asked, "What happened?"

"President Lityny believed I was like you."

"Like me? In what way?"

"Yes, he believed I could dream about the future. When he found out that I only had a slight ability and that you were the gifted one, he lost interest in me and I was given a desk job."

Braun cringed. "Ohh, ouch."

"No, it was fine," said Chenille looking up. "I was able to keep tabs on you there."

"Tabs on me? What are you talking about?" asked Braun turning around.

"I was given a little desk in President Lityny's office and expected to explain everything you said in detail."

"What I said?" Braun was confused, but then he understood. "Are you saying that the EU president was tapping into my conversations with the President just like MD?"

Chenille nodded.

Braun sat down on the step he had just created and shook his head. "I can't believe it! Did the whole world know what I was thinking?"

"We didn't know what you were thinking," said Chenille continuing to dig. "We just heard what you said and saw what you saw and heard what you heard. We couldn't read your thoughts."

"What's the difference?" asked Braun. "Either way, I was being used to further the enemy's plans. Now, everything that I told the President about the future can be used against her. I think America's headed for disaster prematurely because of me."

Chenille shook her head. "No, not because of you, Braun. Think about it. America's been in trouble for a while and it hasn't been because of you. MD has been involved in President MacEntire's political career since before she was elected president."

"I know. She told me that. But since she decided to turn her back on him, I was hoping I could help her make up for past mistakes—but instead, I feel like my presence destroyed all chances for anything good."

"No, Braun," said Chenille. She stood and climbed out of the depression she was digging and approached him. With sincerity in her eyes she said, "No. Everything you did at the White House was good. Believe me. I was impressed. I was secretly clapping almost every day!"

"You were?" asked Braun, feeling less bothered because of Chenille's support.

"Absolutely. You made a difference in the President's life. You touched her heart and now she's different. In consequence, she addressed the nation and encouraged them to plead to God for their welfare."

"She did?" asked Braun, amazed.

"Yes. We heard it on the plane. You were out though."

"Oh," said Braun. He remembered hearing something. He shook his head. "I couldn't tell what was real and what was in my head when I was on the plane."

Chenille nodded and laughed. "That's understandable, but I want you to know I was very proud of your bravery. You got in there and did what you needed to do. I'm sure that was hard and Heavenly Father is pleased," said Chenille as she sat down by Braun.

Braun smiled. He hoped so. With a breath, he changed the subject. "So you knew I had a chip in my head?"

"Sure, I figured it out. I knew about those chips. Remember we discussed them with the Secretary?"

"Right," said Braun nodding. "I remember."

"At first I thought they had bugged you, but then when we could tap in any time, I began to put two and two together."

"Do you have a chip?"

"No."

"That's lucky," said Braun. "I wish...." His voice faltered.

"I know," said Chenille as she put an arm around Braun's shoulders. "I know everything, and I'm sorry. It wasn't fair."

Braun looked into Chenille's eyes. He could tell she was really pained. It nearly choked him up. He had to change the subject if he was going to keep control. "So, tell me, how did you get out of there without one?"

"Matt sent me an encrypted note on my computer."

"And said what?"

"He told me that MD wanted you dead and that I was in danger of the same fate if I stuck around."

"I see," said Braun nodding.

"He asked me if I was willing to disappear with you in lieu of us being murdered."

"I take it you said yes," said Braun with a sarcastic laugh.

"Of course. What choice did I have?" asked Chenille with a shrug, pulling her arm back from around Braun.

"So what did you do to get out?"

"I went to the bathroom and just didn't come back. It was an old dating trick."

"You crawled out the window?" asked Braun with a laugh.

"Sure."

"I was imagining some elaborate sting operation to sneak you out."

"Nope."

"So did Matt help you after that?"

"Yes. I had to go to an out-of-the-way country airport where Matt picked me up."

"How did you do that?"

"I climbed down the fire-escape at the back of the building into the alleyway and caught a cab."

"What about your things?"

"I left everything," said Chenille, "except for my scriptures. Luckily, I had them with me at my desk."

"Your scriptures? How did you climb down the ladder at the end of the fire escape then?"

"I tucked them in my shirt."

"What?" asked Braun, laughing.

"I wasn't going to leave them! It took me years to mark them."

Braun nodded. "Good. So who gave you the survival stuff?"

"Matt arranged the snowmobile, the clothes, and everything else."

"Good old Matt," said Braun sarcastically with a look of disdain on his face.

Chenille studied Braun's face and then said, "He *is* good! He saved your life!"

Braun rubbed his forehead feeling a bruise the size of a quarter from being zapped and said, "Jury's still out on that one."

"You don't know everything he's done for you. If you knew, you'd be grateful."

"OK then, tell me. What *are* all the things that he's done for me?"

"I don't even know," said Chenille with a hand to her chest.

"Then how do you know that he's done anything but dispose of us out in the snow, leaving us with the bare minimum to soothe his conscience?"

"Braun. *Because I know!* I've talked to him over and over and I know he's a good guy. He's been worried about you for a while."

"Then why hasn't he been talking to me?" asked Braun feeling anger welling up inside.

"Braun," Chenille said, giving him a frustrated look. "Duh, think about it."

"What?" asked Braun, still not getting it.

"Do I have to spell everything out for you?" asked Chenille, her eyebrows raised.

"I guess so," said Braun, "because I can't think of anything I like about the guy."

"You had a chip—in your head—if he talked to you, then…"

Braun nodded. OK, now he got it. "Oh, I see, MD would know about everything he talked about."

"Right. And the whole point is to not let MD know *anything*. Our goal here is to live, not get picked off by some sniper or an assassin bug. That's a big deal, I think."

"Only if we survive this snow," added Braun sarcastically.

"We will."

"How do you know?" asked Braun.

"Because I, unlike you, know the whole plan."

"Can you clue me in? That would be the nice thing to do," said Braun. "Then I wouldn't feel so oblivious." Braun held up a hand and gestured to the cave. "I don't even know where we are!"

Chenille looked at Braun for a moment and then took his hand in a reassuring clasp.

She hesitated just long enough to make Braun worried. "What? Don't tell me we're at the *North Pole*!" he joked, trying to lighten the mood.

Chenille looked surprised and then covered her mouth in a laugh.

"What?" said Braun, shaking his head. *"We're at the North Pole?"*

Chenille's eyes flicked around the shelter as her lips parted helplessly. She looked like she was searching for something to say, but nothing came out.

Braun felt like he was in shock as he stood and started to pace. "Chenille, talk to me!"

Chenille shook her head and with a hand out said, "Braun, calm down."

He continued to pace as he scratched an itch under his hat. "Calm down? Calm down? Yesterday I was in Washington, D.C. eating beef Wellington and sleeping under a real goose down comforter and you tell me to *calm down*?"

"Two days ago," said Chenille.

"What?" asked Braun with a pained look. "Two days?"

"With the time change it's two days ago that you were in Washington, D.C."

Braun threw up his arms and said, "Great! Now I've lost another day!"

Chenille stood up. "Now, Braun, you're not yourself yet. Think about this rationally."

"I am thinking about this rationally!"

"No, stop and listen!" said Chenille with convincing strength.

Braun stopped pacing and looked at Chenille in frustration. His life had just been turned inside out and Chenille wanted him to be happy about it? "I'm listening," he said begrudgingly.

"MD ordered you to be killed because you were causing trouble in the White House."

"He ordered me killed because I was causing trouble?" asked Braun, shaking his head.

Chenille nodded. "That's what I was told."

Braun laughed with satisfaction and said, "Good. I'm *glad* I was causing trouble. That meant I was doing my job."

Chenille looked amazed. "You're crazy."

"Maybe," said Braun. "But I've got a clean conscience."

Chenille nodded. "That's good."

"So who was ordered to make the hit?" asked Braun.

"Matt."

A foggy memory flooded back to Braun's mind. Matt stood over him with a gun. He was saying something about his father. "Right," said Braun nodding. "Matt told me that he would have liked me as a brother-in-law and then bang! He shot me in the head with some sort of electricity and sent me here. What a great brother-in-law."

"He didn't shoot you. He disabled the chip that was in your head."

Braun's gloved hand came up to his forehead. "He did?"

"Yes, he did. He did that so his father couldn't track you any more."

Sudden anger took hold of Braun's chest. "And now I should *love* him for that! That *fetcher*! Too little, too late!"

"Braun, what are you talking about?"

"Matt, our great hero, knew what was happening to me the whole time and let it happen! Yes, he's a *great* guy!"

"Braun!"

"No, let me finish! That guy knew that his father recorded every conversation I had with the President and he did nothing! Not only that, he allowed the Secretary General, our friend and the newest convert of the church, to be blackmailed by MD to put that chip in my head! And even then, he still allowed the Secretary General's brain to turn to mush because the damage from the chip in his head had gone too far!!! Yes, that's a great guy!"

"Braun, your anger is misplaced. It wasn't Matt that did all those things, it was MD…"

"Chenille, are you so blind? MD and Matt are the same! When MD dies, Matt will take his place! Matt is just as guilty as his father!"

"Braun, that's not true…"

"It is true! And now, instead of being known as a good Aide to the President, I'm going to be known as the spy that handed the whole country on a platter to MD! Wow, what a *great* history! Do you think my parents will be impressed by that one?"

Chenille took a big breath and nodded. "OK," said Chenille as she stood and approached Braun with her hands up. "I know. This must be a huge shock to you."

"Yes. HUGE! I can't tell you how angry I'm feeling!"

"I can guess."

"Chenille, I'm beyond anger! The President trusted me! She was listening to me! We were making progress!"

"I know," stressed Chenille. "I'm sorry."

Braun shook his head and threw his stick down in anger, and then pushed his hat off his head and ran his gloves through his hair. *"That's so…so…"* Braun made two fists. He was so angry words were inadequate for his feelings.

"I know," said Chenille quietly, trying to calm him down. "But think of it this way: it's over for you now."

"Over? *This* is over?" asked Braun, his hands out looking defeated.

Chenille looked around the cave. "It's not much but at least you aren't dead!"

"No, I'm not physically dead but what about my family? What about my future in the medical field? What about going home? *I might as well be dead! My future is gone! There's nothing left!*"

"You knew what you were getting into," said Chenille with a downward gaze. "You knew the risks."

"Yes, death. REAL death, not fake death. I think I'd be more willing to accept death than—this place. At least if I was dead I'd be warm!"

"Siberia," said Chenille looking away now.

"Siberia?" he exclaimed. *"We're in Siberia? Isn't that where Russians put their prisoners?"*

Chenille shrugged but then shook her head as she seemed to stop trying.

Braun could just see enough of her face that he could tell it changed expression. Pain now was at the surface. Then, all of a sudden, her shoulders began to shake as tears flowed freely.

Braun stopped his tirade. Chenille was crying. Seeing her cry was too hard for him right now. He couldn't take it. "Oh, Chenille, what are you doing? I'm not mad at you. I'm mad at—everything else," he said as he leaned over her shoulder to pull back her hair and look at her face.

She didn't respond but continued to cry with full force with her back towards him.

Braun decided to try again. "Seriously, Chenille, listen. If you're crying because I said something stupid, I'm sorry."

Chenille didn't answer but covered her face as tears fell to the floor.

Braun continued. "Come on, Chenille, tell me why you're crying so I can fix it."

Chenille shook her head.

"Please? ...I'm sorry!" said Braun feeling helpless.

With a shaky voice she said, "I can see this was a huge mistake. I just thought…"

Braun turned Chenille around so she was facing him. "I'm sorry, Chenille. I was angry I didn't consider all the sacrifices you made to help me. Is that why you're crying? I'm sorry. Do you understand me?"

"No, *I* should have realized that everything would continue to be about you. There's no room for anything else in your life except yourself."

"What? What are you talking about? It's not true. I was just blind with anger for a moment, it's over now I told you I was sorry."

"OK, yes, let's talk about what *I* gave up to be here," said Chenille growing angry through her tears. "Do you know what future *I* gave up?"

Braun shook his head again. "No, probably a lot," he said as he attempted to wipe Chenille's tears, but she pulled away from his touch.

"Don't touch me right now," she said angrily.

Braun looked at Chenille in sadness. What had he just done? "OK," he said with both hands up. "We are in the middle of nowhere, so please, let's both try to get along. I said I was sorry. Tell me. What I can do to make it up to you?"

"You can leave me alone," said Chenille with venom in her voice.

"Chenille."

"I'm going to take you to a little fishing community a ways up north but then I'm going back to my life. I'll just change my name and go back. I'm sure Matt will arrange that for me."

Braun dropped his hands to his sides in sadness. This was not what he wanted.

Chenille went back to digging in the snow. She was working angrily.

Braun watched her for a second and then turned back to his step. Picking up his stick from the floor he went back to work too. "OK, Chenille, you do what you feel is right. But—I want to say for the record, that I'm very happy you're here. I was stupid to complain like I did and...I hope it doesn't ruin—the future."

Braun paused for Chenille to respond but she continued to work in silence. He continued again. "And again, just for the record, I missed you. My life has been empty without you. Since the day you left me in the UN prison, I've been hollow inside. So many times I have looked for you out of habit only to realize I was alone. ...I don't want to return to that. It was the worst kind of hell I could imagine. Having you near me, to hear your voice, smell your perfume, to be able to talk to you, has been the answer to every prayer I've uttered since you left. I know you have been hurt by me too many times and it might seem logical to leave me here but please—find it in your heart to reconsider."

Braun stopped talking. He didn't want to go further just in case his words were making it worse.

Braun heard Chenille's pattern of movement change and then she approached him. He turned to look at her and found she was looking at him with hopeful eyes.

"Say that again to my face," Chenille said with emotion.

Braun stopped working, feeling a flushing energy suddenly flow through his body and take away his bad feelings. Turning to Chenille, he probed to see if he was feeling right. "What?"

"I said, say that to my face, not to the wall, or in a prayer or to anyone else. Be a *man* and say it to me. It doesn't count unless you *say it to me*."

Braun moved close to Chenille and looked into her deep blue eyes. He opened his mouth and taking her by her arms said, "*I love you*, Chenille. It is you and only you that I love."

Chenille pushed closer to Braun and said, "Say that again. I didn't quite hear you."

Braun wrapped Chenille tightly in his arms in a full embrace and leaned in until his lips almost touched hers. Then with a whisper he repeated, "I love you, Chenille. I want to be with you forever."

"I think I got it that time," said Chenille with an irresistibly soft smile. "Now kiss me, Braun Rogers. I'm tired of waiting."

Braun hesitated briefly and then pressed his lips to Chenille's. The kiss was exquisite and her breath was sweet. After the first kiss he decided to kiss her again, and again. He found himself amazed with wonder. Her kisses were better than anything he had ever imagined. Oh wow! She was right. Even when cold, his life could be good!

Lessons in Martial Art

Provo, Utah
3:15 p.m.

"Hana, tul, set, net," counted Carea as she punched sharply into the air directly in front of her, alternating fists with every count. "Tasot, yosot, ilgop, yudolp,"[1] she continued in the horse stance. She watched her reflection in the mirror very carefully, making sure every punch was precise; every punch was full of power. It didn't matter that the city had been shut down due to computer glitches and electricity going haywire. Competitions were soon. Each practice had to count, even today.

Carea had grown strong. Her vibrancy had returned. The sickness caused from the chip in her head that had caused her to nearly starve to death, was resolving. She could feel her body centering power and ready to move at her command. She felt good.

"Ahop, yeol, yeol hanna, yeol tul," she continued when suddenly the lights flickered on and then went out again. "Stupid lights," she said under her breath. "Why don't they make up their mind?" But then a movement in the corner of the room diverted her attention.

In the dim, filtered light that came through the windows, Carea knew someone was approaching. She saw it in the mirror. The person was masked. It was a test. What? Did they think the lack of light would change anything?

Carea whipped around and faced her opponent who somehow caught her with a leg throw. She fell sharply on her back. It knocked the wind out of her. She was stunned. How did that happen?

Carea's opponent retreated defensively, to escape her reach. Who was this? Quickly Carea scrambled to her feet. She would not be taken down so easily again!

It was time for a mobile attack. Carea aggressively slid to one side down on the mat, executing a scissor sweep, sending her competitor sprawling through the air onto his back. She heard the rewarding grunt she was expecting. To her that meant her attack had been effective. It was a major mental victory.

The masked person turtled up on his head and rolled.

Carea, rolled to her back, and then used her shoulders to propel herself to her feet to keep the advantage. Once again her opponent was on his or her…no…Carea studied the person in front of her. It was a guy for sure. Once he was on his feet, she could feel his power. Whoever it was, he was strong. As she stared into his dark eyes she noticed he had a scar by his left eye, but she couldn't think of who he was. Had she fought him before?

Carea saw her opponent move one way and then abruptly step back. He attempted to catch her in a complex combination, but she returned with a six kick, block, and thrust technique. She ended with a spinning far-leg trip to a lift and reverse throw. The boy, whoever he was, went sailing over Carea's shoulder, his feet pointed at the ceiling. He landed squarely on his back.

Once again, victory! Carea was pleased but she didn't stop. She pounced on the boy and finished him with a combination straight arm lock-collar choke. Her opponent, obviously shocked, tapped out to avoid having his arm broken and being choked unconscious.

Carea stood, expecting to unmask her opponent but instead he got up and slunk away.

"Hey!" she yelled after him. "Don't run away like a coward! Show me who you are!"

The boy didn't respond but disappeared out the door of the gym.

"What a freak!" Carea said as she breathed deep, allowing the oxygen to catch up with her body.

"You're too hard on them," said her Sonseng[2] as he walked in from one of the back doors.

"*I'm* too hard on *them*?" she asked astonished.

"Yes."

"How?"

"You break their spirits. It's difficult to find one to challenge you."

"I thought the idea was to win."

"No, you are wrong," said her instructor as he began to circle her.

Carea just waited for her Sonseng to finish. It was obvious he wanted to make a point.

"The idea," continued Carea's teacher, "is to achieve harmony with nature and one's self."

Carea shrugged and then smoothed her hair, letting her fingers trace the rubber band that bound her short crop of hair. "Then why do you have these guys sneak up on me?" Carea dropped her hand to her waist. "What do you think I'm going to do? *Hug the helpless buggers?*"

The Sonseng smiled and nodded as he stood before her. "I'm sure they'd like that better."

Carea's jaw dropped. "You've got to be kidding!"

The Sonseng patted Carea on the shoulder. "Of course, I'm kidding."

Carea frowned. "Be serious with me. What do you want from me?"

"It's not what I want. It should be what you want."

"Don't speak in riddles."

"OK, I'll spell it out..."

"In English please," said Carea with a slight smile. Now she was teasing him.

The Sonseng bowed slightly with an intense glare. "In plain English then."

"Thank you," said Carea, feeling like she had won yet again.

"I think you should try to gain a balance. You're off balance in your life. Take back your center."

Carea's mouth flew open in surprise. "I'm not off balance! I've never felt better! I cleaned that guy's clock—in the dark, no less!"

The instructor calmly nodded. "Yes, you are off balance. You're confused and angry. It drains you of your potential."

Carea was confused. What was her teacher talking about? "My combat potential?"

"Your spiritual potential."

"Since when did you become my spiritual leader?"

"Since you lost your way."

"Lost my way?" This line of conversation was creeping her out. Suddenly she didn't want to be at practice anymore.

"Yes. You're at odds with yourself, your beliefs, your direction," continued her Sonseng. "No matter what God you serve, this is one principle we all must follow. We must know our creator and the power that we can achieve through reverence and self-knowledge. That can only be achieved through the quiet stillness of self-discovery of our true self created by God."

Carea looked at her teacher for a moment as she digested what he had just said. "Hmmm." She let her eyes fall to the mat below her feet as she contemplated the implications. Physically she was healed but emotionally, it was true she still felt tattered and shredded into a thousand pieces. She hated to admit it but her Sonseng was right. She was at odds with herself.

With a big sigh she looked up and said, "So how do I gain balance?" It was a blunted question. She didn't want to reveal her true interest.

"Balance is gained by controlling both evil and good forces that swirl around us. A true martial artist knows how to behave in all situations. You should sense your course of action and take it, despite how the surface of any situation appears. Re-learn how to trust yourself. Re-learn how to trust your God. Great knowledge resides within you. Look to it and make yourself one with it."

"How do I do that?" asked Carea.

"Are you meditating?"

Carea shook her head. "Meditation is a waste of good training time," she said with a mocking smile.

The Sonseng shook his head. "That's where you're wrong. Meditation is the key to success in your future and your spirit. Find yourself, Carea. Take the time to get to know yourself and the powers that run the universe."

Carea looked down at her feet and then up at her teacher. She knew he was right. It had been awhile since she sought out God earnestly. Her anger had caused her to lose control of her own center, a balance that only spirituality could restore. Finally she bowed. "I understand your counsel, and you are wise. I will begin to meditate again."

"Good. And as you do, you will evolve. You will learn how to soar through the sky as the sun and the moon and harness the power that moves around us."

"I'd be happy with the gold medal," said Carea with amusement.

The Sonseng turned with a serious expression and began to walk back towards the door as he said, "There's more to life than mere competition." Turning back briefly to Carea he continued, "Look beyond petty symbols of value and into real power." With a finger in the air he finished. "That is where you will find the true strength you seek."

Carea raised an eyebrow. Real power is what she sought. Maybe it was time she put her teacher to the test. Maybe it was time to set things right with God and herself. It was time to heal. "I will, Sonseng. Thank you," Carea bowed again, staying low for a moment. When she looked up, the lights turned back on, but her Sonseng was gone.

Explosive Strategy

In space, over America
Independent of time zones

Grace gazed through the triple thick window. The shuttle, which was the new Air Force One, was 130 miles into the stratosphere. She could see the curve of the planet on the horizon.

She had the International news on her video screen. It was fuzzy and pixilated often, but sometimes she could make the images out.

It looked to her as if the world was struggling to carry on business as usual; however, the extra solar activity had wreaked havoc all over the planet. Many computer systems were still down and were expected to be down for another day. Interconnecting the systems again might take more time after that. Oh, how long was she going to have to stay up in space? She was already going bonkers!

In her mind's eye, Grace imagined what would happen as the banks came back online. At first many would think the inaccurate account balances were a systems glitch. All over America, computer repairmen would be called in to retrieve the data, but it would be no use. Then one bank would call another bank until it would become apparent that the accounts were truly dry. Her explanation of what was occurring would come to all of them, but probably too late, since e-mail messages were probably backing up, or even being deleted right now.

In her mind she counted. Yesterday and today made two days, another day for the computers to come online, another day for them to link, then a week or so as the nation entered a State of Emergency.... She shook her head. She couldn't do that. She only had three day's worth of food up here. What should she do if her food ran out before the computers registered the transfer of funds? She was just wasting her time and would probably have to return right when the violence broke out. Maybe she could have the shuttle land somewhere else—somewhere remote....

Grace looked at her fingernails. She had already peeled most of the polish off. She'd have to have her manicurist…no. There'd be no manicurist to do her nails when she returned to earth. OK, now that was depressing.

She hated this delay. In a way, she wished the whole thing would just happen so she could deal with it, instead of worrying sick over it.

"Oh, I almost forgot," Grace whispered to herself. "I need to put a call out to the Rogers' family. Connect me to Braun Rogers' residence in Utah, please."

"Connec…," partially answered the automated female computer voice. It was having difficulty responding.

Grace waited to see if the phone line would connect. When it did, she prepared herself and reviewed in her mind what she would say. She wouldn't say anything about Braun being a mole, because in her heart of hearts she knew he didn't know he was a spy for MD. She was sure he was tricked in some way. On that premise she would only say good things to his parents. He deserved to be remembered with honor. She could do that for him.

The phone rang four times and then a recording began to speak, inviting her to leave a message.

Grace clenched her fist in frustration but then she forced herself to relax. She didn't want to speak to a recording but she wasn't going to get upset about this too. She'd just leave a message. It was probably her only chance.

"Ahh, Mr. and Mrs. Rogers, this is Grace MacEntire, the President of the United States. I had the privilege of working with your son, Braun. I want you to know he was a delight to have around, not to mention enlightened and wise. I regret to tell you he is missing from his post here at the White House. I would like to tell you that we're doing everything in our power to find him, but to be honest, our country is about to enter a State of Emergency and we can't afford the resources. I'm hoping he has called you and you know where he is. I pray everything will turn out well. Good luck, and good-bye."

The President placed both hands in her lap. Now all there was to do was wait. She had done her part that day and set all the political wheels in motion the best she could.

"Captain of Air Force One, please," said Grace out loud.

"Yes, Madam President," answered the computer, this time without problems.

In a few seconds, a masculine voice answered her. "Madam President. How are you today?"

Grace considered her situation and smiled slightly. "I'm doing fine, Lincoln."

"What can I do for you?" he asked.

"I'm sure you're aware that we're going to stay up here for at least one more day, correct?"

"Yes, Ma'am, I received the State of Emergency plans when we took off."

"Excellent. Yes, as I understand, we're invisible to radar detection, correct?"

"Not invisible, but difficult to detect."

"How difficult?"

"Very."

"Tell me how that works."

"We have re-entrant triangles behind the skin of this machine. Radar waves that penetrate the aircraft get trapped in these structures, bouncing off the internal faces and lose their energy. We also have iron ball paint that covers the shuttle that contains tiny spheres coated with ferrite. This paint converts radar energy into heat and then it dissipates into space."

"So do you feel we're safe from detection up here?"

"Generally. Solar flares also destroy radio waves, so that's another mechanism that disguises our presence."

"Oh, good."

"If we cut our engines, then that will eliminate another way someone can detect us."

"Then let's take the engines down to a minimum."

"Yes, Ma'am. …Ahhh, Madam President?"

"What is it, Lincoln?"

"I do have one concern you should be aware of."

"What would that be?" asked Grace.

"Although solar flares may disguise us, they are also very caustic to the internal technology of this machine and we're receiving quite a pummeling."

"We are?" asked Grace looking outside the window.

"Yes, we are."

"I don't see anything out my windows."

"Ma'am, the electricity is invisible. Radiation is pulsing through our systems as we speak. I'm already seeing some problems that are giving me concern."

"What kind of problems? Don't we have surge protectors on this machine?"

"Yes, Ma'am. We have many safety systems but despite those, I'm still seeing irregular readings and electricity surges. I've even had one system completely go out."

"Which one?"

"Environment control. I can't guarantee your cabin is going to be as warm as you like it."

Grace looked out into the blackness of space and considered returning to earth now. Maybe she could go underground. "Are we in danger?"

"Not as of yet."

"Hmmm," said Grace as she imagined how mad it was going to be around the White House when everyone figured things out. With all the fluctuations in electricity, the security system would probably be undependable and people could storm the building. What if the elevators didn't work and she couldn't get away? Or she was stuck in them a hundred feet down.... Grace shook her head. No, that would not be how she would die. She'd rather take her chances up here, or again, maybe somewhere else. America was a big place.

"Just keep me informed of how things are going."

"Yes, Ma'am," answered the pilot.

The engines powered down, reducing the roar to a constant hum.

A sudden weightlessness caused Grace to rise in her chair, but the belt kept her seated.

"Madam President?" requested the female computer voice.

"Yes?" Grace was impressed. The automated assistant had come back online.

"Mr. Wormwood is on the pho—oo—ne."

Grace was intrigued. With a raised eyebrow she asked, "Mr. Wormwood, huh? Now that would be an interesting person to talk to."

"Yes, Ma'am."

"...Put him through to my private line."

"Y—es, Ma'am."

Seconds later a red phone rang right next to Grace. "Hello, Mr. Wormwood. It's been longer than I expected since your last call...Oh, I understand. How have you been? ...That's good. Yes, I'm safe for now... How did you know I was up here?" asked Grace with a frown. "...I don't know if I like that. If you know where I am, does... *No*?" Relief flowed through her. "Well, good. That's very good. OK...I'm listening. Go ahead," Grace tapped her fingernails as she listened to the man on the line. She nodded as she said, "Yes, I have that capacity. I could do that.... The nearest one?" she asked as she looked out her window. "Got it," she replied, after not seeing what she was looking for but assuming she could find it. "I think that would be a very good idea." Now she was smiling like a Cheshire cat. "*I like how that sounds.* What a great opportunity, thank you. I'm especially attracted to the idea that all the damage will be blamed on the magnetic storm. It's brilliant." Grace paused as she listened. "Yes, yes. I think it just might shake things up a bit in the enemy's camp. ...No, *thank you*, Mr. Wormwood. I believe you've made my day, and it was getting kind of depressing. Maybe all is not lost after all. ...I'll get right on that." Grace smiled and nodded. "It will be my pleasure. Thank you for calling. ...Good luck in all your endeavors." Then thoughtfully, Grace hung up the phone.

Unstrapping herself from her seat, Grace pulled on the window ledge and leaned into the glass as her body began to float slightly. Looking below the shuttle and off to the left she saw the satellite she was looking for. It was just now floating by. Squinting she tried to ignore the glare of the sun on the side of the machine. As it turned, the writing became very clear. In big black letters it identified itself as property of the UN.

"Lincoln, please," she said into the air.

"Yes, Ma-'am," said the computer.

Grace noticed the stutter but ignored it.

"Lincoln here," said the captain.

"Lincoln, my friend, do you see that satellite off to the left of our shuttle?"

There was silence for a moment. "Yes, Madam President, I see it."

"*Destroy it*," said the President emphatically.

"Ma'am…ah…." The voice hesitated; it was obvious the pilot had more to say.

"Yes, Lincoln? Do you have something you would like to say?"

"Yes, Ma'am."

"Proceed."

"Madam President. That is an unmanned satellite belonging to the UN."

"Yes, I am fully aware of that fact," Grace answered.

"I feel obligated to inform you that firing on that vessel unprovoked might be seen as instigating international conflict."

President MacEntire smiled. "No, it wouldn't. Now if I sent my military up here to wipe it out, then I agree with you, it would be seen as an act of war."

"Yes, Ma'am."

"But, Lincoln, I assure you, no one will detect our involvement in this satellite's destruction for two reasons. Number one, we're in the middle of a solar storm, as you pointed out. Anything can go wrong with these satellites right now, am I right?"

"Yes, you are right, Ma'am."

"Number two, we are very difficult to sense, by your words. Therefore, computers would have a difficult time proving our presence. If that satellite blew up, all anyone would be able to prove is that their system was down, don't you agree, Lincoln?"

"Despite those facts, Ma'am, it's my job to tell you that I don't think we should do anything without the approval of Congress. Forgive me for being so bold."

Grace hesitated. "No, Lincoln. This is not a time for lobbying and waiting for a vote. We have a job to do and we're going to do it. If I have to write an Executive Order, I will." She was joking but serious at the same time.

"All right, Ma'am."

Grace listened for the hum of the hydraulics that would open the doors to release the missile that rode beneath her shuttle and the hissing of the launch of the air-to-air missile, but it didn't begin.

"Lincoln?"

"Yes, Ma'am?"

"Do I have to draw you a picture? *I repeat, blast that floating bird out of the sky. Do as I say!*"

"Right away, Ma'am…. Ah, forgive me, but I want to be clear about which satellite you really want destroyed. There are at least twelve on my screen within range. A few have the same markings as the one you referred to."

President MacEntire looked out her window again but she couldn't see any other satellites. "Show me what you're seeing Lincoln. Show them to me on my screen!" The large wall-sized screen directly in front of her flickered for about ten seconds and then finally came to life, giving her a spectacular view of space with not just a few, but many colored, blinking satellites, and another still coming into view on the horizon. Each satellite was enlarged and enhanced by the computer, revealing more machines with similar markings to the first one she had spotted.

After seeing the myriad of satellites, the President said, "Shoot the one that's closest to us. Right there on the left."

"On the left, you say?" asked the pilot.

"Yes, Lincoln, that's right."

"The killer satellite?"

"Killer satellite?" asked the President confused. "That's not a killer satellite. Isn't that a communications satellite?"

"It might be used for some sort of communications but it's also working with 23 other ones just like it in a great web to be able to destroy a tick off your dog while it's in a full run," said Lincoln.

"A killer satellite, huh?" said the President, genuinely surprised. Why hadn't she known this? So the UN had some dirty little secrets? Well, she'd take care of that, thanks to Mr. Wormwood. Secret killer satellites pointed at America should have been taken out a long time ago—no they should have *never* made it into the sky in the first place! "Tell me more about that satellite, Lincoln."

"Yes, Ma'am. It's built for war. I should know. Before my White House days as your pilot, I worked on this model's production for America in the Air Force, although as soon as it was functional, the next administration scrapped it. I'm sure the UN received their pattern from us because they're exactly alike."

The President looked down, shook her head and laughed sarcastically. Clicking her tongue, then she began to nod. Oh, wouldn't destroying a satellite that was the eyes, ears, *and muscle* for MD mess up his plans? What a jackpot!

"Even better reason to shoot it down, don't you think, Lincoln?" said Grace, still smiling and feeling very happy with her good fortune.

"Yes, Ma'am."

"Because doesn't it look like that satellite is pointed at the East coast of the United States?"

"Yes it does, Ma'am."

"The White House maybe?"

"Most probably, Madam President."

"That's home. Hmm, does that make you feel comfortable, Lincoln?"

"If we were being threatened by the UN, then no Ma'am, it doesn't. I have family down there."

"I'm glad you do…you'll understand better what I'm going to say next then."

"What is that?"

"We *are* being threatened by the UN. Not the UN itself, but those who control the UN. We're in a new war. I have been given notice today of an impending attack that will wipe out America's *total* economy. How does that make you feel?"

"Threatened, Ma'am."

"That's right. Threatened. So should we just lie down and take it in the jaw?"

"No, Madam President."

"So I ask you again, what would be the best thing to do with this secret war machine sponsored by the very people who are going to ruin our lives, pointed at the ones we love, in light of this new information?"

"I don't know, nor am I qualified to guess."

"Well, I know, and I'm not going to give them a future chance to take us out with this system. It's time for a response and we're going to give it."

"Alright, Ma'am. Give the order."

"In the name of National Security, and by the authority of the office of the President, *blow it up*!"

"Yes, Madam President."

Grace watched the cockpit's digital scope appear on her screen. With a sure movement the satellite was identified as their target. A long tone emitted and her screen turned amber, letting them know they had missile lock.

"OK, we have tone," confirmed the captain.

"Fire!" said the President with energy as she listened for the sounds of the missile being deployed. She was rewarded by a mechanical purring sound. Next, as she listened a laser-guided missile was launched from the belly of the shuttle with a loud hiss. Within seconds, the satellite was a flaming ball, exploding into pieces.

"Wahoo!" hollered Grace, letting go of some pent up energy with glee.

A few seconds later, another satellite exploded nearby.

"What?" gasped Grace, her eyes wide but totally enthralled. "Another one blew up?"

Then further away another satellite blew up.

"Lincoln, why are those other satellites exploding?"

"I don't know, Ma'am. I shot the one closest to us and that's all."

"Are they all the UN's machines?"

"I believe so, because on my screen, I highlighted all of the UN's satellites to make sure I didn't hit anything else."

"And those exact machines are the ones blowing apart?" asked Grace, anticipating his answer.

"Yes, Ma'am, exactly."

"Yes!" said Grace under her breath as she continued to watch her screen. "There's another one!" she said as she watched a fourth one detonate. "Do you think they're going to all explode?" She hoped they would. That would be a result beyond all her expectations.

"I don't know, Ma'am. I don't know why the others exploded in the first place."

"I don't either, but I don't care. That was a great shot!!"

"Thank you, Ma'am."

After a few moments, Grace said, "I think it's stopped."

"I think you're right. I don't see anymore explosions on my screen," said Lincoln.

"Good, because we don't want to give anyone a reason to snoop around up here. If we blow up too many satellites, someone might start looking for us."

"Yes, Ma'am."

"I didn't want to blow our cover. I just wanted to take that system out."

"I think we've done that, Ma'am."

"*Good*," said Grace ardently.

"Anything else, Ma'am?"

Grace smiled. "No, that will do. Your country thanks you, and so does your Pres...."

There was a loud bang and she was enveloped in darkness.

"Lincoln?" asked Grace into the dark. Her voice was flat and small. "Lincoln?" Grace called again. "Lincoln?"

Silence.

"Oh, no. ...I think we're in trouble," said the President.

Notes to "The Unraveling"

Lessons in Martial Art

[1] The counting is in the Korean language. It is the language many martial artists speak when performing Tae kwan do, even in America.

[2] Sonseng is Korean for "teacher."

[3] "We pay too little attention to the value of meditation, a principle of devotion....Meditation is the language of the soul. It is defined as 'a form of private devotion, or spiritual exercise, consisting in deep, continued reflection on some religious theme.' Meditation is a form of prayer. Meditation is one of the most secret, most sacred doors through which we pass into the presence of the Lord....Let us make God the center of our lives" (David O. McKay, "Elements of Worship", *Teachings of the Presidents of the Church*, Vol. 4, p. 29).

CHAPTER FIVE

WEB OF PAIN

"That every man may act in doctrine and principle pertaining to futurity, according to the moral agency which I have given unto him, that every man may be accountable for his own sins in the day of judgement" (D&C 101:78).

00:03:11, 14:55:29, Zulu
Friday, September 19th

Peter, Peter, Pumpkin Eater

Provo, Utah
2:05 a.m.

Corrynne sat up in bed. She thought she had heard a knock at the front door. She listened intently for it again.... Maybe it was something else, the water heater or one of her boys knocking around to get a drink…. She held her breath to listen for the sound again.

Knock, knock, knock.

There it was again! She looked at the clock. It was two in the morning! Who would be at the door at this hour? "Bo! Wake up!" she said as she poked at his shoulder. "There's someone at the door!"

"What?" Bo mumbled, still obviously asleep.

"Wake up!" said Corrynne with more energy.

Knock, knock, knock.

"Do you hear that?" asked Corrynne, pushing Bo's shoulder this time.

Bo sat up straight in bed. "What was that?"

"Someone's knocking," said Corrynne as she flipped back the covers and moved to the window. "I think there's somebody at the door."

Bo got out of bed. "Do you see anyone?"

Corrynne looked up and down the empty street. There were no cars parked outside. "Noooo," she said as she double-checked.

Knock, knock, knock.

"Well, someone's out there alright, because they're knocking again," said Bo as he pulled on his jeans that had been crumpled on the floor.

"Are you going to answer it?" asked Corrynne.

"I'm not getting dressed for nothing," said Bo as he headed for the open bedroom doorway.

Corrynne pulled her bathrobe from a closet hook, put it on, and then followed behind.

By the time Corrynne was at the bottom of the stairs, Bo had the front door open. She saw him step outside.

"Is anyone out there?" she asked poking her head out the door just as she heard another knocking sound from behind her. "Bo, I think the knocking is coming from a different door. It sounds like there's someone at the kitchen door," she said as she noticed a dark shadow steal across the kitchen door window. *"Bo!"*

"What?" he asked from outside.

"Someone *is* outside the kitchen! I see the outline of a head!"

"So answer the door," said Bo as he stepped back into the house.

Corrynne was shocked. "I'm not going to answer it! That's why I have you!"

Bo threw Corrynne an annoyed look.

Corrynne returned the look and shrugged. "What?"

Bo sighed and then deliberately walked to the kitchen door, pounding the floor with every step. "Who do you think is out there, Corrynne? The bogeyman?"

"You never know," Corrynne retorted.

"I don't think the bogeyman would knock," Bo said as he unlocked the handle and quickly opened the door. There was a momentary pause then he said, "Well, hello, stranger!" with a jolly voice, holding out a thick hand in welcome.

Corrynne stood on her tiptoes from where she was standing. She could see a man whose form looked familiar in the moonlight but couldn't make out his features. She walked forward a few paces and then asked, "Who is it, Bo?"

"It's Matt!" he said over his shoulder with a smile.

Corrynne frowned. Matt was here? She didn't know if she liked that—just a few days previous, she had a phone call from Braun telling her that Matt's father wanted mind-control chips in everyone's head. A bad feeling filled her stomach.

"Come in, son!" continued Bo. "What are you doing outside at this hour? You scared your mother-in-law to death!"

Matt smiled apologetically as he stepped in. "I'm sorry. I knew I might do that."

"Where's Brea?" Corrynne asked, looking beyond Matt but not seeing her daughter. She wondered if Braun had been successful in encouraging her to leave the Daimler mansion. Could she have snuck out? Was Matt looking for her? "Is she with you?" she asked.

"No," said Matt.

"Where is she?" asked Bo.

Corrynne hadn't had a moment to talk to Bo yet about Braun's misgivings about Matt. He'd been gone on ward business.

"She's nearby. She's sleeping. She was exhausted," said Matt.

That didn't make sense to Corrynne. Why was her son-in-law in her home but her daughter somewhere else? Something wasn't right. She was sure Brea would come home no matter *how* tired she was. Corrynne shook her head and asked, "Something's wrong with her isn't there? Where is she really? Is she at the hospital?"

Matt looked at Corrynne with a blank stare and then shook his head. "She's just a mile or so away. She's fine. She's sleeping." Then with a slight frown he said, "Mom, you seem upset. Is there something you're worried about?"

Hearing this man call her "Mom" jilted Corrynne. "Call me Corrynne. I feel more comfortable with that name," she said automatically.

Bo looked at Corrynne with a question in his eyes.

Corrynne glanced back at Bo and moved a single finger of her hand to signal to him that right now was not a good time to question her. He must have got the hint because he turned his attention back to Matt.

Matt shrugged and said, "OK, Corrynne. I assure you that everything's going great. Brea's pregnancy is right on track," he said as he unbuttoned his overcoat. "It's just been a stressful few months at my parents' and we needed to get away."

"What happened at your parents' house?" asked Corrynne, feeling even more uptight now that he mentioned his father.

Matt took off his coat but Corrynne didn't offer to take it.

Bo stepped forward and said, "Here, let me take that for you."

"Thank you," said Matt as Bo hung the coat on a coat hook behind them where the other family coats hung.

"My parents are extremely overbearing. They wore Brea out."

"How?" asked Corrynne imagining a whole host of awful things.

"Time is short, I'd rather not get into that right now," said Matt.

"No, seriously," said Corrynne with a forced smile. "Tell me what has been going on. I'm a captive audience."

Matt was kind but stern as he said, "No, I don't think so. There are other things I'd like to talk about right now. There's a reason I came here in the middle of the night."

"Tell us what's on your mind, Matt," said Bo patiently, motioning to the table, indicating all of them should sit.

Matt studied both Corrynne and Bo for a few seconds and then as he pulled out the bench at the table and sat down, he said, "What I'm going to tell you is going to sound crazy—no it's going to sound *insane*. You're going to have a hard time putting all the pieces together because I can't give you all the pieces, but…"

"Don't beat around the bush," said Corrynne taking on a serious look. She was getting impatient. She didn't like anything about this visit!

"Ummm," said Matt as he thought. He was beginning to look a little nervous.

Corrynne watched his hesitancy. She knew he was trying to find the right words to say. He was being very careful—but why…? Then a thought hit her square in the face! Braun was heading over to Matt's house yesterday when she had talked to him on the phone. Since then, she hadn't heard a peep! Considering how upset her son had been during their conversation, *surely he would have called her after the visit*! "Excuse me, but I have to ask you a question," said Corrynne blurting out her thought.

"What is it?" asked Matt calmly.

"Did you see Braun yesterday?"

Matt nodded. "Yes. I did see him. That's why I'm here to talk to you. I have news concerning him."

"I knew it!" said Corrynne jumping up from her place at the table and pounding it with a fist at the same time. *"He's hurt, isn't he? What did you do to him?"*

"What's wrong with you, Corrynne?" asked Bo with a frown. "Sit down. Let Matt talk."

Corrynne looked at Bo and then back at Matt. With her finger pointed she said, "Braun called me yesterday, Bo. He called me in a panic. He was on his way to Matt's house to get Brea. He thought Brea was in danger."

Matt's eyes widened and suddenly, he looked a little sick.

"What? Why would Braun be in a panic?" asked Bo looking back and forth between Corrynne and Matt.

"Because he discovered that Matt's not an investment banker as he has lead us to believe. He's the son of the man who runs the IMF, Matthew Daimler, the same man who wants to put the chip that's in Carea's head, in every person's head on the planet. Including yours and mine!"

Bo's face changed shades as he looked at Matt. "Is this true? Is your father behind the chip that's in my daughter's head?"

Matt swallowed as he held up his hands. "OK, now things are getting out of control…"

Bo stood up, pushing his chair out from behind him and towered over Matt. *"No, they're not out of control unless you don't level with us,"* said Bo in the most authoritative voice Corrynne had ever heard.

Matt looked down at the table and then back up at both of his in-laws. "Please sit down, both of you. I'll tell you everything."

Corrynne and Bo looked at each other and then slowly took their seats.

"OK, yes," began Matt, "my father is a supporter of the bio chip and Carea does have a prototype of the kind that would be implanted—but…"

"Talk faster, before I throw you out of my house," said Bo becoming enraged. *"And you better say something I like!"*

"What's happened to Braun? What's happened to my son?" asked Corrynne revealing a shaky voice. She couldn't help it. She was near tears.

Matt shook his head as he held up his hands defensively. "Your son is alive and well. Things aren't perfect concerning him, but he's safe and that was my primary objective."

"What in the heck are you talking about?" demanded Bo with an angry stare. "What do you mean *'that was your primary objective'*?"

"Just hear me out before you get any angrier," said Matt. "I think you'll find that I'm a good ally."

"Leave that judgment to us," said Bo maintaining his aggressive attitude.

Matt nodded. "OK. I guess that's all I can ask." Matt took a deep breath and said, "Soon, you'll receive a communication from the President telling you that your son is missing…"

"Missing?" interrupted Corrynne, then covering her mouth with her hand as she looked at Bo.

"Yes, missing," said Matt again. "I'm surprised she hasn't already."

Corrynne looked at Bo and tried to remember the previous day. A memory clicked. "I received a strange phone call yesterday from an unlisted, private number but I couldn't understand it. The voice sounded official but there was too much interference to understand what was being said. Do you think that could have been the President?" she asked Bo.

Bo shook his head. "How would I know?"

"If it was," said Matt, "she'd be telling you that Braun had disappeared from his quarters near the White House, but he's not missing. He's in hiding."

"Hiding?" asked Bo. "From what?"

"From my father."

"Your father?" asked Bo.

"I knew it!" said Corrynne.

"Yes," said Matt with a serious look. "I'm sad to say that Braun was right to warn you about my father. He is a dangerous man with more power than any one person should have."

"Braun told me that exact thing yesterday. He said that he was evil," said Corrynne, now with worry.

"Yes," said Matt nodding. "I would agree with that."

"But in my mind there's a difference between being evil and dangerous," said Bo. "Which is it?"

"There's no difference," began Matt. "Evil is what makes people dangerous and my father is both evil *and* dangerous."

"So Braun was right," said Corrynne. "I was hoping he was just over-exaggerating."

Matt nodded and said, "Braun was right. Braun's been right about everything that I've ever heard come out of his mouth. He's a great guy. And that's why I took it upon myself to protect him. It was the least I could do."

"Why would Braun need protection?" asked Corrynne, feeling like she was wilting from shock. "Did he offend your father?"

Matt looked up at the ceiling and said, "Let's just say he was getting in the way of my father's plans. He doesn't tolerate that very well. Patience is not one of his strengths."

"Braun was in the White House," said Bo. "What does your father have to do with the White House?" he asked, but then a look of understanding crossed his face. "Are you saying your father controls the White House?"

Matt shrugged. "No, he doesn't control the White House any longer and that's the problem."

"I see," said Bo. "The President isn't following the script any longer is she?"

Matt smirked a little and then said, "No, and Braun's great discussions about turning the nation back to religion didn't sit well with him."

"Because the President was listening to Braun," said Bo with a hint of a hidden, satisfied smile.

Matt nodded. "Yes, because she was listening."

"That's my boy!" said Bo with a laugh. "He put it all out there and he made a difference!"

Matt smiled. "He made more than just 'a difference,' he stirred the pot and everything started to boil."

"Yes!" said Bo, obviously very happy about his son's effect.

"How did your father threaten Braun?" asked Corrynne, anxious to get to the meaty details.

With a serious look Matt said, "He asked me to kill him."

"Are you kidding?" asked Corrynne, shocked beyond belief.

"No, I'm not kidding," said Matt shaking his head. "I was given the order and my father expected me to follow through to prove my allegiance as his son and heir. It was a test."

"Because Braun was Brea's brother?" asked Bo.

"Yes, that was one contributing factor. My father knew it would be near impossible for me to carry out the hit. He enjoyed watching me squirm."

"So what did you do then?" asked Bo.

Matt looked straight into Bo's eyes and said, "I gassed him and sent him to Siberia."

Bo let out a laugh and hit the table. "That was a good one," he said, but then returning to a more somber mood he said, "Now tell me what you really did."

"That's what I did," said Matt. "He's in Siberia."

Bo's face contorted into confusion. "Russia—Siberia?"

Matt nodded. "Yes, the Siberia in Russia."

"Why?" asked Corrynne, horrified.

"Because that was the only way I could make Braun 'die' convincingly. In Siberia technology doesn't exist. My father's power comes through technology and to hide someone, they must be untouchable, unreachable, untrackable, and that means no technology. Now, because my father can't find him, he's dead. With that plan, I win, my father wins, and Braun wins. No one loses."

"When will he come back?" asked Corrynne.

"When it's safe."

"When will it be safe?"

Matt paused. "When I have power over the IMF."

"Ahh," said Bo with a spark of understanding beginning in his eye. "You're planning a take-over."

"Every hour of every day," said Matt with resolve.

Quiet filled the room as each person digested the reality of what was being said.

After a few moments, Matt leaned forward and asked, "Would you like to hear about your other sons?"

Bo furrowed his eyebrows. "What?"

"What are you talking about?" asked Corrynne, trying to figure out what was happening here. Was he trying to divert their attention?

"Do you remember that Braun could use satellites to see anything he wished, anywhere in the world?"

"Yes," said Corrynne, as she watched Matt carefully.

"He watched the flooding in Provo from the UN," said Bo.

"Right," said Matt. "I could do the same thing until a few hours ago."

"What happened a few hours ago?"

"The systems went down from the solar storm. I'm sure they'll be up again soon, but right now they're down."

"So, you have access to the UN's satellites," said Bo with a nod.

"Yes," said Matt.

"What have you seen?" asked Corrynne beginning to be interested now.

"Well, Conrad is doing very well. He's helping build the new Jewish temple."

"He still is?" asked Corrynne, enthralled.

"Yes. He's outside nearly every day working on the building. It's looking good."

"I wish I could see him," said Corrynne.

"You will," said Matt. "You'll probably be interested to know that he's still in close contact with the apostles."

"So you see them too?" asked Corrynne.

"I do."

"Wow. Wouldn't that be so amazing to just look in your crystal ball and see whatever you want?"

"It can come in handy."

"What about Dane?" asked Bo.

"I've watched Dane travel around America, being a good steward over the people," continued Matt. "He's in New York right now, keeping the peace in that city."

"New York? I thought he was in Michigan," said Corrynne a little confused. "Or was it California?"

"Nope, I looked yesterday. He's in New York."

"New York?" asked Bo. "A lot happens in New York for our family, doesn't it?"

"It seems to," said Matt. "But New York needs him. There's trouble brewing because the electricity keeps going out. It's becoming a free-for-all."

"That's dangerous," said Corrynne.

"It could be, but Dane is well armed. He'll be fine."

"I hope so," said Corrynne worriedly.

"I was thinking, as I watched him this morning," continued Matt, "that even though I've never met him, I can tell that he's a good kid. He doesn't give up. He's the perfect soldier, doing his best for his country."

"That sounds like Dane. He's always trying to be better than he was the day before," said Bo.

"You'd be proud of him then. He's doing very well."

"He told us in his last letter that he hasn't been injured," said Corrynne. "He's convinced he has a guardian angel watching over him. Most of his buddies have been hurt already."

Matt nodded. "I believe it."

"Sometimes I think I worry too much," said Corrynne. "Mainly because what we see on the television looks pretty ugly, especially in the bigger cities."

"I know what you mean," said Matt with a nod.

"So tell us your plans for you and Brea," said Bo.

Matt smiled and then said, "Before I get into that, may I have a drink of water?"

"Sure," said Corrynne getting up from the table to serve her son-in-law. He had answered all of her questions honestly and she was feeling more trust for Matt. Corrynne handed him a full glass of water which he drank right down.

"Thirsty?" asked Corrynne with a smile.

"Yes, talking like this makes me crave water," said Matt as he wiped the excess water from his mouth with his hand.

"That's the stress response," said Corrynne. "It turns your tongue to cotton. You've revealed yourself through that glass of water, whether you meant to or not."

"What's that?" asked Matt.

"Because your mouth is dry, I can tell you're just as stressed as we are," said Corrynne with a laugh. "You have to be telling the truth."

"Not necessarily," said Bo. "Lying causes stress too."

"Oh, I know," said Corrynne. "I was just joking."

"I'm not lying, if that's what you're getting at," said Matt in seriousness. "I'm putting myself out there. I'm risking everything in hopes you'll begin to trust me."

"Things are improving in my mind," said Corrynne. "I'm feeling much better. Aren't you, Bo?"

Bo didn't say yes or no. He was reserving his opinions.

Matt looked from Bo to Corrynne and said, "I'm glad we're beginning to connect, because there's a lot I need to tell you concerning my relationship with Brea."

"Why? What's wrong?" asked Corrynne sitting back down and feeling her worries return.

"I'm building a home in the cleft of a mountain just north of this valley."

"Up Provo canyon?" asked Bo.

Matt nodded. "Yes."

"That's a good thing, right?" asked Corrynne. "You'll be close by."

"Yes, but here's the bad news. Brea will be staying at the house and I'll be living in Germany."

"Germany? What's in Germany?" asked Corrynne.

"That's where the business is being moved."

"What does this mean?" asked Bo.

"That means Brea and I have made a decision to live apart for a while."

Corrynne frowned. "What's happening here?"

Matt hesitated and then said, "I'm caught in a web and it has both Brea and I captive,[1] and once again, the spider is my father—I have an influential position in the IMF but still, he trumps me by a long shot."

"I see," said Corrynne. "And he doesn't like Brea in your life, does he?"

Matt looked at Corrynne with a question in his eyes.

Corrynne continued, "Brea suspected that was the case even before she went to New York."

Matt nodded and took a breath. "I wish she'd been wrong, but she ended up being pretty accurate in her assessment. You see, my father demands control over everyone in his life, privately, politically, and professionally."

"That's a lot of control," said Bo.

"Yes. But what makes matters worse is that if anyone in his circle exhibits the tiniest bit of independence, then he takes it upon himself to squash it before it can get out of control."

"Are Brea and your father not getting along because she's independent?" asked Corrynne.

"No, I'm saying something much worse than that."

"What are you saying? Spit it out," said Bo with a stern look.

Matt fiddled with his wedding ring. "Brea's in danger, just like Braun was."

"No, don't tell me that," said Corrynne as she shook her head with her hand to her forehead.

"Why?" asked Bo.

"Because she interfered in my father's plans."

"How could Brea do that?" asked Corrynne.

"By influencing me for good."

"What?"

Corrynne shook her head. "This is stranger than anything I've ever heard!"

Bo got up from the table and began to pace. "What kind of baloney is this?"

After a few moments Matt looked at Bo and said, "I've been praying about..." Matt stalled as if he changed his mind about what he was going to say and then shook his head. "I'm sorry, this is difficult. I have to be very careful because I don't want to put you in danger, too."

"Us?" asked Corrynne feeling dizzy with anxiety. "Your father would come after us?"

"Yes, if you knew too much, or, like Braun and Brea, if you affected his power or control in any way."

"Why would we do that?" asked Corrynne looking back at Bo.

"I'd do that," said Bo with hot anger in his face.

"No you wouldn't," said Corrynne.

"Yes, I would. Someone has to stop that man."

"Not you," said Corrynne getting angry now.

"I'm going to stop him," said Matt calmly.

Both Bo and Corrynne turned and looked at Matt for an energy-charged moment.

Then Bo frowned and said, "And I'm supposed to believe you? You tricked Brea into marrying you. If you had been honest and told her what she was getting into, she never would have trusted you."

Matt looked passively at Bo. Then with a calm voice he said, "I assure you I am who I seem to be."

"No you're not..." said Bo, a finger pointing at Matt.

Matt continued despite Bo's comment. "I went on a mission, I attended BYU, I love your daughter, I'm a faithful member of Christ's church. I have a testimony of the Savior and I want nothing more in the world than to protect my family, but it's becoming increasingly difficult."

"You're a chameleon, a deceiver, *a chip off the ol' block*!" said Bo with vehemence.

Matt lowered his head while shaking it slowly.

Corrynne shot Bo a frustrated look. In her opinion, he had been too hard on Matt. That last comment was a low blow.

After a few moments, Matt raised his head and said, "My father has asked me to leave Brea."

Neither Bo nor Corrynne responded but just looked at each other in anticipation.

"I'm to divorce her before I leave Utah…." said Matt seeming to falter a little.

This was the first time Corrynne saw any emotion come from Matt. She could feel his heart and it was breaking. It made Corrynne sad. "Divorcing Brea during the last few weeks of pregnancy won't be good for her adjustment during delivery and post partum. You can't do this now," offered Corrynne. "She could spin into a post partum depression that could end up in psychosis."[2]

Matt nodded and looked down at the table again. "I have to. Brea understands. She'll be OK."

"No, Brea is just being strong. I know her. She's like me. She'll say she'll be fine, but she won't be. One can only handle so much stress."

Matt held up one hand. "No, she'll be fine, and I'll tell you why. We'll be divorced only on paper. I'll have two sets created. On the records of the government, we'll be divorced but she'll have the genuine paperwork in her possession declaring that we are married. It has to look legal so if my father researches it he'll be able to find the proof of my word to him…"

"Proof of your deception to him?" asked Bo with a cynical eye. "In that case it shouldn't be hard."

"Bo, that's enough," said Corrynne in a warning voice.

Matt ignored Bo's statement and continued. "There's more that you should know about," he said looking at his mother-in-law.

"Go ahead," said Corrynne with a supportive nod.

An aggrieved look returned to Matt's face. "OK, bear with me here."

Bo crossed his arms as a sign that he wouldn't be won over by any kind of emotion.

"I am my father's heir whether I like it or not. I cannot escape my duties. My father believes Brea has made me vulnerable to my enemies and clouded my vision of my future. He offered to eliminate her if I couldn't."

Corrynne felt as if she had been punched in the stomach. "Why would he do that? She isn't a threat! She's carrying his grandchildren!"

"I know. That's why I have to protect her, too."

"Are you going to send her to Siberia?" asked Bo with a sneer.

Matt looked at Bo and smiled patiently. "No, I'm not going to send Brea to Siberia. She'll stay here, in her own home, like I said. But the point I want to make is this, I had to bargain for her safety, and my father likes people to have pain, especially me, so it was a painful bargain. There was a huge price requested."

"Just use your MasterCard," said Bo now leaning against the wall as if he was bored.

"Bo, stop it!" said Corrynne. "There's enough suffering in this room. Make things *better*, not worse." Then turning back to Matt, Corrynne said, "Tell us what you had to do," she said kindly.

Bo looked like he was thinking about saying something but then he stopped himself.

Corrynne was grateful.

Matt took a deep breath and started. "Part of the bargain to assure Brea's safety was to allow my parents to raise one of our children as theirs."

Corrynne felt her cheek twitch as she covered her mouth in disbelief.

Bo, suddenly getting angry again, exclaimed, *"I've heard enough!"*

Matt held his hands up and said, "I know how this sounds, but my father has elected to raise my child to take my place if I don't turn around. It's his leverage to make me bend to his wishes."

"What?" asked Corrynne. "I've never heard of such a thing!"

"In my father's mind, since my child has his blood running through his veins, he would be a perfect heir if I didn't work out. He'd just get rid of me and life would go on as he planned it."

"Your father is insane," said Bo shaking his head.

Matt nodded with a blank face. "He definitely doesn't have the natural affection a father would have for a son."[3]

"So he wants a *daughter* to take your place?" asked Corrynne.

Matt shook his head. "No, he'll take my son."

"Your son?" asked Corrynne in confusion. "You're having twin girls."

"No," said Matt. "An ultrasound has verified Brea's going to have a boy and a girl."

"It did?"

"Yes."

"I didn't know that. When was that?"

"We had it done at a mall on the way here."

"The mall?" asked Corrynne with a confused look. "Why the mall?"

"Because we needed to know. The previous ultrasound, as you know, led us to believe that we were having girls. My father requested me to hand over my first born son in return for Brea's safety. Now we can do that."

"Wow," said Corrynne, astounded by what she was hearing. She shook her head in shock and mumbled, "I just don't know how…." but never finished her thought.

Matt picked up the conversation. "My thoughts are that if I can't have Brea, then at least I can have a part of her to remind me of her. Even though our son will not be legally ours anymore, I can watch over him and use my influence to guide him in my own way."

"What's going to stop your father from turning him against you?" asked Bo, his eyes narrowed to slits.

"I don't know," said Matt. "I'm hoping that with the Lord's help, I can figure that one out. I don't really have choices right now. I just have to go with the current and plan as I see how things pan out."

"This sounds like…like…" started Corrynne feeling a loss of words.

"I know how it sounds," said Matt. "I'm not happy about this arrangement either. It makes me sick, yet I understand it. I'm sure hearing this information for the first time must be difficult for both of you, but I guarantee it's harder on Brea and me."

"I'm just saying…" started Corrynne but Matt held up a finger. He wanted to finish his thought.

"We have had our lives ripped apart by those who should have protected us. We will not have the future we expected and every one of our plans will go on hold until I can free us from my father's grasp." Matt made fists and his voice grew more intense. "In the mean time, we'll have anger, loss, despair, and mourning. I of all people understand how this sounds and I of all people am not happy with how things are turning out, but as I said before, my hands are tied. If I want Brea to be safe and free, I must make sacrifices now. That's the only way she can heal.[4] We must hide her along with one child and I must take the other back with me to Germany where I will allow my mother to raise him."

"So you're planning to take Brea and your son as well as your life back at some later date?" asked Bo.

Matt looked surprised. "Of course I am! Is there any question?" he asked as he looked back and forth between Corrynne and Bo. "The sooner, the better!" Matt sighed as he shook his head. Then he said, "My plan is to visit once in a while, but I'll have to do it at off times when I know my father's attention is distracted. My visits will probably be intermittent and there might be periods where I won't visit at all. It just depends on what's happening and what excuses I can make to pass through Utah without anyone suspecting I'm still in love and married to Brea."

"We understand," said Corrynne trying now to be supportive.

"The house is being built into the side of the mountain. It will be camouflaged so that no one will know that it's there. It will be impenetrable to my father's sensing and spying devices, so no matter if he looks here, he won't find her."

"You know he'll look here first," said Bo.

"Yes, I know, but considering everything, I realized Brea must have her family. With your help, I'm sure she'll be better off here than anywhere else in the world."

"So you're sure the house you're building will be safe for her?" asked Corrynne.

"Positive. That's one benefit of being my father's son and being involved in the business. I understand his ways and can find ways around his ways. It will be a very nice place. She'll have all the luxuries of life and anything money can buy." Matt continued, "I want you to know I love your daughter more than anything else in this world! She, our children, and I—we're a family!"

"So what happens if your plan to take over his business fails?" asked Bo. "It seems your father has quite a bit of power and hasn't been dethroned yet. You might not be able to dethrone him either."

"Well…" Matt paused with a blank look on his face. "Sooner or later Brea and I will be together, even if I have to wait for my father's death."

"So until then Brea will live underground in hiding?" asked Bo.

"Yes. It's the best solution I can think of. It's the only way we can maintain what we have."

"Selfishness aside, what kind of life will that offer?"

"Bo!" exclaimed Corrynne with a shocked look. Her husband was making a bad situation worse!

"The best possible," said Matt emphatically. "It's not ideal but it's better than no life at all."

"Right," said Corrynne looking back and forth between Bo and Matt. "Anyway, how bad can it be? How old is your father? I've never even seen him before, so I don't know."

"He's in his fifties."

"Fifties?" asked Corrynne, surprised by his answer. Before she could stop herself she blurted out, "He could live for another forty years!"

"I know," said Matt with a far away look on his face.

"At what point will you decide Brea deserves better than your plan?" said Bo.

"I don't know. Not right now and not in the near future."

"There has to be a better solution," demanded Bo.

"There isn't," said Matt with a stern look and a tight jaw.

"So Brea is just supposed to waste away her life waiting for you to take over or for your father to die?"

"Yes."

"You know she won't be a part of a community, or be able to walk out in public."

"Right, I know."

"She won't be able to interact with anyone."

"Yes. I know."

"You might as well put her in *prison*! Is that the price you want your family to pay for your shortsighted needs?"

Matt looked dumbfounded, as if he might be going into an emotional shock. It seemed either he didn't want to answer, or he couldn't.

"We'll take care of her, Bo. We'll make it work," said Corrynne as she smiled gently at her husband. She was sending him a signal to stop being so hard on the boy.

Bo ignored Corrynne's hint and continued. "I know, but we shouldn't have to. When this man took my daughter as a wife, he promised to put her first! To love her, to cherish her, to protect her!"

"Bo! You're going to wake the children! Be quiet," warned Corrynne.

Bo continued, unaffected by his wife's continued suggestions. With a finger pointed at Matt he ranted, "He promised to give her children and a future, not to put her in a hole for safe keeping!"

"I know, Bo, but right now, let's focus on the stresses at hand. Brea is due in December. We have to figure out how to deliver those babies safely while keeping her anonymity," said Corrynne. "I think this is best."

"This is *bull*!" Bo's face was turning red.

"Bo," said Corrynne with a pleading look.

"No, Corrynne! This man should do the right thing and cut Brea loose. He should allow her a chance at a normal life. He *should* divorce Brea and not carry on this charade. His father has promised not to hurt Brea if he takes a child back with him. I say let him do that and let it be the end!"

"Bo, that will break her heart! At least with Matt's plan, Brea has a chance of having her life back some day. And by the way, that's your grandchild you're talking about!"

"Grandchild? No, Matt is giving away our grandchild. Now it will be someone else's grandchild…"

"Oh my goodness, Bo! What's wrong with you?!" asked Corrynne getting angry at how everything was spiraling out of control.

"And as far as someday, Corrynne, Brea will be better off without this guy!" he said continuing to point at Matt. "She could meet another man, worthy to take her to the temple, and start over. That's not such a bad option!"

"What about the children?" asked Corrynne.

"There'll be other children, Corrynne. If she marries someone else she'll be able to have many more children. If she stays married to this guy, that's the end. No more children, unless they're planning on secretly having more children, but that will seem kind of strange being that she's 'divorced'," exclaimed Bo, using his fingers to make quotation marks in the air. "Unless Matt is expecting Brea to wear a scarlet letter 'A' on her chest, this whole plan is ridiculous, unhealthy, and selfish."

"OK, now you're being cruel, Bo."

Matt looked down at the table, took a deep breath, and stood up. "I'm sorry you feel that way, but this decision has been made by both Brea and I. We are two consenting adults who have come up with a solution that seems best for everyone under the present circumstances. I had hoped you would understand and support us in our efforts to keep our family together and whole."

Bo stood firm with a grim look on his face and his arms folded. "Well, considering you knew about your father before you married my daughter and that you chose to put her at risk, representing yourself as something you weren't, I'm sorry, I can't support *or* trust you."

"Bo! Come on!" exclaimed Corrynne.

"But you do trust your daughter, right?" asked Matt.

"Without reservation."

"Then I hope, as we go forward with our plan that you will be there for her as she seeks peace in her life."[5]

"I will indeed."

"That's all I can ask. Good enough then," said Matt as he retrieved his coat from the coat hook. "You'll be hearing from Brea soon."

"No, no, no. This is not a good way to end things!" said Corrynne standing up now too. "We need to figure things out. We're family. We can't just decide to be angry and stomp off."

But it was too late. The kitchen door opened and closed, leaving Bo and Corrynne alone in the kitchen.

Corrynne used that opportunity to give Bo the angriest look she could muster and then stomped up the stairs to their bedroom.

"I thought it wasn't right to be angry and stomp off!" called Bo after Corrynne.

In response to him, the door to the bedroom slammed.

Notes to "Web of Pain"

Peter, Peter, Pumpkin Eater

[1] All of us at one time or another has suffered from an abusive experience. To recover from such is very difficult. The following quotes deal with one's healing from *any* unhealthy, abusive relationship with another. In the text, Matt has distanced Brea and their future family from MD to avoid the destructive influences of MD. This was a very important first step toward healing. The next step, to distance one's self from the pain and suffering of the abuse, they must learn and understand the following eternal principles:

"Your abuse results from another's unrighteous attack on your freedom. Since all of Father in Heaven's children enjoy agency, there can be some who choose willfully to violate the commandments and harm you. Such acts temporarily restrict your freedom. In justice, and to compensate, the Lord has provided a way for you to overcome the destructive results of others' acts against your will. That relief comes by applying eternal truths with priesthood assistance. Know that the wicked choice of others cannot completely destroy your agency unless you permit it. Their acts may cause pain, anguish, even physical harm, but they cannot destroy your eternal possibilities in this brief but crucial life on earth. You must understand that you are free to determine to overcome the harmful results of abuse. Your attitude can control the change for good in your life. It allows you to have the help the Lord intends you to receive. No one can take away your ultimate opportunities when you understand and live eternal law. The laws of your Heavenly Father and the atonement of the Lord have made it possible that you will not be robbed of the opportunities which come to the children of God. You may feel threatened by one who is in a position of power or control over you. You may feel trapped and see no escape. Please believe that your Heavenly Father does not want you to be held captive by unrighteous influence, by threats of reprisal, or by fear of repercussion to the family member who abuses you. Trust that the Lord will lead you to a solution. Ask in faith, nothing doubting. (See James 1:6; Enos 1:15; Moro. 7:26; D&C 8:10; D&C 18:18.)" (Richard G. Scott, "Healing the Tragic Scars of Abuse," *Ensign*, May 1992, p. 31).

[2] "Unless healed by the Lord, mental, physical, or sexual abuse can cause you serious, enduring consequences. As a victim you have experienced some of them. They include fear, depression, guilt, self-hatred, destruction of self-esteem, and alienation from normal human relationships. When aggravated by continued abuse, powerful emotions of rebellion, anger, and hatred are generated. These feelings often are focused against oneself, others, life itself, and even Heavenly Father. Frustrated efforts to fight back can degenerate into drug abuse, immorality, abandonment of home, and, tragically in extreme cases, suicide. Unless corrected, these feelings lead to despondent lives, discordant marriages, and even the transition from victim to abuser. One awful result is a deepening lack of trust in others which becomes a barrier to healing" (Richard G. Scott, "Healing the Tragic Scars of Abuse," *Ensign*, May 1992, p. 31).

[3] "This know also, that in the last days perilous times shall come. For men shall be lovers of their own selves, covetous, boasters, proud, blasphemers, disobedient to parents, unthankful, unholy, Without natural affection, trucebreakers, false accusers, incontinent, fierce, despisers of those that are good, Traitors, heady, highminded, lovers of pleasures more than lovers of God; Having a form of godliness, but denying the power thereof: from such turn away" (2 Timothy 3:1–5).

[4] "Recognize that you are a beloved child of your Heavenly Father. He loves you perfectly and can help you as no earthly parent, spouse, or devoted friend can. His Son gave his life so that by faith in him and obedience to his teachings you can be made whole. He is the consummate healer. Gain trust in the love and compassion of your elder brother, Jesus Christ, by pondering the scriptures. As with the Nephites, he tells you, 'I have compassion upon you; my bowels are filled with mercy. … I see that your faith is sufficient that I should heal you.' (3 Ne. 17:7–8.) Healing best begins with your sincere prayer asking your Father in Heaven for help. That use of your agency allows divine intervention. When you permit it, the love of the Savior will soften your heart, break the cycle of abuse that can transform a victim into an aggressor. Adversity, even when caused willfully by others' unrestrained appetite, can be a source of growth when viewed from the perspective of eternal principle. (See D&C 122:7.) The victim must do all in his or her power to stop the abuse. Most often, the victim is innocent because of being disabled by fear or the power or authority of the offender. …Forgiveness can be obtained for all involved in abuse. (See Article of Faith 1:3.) Then comes a restoration of self-respect, self-worth, and a renewal of life. As a victim, do not waste effort in revenge or retribution against your aggressor. Focus on your responsibility to do what is in your power to correct. Leave the handling of the offender to civil and Church authorities. Whatever they do, eventually the guilty will face the Perfect Judge. Ultimately the unrepentant abuser will be punished by a just God. The purveyors of filth and harmful substances who knowingly incite others to acts of violence and depravation and those who promote a climate of permissiveness and corruption will be sentenced" (Richard G. Scott, "Healing the Tragic Scars of Abuse," *Ensign*, May 1992, p. 31).

[5] "You cannot erase what has been done, but you can forgive. (See D&C 64:10.) Forgiveness heals terrible, tragic wounds, for it allows the love of God to purge your heart and mind of the poison of hate. It cleanses your consciousness of the desire for revenge. It makes place for the purifying, healing, restoring love of the Lord. The Master counseled, 'Love your enemies, bless them that curse you, do good to them that hate you, and pray for them who despitefully use you and persecute you.' (3 Ne. 12:44; italics added.) Bitterness and hatred are harmful. They produce much that is destructive. They postpone the relief and healing you yearn for. Through rationalization and self-pity, they can transform a victim into an abuser. Let God be the judge—you cannot do it as well as he can. To be counseled to just forget abuse is not helpful. You need to understand the principles which will bring healing. I repeat, most often that comes through an understanding priesthood leader who has inspiration and the power of the priesthood to bless you" (Richard G. Scott, "Healing the Tragic Scars of Abuse," *Ensign*, May 1992, p. 31).

CHAPTER SIX

MORTAL STRIFE

"For the time speedily cometh that the Lord God shall cause a great division among the people, and the wicked will he destroy; and he will spare his people" (2 Nephi 30:10).

00:03:11, 07:30:43, Zulu
Friday, September 19th

Violence in the Streets

Manhattan, New York
11:30 a.m.

"My money's gone!" yelled a woman who looked like she was going to faint and had fallen to one knee. "It's gone. *Completely gone!*"

Dane, who was standing at his post outside the bank, moved to help the woman.

With tears in her eyes, the woman said, "Soldier, they've taken all my money. Can't you do something?"

Dane pulled the woman to her feet and asked, "Are you saying you've been robbed?"

The woman nodded. "Yes, I've been robbed. The bank took all my money. Now I have nothing! *Nothing! Do you hear me?*"

"The *bank* took your money?" asked Dane, not quite understanding.

"Yes! Yes! It's gone!" she said as she dissolved into tears.

Right at that moment hordes of angry people began to pour out of the bank. *"We have a crooked president!"* yelled one angry man with a fist in the air. *"She took our money to pay* ***her debts****. She's the worst kind of criminal!"*

"Why do we keep trusting politicians?" said another man, equally furious. "They don't care about the people! The political system is a *joke*!"

Dane watched in confusion. Finally he held up his hands and stopped a gentleman to ask, "I'm sorry, can you tell me what's going on here? What's everyone so upset about?"

"They're kicking us out of the bank at gun point," the man said.

"Who is?" asked Dane.

"The bank security."

"What? I'm sure you're mistaken."

"I'm not."

"Why would they do that?" asked Dane.

"Because there's no money left! Most of it has been taken by the IMF to pay America's international debts and the ten percent the government has promised us won't be here for weeks!"

"OK, slow down. Who did this? The IM—who?" asked Dane. Now he knew something was terribly wrong but he didn't know what he was supposed to do about it.

Gunshots rang out inside the bank and Dane pushed through the sudden flow of people who were trying to escape the building. He had to force his way through the crowd, squeezing between men and women, pulling free from their hands as he passed. A cacophony of noises erupted; people were yelling and crying. Some were on the floor, others were fist fighting. The security guards had their guns in the air, shooting, obviously attempting to bring some sort of order to the chaos.

A business man with a red face suddenly punched one of the security guards. The guard fell with a thud and his gun was kicked across the floor.

Dane dove for the gun. It wasn't good to have a loaded weapon loose on the floor, but he was too late. A teenager picked it up and slipped it in the back of his jeans.

Dane pulled his gun and pointed at the boy. "Give up the gun."

"What gun, dude? You're imagining things," the teen said belligerently.

"I'm not imagining things. Give me the gun."

"Dude, you're high or something. All I have is a piece of paper that says I'm broke."

"Hands up!" yelled Dane. *"I'm not playing with you!"*

"Fine!" said the boy as he pulled the gun from his pants and acted as if he was going to hand it over, but at the last second he darted into the crowd.

Dane pointed his gun after the teen but he couldn't fire because of the mass of people running back and forth. So instead he pushed into the crowd once more and ran after the boy. Once he got outside, the main entrance was thronged with people, and in the mess of to and fro movement there was no sign of the delinquent.

Dane stepped back to the wall of the building, out of the way of the angry masses, and called his commander. "This is Joey Fodder calling for Salamander. Do you copy, Salamander? Over."

"This is Salamander, over."

"Salamander, this is a 9-1-1. The streets are a mass of confusion. There are gunshots at East 49th Street and 1st Avenue South. We have some injured and I am unable to keep order. I need back up. Repeat. This is a 9-1-1. I need back up. Over."

"That's a negative, Joey Fodder. There are no troops available to back you up. Violence has broken out everywhere. Just sit tight and do your best. Over."

"Do I break up the fights that are around me? Over," asked Dane as two men began tussling out on the sidewalk, knocking over other people.

"Only in the case where it looks like there might be a loss of life. Otherwise, stay out of the way. Over."

"Copy," said Dane feeling overwhelmed.

"Over," said his commander.

"Over," said Dane wondering if this kind of thing was happening everywhere or only here in Manhattan. He wished he had his cell phone from home. He could search the net. Then he saw through the bank window a television screen mounted up on the wall. He couldn't hear what was being said, but all the images that flashed on the screen displayed his worst fears. This outbreak was not just local, it wasn't just one bank that had been emptied of all its funds; it was every bank in America! How could this have happened? What did this mean?

Dane's mind went numb. He couldn't even fathom the consequences of no money in America; the land of the free; the land where dreams came true.

Dane slid down the brick wall and hunched low, putting his automatic rifle behind him. It was clear there was nothing he, nor anyone else, could do to stop this avalanche. Oh, how he wished he were home.

Handcuffs

Provo, Utah
9:40 a.m.

"The proliferation of electronic stock markets created a valid reason for restructuring the U.S. stock market system."

Carea yawned as she drew a picture of a masked ninja on the edge of her economic notes. She didn't know if she wanted the ninja to be a girl or a boy yet as she drew the hooded mask. It reminded her of her exchange at the gym. It irritated her to think that she still hadn't a clue who she'd fought.

"Ben Wright, the current chairman of the Securities Exchange Commission, believes the current system is too fragmented and perplexing for the average investor," the teacher droned.

Carea dropped her pencil and lifted up her arms, elbows bent, to stretch her back over the top of her chair. She had been sitting in one position too long.

"Yes, Miss Rogers?"

Embarrassment colored Carea's cheeks as she felt the class turn and look at her. She immediately pulled her arms down to her chest. She wasn't asking a question.

"Did you have a comment?"

Carea shook her head. "I'm sorry, I was just stretching. I didn't mean to interrupt."

The teacher nodded and then thoughtfully continued as he turned to pace the other direction at the front of the class. "The SEC would like to 'synchronize' the system and somehow create a fundamental market to increase efficiency."

Out of the corner of her eye, something black and shiny caught the afternoon sun outside the classroom window where a main street went parallel to the high school. The light quickly traveled around half the room and then disappeared. She was used to the cars catching the light as they passed by and didn't pay any particular attention to it. But then another blinding light blasted into the classroom and traveled the walls, followed by another.

Carea turned to look out the window just in time to see three black SWAT vans pull into the school parking lot and drive out of sight. Sitting up, she wondered what was going on. She tore a piece of paper from her notebook and wrote a note to David, the boy who sat across from her in this class and someone she liked to tease. It said, "Did you see those SWAT vans in the parking lot?" Then she drew an arrow pointing to the window under the words, wadded the piece of paper up, and when the teacher wasn't looking, lobbed it over to David.

The paper hit David square on top of his head. It bounced off and landed on the floor next to him. He frowned and then gave Carea an irritated look.

Carea laughed at his expression but quickly looked down and shielded her face with her hand so she wouldn't alert the teacher. She knew David thought she had taken a risk. This teacher was brutal if he caught students passing notes. If someone wrote a note in this class, it had to be worth the risk of getting caught.

"Read the note," mouthed Carea as she pointed, keeping one eye on her teacher.

The boy waited until the teacher turned to pace the opposite direction as he lectured and then used his foot to pull the piece of paper close to him. Slowly, David leaned down and picked up the paper. Under the desk he smoothed the paper and read the note. Next, he looked out the window, suddenly very interested. After searching the outside, he took a pencil and scribbled something down on another piece of paper. Then he too scrunched it up and threw it back to her when the coast was clear.

Carea knew the note was coming so she caught it and then held it in her lap until it was safe to unwrap it. The note said, "Number one: If there were SWAT vans in our parking lot that would be cool. But I don't see them so I think you're just imagining things. Number two: If there were SWAT teams here, they would be here to take you away. Ha, ha."

Carea gave David a menacing look. She knew he was just joking, but gave the look just to play along.

Suddenly, the door of the classroom flew open and men in black clothing with bullet proof vests and helmets on came into the room. On their vests it said SWAT in large letters

Carea was shocked at first, but then she looked at David with a smile. "I wasn't making it up," she whispered.

David didn't reply. He just watched the men circle the classroom with their automatic weapons held in front of them with the muzzle pointing towards the ceiling.

An officer spoke in low tones with the teacher and then showed him what looked like a list and then another piece of paper, which might have been a warrant.

Carea watched as the teacher nodded and took a step back against the front wall, out of the way.

As soon as the teacher stepped back, the officers pulled out mini-computers from their pockets. They looked from the screens back to the people in the room. A boy in the corner, dressed in a leather jacket characteristic of the Bats, was the first to be confronted. He wasn't a Bat any more, since the group had been disbanded locally, but he still dressed like them.

"Cooperate and you won't get hurt," said the officer to the boy, whose name was James.

The boy nodded with wide eyes. It was obvious he was frozen with fear.

The officer took a plum-sized, sleek, silver object from his pocket and pointed it at James' hand that was resting on his desktop. It let out a high piercing alarm.

Carea shifted in her chair uncomfortably. She knew what that silver object was used for. It had been waved over her head at the Imam Mahdi mansion. It was a chip detector. Carea shook her head. Even though James was clean now, he was going to be lumped with all the other Bats in the world. It wasn't fair. He was a cool kid now but since he had a chip in his hand, just like all the Bats, he would probably be taken away somewhere.

A spasm of panic rippled through her. Would that mean she would be taken away? That couldn't happen. What could she do? She looked around the room for some sort of get-away. There were officers everywhere, and she had the feeling these guys would shoot first and interview afterward.

Carea felt under the desk, as a nervous impulse. Was there gum under there? Yes, she found some! Ignoring any normal reaction to touching post-chewed gum she began chipping away at one piece with her thumbnail. Maybe if she found a piece that matched her skin color and stuck it to her forehead, she could fool the machine. Her hair was just long enough to hide it…

"Miss Rogers?" came a booming voice next to Carea's ear that made her jump.

"What?" she asked reflexively feeling her heart beat wildly.

"Sit still." The officer waved the silver object over her head. Her heart pounded. The alarm screamed. It was over.

Carea could feel David's eyes on her.

"Carea?" she heard him whisper.

She didn't have to look at him to know he was stunned. No one knew she had a chip in her head. She had always been anti-Bat, so to find out she had a chip in her forehead—she knew the news would shock everyone.

Carea kept her head down. She wished she could just disappear.

"Please put your fingers on the screen," directed the officer.

Carea did as she was told with stinging eyes. She looked up briefly to see all her personal information flash on the screen above her fingers.

"Come with me," he stated as he took her arm.

"I'm not a Bat," said Carea through gritted teeth. She was trying not to cry. She needed to talk to her mom. She needed to talk to the Chief of Police, Chief Morgan! Maybe they could get her out of this. "I want to talk to Chief Morgan!"

"Come with me, Miss," said the officer as he lifted her out of her chair forcibly. "The Chief has nothing to do with our operation."

"She's not a Bat," said David who was standing next to his desk now. "There's a mistake, your machine's messing up. She'd never be caught dead doing what the Bats do."

The officer didn't pay attention. He twisted Carea's arms behind her back and handcuffed her.

Carea began to cry silently. She was so frustrated!

"Did you hear me? You've made a mistake!" said David getting bolder.

"Yeah!" said someone from the back of the room. Carea wasn't sure who it was, but it was nice that her friends were standing up for her.

The comments must have made the officer angry because his grip became tighter. "So what's this then?" he asked, sneering at the classroom, exposing Carea's right shoulder blade and the letters "B. A. T." boldly in black.

Carea was shocked! How did he know about the tattoo on her shoulder? Then she realized her square necked shirt must have bowed as he handcuffed her hands behind her back, exposing her tattoo to his view.

Carea swallowed and shrugged hard as she imagined the astonishment of everyone in her classroom. How could she deny being a part of the Bats now? No one would believe her. No one would understand.

David shut his mouth and sat back down as Carea was escorted out.

At the last moment before the door closed to the classroom, Carea looked back. The shock on David's face and the remaining class members' faces cut into her heart. It was the worst hurt she could imagine.

Out of Control

Manhattan, New York
1:10 p.m.

The traffic had come to a standstill as thousands of people were standing outside the bank and spilling down the sidewalk and out among the stopped cars. Horns were honking. Phone circuits were jammed. Communication had stopped. The city was crippled.

Dane was in a daze. He didn't know what was happening. It was some sort of disaster, but without outward destruction. No earthquake, no bombs, no airplanes. The sky was blue, the sun was bright; by all logic, it should be a beautiful, happy day, but it wasn't. All the people around him had looks of shock. Numbness filled the air. Dane wondered how his own parents were doing. Were they standing outside a bank too? Were they embroiled in an angry mob that was only getting angrier?

Dane looked around at all the angry people. He watched a man punch a window with his bare hand and come away with glass sticking out of his flesh. What was he supposed to do about all this? What could he do? He was only one man—no, he wasn't even a man. He was still a kid expected to act like a man. Dane shook his head in disbelief. How did he get caught up in all this confusion? But the bigger question was, how could he get out?

Across from him, one man hit another man in the face. Dane could hear the sickening thud as the second man's head hit the sidewalk. Dane jumped to his feet. This was crazy! He was told to stay out of the way, but how could he? These people were acting like animals! What was wrong with them? Why did they think punching each other would fix anything? Some people were so stupid!

Dane was sick of it all. He moved from his corner and he thrust himself into the mass of people outside the bank. He walked with his hands up and his automatic machine gun in the air. He wanted people to know that enough was enough. *"OK, people! Calm down! There's no need to get violent! It doesn't help anything. The enemy is not out here, it's whoever took your money, so stop beating on each other!"*

With Dane's loud voice, it seemed like he was getting through. The people around him stopped shoving each other and began listening to him. But then that was a problem. He didn't know what else to say. He searched his mind to deliver some important message to these lost and worried people. As he filled his lungs to call to the people around him his radio receiver buzzed loudly in his ear.

"Jo-ey-Fodd-er? Do you copy? Ov-er." The reception was shoddy at best.

Dane looked down at his receiver and pushing the button, he retreated back to the wall for some privacy. "I'm here. Over."

"Re-ttreat to base nnow. Do you copy? Retreat to base…."

Dane knew what the missing word was, so he responded. "Base? That's a negative. There are riots out here. People are hurt, cars are damaged. Windows of stores are getting bashed in…"

"We're aware…but…order's the ss-ame. Retreat. You are being…assigned. Return to base uunn-less you receive other orders…mean time. Over."

Dane looked at the chaos around him. He could see that he wasn't making a difference anyway, so might as well not fight to stay. "Copy that. Over."

Looking around at the anarchy, he decided he'd give one last warning. Just in case anyone was listening to him. *"People, listen! The bank has no money. It's closed. You'll have to come back another time. No one can help you here. I suggest that all of you seek shelter. Get out of the way. Go home!"*

A bottle sailed through the air and crashed on the other side of the crowd, punctuating Dane's words.

"We want our money!"

"Tell them to open up!"

"I know this is hard. It's hard for me too," said Dane, trying to be calm, "but please, so no one gets hurt, go home or work. I don't care which."

"Work? Why would we go there? *All my bosses are here!*" said a New York woman wagging her head in contempt.

Dane looked at her and said, "Then your bosses need to leave, too." Addressing the crowd next, he said, "Go home! The bank isn't open! All standing here is going to do, is get someone hurt."

Suddenly, off to Dane's left a loud voice broke out, *"I'm not leaving till I get my money!"* The businessman turned around and with an angry face, his veins popping out, he screamed at the people behind him. *"Stop shoving! We're all stressed! Let's just be civilized and not raging lunatics!"*

A younger man behind, with longer hair and in street clothes, received most of the screaming face to face. With a powerful push he knocked the businessman out of the crowd and down to the ground. "Don't yell at me! I wasn't the one that pushed you, but since you thought I was, I thought I'd make you honest!"

Dane moved to help the businessman up but the crowd was erupting in more angry screams and the pushing and shoving intensified. Soon there were two fist fights on the fringe of the mob.

"I can't deal with this!" said Dane to himself. ***"People! Stop!"*** he yelled, but no one stopped. Anger was hot and tempers were rising.

Nearby the crash of a store glass window tinkled on the cement at the same time that someone threw a man on top of the hood of a car. Dane shook his head as he released the safety and pulled the trigger twice.

The people nearest him ducked and covered their ears. A baby started crying.

"Listen to me!" he yelled. "I have the authority to shoot anyone who harms someone else!"

"Then shoot him first!" yelled the businessman, directing his remarks to the longhaired man who had assaulted him. "This is an Armani suit. It cost me thousands of dollars and now it has a *hole* in the knee."

Dane ignored the businessman but shot his gun again in the air. "Go home!" he said. "Being here won't help you. I promise if you stay, more will get hurt. You might even get killed. *Go home!*"

Then in frustration he just walked away without looking back. He'd go south, towards the old UN building that now housed the National Police base camp in New York. Enough was enough!

Shake-Down

Salt Lake City, Utah
11:15 a.m.

"I want to go home!" exclaimed Carea. "You can't keep me here!"

"Hands up," said the policewoman. She was a heavyset black woman with a flipped-up hairstyle. She smiled sarcastically as she waved the metal detector across Carea's front. "Oh, yes we *can* keep you here. You're in a gang and everyone who's in a gang goes to a containment camp. And if you ask me, we should have done this years ago."

"I'm not in a gang!" said Carea emphatically. "I hate gangs! I'm on the anti-gang committee!"

The woman took a step back and looked Carea up and down. "Uh-huh." Nodding with a tongue in her cheek she added, "Sure you are."

"I am! You've got the wrong girl!"

"Whatever," the woman said as she sighed and shook her head. Putting the wand in a holster, she said, "Arms out to your side."

Carea complied and said, "Listen to me. I'm not one of them," gesturing to the rest of the hard-looking girls, clad in black with multiple piercings and tattoos. "I'm sure you see the difference."

"It doesn't matter if I see the difference. Eyes lie. I've seen all types come through that door and you're no different," said the woman as she patted Carea's arms and upper torso.

"What can I do to convince you?" asked Carea. She was trying to sound calm as the woman moved to pat down her legs.

The officer stepped behind Carea and began to pat her back and hips. "You can't convince me, and even if you did, it wouldn't matter. I don't make the decisions around here."

"Who can I talk to?" asked Carea over her shoulder as the woman looked at the bottoms of her shoes.

"No one," said the woman standing up and stepping back in front of Carea. "You're here for a reason and the earlier you accept that, the faster you'll adjust."

"I won't accept that!" said Carea folding her arms. "My parents will sue whoever ordered this operation! I know the Chief of Police!"

"I don't care who you know, if your parents want to sue someone, they'll be suing the President of the United States," said the woman as she pressed some buttons on a hand-held computer. "I'll tell you, you might as well make the best of things. There isn't a court in the land that will change anything for a while, not as long as there's fighting in the streets, even if we did get the wrong girl."

"Uhhhhgh!" said Carea under her breath in complete frustration. She could feel tears coming to her eyes, which she quickly wiped away.

"A little advice to a pretty little thing like you," said the officer pointing a stylet at Carea. "Don't complain. Don't fight. Don't try and be funny. Just be good. You be good, you'll have a greater chance of getting out of here. If you put on an attitude, you'll just stay that much longer or get killed by someone with a bigger attitude."

"You'd let that happen?" asked Carea, surprised.

"No, we don't let anything happen, but if it does when we're not looking, what can we do?"

Carea couldn't believe what she was hearing! Was there no protection? *"That sounds pretty lame!"*

"Lame or not, we don't have enough resources to keep everyone safe. It's your job to figure out the rules of the game and play by them. That's how you stay healthy and happy. Where you're going, the camp is run by the inmates, so you have to learn to get along!"

"Or learn who's the biggest bully," said Carea.

"Maybe," said the woman shrugging. "Sometimes that's how it works, I don't deny that."

"I want to call my parents," said Carea.

"The phones are out. You can call them from Alaska," said the woman as she unlocked a cabinet on the wall.

"Alaska? Why do I have to go to Alaska?" asked Carea, completely shocked. "Why can't I stay here?"

"There's no room. This place is just for hardened criminals. You'll be going to a low security camp. It's the only federal facility big enough for everyone we're picking up in these sweeps. Now, here's a jumpsuit," the police officer handed Carea a bag and what was supposed to be an orange jumpsuit. It looked more brown than orange due to age and mildew stains.

"Put this on. Take everything else off, except for your underwear, and put them in the bag and bring the bag back here."

Carea gave the policewoman an angry stare, not knowing what else to say.

The woman simply looked bored and then pointed into the next room.

Carea unhappily moved through the next set of doors into a room full of young women changing. The room was a square cement shower room with old, crusty showerheads sticking out of the walls. She picked a corner to change. Self-consciously she took off her pants as she faced the corner of the room. Slipping the bottom part of the jumpsuit on, she pulled it up to her armpits and then pulled her shirt off and quickly slid her arms in, being sure to stay as covered as possible. She worried about who was watching her. Just because she was in the women's portion of the prison didn't mean she was safe. She had heard horror stories about prison and stalkers. Women, she heard, were just as bad as the men. That thought scared her the most.

Carea zipped her jumpsuit and put her clothes in the bag that she had been given. The pungent smell of mold met her nose as she moved. Carea sniffed the collar of her orange suit and frowned. It smelled as bad as it looked. Obviously, this suit had been in storage too long.

Carea walked back to a different wiry policewoman who had thick black-framed glasses because the first one was busy. After waiting in a short line, she said, "This outfit is moldy. I need a different one."

The woman looked at Carea with an irritated frown. "Sorry, no new suits. You take what you're given."

"Come on. Just give me a different one," pleaded Carea. "I saw that you have a whole cabinet full of different ones."

Suddenly the policewoman squared her shoulders and in her most authoritative tone yelled, "You'll wear what we give you and just *shut-up* about it!"

Carea frowned. Why did this woman yell at her? She didn't do anything to her. She didn't even do anything wrong! Then with the kindest voice she could muster, she said, "I think someone should teach you manners."

The policewoman grabbed Carea by the arm and took her down the hall. "I'll teach you manners!"

"Where are we going?"

"To solitary!"

"Why?"

"Because you won't shut up. I can't take a whiny, rich girl."

The policewoman stopped, unlocked a barred entry, and shoved Carea through the narrow opening. As she stumbled through, Carea tripped on the cement ledge in the floor and went down hard.

"There you go!" said the woman as she slid the bars closed and locked them. "Now you can talk all you want and I won't hear you."

Carea crawled to the nearest wall and pulled up her suit leg to look at her stinging knees and shins. She hadn't really hurt anything though, except her pride. Her knees might be a little bruised, but that was nothing to cry about. Despite those thoughts, she buried her head in her arms propped on her bent knees and cried. She figured she deserved a good cry. After all, there wasn't anything else to do.

Fire

Manhattan, New York
2:15 p.m.

Dane gasped for breath. He had run the last few blocks. He had to get to the UN building and out of the madness. He could see the building now. It was only one block away.

Baaaarrrrrrrhhhhhhuuuuuummmmm!

The blast was deafening, reaching through Dane's body and shaking every atom! An explosion ripped the ground open and Dane lost his footing. The next part was all a blur. Dane sailed through the air and crunched to a stop on a parked car. His head whiplashed slightly, and then he rolled backwards. His feet flew over his head as he rolled down the windshield and onto his stomach. He finally came to a stop on the hood with his legs half hanging off the front of the car. He was marginally aware of something else falling out of the air. It landed on the sidewalk beside the car with a sound like a wet thump.

Dazed, Dane lay on the hood with his eyes shut and his ears ringing like a thousand bells. His instincts told him to keep his head down. After a few seconds, he opened his eyes and lifted his head slightly, just enough to look at his hands that were beside his face. He looked at each finger. They were all intact. That was good. He flexed his legs. They seemed fine. No injuries that he could feel. He felt for the strap of his gun. Good, it was still on him. Seeing other people beginning to sit up or stand, he slid off the hood of the car and crouched in front of it.

Using the car as a protective barrier, he peeked around the bumper at the UN building he had almost entered. It was now enveloped in fire and black smoke was filling the air. He shook his head with his mouth open in astonishment. A few more minutes and he would have been toast! More than toast! He would have been splattered!

What had just happened? ...What had exploded? Was it a bomb...a suicide bomber, or...was the city under some sort of aerial attack?

Dane looked into the sky for a plane. There was a low-flying plane, but it wasn't a war jet. It looked more like a small prop plane. It was headed out of the city. It definitely wasn't the type to have dropped any kind of explosive large enough to demolish a building!

Then Dane had a strange sense of numbness. His thoughts were all jumbled up. He didn't know what to do next. What was he supposed to do? If his post was gone, who would he answer to? Where should he go? The moans of people nearby broke through his stupor and got his attention. He looked around. Maybe he could help someone. Yes. That would be appropriate for the National Police—for him.

Dane knelt down on his knees and looked under the six lanes of cars. From his vantage point, he could see the people lying in-between cars. Very few of them were moving; those who could had already begun to evacuate.

Right then, there was another deafening explosion. Dane responded quickly, squatting up against the car. He raised his arms to protect his head and scrunched into a ball to make his body into a smaller target. Debris fell around him, including a brick that bounced off of the roof of the car and arched over him, landing five feet away. Dane looked at the brick that had come to a stop under the back tire of the car next to him. He had to get out of there! *Everyone* had to get out of there!

Quickly, Dane looked up. Nothing else was falling. He stood up a bit, still crouched over. *"Everyone out! Leave! If you can walk, get someone else out that can't!"* he added, knowing he couldn't help everyone himself.

All of a sudden Dane remembered that something had fallen out of the sky and landed near him after the first explosion. With a sudden jolt he wondered if it could have been a person! He pivoted and moved around the car in the opposite direction. Yes, he had been right. A man lay motionless, crumpled on the sidewalk. Was he still alive? Dane looked down the sidewalk and saw masses of people running his way. He needed to move the gentleman out of the way of foot traffic so he didn't get trampled!

Slinging his gun strap over his head so that the gun was secured on his back, he took hold of the man's feet. Dane dragged the stranger around the bumper to his place of safety in front of it. He turned the man over. Seeing a large indented gash on the side of his head, Dane checked the man's neck for a pulse, but couldn't find any. He repositioned his fingers higher on his neck and tried again, but still, there was nothing.

"Hey! Do you hear me?" Dane yelled into the man's ear, in case he just wasn't good at feeling pulses, but the man lay lifeless and didn't answer.

Pained, Dane pushed the button on his radio. "Salamander! Salamander! Do you copy? Over!" he yelled above the screams of the people rushing by him.

Dane was met with static. There weren't any voices on his radio. All of them had fallen silent. Did that mean the tower had been hit? Or maybe his radio was busted. Dane took the radio out of its holder and hit it in his hand, but it didn't change anything. The static continued.

He tried again. "Salamander! There are injuries out here! Someone copy! Send help! Over!"

A third explosion rang out and the ground shook. Dane ducked down as glass and chunks of cement rained down on him again. Papers floated to the ground as dark smoke loomed above. Smoke billowed high above him to the East. Something else had exploded. Now fire was threatening everything.

"Help me," said a small, thin voice nearby.

The plea stung Dane's mind. It was a child! There was a child somewhere near! In poignant worry, he dropped to the ground to search under the cars. The voice was coming from below him. Was he or she under the car? It was very close. "Where are you?" yelled Dane, seeing no one.

"I'm here."

"Where's 'here'?" he asked crawling on the ground, following the sound.

"Here in the water. My brother put me here!"

"What water?" asked Dane. There wasn't water anywhere on the ground. "I hear you, but I don't see any water..." But then his breath caught in his throat—his eyes fixed on the grate leading down into the sewer. Could she be down there? He rushed to look through the metal bars to see the cute tear-stained face of a little girl maybe five or six years old. She had curly blonde hair with a shiny pink bow on the side of her head. "What are you doing down there?"

"My brother's hiding," she said wiping a tear from her face. "I can't get out to find him! I tried. I'm too little."

Dane stuck his hand through the larger opening between the sidewalk and the grate. "Take my hand."

Dane felt little fingers grasp his. He stretched so he could grab onto her wrist instead, then leveraging his body against the side of the curb, he pulled the little girl up high enough so she could grab hold of the grate and help him pull her through the hole.

"Where's my brother?" asked the little girl wiping her face again with the back of her hand as she watched the people pass by with a frightened stare.

Dane looked around helplessly. "I don't know."

"Where's Mommy and Daddy?" she asked looking around.

Dane shook his head. "I don't know who your Mommy or Daddy are but we have to get out of here! Come with me!"

"No!" yelled the little girl. "My brother's coming back!"

Dane shook his head and stood. He pulled on her hand gently to urge her away from the smoke that was beginning to fall around his ears, coating his nose with its foul odor. Soon it would be in their lungs if they didn't leave now. "Come on! Let's go find your brother," he said smiling and nodding. Coaxing her away from the sewer.

The little girl shook her head and pointed. "He's not that way, he's the other way. I heard him run the other way!"

Dane couldn't take time to reason with her. He knew they had to leave or die. With a sweep of his arm, he picked her up and ran down the street.

The little girl began to scream and kick in Dane's grasp.

"There's a fire behind us and we have to get out of here!" explained Dane, but it didn't do any good.

The little girl continued to flail about and scream at the top of her lungs.

Dane tightened his grip and kept running. He had done this a hundred times to belligerent little brothers, so this wasn't difficult. He knew just what position to hold the little girl so she couldn't bite his arm. Good thing he was a good guy.

Soul Decision

Salt Lake City, Utah
12:35 p.m.

Carea sniffed and looked around her cell. "Nadia was here," was carved into the wall. There were other words on the walls, nonsense words. Maybe it was a code of some sort. Carea stopped trying to make sense of them when she realized there was nothing of value to her in them. Only the person who wrote them understood their meaning and they were probably going insane when they wrote them.

Turning her thoughts inward, Carea looked down at her stocking feet. They had let her keep her socks on. She lifted her big toe on the right foot and then the left. Then she sniffed again and let her head fall onto her forearms that were wrapped around her knees.

In silence Carea considered subjects of the gospel she had been taught her whole life. As she understood it, someone like her wasn't *ever* supposed to end up in prison! God's world was governed by natural laws with predictable outcomes.[1] She had been taught that if you lived your life well, obeying the commandments, staying out of trouble, then life was generally good. You got to steer clear of the major hazards—*like prison.*[2] Oh, yes, there'd be bad days[3] like when a pet died, or when a big zit grew on your nose on the day of prom, but nothing truly terrible would happen.[4] You'd grow up, go to college, get married, have children, become a grandparent and maybe go on a mission, and then die, inheriting celestial life and have joy forever.[5] That was about it. That was the pattern of life.[6] Of course you could add frills to your mortal life if you wanted to, by the kind of degree you chose, how much money you made, if you became the PTA president, but those things were just extra and didn't really matter.[7]

Mainly, the cycle of life was the same for everyone, unless you chose to fight God's laws.[8] Then life would kick you in the pants to teach you by the consequences of your bad choices to go back to obeying the laws and get you back on the beaten and proven path.[9] That's what she thought prison was for. It was the government's punishment for disobeying laws that were based on Christian principles,[10] at least in America. That meant, if you obeyed the commandments, naturally, you'd never go to prison because you'd never be breaking the law! People who stole, lied, and killed deserved to be locked up. But not her! People who didn't want to obey the laws had their freedom taken away, but that wasn't her! She had been a law-abiding person her whole life! Why then was she here? *What had gone wrong?*

Carea considered how she received the chip in her head. She had been drugged and kidnapped. That wasn't her fault! A freak had picked her out of a crowd for who knows what reason and then played games with her head. How fair was that? What would God do with that scenario? Justice would say, Imam Mahdi should suffer for doing that to her. Punish the offender, not the offended! If God was a just God, why didn't he work things out so that could happen? It seemed like that's what *should* happen! She *deserved* to be protected! She *deserved* to have some kind of miracle happen that would have made that stupid machine fail when the SWAT policeman waved it over her! Now God's natural laws were backfiring all over her for no fault of her own!

Carea looked up at the ceiling, talking to God, "What are you going to do about *that*, Heavenly Father?"

Carea waited, looking up at the cement ceiling, seeing water stains in the corners and a stark white light bulb under a mesh screen. She waited for an answer but didn't feel or hear anything. Automatically, she imagined what her mother would tell her. She could hear her voice in her head saying, "Sweetheart, Imam Mahdi will be punished and you will be set free…eventually."

Carea frowned. "That doesn't do me any good right now!" she answered back in her head.

"But right now isn't what's important," her mother would say.

"Then what is? And don't tell me this *crappy* experience is for my good!"

Carea imagined her mother's expression change from empathy to disapproval with her choice of words, but then back again. Carea knew her mother would forgive her, considering the circumstances. "Sweetheart," she would say as she would touch her hair gently. "The Lord understands the beginning from the end. He's in charge. We have to trust him and do the best we can in the situation we're in. You'll grow strong through this experience."[11]

"Yeah, *whatever*!" yelled Carea out loud. *Life stunk*, she decided. If this imprisonment was for her experience, then that stunk more than a pile of rotting manure! She had had enough experience the first abduction around. What was she supposed to learn this time?

Carea searched her mind for something to hold on to. There had to be something else; some other answer to her woes than "it will be for your good."

Now, wait! A thought came to Carea…. Didn't she and God have a deal? Wasn't he bound by his own word?[12] Yes, that was right! He was! She remembered the covenants she had made at baptism that in return for obedience, wasn't she supposed to be blessed? She thought as she stood as a witness[13] for Christ, in his name, miracles would happen in her behalf.[14] Wasn't that how it worked? So, if he was bound by his word, then when would her blessings come? When would her miracles come? She had to believe they would! Even though she was locked away, miracles were bound to come because God could not lie![15] If he did, he would stop being God, and since the world was still spinning and the sun was still shining,[16] she was pretty sure he was still God.

Carea looked back down at her feet. She wondered if Heavenly Father would be angry with her for questioning all that she had been taught. Or maybe he wouldn't be angry at all, because he wasn't listening...was he listening? She was told he always listened. Was it true?

Carea closed her eyes and concentrated on heaven. "Hello!" she said in a whisper. "Is someone up there? Are you watching out for me?"[17] Fleetingly she wondered if angels actually listened to prayers and then took notes for Heavenly Father. Maybe Heavenly Father didn't know what was happening to her because she had a really bad angel following her. Maybe that's why no miracles were happening for her....

Carea shook her head ever so slightly. No, she knew Heavenly Father was aware she was being held in prison unjustly, because he knew everything.[18] The answer to her question of why it was happening to her was because he was allowing it to. He could change everything if he wanted to, but he chose not to. He was allowing her to be subject to other people. So, if that was true, then why?[19] What could be accomplished by her being in prison? Carea thought for a moment, searching what she had learned through her life. A memory of her conversation with her parents about Imam Mahdi and why bad things can happen to good people at the hands of evil surfaced. She remembered talking about Joseph Smith and how, he being a prophet of God, had suffered so much. How he had been thrown in prison often and made to live in inhumane conditions.[20] Carea looked around her cell. It wasn't the Marriott, but it wasn't inhumane. In that regard she was lucky she didn't have to suffer like he did. Then she thought about Jesus Christ. He was the Son of God and he had to not only suffer for the sins of all humanity, but after that, he had to be beaten, and crucified.[21] Carea shook her head. No, that wouldn't be happening to her either. What about Abinadi? He was burned for his words as he fulfilled the Lord's will.[22] That would be painful, she thought. She knew burning wasn't an approved activity in prison, so again, she was lucky compared to him. Then there was Joseph, who was sold into Egypt by his own brothers as a slave.[23] Even there, she was better off. She wasn't a slave and her siblings loved her...that thought made her smile—just a little.

So, then, what could be the reason she was put in this situation? After thinking about things for a while, she came to the conclusion that there must be a master plan somewhere. It was the only answer. God didn't just let stupid things happen, did he?[24] There was a reason Joseph suffered for the Church. There was a reason Christ suffered for humanity, there was a reason Abinadi suffered for the Christians. What was her reason and who was she suffering for?

These questions stirred strong feelings in her heart. The feelings were warm and they made her happy. They sank deeper and deeper until it felt like they merged with her, making her profoundly content.

She asked the questions again to herself, as if to test these feelings. Who was she suffering for? What were the reasons? Was there a purpose? If she was like Joseph, could she become something great like he did by enduring this trial well? Was this a test? And if it was, could she pass it?

Carea allowed herself to think about Joseph of Egypt a little while. He and she had many things in common. He was an innocent victim. All he was guilty of was being in the wrong place at the wrong time. That was like her! He was only a kid when he was made a slave and then imprisoned, as she was now.

"Heavenly Father," she began, reverently this time. "Is there a purpose to my being here?" She waited for an answer. The happy feeling remained. She thought about that. Was she making it up? Was it an answer to her questions? Could it be a miracle on her behalf, or could she be fabricating an answer from God in her stress and out of desperation?

Carea looked around the dark concrete cell. Her good feeling continued. She was truly happy! This was so strange! Smiling, she shook her head. No, she was sure the feelings weren't being inspired from the dank dungeon she was in, or the atmosphere! She hadn't even eaten, so they couldn't be feelings of physical satisfaction. Carea looked down the hall at the woman who had incarcerated her. And it definitely wasn't coming from her!

Carea continued to smile. Yes, she could now say she felt she was getting an answer to her prayers! Oh, that made her happy! So there *was* a purpose to her being in this situation! She liked that! Being like Joseph of Egypt was kind of cool!

Nodding, Carea realized her next step was to make a plan. She wanted to be prepared to capture any opportunity the Lord threw at her. That's what Joseph did and that's how he conquered his trials. She wanted to be just as diligent, righteous, and honorable as he was. She would make a difference and then just watch what would happen!

"We're moving these people out now," said one officer to another from down the hall. "Load them in the vans!"

Carea stood up, feeling like an entirely different person. She was actually feeling excited for what the future held. Could that be possible? Was she going insane now? She smiled and chuckled a little. Maybe the people held in this cell before her were a little insane, but she was not. No, she was going to come out the winner in this situation—she could feel it as peace filled her.[25]

"Let the games begin," said Carea to herself.

Notes to "Human Strife"

Soul Decision

[1] "There is a law, irrevocably decreed in heaven before the foundations of this world, upon which all blessings are predicated—And when we obtain any blessing from God, it is by obedience to that law upon which it is predicated" (D&C 130: 20–21).

---

[2] "The more faithfully we keep the commandments of God, the happier we will generally be" (James E. Faust, "Our Search for Happiness," *Ensign*, Oct 2000, 2).

[3] "Critical to our knowledge of the plan of happiness is an understanding of the great governing principle of agency. A person does not have to spend much time in the schoolroom of mortality to realize that Heavenly Father's plan does not provide for blissful happiness at every step along our mortal journey" (M. Russell Ballard, "Answers to Life's Questions," *Ensign*, May 1995, 22).

[4] "Consider on the blessed and happy state of those that keep the commandments of God. For behold, they are blessed in all things, both temporal and spiritual; and if they hold out faithful to the end they are received into heaven, that thereby they may dwell with God in a state of never-ending happiness" (Mosiah 2:41).

[5] "Behold, I am the law, and the light. Look unto me, and endure to the end, and ye shall live; for unto him that endureth to the end will I give eternal life" (3 Nephi 15:9).

[6] "Happiness is found only along that well beaten track, narrow as it is, though straight, which leads to life eternal" (David, O. McKay, *Conference Report*, Oct. 1919, p. 180).

"The treasure house of happiness is unlocked to those who live the gospel of Jesus Christ in its purity and simplicity. Like a mariner without stars, like a traveler without a compass, is the person who moves along through life without a plan. The assurance of supreme happiness, the certainty of a successful life here and of exaltation and eternal life hereafter, come to those who plan to live their lives in complete harmony with the gospel of Jesus Christ—and then consistently follow the course they have set" (Spencer W. Kimball, *The Miracle of Forgiveness*, p. 259).

[7] "Those things which we call extraordinary, remarkable, or unusual may make history, but they do not make real life. After all, to do well those things which God ordained to be the common lot of all mankind, is the truest greatness. To be a successful father or a successful mother is greater than to be a successful general or a successful statesman.... Let us not be trying to substitute an artificial life for the true one" (Joseph F. Smith, *Juvenile Instructor*, 15 Dec. 1905, p. 752-753).

[8] "The Apostle Paul clearly forewarned us of the price of unwisely using our agency: 'The wages of sin is death' (Romans 6:23). Each time we misuse our moral agency, there is a penalty attached: By offending the Spirit, we withdraw from his companionship; and when we persist in our deviant course of action, we experience a spiritual death, and with certain sins death may be physical as well as spiritual. Alma taught that 'wickedness never was happiness' (Alma 41:10; emphasis added), a reality more powerful than gravity. Unhappiness is another price to be paid for misusing our agency. To some of the recalcitrant generation of his day, Helaman explained, 'Ye have sought for happiness in doing iniquity, which thing is contrary to the nature of that righteousness which is in our great and Eternal Head' (Helaman 13:38)" (Spencer J. Condie, "Agency: The Gift of Choices," *Ensign*, Sep. 1995, p. 16).

[9] Alma the Younger experienced what it was like to disobey the laws of God, see his potential dark end, but then seeing this, repented to find glory and the right hand of God! From his own words.... "I was racked with eternal torment, for my soul was harrowed up to the greatest degree and racked with all my sins. Yea, I did remember all my sins and iniquities, for which I was tormented with the pains of hell; yea, I saw that I had rebelled against my God, and that I had not kept his holy commandments. Yea, and I had murdered many of his children, or rather led them away unto destruction; yea, and in fine so great had been my iniquities, that the very thought of coming into the presence of my God did rack my soul with inexpressible horror. Oh, thought I, that I could be banished and become extinct both soul and body, that I might not be brought to stand in the presence of my God, to be judged of my deeds...Now, as my mind caught hold upon this thought, I cried within my heart: O Jesus, thou Son of God, have

mercy on me, who am in the gall of bitterness, and am encircled about by the everlasting chains of death. And now, behold, when I thought this, I could remember my pains no more; yea, I was harrowed up by the memory of my sins no more. And oh, what joy, and what marvelous light I did behold; yea, my soul was filled with joy as exceeding as was my pain!" (Alma 36:12–15, 18–20).

[10] It's a broadly accepted fact that the Ten Commandments, the core of Judeo-Christian beliefs, are the core of the moral and legal system established in America, thus the basis behind the display of the Ten Commandments monuments around the nation at court houses and establishments of law. It is true that the constitutionality of the monuments has been challenged in Van Orden v. Perry, and it was tried in the Supreme Court, June 27, 2005 with a vote of 5 to 4, finding it constitutional.

[11] Living through difficult adversity, especially at the hands of evil people may lead us to the impression that God has abandoned us. The best of us, even Joseph Smith felt that feeling in the Liberty Jail. God's response to him, his prophet, demonstrates his desire for us to endure everything we are faced with in humility, realizing all experiences here on earth are for our good.

"If thou art called to pass through tribulation; if thou art in perils among false brethren; if thou art in perils among robbers; if thou art in perils by land or by sea…If thou art accused with all manner of false accusations; if thine enemies fall upon thee; if they tear thee from the society of thy father and mother and brethren and sisters; and thou be dragged to prison, and thine enemies prowl around thee like wolves for the blood of the lamb…And if thou shouldst be cast into the pit, or into the hands of murderers, and the sentence of death passed upon thee; if thou be cast into the deep; if the billowing surge conspire against thee; if fierce winds become thine enemy; if the heavens gather blackness, and all the elements combine to hedge up the way; and above all, if the very jaws of hell shall gape open the mouth wide after thee, know thou, my son, that all these things shall give thee experience, and shall be for thy good" (D&C 122:6–7).

[12] "I, the Lord, am abound when ye do what I say; but when ye do not what I say, ye have no promise" (D&C 82:10).

[13] "…Stand as witnesses of God at all times and in all things, and in all places that ye may be in, even until death, that ye may be redeemed of God, and be numbered with those of the first resurrection, that ye may have eternal life" (Mosiah 18:9).

[14] "For I am God, and mine arm is not shortened; and I will show miracles, signs, and wonders, unto all those who believe my name" (D&C 35:8).

[15] "Lord, I know that thou speakest the truth, for thou art a God of truth, and canst not lie" (Ether3:12).

[16] Because of God and his laws, all things, including the earth and even our own bodies exist from moment to moment.

"He comprehendeth all things, and all things are before him, and all things are round about him; and he is above all things, and in all things, and is through all things, and is round about all things; and all things are by him, and of him, even God, forever and ever" (D&C 88:41).

"And if these things are not there is no God. And if there is no God we are not, neither the earth; for there could have been no creation of things, neither to act nor to be acted upon; wherefore, all things must have vanished away" (2 Nephi 2:13).

[17] "Learning the language of prayer is a joyous, lifetime experience. Sometimes ideas flood our mind as we listen after our prayers. Sometimes feelings press upon us. A spirit of calmness assures us that all will be well. But always, if we have been honest and earnest, we will

experience a good feeling—a feeling of warmth for our Father in Heaven and a sense of his love for us. It has sorrowed me that some of us have not learned the meaning of that calm, spiritual warmth, for it is a witness to us that our prayers have been heard. *And since our Father in Heaven loves us with more love than we have even for ourselves, it means that we can trust in his goodness, we can trust in him; it means that if we continue praying and living as we should, our Father's hand will guide and bless us*" (Spencer W. Kimball, *Teachings of Presidents of the Church*, p. 56–57, italics added).

[18] "O how great the holiness of our God! For he knoweth all things, and there is not anything save he knows it" (2 Nephi 9:20).

[19] "Trying to comprehend the trials and meaning of this life without understanding Heavenly Father's marvelously encompassing plan of salvation is like trying to understand a three-act play while seeing only the second act. Fortunately, our knowledge of the Savior, Jesus Christ, and His Atonement helps us to endure our trials and to see purpose in suffering and to trust God for what we cannot comprehend....Daily life's repetitiveness actually occurs for a reason. President Brigham Young reflectively observed: 'Men are organized to be independent in their sphere, ...yet they have, as soldiers term it, to run the gauntlet all the time. They are organized to be just as independent as any being in eternity, but that independency... must be proved and tried while in this state of existence, must be operated upon by the good and the evil' (in Journal of Discourses, 3:316). So often in life a deserved blessing is quickly followed by a needed stretching. Spiritual exhilaration may be quickly followed by a vexation or temptation. Were it otherwise, extended spiritual reveries or immunities from adversity might induce in us a regrettable forgetfulness of others in deep need. The sharp, side-by-side contrast of the sweet and the bitter is essential until the very end of this brief, mortal experience. Meanwhile, even routine, daily life provides sufficient sandpaper to smooth our crustiness and polish our rough edges, if we are meek. Anne Morrow Lindbergh wisely cautioned: 'I do not believe that sheer suffering teaches. If suffering alone taught, all the world would be wise, since everyone suffers. To suffering must be added mourning, understanding, patience, love, openness, and the willingness to remain vulnerable' ("Lindbergh Nightmare," Time, 5 Feb. 1973, p. 35)" (Neal A. Maxwell, "Enduring Well," *Ensign*, Apr 1997, 7).

[20] "In our dispensation, the Prophet Joseph Smith endured all manner of opposition and hardship to bring to pass the desire of our Heavenly Father—the restoration of The Church of Jesus Christ of Latter-day Saints. Joseph was harassed and hunted by angry mobs. He patiently endured poverty, humiliating charges, and unkind acts. His people were forcibly driven from town to town, from state to state. He was tarred and feathered. He was falsely charged and jailed....Imprisoned at Liberty, Missouri, and experiencing deep, emotional temporal feelings that his own hardships and the tests and trials of the Saints would never cease, Joseph prayed: 'O God, where art thou?...Yea, O Lord, how long shall they suffer these wrongs and unlawful oppressions, before thine heart shall be softened toward them, and...be moved with compassion toward them?' (D&C 121:1,3) Joseph was told, 'My son, peace be unto thy soul; thine adversity and thine afflictions shall be but a small moment' (D&C 121:7)" (Robert D. Hales, "'Behold, We Count Them Happy Which Endure'," *Ensign*, May 1998, p. 75).

[21] "Examples of faithfully enduring to the end are taught by prophets of all ages as they demonstrate courage while enduring trials and tribulations to carry forth the will of God. Our greatest example comes from the life of our Savior and Redeemer, Jesus Christ. When suffering upon the cross at Calvary, Jesus felt the loneliness of agency when He pled to His Father in Heaven, 'Why hast thou forsaken me?' (Matt. 27:46). The Savior of the world was left alone by His Father to experience, of His own free will and choice, an act of agency which allowed Him to complete His mission of the Atonement. Jesus knew who He was—the Son of God. He knew His purpose—to carry out the will of the Father through the Atonement. His vision was eternal—'to bring to pass the immortality and eternal life of man' (Moses 1:39). The Lord could have called on legions of angels to take Him down from the cross, but He faithfully endured to the end and completed the very purpose for which He had been sent to

earth, thus granting eternal blessings to all who will ever experience mortality. It is touching to me that when the Father introduced His Son to prophets in dispensations since, He would say, 'This is my beloved Son, in whom I am well pleased' (2 Pet. 1:17), or 'Behold my Beloved Son,...in whom I have glorified my name' (3 Ne. 11:7)" (Robert D. Hales, "'Behold, We Count Them Happy Which Endure'," *Ensign*, May 1998, p. 75).

[22] "Now Abinadi said unto him: I say unto you, I will not recall the words which I have spoken unto you concerning this people, for they are true; and that ye may know of their surety I have suffered myself that I have fallen into your hands. Yea, and I will suffer even until death, and I will not recall my words, and they shall stand as a testimony against you. And if ye slay me ye will shed innocent blood, and this shall also stand as a testimony against you at the last day. And it came to pass that they took him and bound him, and scourged his skin with faggots, yea, even unto death. And now, when Abinadi had said these words, he fell, having suffered death by fire; yea, having been put to death because he would not deny the commandments of God, having sealed the truth of his words by his death" (Mosiah 17:9–10, 13, 20).

[23] "Come, and let us sell him to the Ishmaelites, and let not our hand be upon him; for he is our brother and our flesh. And his brethren were content. Then there passed by Midianites merchantmen; and they drew and lifted up Joseph out of the pit, and sold Joseph to the Ishmaelites for twenty pieces of silver: and they brought Joseph into Egypt" (Genesis 37: 27–28).

[24] "God controls our lives, guides and blesses us, but gives us our agency. We may live our lives in accordance with His plan for us or we may foolishly shorten or terminate them. I am positive in my mind that the Lord has planned our destiny" (Spencer W. Kimball, "Tragedy or Destiny," Taken from a devotional delivered at Brigham Young University, published by Brigham young University, 1955).

[25] "My peace I give unto you: not as the world giveth, give I unto you. Let not your heart be troubled, neither let it be afraid" (John 14:27).

CHAPTER SEVEN

EVIL DESIGNS

"...When the devil shall send forth his mighty winds, yea, his shafts in the whirlwind, yea, when all his hail and his mighty storm shall beat upon you it shall have no power over you to drag you down to the gulf of misery and endless wo, because of the rock upon which ye are built, which is a sure foundation, a foundation whereon if men build they cannot fall" (Helaman 5:12).

00:03:11, 04:25:21, Zulu
Friday, September 19th

To Dust Ye Shall Return

Manhattan, New York
2:35 p.m.

"Put me down!" yelled the little girl in a shrill screech, for the hundredth time. Her bow was barely hanging on by a strand of hair and was flicked about as she flip-flopped her body in Dane's grasp.

He stepped into an alleyway, out of the way of the people running out of Manhattan. They were nearly back to the bank where Dane had been called off his post. The little girl was getting heavy. He was relieved to take a break.

Dane let the little girl slide down his side as he squatted to look at her at her level. "Tell you what. I'll let you stay on the ground if you don't run away. I have to protect you."

"No! I want my mommy!" the little girl screamed. Then she wiped her runny nose and tears on her sleeve.

Dane was feeling frustrated. "I know you want your mommy. I want you to have your mommy, but I don't know where she is!"

"She's back there!" the little girl said, pointing behind them.

Dane didn't know what to say to this little girl. She didn't understand what was happening. He tried something else. "What's your name?"

"Nebraska."

"OK, Nebraska, you're right. It could be that your mom is back behind us, but do you know where?"

"In the hotel with the bi-big bathtub!" she said with a reflexive heave from crying too long.

"Every hotel has a big bathtub," said Dane growing frustrated. "Look, I can't just let you walk around this city, looking for your mom."

"Why not?" Nebraska asked as she wiped her nose again. Her nose was really running.

"Because you'd be killed," said Dane as he took a tissue from his pocket and offered it to her.

"Why?" asked Nebraska before she blew her nose in the tissue.

"Because buildings are on fire. People are running everywhere, look!" he said pointing toward the street where there were so many people they couldn't see anything else. "You'd get trampled!"

Nebraska finished blowing her nose and then looked out at the people passing by with a blank face.

"Also, there's dust and dirt in the air from the explosions."

"I don't see any," said the little girl as she wadded up the tissue and dropped it on the ground.

"You can't see it, but it's there. And it's only going to get worse. All the smoke from the fire's coming this way," said Dane as he leaned over and picked up the tissue. Putting it in his pocket, he continued. "We have to get away from the bad air filled with smoke and dirt. We can't breathe that stuff. It will kill us. Do you understand?"

"I can hold my breath," Nebraska offered.

"I'm sure you can, but you can't hold it long enough to find your mother."

"I can run fast. See my feet? My shoes are fast," said the little girl, holding up her pink and white athletic shoes one at a time.

"I know you can, but look, those people run faster," said Dane pointing out of the alley at the rampaging people. "They'll step on you and squish you," said Dane, suddenly feeling something trickle down his lip.

With a finger he touched the liquid. Did he have a bloody nose? The liquid was clear. No, it was just a runny nose. The smoke must be making their noses run. Taking out another tissue, he blew his nose too. "Also, bad men might kidnap you. I have to protect you from them."

"Are you a bad man?" she asked, her eyes wide and frightened.

"No. I'm not a bad man. I'm a soldier. I'm here to protect you."

"Nah ahh," said Nebraska shaking her head defiantly with her hands on her hips. "If you were a good man, then you'd find my mo-mmy!" she said as her nose began to run again.

Dane handed her another tissue from his pocket. "Blow your nose."

"I did," she said with a confused look.

"Do it again," said Dane, still holding the tissue out.

Nebraska did as she was told, and then tried to hand the tissue back.

"Why don't you put that tissue in your pocket? It looks like you're going to need it."

Nebraska wadded it into a ball then put it in the pocket of her jeans.

"Tell me, do you live in New York?"

Nebraska shook her head.

"Where do you live?"

"92234 Los Alameda Avenue," said Nebraska. Obviously she was well rehearsed.

"In what state?"

"What?"

"What's the rest of your address? Alameda Avenue—what?"

Suddenly, Nebraska understood what Dane was asking. "Rancho Cucamonga, California," she said matter-of-factly.

"Oh," said Dane feeling discouraged. He looked around with his hands on his belt as he thought about the situation. How was he going to get this little girl to her family? He didn't even know where to begin. It seemed an impossible task. How long would he have to tote her around with him? He took a deep breath, but that was the wrong move. It made him start to cough. His chest was unusually tight. It was probably all the smoke.

"Are you OK?" asked the little girl as she watched Dane continue to cough uncontrollably.

Dane took a folded rubber mask from a deep pocket in his vest. With his eyes tearing from too much coughing he rasped, "I think I need to wear this now. It's getting hard to breathe," said Dane as he slipped it on and tightened the clamp at the back of his head.

Nebraska laughed. "You look like an Alene."

"Alene? You mean an alien?" asked Dane, his voice dampened by the rubber.

"Yes," said Nebraska, correcting herself, "an alien. I want an alien mask, too."

"I don't have another alien mask, but I do have a robber mask."

Nebraska jumped up and down and clapped her hands. "I want to be a robber! I want to be a robber!"

Dane took out a handkerchief and tied it around Nebraska's face. "There, that will keep all the dust out of your lungs."

Nebraska's eyes smiled. "Do I look like a robber now?"

"Yes, a real cute one."

"Stick 'em up!" she said, pointing a finger at Dane.

Dane held up his hands. "No, don't shoot!" he said in a sing-song voice.

"Bang!" said Nebraska, giggling.

"Hey! You're not supposed to shoot if I put my hands up."

"Oh, sorry!" said Nebraska, covering her masked face to laugh again.

"So, Nebraska," said Dane hunching down. "Is your family visiting anyone here?"

"No."

"Like a cousin, a grandma, a…"

Nebraska's face lit up. "Grandma Jenkins!" she said jumping and clapping.

"Yes!" said Dane. "Where does Grandma Jenkins live?"

"In washing machine CC."

"Washington, D.C.?"

"Uh, huh," said the little girl nodding. "Washing machine CC."

Dane stood up and looked around. The sky was getting darker. "Washington, D.C.," he mumbled as he scratched his head. "How far away is that from here?"

Nebraska saw a dog run by. "Doggie!" she yelled and took off after the dog.

"Nebraska! Stop! You're going to get lost again!"

Nebraska looked back momentarily at Dane but pointed excitedly after the dog and disappeared, squeezing between the legs of the people in the crowd.

Dane rushed into the throng of people to catch Nebraska, but now she had disappeared. She was too short to spot in the sea of people. *"Nebraska!"* he yelled in one direction. *"Nebraska!"* he yelled in another direction. He tried in vain to see her among the people. Then, by some miracle he saw the tail of the dog just ahead. Dane took off towards the dog. He knew if he could find the dog, Nebraska would be close by. *"Nebraska!"* he yelled when he had caught up to what looked like a miniature collie.

"What?" said a little voice near him.

Dane whirled around. "Where are you?"

"I'm right here!"

The voice was coming from his right. Dane turned and relief hit him as he saw little Nebraska looking up at him, her eyes smiling over the bandana. Dane caught her wrist and pulled her close.

"I just wanted to pet the doggie," she said in an innocent voice.

"I know," said Dane feeling like he couldn't bear the thought of Nebraska being lost in New York. Picking her up he said, "But I almost lost you. You can't chase the doggies right now. It's just too dangerous. There are too many people…"

"The doggie needs a mask too," interrupted Nebraska with a worried look as she pointed in the dog's direction.

Dane laughed. "I can't make the dog a mask. He wouldn't keep it on."

"Everyone needs masks so they can breathe," said Nebraska.

Dane nodded and shrugged. "Yes, they do, but I don't have enough for them," he said, as the crowd suddenly slowed and then halted.

"What's going on?" Dane asked a man beside him who was taller than he and wearing a Hawaiian-style orange shirt.

The man stretched to look over the heads in front of him. Then he said, "I don't know, but I've got to get out of this city." Then he dove into the standing crowd, pushing his way through and disappearing from Dane's view.

"Maybe *you* can tell me why everyone's stopped," said Dane as he lifted Nebraska up onto his shoulders. "What's going on out there? Can you see? What's holding everyone up?"

Nebraska was quiet a few moments and then said, "A bunch of people are sleeping on the ground."

"Sleeping?" asked Dane. "You mean lying on the ground? Are they hurt?"

"I don't know."

"Is anyone bleeding?" asked Dane.

"No," said Nebraska.

Dane looked around for clues. All the buildings were intact. The fire was burning strong behind him but ahead of him was clear. He noticed the cross streets. He was at 48th and 50th. One block north of the bank he had been guarding earlier that day. Then he noticed a change. The people standing around him looked ill, like they were getting sick. Abruptly, one man to his left vomited, and then he heard another do the same thing, behind him. Next, people around him began to sink to the ground. They were fainting! The whole crowd was losing consciousness!

"What's happening?" asked Dane, very bewildered. He decided something must be in the air, because he wasn't affected. The mask was filtering out whatever poison was floating around. "How you doing, Nebraska?" He asked, now worried as he felt Nebraska's weight change on his shoulders. She was leaning heavily on his head. "Nebraska! Are you OK?"

The little girl didn't answer.

"Nebraska!" exclaimed Dane as he pulled her off his shoulders, careful not to dislodge his mask. She was unconscious too! The handkerchief mask he had made for her had not protected her.

"Nebraska!" called Dane, as he shook the little girl gently. Could everyone be smoke intoxicated? Dane looked around. No, Nebraska was right. The air was clear around here. There wasn't any smoke or dust in the air. This was much more than smoke intoxication.

Suddenly Nebraska started twitching and spit began to bubble out of her mouth.

Then, in a moment, clarity cut through him like a knife. He knew what was happening! *This area had been gassed!* A nerve agent would do this! He recognized the signs from training. "Yes!" he exclaimed as he looked through his medical pack that was in another vest pocket. His mask protected him from the poison because it was a *gas* mask! Dane ripped through his pack. Where was the purple tube with the yellow top? It was the antidote for gas poisoning. Nebraska needed it *now*!

Dane blinked twice. It was getting difficult to see. It was as if the sun was being covered by clouds. Dane looked around. He could only see directly in front of him. He was losing his peripheral vision.

"I've been gassed too!" he gasped out loud, being completely surprised. "I must've inhaled the gas when I was running away from the fire!" That would explain the coughing and his running nose. Dane knew he had to work fast, or he too would lose consciousness. Where was the antidote…?

Nausea began to build inside him as Dane finally located the purple tubes secured in a protective case. He had five of them. He pulled one out and flipped off the cap with his thumb. Then he put the end against his thigh and pushed the end of the tube. He felt a sharp stab as the needle hit his muscle and the fluid was injected. Almost immediately his symptoms began to recede.

Next, Dane pulled out another tube and flipped off the protective end. Putting it on Nebraska's thigh, he deployed it into her muscle. Now he knew he had to get her out of this area. He didn't have another gas mask for her and he couldn't give her his mask because the only way she was going to survive was if he stayed alive to help her.

Dane stood up, feeling his strength return. With Nebraska in his arms, he ran through the people that lay on the ground. He began to pray fervently. "Please, Father, help me get this little girl to safety," was all he could say. It was a prayer he repeated over and over again, wanting to make a difference in at least one person's life.

Dane headed for the East River that was just a couple blocks over. There was fresh air and a mild breeze, enough to blow away the toxin. Quickly he turned right and rushed across the street and down the sidewalk, jumping over and weaving around unconscious people. Dane kept his eyes averted. He didn't want to look at the people. He couldn't help any of them. He had to help Nebraska. He had to get her to safety. He had to stay focused.

Dane saw the water. He was almost there, but he was exhausted and hungry for air. The mask felt like it was suffocating him. He couldn't get enough oxygen through the filters. He wanted to rip it off his face, but he didn't dare.

Nebraska started to stir.

Dane stared at her. Was she waking up?

Next, she opened her eyes and then her eyes smiled at Dane. He was so happy! "Nebraska! You're better!" he exclaimed.

"Put me down," she said.

Dane put her down but said, "We have to keep moving. There's poison in the air. We have to get out to the wind.

"OK," she said as she tried to walk but stumbled.

Dane caught her. "Be careful. You're still weak."

"My legs aren't working right," she said simply.

"I know. Let me carry you for a while more," replied Dane.

Nebraska turned to Dane and held up her arms.

Dane picked up this little girl that an hour before had been a stranger. Now he felt great protective love for her. He hugged her close and thanked his Heavenly Father for her. He needed to find Nebraska's grandmother and keep her safe. Right now, that was the most important thing he could do.

Prison Van

Salt Lake City, Utah
2:30 p.m.

"I want to talk to my mother!" Carea yelled through the bars of the prison bus, trying one last time to get to communicate with her parents before they took her away. *"You can't take me away without my parents knowing what's happening!"*

"Where were your parents when you were out on the streets?" said a man's snide voice from outside. "If your parents really cared about you, you wouldn't be here."

Fury exploded in Carea. *"My parents do care—it's you who couldn't care less!"*

"Shut up!" the man yelled.

"I'm entitled to a lawyer. I'm entitled to a trial. I'm entitled to..."

A billy club hit the bars hard, startling Carea. She fell back, stepped on someone's foot, lost her balance, and fell on the floor.

"Sit down! It's going to be a long, long ride, *street scum.*"

A gruff looking Asian girl with strange, icy blue eyes, laughed at Carea. She had tattoos of skulls and other death symbols on her arms and sported a red bandanna on her head. With two rings on her upper lip and two on her lower, she looked very much like a vampire. Carea couldn't help but stare.

"So, you *think* you're entitled?" the girl asked with a sneer. "You think you have rights?"

"Sure. Why not?" said Carea, standing, shaking off her amazement and brushing herself off.

"Because we're in a State of Emergency, stupid," replied the girl with a side bob of her head.

"Who is?" asked Carea. She wasn't going to let being called stupid get to her.

"America is."

"Since when?"

"Since this morning. That's why you and all of us were welcomed into Hotel Utah so warmly."[2]

Carea looked around the vehicle for a place to sit. There wasn't any. There were wall-to-wall girls, and not the kind she wanted to sit next to. They were all scary in one way or another.

"I thought I was here because of the Bats," she said as she pushed into a seat beside the least threatening girl she could find. "But I'm not a Bat."

The Asian girl looked at her sideways and shook her head. "I believe you. You don't look like one either. Bats are mean. They'd sell their momma if asked to, but I bet you wouldn't."

"I wouldn't,"[3] said Carea, shaking her head.

"That's my point. You look too *nice*. You'll be eaten up out there at the camps. *Nice* knowing you."

Carea tried to smile. "No, I won't. I'm going to get out of there."

"No, you're not."

"Yes, I am."

"How?" asked the girl with an intense stare.

"When my parents find out where I'm at, there'll be trouble to pay. I just have to hold on till that happens."

"So there'll be trouble to pay, will there?"

"Yes."

"By who?"

"I don't know. The government."

"Well, that's where you're wrong. During a State of Emergency the government doesn't care about the people. You're nothing to them and they don't owe you anything."

"What? I've never heard of such a thing. We are the government. They owe me justice."

"You must be a sad person."

"Me?" asked Carea surprised. "I'm not sad."

"You must be. You believe everything everyone tells you—if you're not sad now, you will be as soon as you realize what's real and what's not."

"What are you talking about?"

"We're in what you call martial law. During martial law, there are no judges listening to parents, no justice for the downtrodden and no freedom for *you*! You're going to have to tough it out just like the rest of us."

"OK. Stop. What's martial law?" asked Carea. She remembered hearing about it but couldn't remember from where.

"It's when the country, or the police, can do anything they want to anyone they want as long as they think they're a threat. Including putting your sassy butt in prison for wearing the wrong shoe color."

"That can't be true," said Carea, shaking her head.

"Then why are *you* here? *Worm*."

"I don't know," said Carea. "But I don't have to resort to names to get my point across."

"Why not? Labels make the world go round, haven't you heard?" The Asian girl stood up and began pointing around the van. "I'm a Blood, she's a Rocker, that one over there is a Pot Head—Skater, I think we've got some Goths in here that go great with the Bats. And you...if you're not a Bat, then you're a worm and you'll get eaten in the circle of life."

"Not if everyone refuses to eat meat. We can all become vegetarians and live together in peace," said Carea smiling bravely, trying to be quick with a comeback.

There were a couple of girls that laughed quietly at Carea's joke.

The Asian girl looked around at the bus. Everyone was staring. The girl scrambled to keep the upper hand. "No. We *like* to eat fresh meat. Get used to it. It's who we are. We can't help ourselves."[4]

"What? Who you are? That's the most ridiculous thing I've ever heard! You aren't a gang member from birth, you choose to be one,"[5] said Carea. Then she held up a peace sign as if politicking and exclaimed, "You can change. *No red meat! Eat your veggies!*"

Again, girls laughed up and down the bus. This made the huge girl with the tatoos seem a little nervous. With sudden anger the girl growled, *"You better watch it!"*

"Meaning...?" asked Carea being passively defiant.

With clenched teeth the girl said, "Meaning, *fall in line or become the line*."

"Are you telling me to conform?" asked Carea as if surprised. She knew she was walking the line between sarcasm and genuine inquiry, and honestly, she was teetering on which one she was being.

"Yeah. If you know what's good for you,"[6] said the girl pushing forward as if to attack Carea. The girls around her held her back. *"And if I were you, I'd be afraid,"* said the girl, continuing her intimidation tactics.

"Hmmm," said Carea as she studied the frightening girl who was almost a woman. Actually—she seemed more like a man than a woman to Carea. "So what happens if I'm afraid?" she asked, really wanting to know.

"I won't hurt you," said the girl, letting up a little.

"What happens if I'm not?" asked Carea, wondering how far she could push this without getting in too much trouble.

"You might not see tomorrow," said the girl with a sneer.

"Hmmm," said Carea, trying to figure out what to do. If it was true that she was stuck with these people, then she better start making plans right now for survival. In a moment of sheer inspiration, she stuck out her hand and said, "My name is not worm and neither is my label. My name as well as my label is Carea. Nice to meet you. Oh and by the way, I *am* afraid of you, so you can let me live. I hope we can be friends." Carea smiled politely.

The girl looked at Carea with sudden boredom. "Are you trying to be funny again?"

"No, I'm trying to play the game by your rules. You want me to have a label, I've got one. It's Carea. That's what you can call me."

The gang member seemed to grow a few shades of red again, and then as if she were a volcano that was about to blow she yelled, *"OK. I'm going to give you one chance to cut out the cute stuff. From this moment on, you don't speak unless I say so. You don't have an opinion unless I grant it. You don't even have a desire to do anything unless I tell you, you can. I'm the law around here. Do you understand me?"*[7]

"Oh, but you're wrong," said Carea confidently, seeing now that this girl really didn't want to attack her or she would have already. She was gaining the upper hand, plus she knew she could hurt this girl if she had to defend herself. She hoped she didn't but at least she had that knowledge. "I have my own mind and in fact, I use it often."

"Ah ha ha," laughed the girl. Then she called Carea a name meant to offend her.

"I don't think I like how you just spoke to me," said Carea setting her jaw. She knew that if she allowed this girl to bully her, it would never end.

The girl sized her up. Carea could feel her estimating Carea's strength, then with a condescending look the Asian girl said, "You're not very smart, are you?"

Carea frowned as she felt the emotional current change. She could feel the girl beside her cower away as others ducked. The other girls thought she was going to get hit! They were trying to clear the way! But she wasn't going to be intimidated by gorilla-girl. She needed to establish herself as strong, ASAP. This was her chance to make an impression! To change the course of the future![8] She would continue to press her luck.

"I'm smart enough. Probably smarter than you," Carea shot back.

The girl stood up and Carea was surprised. She was huge. She bore her teeth in a sort of frighteningly quiet growl and then said, "Oh, you're *dead*."

"Why?" asked Carea, seemingly unaffected although she was starting to shake inside. She was wondering if she could defend herself in this small, enclosed space. That girl only had to sit on her and she'd die from asphyxiation. Maybe she had made a mistake, but still she had to make it look like she was in control.

"Why am I dead? Because I state the obvious?" Carea added.

The girl bounded out of her bench and lunged for Carea but Carea ducked just as the van started to move. The girl went sprawling to the back of the small bus, tripping over many feet that stuck out in the isle. When Carea looked again, she saw that the girl's ankles were around her ears. She knew that must have been very embarrassing for the gang leader and Carea instantly felt sorry. Getting up, she held out a hand as the girl tried to untangle herself from all the legs.

"Here, let me help you up," Carea offered as she steadied herself with the van wall. She wanted to fix this relationship as soon as possible. She didn't want enemies in a prison situation. Her survival depended on most everyone being her friend.

The girl looked at her angrily and said, *"I don't need your help. I'm not a cripple!"*

Carea nodded and put her hands up. "I know you're not a cripple. I'd just like to be friends."

The girl finally stood up and said, "*I don't have friends.*"

Carea nodded and said, "Yes, you do. You're looking at one."[9]

The large girl clumsily moved back to her seat as she swore a string of harsh expletives.

Carea, too, returned to her seat smiling inside. Maybe the girl wasn't anxious to take Carea up on her word but she knew she surprised her by both her boldness and her kindness. It wouldn't be long till the prison bully was on her side.[10]

Yes, thought Carea. That would be her first goal, other than speaking to her parents, of course. She would build a group of friends. Big friends, big scary friends just like the girl in front of her. And Vampire Gorilla-girl was first on her list.

Escape from New York

Manhattan, New York
5:05 p.m.

"Umm, what's your name?" asked Nebraska, pointing at Dane with her little index finger as they walked together along the banks of the East Manhattan River.

Dane was surprised. Hadn't he told her his name? "My name is Dane," he said with a little chuckle. "Dane Rogers."

"Dane Rogers, I'm cold," said Nebraska looking up at him.

Dane noticed that she was shivering and had slightly blue lips. He squatted down and rubbed Nebraska's damp arms. "Is that better?"

Nebraska shook her head with a sour look. "Dane, I didn't like it when we jumped in the water. I didn't want to go swimming."

Dane smiled and nodded. "I know, but there was poison all over you. If we didn't jump in and wash it off, both you and I would have become sick again. We had to go swimming, but now we're done and see?[11] You're healthy."

"But I'm really cold, and my bow floated away," said Nebraska looking out at the water.

Dane hugged Nebraska and with the most comforting tone he could muster he said, "I'll make you a new bow.... Come here, I'll warm you up."

Nebraska came close to Dane and he unzipped his damp jacket. Holding her close, he wrapped his vest around her. She was small enough that he could almost cover her entire body with either his arms or his vest.

Nebraska snuggled into his chest and let Dane comfort her and that made him contented.

Dane stood up, supporting Nebraska's weight in his arms and continued to walk slowly along the East bank of the Manhattan River. He allowed his mind to go through the events of the day. He shook his head. All of it was unbelievable. He was grateful that there were no fallen people down by the river. Nebraska didn't need to see any more sadness that might cause her trauma.

Dane gazed at Nebraska's golden hair. She was so sweet and innocent. He felt a strong desire to protect her, but just how, he didn't know. Now that he was out of immediate danger he had to figure out what was the best thing to do next. With silent prayers he discussed the situation with Heavenly Father.

"Dane?" said Nebraska in almost a whisper, breaking the silence.

"Yes?"

"I'm hungry."

"I bet you are," said Dane. "We've had a hard day, haven't we?"

Nebraska nodded.

"I have some raisins. Would you like those?"

She nodded again.

Dane held Nebraska with his left arm as he fished in his vest pocket for the raisins. As he blindly felt through the emergency rations in a side zipper pouch, a poignant realization hit him. Because of the military, he was the only person in New York who could have possibly helped this little girl! He had the atropine, he had emergency supplies, and he had the knowledge to survive. He had the very things that Nebraska needed to stay alive. What were the odds of that? One in 19 million? What luck! Then, instantly, he knew, it wasn't luck. He had been blessed with the capacity to do a work.[12]

Dane found his raisins and handed them to Nebraska through the opening in his vest.

"Thank you," she said, already sounding happier.

"You're welcome," said Dane, amazed at this miracle that was unfolding at his hands. Dane was sure God's hand was in her survival. Now he not only wanted to assure her safety, he *had* to. It was his obligation. With the Lord's help, he knew he would.

"So, tell me again how you got down in that sewer," requested Dane wondering how a little girl could possibly get down in a sewer in the middle of Manhattan.

"What's a sewer?" asked Nebraska.

"A sewer is where all the old water goes from the street. You were down in a sewer when I found you. How did you get there?"

"My brother and I were playing hide and seek and I got stuck. I was supposed to go find him but I couldn't get out."

"But how did you get down there?"

"My brother put me down there. He said he didn't want me to peek."

"Where was your mom?"

"She was in the store."

"Sounds like your brother isn't very nice."

"Yeah, sometimes he's mean," said Nebraska. "Where are we going?" she asked as she chewed happily on her raisins.

"I think we should go to Washington, D.C., to find your grandmother."

"Yea! Are you going to walk all the way?"

Dane smiled as he pulled her weight back up inside his vest. "Am *I* going to walk all the way?"

"Yes," she said with a little giggle. "Your legs are longer."

"Yes, but they get tired too," said Dane.

"Maybe I'll carry you," said Nebraska. "Then you carry me, and then I carry you."

Dane laughed. "Maybe," he said. "That would be nice."

"Is it a long ways?"

"Yes," said Dane, noticing that he was hearing a motor and it was getting closer as they walked. He looked behind them but he didn't see any boats approaching; the whole river seemed empty of life.

"How long?"

"I don't know."

"How do you know which way to go?"

"I don't," said Dane, "but I'll find out. I'm a soldier. Soldiers are very smart."

"I'm very smart," said Nebraska. "My mom says so."

"That's great," said Dane smiling. "I can tell."

"Will my mom be in washing machine CC?"

"It's *Wash-ing-ton, D.C.*," said Dane, trying to be clear about the words, while concentrating on the motor sound. They were almost on top of whatever it was that was making the noise.

"Will my mom be in *Wash-ing-ton, D.C.*?" said Nebraska, very careful to enunciate every syllable.

"Maybe," said Dane, but knowing in the pit of his stomach that Nebraska's parents, as well as her brother, were probably dead from the toxic nerve gas. He would hope that they weren't. After all, he didn't really know.

Nebraska swallowed and said, "Do you have any more raisins?"

Dane felt in his pocket. "No, I don't."

"What do you have?"

"I have a protein bar."

"I don't like protein bars. My mom eats those."

Dane snickered. "Yeah, they aren't quite like candy bars are they?"

Nebraska shook her head. "Nope. I like candy bars. Do you have any candy bars?" she asked, looking up at him and tapping her index finger on his chin.

Dane shook his head, "Nope."

The whirring motor sound was becoming deafening.

"Do you have…" yelled Nebraska, paying no attention to the reason she was having to yell.

"Wait," said Dane to Nebraska. "Do you hear that loud noise?"

"Yes."

"What do you think that is? Do you think it's a—boat? I think that sound is coming from a boat," said Dane, scanning the empty river again.

"Or it's a car that ran into the water. Whatever it is, it's right below us. What do you think?"

"Where?" asked Nebraska looking around.

Dane put Nebraska down. On his hands and knees he leaned over the ledge they were standing on that extended about ten feet above the river.

There below the ledge was a small, marooned, brightly colored speedboat. It had flames painted up its side. It was obvious the nerve gas had killed the owner and it had run into the embankment with the throttle still engaged.

Looking back at Nebraska, Dane said, "Yep, there's a boat down there."

Nebraska got down on her stomach and looked, too. "Yep. There is."

"I'm going to go down there and see if we can ride in it. Would you like to ride in a boat?"

"Are there candy bars?" asked Nebraska, looking sideways at Dane.

"Maybe. I can check."

"Go check," said Nebraska with excitement in her voice.

"OK, you sit right here on the ledge. Don't go anywhere."

"OK," she said as she sat down and swung her legs over the ledge.

Dane scaled the ledge and approached the boat that was cocked to the right and tipping from the force of the engine driving it into the embankment. Climbing carefully onto the boat's bow, he dropped over the windshield, into the open cabin. Pulling the throttle back, the motor slowed to an idle. As soon at that happened, the boat equalized its balance and the back end floated gently in the water.

The owner was on the floor of the boat. It looked like he had fallen from his seat when he had passed out. Dane didn't want the dead man to scare Nebraska, so he picked up the body and quietly put him in the water. He wished there was something else he could have done that was more respectful, but considering the dire situation New York was in, the water was the best place he could think of.

"Where are you going?" asked Nebraska.

Dane looked up at Nebraska and noticed the scared look that was beginning to form on her face.

"Nowhere," said Dane realizing the boat had become caught in the river's stream and was floating away. He quickly went to the controls of the boat and drove the boat back to Nebraska. "I'm coming," he called. "I just have to tie the rope so the boat doesn't get away."

"OK," said Nebraska.

Despite repeated attempts, Dane could not get the boat to stay put near the bank long enough for him to jump out. The river was just too swift. So finally, he just pushed the throttle up again and let it drive itself into the bank. Because it was a steep drop from the bank into the river, the boat stayed pointed into the bank, caught on tree roots that jutted out into the river.

With one hand, Dane took hold of the anchoring rope and then he jumped out.

"Hurry, Nebraska! Jump!"

"Did you find candy?" she asked standing up.

"Not yet. Come on down. You can look."

"OK," she said as she held out her hands for Dane.

"Jump! I'll catch you!"

"OK!" she said with a hop and then she landed safely in Dane's arms.

Dane rushed to the boat and carefully climbed on the bow. He gently placed Nebraska in the boat and then he too climbed in.

Nebraska immediately set about looking around the boat. Right off she found a bag. "Is this pop?" she asked.

Dane looked back as he backed the boat out from the branches. He saw Nebraska holding up a six pack of beer. "No, that's not pop. You don't want that stuff."

"What is it?" she asked looking at the label.

"It's alcohol."

"What's alcohol?"

"It's a drink made from rotten food."

Nebraska made a face. "Yuck! Who'd like that?"

Dane laughed. "I don't know," he said as he turned the boat around and pushed on the throttle to head out into the river.

"Here's some chips," said Nebraska, holding up some Doritos.

"Good, let's eat them," said Dane, relieved there was food onboard. That would make his rations last longer.

"Can you open them?" yelled Nebraska. The wind was blowing her hair into her face as she tried to walk toward him.

Dane looked back at the little girl and said, "No, it's not hard. You just pull on the sides of the bag and it opens. But sit down right now and put on your safety belt. I don't want you to fall overboard. Do it before you open the bag."

"OK," said Nebraska. She climbed into the seat beside the captain's chair.

Dane stretched to help her put on her belt then looked out into the horizon. They were going east. He knew the river would lead him out to the Atlantic Ocean.

Dane studied the gas tank level as Nebraska chomped on her chips. It was about three-quarters full. He didn't know how far that would get him, but he hoped it would at least get him to Washington, D.C. He estimated it was about a 200 mile trip.

Dane looked at his little companion. Her right hand was orange already from the cheese flavoring. She held it up in the air, poised to take another dip into the bag. He was intrigued at her resilience. A couple hours before, she was near death, but now, she was enjoying a boat ride and eating Doritos!

"Blessed are the little children…for they shall inherit the kingdom of God," he said as he drove with the sun setting behind him.

Media Failure

Provo, Utah
3:20 p.m.

"Get him, Roc!" yelled Ry as he pushed the buttons on his controller furiously.

On the television screen, digital characters fought each other with supernatural powers.

"Oh, low blow!" exclaimed Jax, laughing at how his miniaturized robot waddled around in a circle. It had just been blasted with the power of Zoar, Rocwell's online character. They were playing a three-player video game that networked with both the television and the Internet.

"I told you I could beat you," said Roc with an indulgent laugh. "I'm good at this game."

Suddenly, the television went black.

"Aaahhk!" screeched Roc. "What happened?"

Ry looked over at the outlet to see if the plug had been ripped out, but it hadn't. "The television is still plugged in."

"The power's out again," said Jax as he dropped his controller dramatically on the floor after looking at the clock on the refrigerator. "No television channels and now no electricity."

"What's wrong with everything?" asked Ry. "Why doesn't anything work now?"

"I don't know," said Jax. "I think it has to do with the sun. Who knows."

"We need to get a sun protector," said Roc, turning on and off the television set.

"That's called a surge protector and we've got one, it's just that all the electricity is off. It'll come on again later," said Jax. "Who knows when we'll get channels again."

"Well, I'm going to Nate's house," said Roc.

"He doesn't have TV either," said Jax.

"I don't care," said Roc. "He has hamsters."

"Dad will be home any time."

"I know," said Roc as he opened the front door. "I'll be back by five thirty," he said. Then he closed it.

Ry walked over to the window and looked out. "I think I'll go outside too. I'm going to go shoot some hoops. Do you want to go?"

Jax shook his head. "I can't. Remember? I'm watching the twins till Dad gets home."

Ry laughed. "Oh yeah. Good thing I've already had my turn. See ya!" he said as he opened and closed the door with a slam.

Jax looked around the near-empty house. It was silent except for the high-voiced babble coming from under the stairs where the twins were playing with Legos. It was strange to be the oldest one in the house now. Everyone had left. He didn't like it. He felt lonely all the time—no, not really lonely, but like everything wasn't complete.

Jax saw Strykker try and fit two pieces of Legos together but was having a difficult time in the little alcove under the stairs. He loved to play there.

Jax moved to the stairs and sat down with the twins. "I can make you a tall tower," he said to Strykker. "Do you want me to make it for you?"

Strykker nodded.

"I want a fower," said Striynna. She was on her knees wedged back in the corner of the wall and the stairs.

"OK, I'll make you a tower," Jax said to Strykker, "and a flower for you."

"Yea!" said Striynna clapping.

Strykker just watched with eager eyes.

So what if there wasn't any electricity. There was always something else to do, thought Jax as he began building for his brother and sister.

Notes to "Evil Designs"

To Dust Ye Shall Return

[1] There are several types of nerve gases that are organophosphates that can be easily absorbed through the skin, by means of inhalation or ingestion. The symptoms of the poisoning are similar, regardless of the route of introduction. Upon inhalation, for instance, the symptoms in order of occurrence include: runny nose, bronchial secretions, tightness in the chest, dimming of vision, pin-point pupils, drooling, excessive perspiration, nausea, vomiting, involuntary defecation, urination, muscle tremors, convulsions, coma, death. Primary treatment for nerve agents is Atropine Sulfate. It is commonly carried in auto-injectors by military personnel in dosages of 1-2 mg. Nerve agents are thought to be in the stockpiles of several extremist nations and terrorist organizations, including Iran, Iraq, Libya, Lebanon, and Syria. For more information see http://www.fema.gov/hazard/terrorism/chem/index.shtm.

Prison Van

[2] "During World Wars I and II, many people deemed to be a threat due to enemy connections were interned in the US. This included people not born in the U.S. and also U.S. citizens of Japanese (in WWII), Italian (in WWII), and German ancestry. In particular, over 100,000 Japanese and Japanese Americans and Germans and German Americans were sent to camps such as Manzanar during the second World War....In reaction to the bombing of Pearl Harbor by Japan in 1941, United States Executive Order 9066 on February 19, 1942, allowed military commanders to designate areas 'from which any or all persons may be excluded.' Under this order all Japanese and Americans of Japanese ancestry were removed from Western coastal regions to guarded camps in Arkansas, Oregon, Washington, Wyoming, Colorado, and Arizona; German and Italian citizens, permanent residents, and American citizens of those respective ancestries (and American citizen family members) were removed from (among other places) the West and East Coast and relocated or interned, and roughly one-third of the US was declared an exclusionary zone....Almost 120,000 Japanese Americans and resident

Japanese aliens would eventually be removed from their homes, and relocated" ("List of Concentration and Internment camps," *Wikipedia*, http://en.wikipedia.org/wiki/List_of_concentration_and_internment_camps#WWI_and_WWII).

[3] What is the recipe to create strong youth that will not bend to peer pressure?

"Powerful forces in society are attacking gospel values, demolishing families, and corroding the principles and integrity of some leaders in business and government. ...What course will we set in the future? What will be our compass in the midst of the storms of life? What will be our anchor to keep us from drifting off the course that will lead us to eternal life? 'If we start right, it is easy to go right all the time' (Teachings of the Prophet Joseph Smith, p. 343). We must live by this legacy of faith and must pass this legacy on to our children so the Church will always have faithful men and women who can continue to prepare for the second coming of our Lord Jesus Christ" (M. Russell Ballard, "Anchored by Faith and Commitment," *Ensign*, July 1995, p. 12).

[4] "In their search for identity and belonging, too many supposedly savvy teens are now confined to the solitude of a lonely gang. What is the lasting advantage of becoming streetwise if one is on a street to nowhere? Gangs mark the failure of both families and communities as well as symbolizing the pervasive revolt against authority" (Neal A. Maxwell, "'Behold, the Enemy Is Combined' (D&C 38:12)," *Ensign*, May 1993, p. 76).

[5] "Satan would like us to believe that we are not responsible in this life. That is the result he tried to achieve by his contest in the pre-existence. A person who insists that he is not responsible for the exercise of his free agency because he was 'born that way' is trying to ignore the outcome of the War in Heaven. We *are* responsible, and if we argue otherwise, our efforts become part of the propaganda effort of the Adversary" (Dallin H. Oaks, "Free Agency and Freedom," *Brigham Young University 1987–88 Devotional and Fireside Speeches*, pp. 46–47).

[6] "Some time ago I read a letter to a newspaper editor which was highly critical of the Church. I have forgotten the exact language, but it included a question something like this: 'When are the Mormons going to stop being different and become a part of the mainstream of America?' About this same time there came to my desk a copy of an address given by Senator Dan Coats of Indiana. He spoke of a study made by 'a commission of educational, political, medical, and business leaders' dealing with the problems of American youth.' The committee issued a report called *Code Blue*. That report, according to the Senator, concluded: 'Never before has one generation of American teenagers been less healthy, less cared for, or less prepared for life than their parents were at the same age.' He went on to say, 'I have seen the parade of pathologies—they are unending and increasing: "Suicide is now the second leading cause of death among adolescents, increasing 300 percent since 1950. Teen pregnancy has risen 621 percent since 1940. More than a million teenage girls get pregnant each year. Eighty-five percent of teenage boys who impregnate teenage girls eventually abandon them. The teen homicide rate has increased 232 percent since 1950. Homicide is now the leading cause of death among fifteen- to nineteen-year-old minority youth." ...Every year substance abuse claims younger victims with harder drugs. A third of high school seniors get drunk once a week. The average age for first-time drug use is now thirteen years old.' The report reached a shocking conclusion. It said: 'The challenges to the health and well-being of America's youth are not primarily rooted in illness or economics. Unlike the past, the problem is not childhood disease or unsanitary slums. The most basic cause of suffering...is profoundly self-destructive *behavior*. Drinking. Drugs. Violence. Promiscuity. A crisis of behavior and belief. A crisis of character' (*Imprimis,* Sept. 1991, p. 1). When I read those statements, I said to myself, 'If that is the mainstream of American youth, then I want to do all in my power to persuade and encourage our young people to stay away from it'" (Gordon B. Hinckley, "'A Chosen Generation'," *Ensign*, May 1992, p. 69).

[7] "The moment a man or woman becomes angry, they show a great weakness" (Wilford Woodruff, *Journal of Discourses,* Vol. 4, p. 98).

[8] "I appeal to the youth to be courageous in maintaining the moral and spiritual values of the gospel of Jesus Christ. The world needs moral heroes! ...Even though the tasks of life become heavy and sorrow weighs upon you, may the light of the Christ life beckon you on still undismayed. With moral courage, we can overcome life's adversities. Courage is that quality of the mind which meets danger or opposition with calmness and firmness, which enables a man to face difficulties that lie in his pathway to righteous achievement....Courage implies facing difficulties and overcoming them. ...When one knows what is right one should always have the courage to defend it even in the face of ridicule or punishment. Let us be courageous in defense of the right. Be not afraid to speak out for the right. Let us be true. May God give us courage to choose the right, ability to appreciate the good things of life, and power faithfully to serve Him and our fellow men. Truth is loyalty to the right as we see it; it is courageous living of our lives in harmony with our ideals; it is always power" (David O. McKay, "Chapter 18: Courage to Live Righteously," *Teachings of Presidents of the Church,* p. 171).

[9] "I invite you to learn about and apply the Savior's teachings about interactions and episodes that can be construed as offensive. 'Ye have heard that it hath been said, Thou shalt love thy neighbour, and hate thine enemy. But I say unto you, Love your enemies, bless them that curse you, do good to them that hate you, and pray for them which despitefully use you, and persecute you....For if ye love them which love you, what reward have ye? do not even the publicans the same? And if ye salute your brethren only, what do ye more than others? do not even the publicans so? Be ye therefore perfect, even as your Father which is in heaven is perfect' (Matthew 5:43–44, 46–48). Interestingly, the admonition to 'be ye therefore perfect' is immediately preceded by counsel about how we should act in response to wrongdoing and offense. Clearly, the rigorous requirements that lead to the perfecting of the Saints include assignments that test and challenge us. If a person says or does something that we consider offensive, our first obligation is to refuse to take offense and then communicate privately, honestly, and directly with that individual. Such an approach invites inspiration from the Holy Ghost and permits misperceptions to be clarified and true intent to be understood" (David A. Bednar, "And Nothing Shall Offend Them," *Ensign*, Nov 2006, pgs. 89–92).

[10] "'...Love your enemies, bless them that curse you, do good to them that hate you, and pray for them which despitefully use you, and persecute you' (Matthew 5:44). What is our response when we are offended, misunderstood, unfairly or unkindly treated, or sinned against, made an offender for a word, falsely accused, passed over, hurt by those we love, our offerings rejected? Do we resent, become bitter, hold a grudge? Or do we resolve the problem if we can, forgive, and rid ourselves of the burden? ...It is required of us to forgive. Our salvation depends upon it....But not only our eternal salvation depends upon our willingness and capacity to forgive wrongs committed against us. Our joy and satisfaction in this life, and our true freedom, depend upon our doing so. When Christ bade us turn the other cheek, walk the second mile, give our cloak to him who takes our coat, was it to be chiefly out of consideration for the bully, the brute, the thief? Or was it to relieve the one aggrieved of the destructive burden that resentment and anger lay upon us? Paul wrote to the Romans that nothing 'shall be able to separate us from the love of God, which is in Christ Jesus our Lord' (Romans 8:39). I am sure this is true. I bear testimony that this is true. '...even as Christ forgave you, so also do ye' (Col. 3:13)" (Marion D. Hanks, "'Even as Christ Forgave'," *New Era*, Jun 1974, p. 4).

Escape from New York

[11] To decontaminate from a lethal chemical exposure, washing everything is necessary. See http://www.fema.gov/hazard/terrorism/chem/index.shtm for further information.

[12] "Be ye strong therefore, and let not your hands be weak: for your work shall be rewarded" (2 Corinthians 15:7).

CHAPTER EIGHT

URGENT NEEDS

"And my soul hungered; and I kneeled down before my Maker, and I cried unto him in mighty prayer and supplication for mine own soul; and all the day long did I cry unto him; yea, and when the night came I did still raise my voice high that it reached the heaven" (Enos 1:4).

00:03:11, 0:48:49, Zulu
Friday, September 19th

Anger

Provo, Utah
4:12 p.m.

Bo paced in his office at the church. Another interview hadn't shown up. That was the second one today. He had taken an extra day, *a Friday, no less,* out of his life to serve the youth of his ward and was rewarded by wasted time! Nothing bothered him more than wasted time!

Frustration was layering his thoughts like silt after a volcanic explosion. Matt's visit in the early morning hours had made him angrier than he had been in a long, long time. Wasting time in his office was only making things worse.

Bo looked at his watch. It was just after four in the afternoon. His stomach grumbled. Then Bo looked at his interview sheet. He had youth temple interviews scheduled for another hour.

Bo sat down in his office chair and folded his hands on his desk. He wondered what he should do with this extra time. He looked at his scriptures. He could read them, but then, he had already done that today; anyway his thoughts were too erratic to concentrate on the scriptures.

He picked up his cell phone and tried to access the Internet to look at the news, but once again his phone was not receiving a signal. Phone service was becoming a joke.

Bo sat in his chair and traced the shape of his fingernails with his eyes. The memory of how his son-in-law had come to his door in the middle of the night invaded his thoughts. He marveled how he had so willingly taken Matt's coat and blindly offered him a seat at his table…Bo shook his head in frustration. At that time, he had thought Matt was family; a welcomed guest. Now that Bo knew the damage Matt had wreaked in his family he imagined slamming the door in his face! He was a home wrecker, *a leech*! He deserved to be shut out.

Bo closed his eyes hard as the reality of everything Matt had told him the night before began to sink in. Brea was a prisoner in her own life, his son Braun had been banished to one of the most unlivable portions of the planet, one of his grandchildren had been given away as a bargaining chip, and Matt hadn't really apologized for any of it!

Bo opened his eyes and looked at the ceiling. He remembered the look on Matt's face as he explained what he had done to his oldest son, supposedly to "protect" him. At that moment, Bo realized that Matt not only *wasn't* apologetic, he actually expected to be *thanked* for his efforts in Braun's behalf! Now, Bo was *really* mad. Thank him? *Thank him for what?* For ruining what he had built? For stealing his children? For making it so he couldn't see Braun, or talk to him for who knows how long? Or maybe Matt wanted to be thanked for bringing his daughter back in worse shape than he had received her? Which was it? No way! No way! *No way* was he *ever* going to thank that man. In fact, he'd be surprised if he could even *stomach looking at him again*!

Bo made fists with his hands as anger ripped through him, wounding his spirit. He felt his muscles tense and his neck grow stiff. His angry thoughts continued. He hadn't labored his whole married life to raise his children just to have them destroyed in a single blow by some slick talker! His children were unique! They had gifts and talents! They had value! They had things to do on the earth! He had been told in a dream that they were chosen and blessed people meant to serve in specific capacities! What about that now? Was Matt binding their potential? Was he getting in the way of their futures?

Bo stood up and paced again, energy escalating inside him. The desire to defend his children was now irresistible. He wanted to set them free from the bondage! But—how could he do that? How could he eliminate Matt and MD from his family's lives forever? Obviously, Matt was not an easy one to get rid of. He seemed bent on staying attached to Brea, despite his botched-up attempt at marriage.

Bo shook his head. *"What a loser!"* he found himself saying, but then felt guilty. His emotional outburst wasn't the proper attitude for a bishop. He knew he needed to be patient in his afflictions but who could be patient in his circumstance?

Bo re-considered recent events. It hadn't been easy. It wasn't easy when Carea was sick. It wasn't easy when Dane almost died. It wasn't easy when they lost their house in the flood and had to build a new one. It wasn't easy when he lost his job at the time he needed it the most. His life wasn't easy when he had to endure the humiliation of Corrynne supporting the family, and the price of gas going so high they could hardly afford to eat anything but the food storage they had dug out of the mud! It wasn't easy when Dane left for the service, or when Conrad couldn't come home, and now the loss of Braun in his life? How could anyone take all of *that* and stay sane?

Bo's anger turned to hot mourning. With fists shaking, he fell to his knees in the middle of his office. ***"Why?"*** he questioned looking up at the ceiling, communicating to heaven. ***"Why? Why? Why?"*** Then great tears fell from his eyes. ***"Father, why do I have to go through so much?*** *...Why does life have to be so hard? Why do I have to* ***sacrifice*** *so much? Why am I expected to take every blow without* ***fighting back****? I can't keep on smiling when I'm* ***bleeding to death*** *inside!* ***...Father****! My burden is* ***too hard*** *for one person to bear! Tell me* ***why*** *I have to deal with these things!* ***Am I being punished?*** *Is there some personal flaw that I still have?* ***Is something evil not burnt out of me yet?"*** he demanded as he thumped his fist on his chest.

Bo waited for an answer but nothing came. ***"If it's flesh you want, take it! Take it all now! Don't kill me piece by piece! Just get it over with! I'm tired of this continual pummeling! I—don't—deserve—it!"*** he spoke with energy and gritted teeth, wanting to yell but worried about who might be outside the door. Then feeling lost in despair Bo bowed his head and wept openly, clasping his hands together in angry fury.

Bo cried on the floor for about fifteen minutes until all the anger was drained out of him. Getting to his feet, he looked at his watch. His next interview was going to be showing up any moment. He picked up the phone to call his first counselor, but again, there was no service.

On a piece of paper he wrote a note. "The bishop has fallen sick. Please reschedule your appointment."

With two pieces of tape he hung it on the outside door, locked up, and went home.

Inhospitable Desperation

Provo, Utah
6:25 p.m.

"OK, the patient is coming off by-pass," said Dr. Ashcroft, the cardiothoracic surgeon. "He's had five grafts. Is the balloon ready?"

"It will be," said Corrynne as she powered up the balloon pump machine that would inflate and deflate a balloon in the patient's aorta. It was a machine that would support and oxygenate a weak and injured post-bypass heart.

The machine turned on, the screen blinked a moment, then went black. Corrynne looked at it, waiting for it to light up, but nothing happened.

"Where's that balloon?" called the surgeon. "We're off pump!"

"It's coming," said Corrynne, flipping the power switch off and on again.

"We need it now!" said the surgeon looking at the waning vital signs on his overhead thirty-inch display.

"I know. The machine is having a problem."

"We can't afford problems," said Dr. Ashcroft. "If we wait too much longer, this patient's brain is going to die. Get the thing working!"

Corrynne waited for the machine to boot up again. The screen flashed and then finally, Corrynne saw some lights that she recognized. "OK, it's coming online," she said, then she whispered to herself, "Please, please, please work."

Corrynne put the machine on "auto" so it would sense the patient's blood pressure and pump at the appropriate time, but the machine started to alarm, telling her that there was no trigger. The patient's blood pressure was too low. The machine wouldn't pump, therefore, the patient's heart would continue to suffer from lack of oxygen.

"Come on! What's it going to take?" called the surgeon. "We have to have some blood pressure! Give me some blood pressure!"

"The machine can't sense when to pump," said Corrynne as she switched the machine to semi-auto and selected the EKG to initiate pumping.

"I need more pressors! Turn up the Neo! Put on some Epi!" Dr. Ashcroft demanded of his anesthesiologist, Dr. Deen.

"I have them maxed out," said Dr. Deen as he started hanging another drip. "I'm putting up Dobutamine."

"Fine," said the surgeon. "How's that pump coming, Corrynne?"

"Dr. Ashcroft, the machine is pumping now."

Dr. Ashcroft looked up at the monitor to see ugly wave forms and a lethal blood pressure. *"What's that?"* he asked. "Are you sure the balloon is pumping?" he asked again.

Corrynne was getting irritated. "Yes, doctor. It's pumping. The patient doesn't have a systolic blood pressure so the wave form doesn't look like it should, but I assure you it's working. Whatever you see up there is my machine."

"No. I think we have pump failure," said the surgeon.

"I agree, or we have *operator failure*," said Dr. Deen, not helping the tense situation. "That pump isn't regular enough for it to be functioning properly. There's something wrong. Maybe you have it in the wrong mode."

Corrynne looked up at the doctors over the patient. "No, I have it in the right mode for this situation. I am pumping off the EKG. The pump is irregular because every time you touch the chest, the machine can't sense the EKG so it pauses. Aside from that, it's doing what it's supposed to."

"Get me a new pump!" yelled the surgeon. *"Go back on bypass till we can figure this out. Pump off!"*

"Going back on by-pass," said the technician working the by-pass machine as he turned dials and pushed buttons. The tubes of the heart and lung by-pass machine filled with red blood.

Corrynne took a deep breath as she looked at the clock and turned off her pump. Her shift was almost over. Only thirty more minutes of these pompous, arrogant doctors. Only thirty more minutes of this abuse and then she could walk out of the OR and let someone else deal with this patient who obviously wasn't going to survive this procedure.

Corrynne was helping in the OR because the surgeon's regular balloon pump nurse was sick that day. Shame on her for being so willing to substitute and coming in on a day shift! She wouldn't be so willing next time, she thought as she burst through the double OR doors.

Running down the halls outside the OR suites, she fished for her badge inside her OR suit which was zipped up over her scrubs. Passing the badge near a small light on the wall opened the locked doors into the ICU.

"What's wrong, Corrynne?" asked an RN who was a co-worker. She was attending to a patient in the room that housed the extra balloon pumps.

"Oh, we're having difficulties in the OR," said Corrynne as she pulled open the cupboard doors and pulled out another machine.

"Did your pump fail?" the nurse asked.

"No. But the doctor thinks it did. I'm just getting another one and we'll have the same problems—you know how it goes. I hate surgeon egos," replied Corrynne as she powered up the new machine to assure herself that it would work and that the helium tank that would inflate and deflate the balloon was full. "Then I can say, 'I told you so,'" said Corrynne smiling sarcastically as she pulled the machine back out into the hall and rushed back toward the OR.

"Good luck!" called Corrynne's friend.

Corrynne smiled to herself. Only fifteen more minutes of good luck as she swiped her badge next to the light again.

The doors swung open and Corrynne pushed the machine back into the OR.

"What do you think about a bi-VAD?" Dr Ashcroft asked Dr. Deen.

"No, this patient is not a good candidate. He'll never come off it."

"I know, but it will get him out of the OR at least," said Dr. Ashcroft. "We don't want him dying on our table."

"It might be already too late," said Dr. Deen.

"I hope not," said Dr. Ashcroft as he stared into the chest of his patient. "His cardiac wall function looked better than that pressure we were getting on the monitor."

"I agree. It did."

Corrynne finished hooking up the last wire and stood up from behind the machine. "The new pump is ready to go."

"Does that one work?" asked the doctor sarcastically.

"Yes," said Corrynne. "The first one worked too."

"No, it didn't. I don't care what you say, that pump wasn't working," he said as he reversed the by-pass blood connection.

Corrynne selected the semi-auto function, but allowed the machine to stay on stand-by. "I'm sorry, but I have to have a blood pressure to give you a blood pressure."

"No, you don't," said the surgeon as he looked up at the monitor. "Start pumping."

Corrynne pushed the start button and said, "My machine was made to augment blood pressure, not deliver blood pressure. If the patient has no blood pressure, I can't give you blood pressure, no matter how well the machine works..."

The lights in the OR flashed and then went out.

"What the—" started the surgeon.

Something in the room was glowing enough for Corrynne to see that the surgeon's sterile hands were in the air as he looked around the room at the lifelessness of his tools.

The backup energy came on and the monitors lit up again but the waveforms were in the wrong place and triple the size. The numbers that communicated pressures were off the screen.

"Fix that screen!" The surgeon yelled, but everyone in the room was sterile except for the by-pass technician, anesthesiologist, and Corrynne. Each of them just looked at each other helplessly. It was obvious that none of them would be able to do as the surgeon demanded. None of them were computer techs.

"Can anything else go wrong?" yelled the surgeon.

Corrynne bit her lip as her balloon pumped a heart that had been too long without blood pressure. She knew the end was near for this patient. There was little left to do.

"Do you have any blood pressure on your machine?" called the doctor.

"Yes, I have a systolic of 38 over a diastolic of 15, and that's all pumping pressure. I still don't have a native systolic pressure. Also, we now are in atrial fibrillation so even that is irregular."

"Can we go back on by-pass till we can fix these monitors?" the surgeon asked the perfusionist.

"No. The power glitch must have blown something in the circuits. The by-pass machine is out of order."

The surgeon looked around the room and asked, "Any suggestions?"

The team was silent. No one met the doctor's eyes.

"I guess, by your overwhelming response, that we're done here. Time of death 19:01."

Corrynne turned off her machine. The battle had been lost.

ξξξξξξξ

"Home," said Corrynne as she slid into her car.

The car did not respond.

"Home," said Corrynne again. Maybe she hadn't said it loud enough.

The car didn't even light up.

"What's going on?" asked Corrynne, feeling too tired to deal with stupid computers any more that night. She touched the thumb pad to turn on the car but again, it lay silent and dead.

Reaching over to the glove box, she retrieved a key that in emergency situations would override the auto start function. She put it into the ignition hole and turned it, just like she was starting the truck.

The Suburban suddenly came to life.

"Yes," said Corrynne smiling. "You just have to be smarter than the car."

Out on the main road, Corrynne noticed that all the street lights were flashing. She deduced that there must have been a city-wide power outage again, but she was getting used to that.

Turning on the radio she switched to her favorite local talk radio station. Maybe they'd have the news on right now.

"...riots continue all over...." Then there was static.

Corrynne leaned forward. Riots? wondered Corrynne. Where were there riots?

"...Bats were taken into custod..." Static.

"What?" said Corrynne as she frowned and hit her radio display. "Work! I have to know what's going on! I'm going to go crazy!"

Corrynne looked up into the sky that was beginning to turn dusky. Was there another solar flare? Was that why the computers and radios weren't working right?

"...elect...energy...out..."

"Electric energy out? Is that what you said?" Corrynne asked her radio.

"...emergency broad...system..." sputtered the radio.

"You're useless!" Corrynne exclaimed, and then she turned the thing off. She'd wait till she got home. Bo would probably know what was going on.

Jax's Burden

Provo, Utah
7:45 p.m.

Corrynne walked into a house full of chaos. Her boys were throwing a baseball in the living room, Striynna was standing over the bucket of flour with most of it all over her and the floor, and Strykker was hiding under the table watching his brothers play.

"What is going on in here?" she asked, almost at her emotional limit for the day.

"Hi, Mom!" said Rocwell.

"Hi, Mom!" said Ry. He didn't even sense that something could be wrong as he tossed the ball to Roc.

"OK, who's in charge here?" asked Corrynne picking Striynna up from the floor and taking her to the sink to wash her off.

"Dad is," said Ry.

"Oh, yeah? Where is he?" asked Corrynne putting her daughter down and grabbing a broom.

"He's in bed," said Roc.

"In bed? Why? Is he sick?" she asked. She swept up the flour as Striynna tried to dip her hand in Corrynne's flour pile on the floor. Corrynne pushed Striynna back with her foot, which caused the baby to fall hard on her bottom.

With a look of shock Striynna turned down her lip and began to cry as the baseball the boys were throwing sailed into the kitchen and hit Corrynne right on the head.

"OK! OK! That is quite enough!" said Corrynne with an angry stare. Pointing at her middle sons she said, *"Boys! Stop throwing balls in the house! I have told you over and over again not to do that!"*

"Sorry," said Ry with a grimace. "We didn't mean to hit you."

"It doesn't matter what you meant to do, the fact is, that you did and now I'm upset! I've had a hard day and this is not what I want to come home to!"

"Sorry, Mom," said Roc with the same grimace as his brother.

"Now, you boys, take Striynna and Strykker upstairs to your bedroom while you get ready for bed."

"What?" asked Roc, his mouth open in shock.

"What?" echoed Ry with the same look. "What'd we do? You're sending us to bed?"

"Yes," said Corrynne. "It's time for bed, at least for quiet time. *Everyone to their bedrooms!*" But then Corrynne realized the kids probably hadn't eaten dinner if Bo was asleep. "Ahh, OK, on second thought, go to your rooms while I figure out where everyone is and throw some food on the table. I'll call you when it's done."

"We ate tortillas and cheese for dinner," said Jax, who magically appeared from around the corner of the kitchen.

Corrynne looked at him and made a face. "You did? That's not a very good dinner."

"Well, Dad told us to make our own. He's sleeping and didn't want to get up."

"OK, then, back to plan A. Ry, Roc, take Striynna and Strykker now! Go up to your room and play with them awhile. If you do well, I might change my mind—in fact, if you put new diapers on them and got them ready for bed, I know for *sure* I'll change my mind, but only after you give me a good quiet time."

"How much of a quiet time?" asked Ry.

"About an hour," said Corrynne.

"How about we give you an hour and a *half* of quiet time and you let us stay up an hour extra," suggested Ry, trying to wheel and deal.

Corrynne was impressed with Ry's thinking. She liked the proposal. "Put the twins to bed, that means pray with them and sing to them until they're asleep, and you've got a deal," she said.

"Deal!" said Ry.

"Yeah, deal!" said Roc.

"I dibbs Strykker," said Ry.

"OK," said Roc. "Come on, Striynna," he said in a high voice, holding his arms out.

Striynna looked up at her mother with tears in her eyes.

Corrynne was filled with compassion and knelt down. Her babies ran into her arms and she hugged and kissed both of them. They in turn clung to her, wrapping their little arms around her neck. Corrynne needed this and she allowed the moment to linger, taking in their little spirits.

"Mom!" said Roc after a few moments.

Corrynne looked up at her sons. "What?"

"We have to take the twins so we can start our time," said Ry with an apologetic smile.

Corrynne nodded and pulled back. "Go with Roc and Ry, OK?" she asked her babies as she smiled.

"No!" said the twins in unison.

"It's going to be bedtime soon. You can play upstairs and then they'll sing with you. You'll like that," said Corrynne, still trying to make them happy.

"No! No! No!" yelled Striynna as she began to jump up and down and then dropped onto her diapered bottom.

"Yes, it's time," said Corrynne. "Go ahead boys, take the twins. They're going to cry no matter what. I'll come into their room in a little while and say goodnight. You'll probably have to pick them up. I don't think they'll go with you willingly."

"OK," said Ry as he picked Strykker up.

"OK," said Roc as he in turn, picked Striynna up but she wiggled so she slid in his arms up to her torso.

"Mommyyyyyyy!" Striynna whined as Roc lugged her whining body up the stairs.

"I'll hug you in a little while, Striynna. Just play with Roc right now," said Corrynne, her voice kind. "I've got to figure some things out, and then I'll come up."

Corrynne turned back to Jax who had been patiently watching the family drama as he leaned against the wall. "Where's Carea?"

Jax shrugged. "I haven't seen her. She hasn't come home from school yet."

Corrynne looked at her watch and shook her head. "It's nearly eight at night! I'm sure she did and she's probably in her room taking a nap, too."

"No, she isn't," said Jax. "I checked. My friend's brother says that she's in prison. He says he saw the police take her away in a SWAT truck."

Corrynne's memory was pricked. Was that what the radio was talking about? She rushed to Jax and took him by his arms. *"Are you sure?"*

Jax nodded and said, "They said she was a Bat. ...She's not, is she?" he asked with a worried look.

Corrynne shook her head, catching Jax's sudden change in demeanor. "No, Jax. She's not a Bat. The Bats tried to make her one of them, but she wouldn't let them. She was strong. Remember?"

Jax nodded but then his eyes welled up in tears. "Mom, what if it's true? What if they have Carea? *What if they won't give her back?*"

Corrynne didn't know. She looked into Jax's eyes and said, "I don't know, Jax, but I'll find out." She wiped her son's tears. "No matter what happens, remember we're a family, and families are forever."[1]

"But..." said Jax.

Corrynne put a finger over his lips and said, "No, Jax, listen. No matter what happens to any of us, if we get sick, if we die, if we're taken to prison, or lost, it doesn't matter because the Lord has promised that he will fix all those terrible things[2] that might happen to us[3] and bring us back together."[4]

"But we have to wait till we die for that to happen."

"Not necessarily. The Millennium is just around the corner. The signs are all around us![5] We're lucky! We won't have to wait long at all!"[6]

"You sure?"

"Of course I'm sure. Now, I want you to think about something very important."

"What?"

"I want you to focus on yourself," she said as she gently placed a hand on his shoulder.

"What does that mean?"

"I want you to do the best *you* can do every day. Try not to let others affect you. Be as good as you can and always choose the right. In this world of ours, it's the only thing you can control.[7] And if you learn how to control your choices, you will have every blessing you've ever wanted,[8] including every person in our family right by your side. I promise!"

Jax wiped his own eyes with the back of his hand. With an intense look he said, "That's if every person in my family *chooses* to be good."

Jax's statement caught Corrynne off-guard. She nodded and shrugged as she tried to find appropriate words. "Well—well, everyone *will* choose to be good," she finally said.

"How do you know?"

Corrynne hesitated as she thought. Jax was really putting her on the spot. She blinked twice as she realized he was right. She *didn't* know. She *hoped* everyone in her family would continue to choose the right[9] but that's all she could do. The rest would be left to each individual person in her family to choose for themselves.[10]

"Well, Jax. You're right," she began, letting her hand drop to her hip. "I don't know. And you're right, Satan doesn't want our family to be eternal and so he'll do everything to separate us, make us angry, or distressed.[11] He hopes he can drive us from righteousness so we'll lose our blessings,[12] but we are the ones who choose if he wins or not. *We are, not him!* We are in control of that outcome. Do you understand?"[13]

Jax nodded, his eyes wide.

"I pray every single day, that everything that Daddy and I have taught you and your brothers and sisters will help you all make good choices. We pray that you will always choose the right so all of us can enjoy eternal blessings together. So far, our family has been very blessed. Everyone is on the right path. That should show you that teaching your children when they're young *works*! And I hope that when you grow up you'll teach your children every day also. You'll read the scriptures with them daily. You'll have Family Home Evening. You'll go to church and pray with your children in family prayer. Through those moments you'll teach them right from wrong. If you do this, it will work for you, too."[14]

"OK," said Jax, still crying but trying to stop.

"Joseph Smith promised parents that were sealed in the temple and who labored all their life to teach their children truth that if the children stray away for a little while from the truth, that eventually, they'll come back."[15]

"He did?"

"Yes, he did," said Corrynne taking her growing son in her arms. She stroked his hair. He was feeling such pain at such a tender age. "He has given us many blessings and now we need to remember those blessings."

Jax nodded.

"It will help us deal with whatever is sad in our lives. Think of the good and be patient with the bad. In the end, all things will be restored to us and we will have happiness forever."[16]

"OK, Mom."

"Now, I need you to do something for me," said Corrynne taking Jax by the shoulders again.

"What?"

"I need you to be my right-hand man, can you do that?"

"What's a 'right-hand man'?"

"I mean that, if it's true that Carea has been taken by the police, we're going to have some bad days ahead. I think they'll be pretty hard to live through for a while. That means I need you to be strong and think positively. You're the oldest one around here now and I need you to be protective and a good example to your brothers and sister. Will you pray to be able to do that?"

"OK," said Jax, sniffing.

"The Lord will help you."[17]

"OK," he nodded again.

"Now, I'm going to go upstairs and talk to Dad. He must be having a bad day, too. You just do something you enjoy for the next little while. The babies are taken care of so go take a hot bath or something. Pour in lots of bubbles."

Jax looked like he was considering his mother's advice then he nodded. "I think I'll do that."

"Good," said Corrynne as she rushed up the stairs, pulling her phone from her scrubs pocket. She dialed Chief Morgan's number. He'd know if Carea had been arrested. She might as well go to the source and stop wondering.

Men in White

Siberia, Russia
5:50 a.m.

The snowmobile stalled in the middle of a large, flat plain.

"What's wrong?" asked Braun.

Chenille was quiet and then she said, "We have to walk from here."

"Why?" asked Braun. "The snow is still deep enough. The snowmobile will still carry us."

"We're out of gas," said Chenille looking back at Braun with worried eyes.

Braun looked at the gas gauge over Chenille's shoulder. She was right. The needle for the gas tank sat on empty. Braun looked at Chenille who was looking down as if thinking. "So which way do we have to go now?"

Chenille reached into her deep pocket and pulled out the GPS device. She turned it on and looked at it for a while. "I'm not sure anymore. This thing stopped working."

"That's not good," said Braun as he got off the snowmobile and scanned the horizon.

"Now, I'm disoriented," Chenille said looking around. "I thought we were going east, but now I think we've been veering north. It's hard to know when the land is so flat, without any markers to help me know which way I'm going. All the clouds don't help either. I can't see the sun."

"Hmmm," said Braun. He didn't have a single idea of what to do. He felt crippled without computers and cell phones. "Well if we had a computer I could do a Map Quest search," then he smiled at Chenille.

Chenille didn't smile back. "You don't understand. This tank of gas was supposed to get us to camp."

Braun nodded and fell silent Chenille was beginning to panic. If he got excited, he would make it worse. Trying to stay calm, he asked, "So what's plan B?"

Chenille pulled off her hat and put her fingers through her hair as she continued to look around in every direction. "I don't know, Braun. To be honest, I think we're in big trouble. We have just a tiny bit of food left and no idea where to go. I mean, it's not like we're in America where we could just start walking and run into a town. Here, the wilderness goes on forever. We'll die before we meet a single person!"

Braun pulled Chenille close and wrapped his arms around her, hugging her tight. With a gentle voice he said, "If this is the end, that's OK with me. I'm happy now that I have you again in my life."

"Braun!" said Chenille pushing away from him. "Be serious."

"I am being serious. I am the happiest man in existence, alive or dead. Dying won't stop any of my goals. I plan on being with you forever. The Lord will make sure that happens."

Chenille studied Braun and then said, "Are you saying you want to marry me?"

Braun smiled and touched Chenille's cheek. "I was thinking seriously about it."

Chenille looked down and shook her head. "What a time to finally think about it: out *in the middle of Siberia, without a temple, let alone anyone to perform the ceremony*!"

Braun chuckled and said with a shrug, "Better late than never, maybe?"

Chenille threw back her head and shaking her doubled fists in the air, let out a loud scream that didn't even echo.

"What was that for?" asked Braun, feeling kind of unnerved.

"You drive me mad!" said Chenille with angry eyes. "I can't believe this. We're on the verge of being starved popsicles and you, *Mr. Dreamer*, can only talk about something I've wanted you to talk about for a year! And now it probably will never happen! You figure it out!"

"Chenille, settle down."

"Settle down?" asked Chenille with a gasp and an open mouth. "I think coming to terms with the end of all my hopes and dreams for my life is a big deal. I'll never be married, I'll never have children, I'll never grow old…"

"Stop," said Braun with his hands up. "There's an option you haven't considered."

"What's that?" asked Chenille with a hand on her hip.

"We haven't prayed for help yet," suggested Braun.

Chenille's face suddenly softened. "Prayer?"

"Sure. God knows where we are. He knows how to get where we need to go to survive. I think if we pray, he'll give us some inspiration that might show us which way to walk."

Chenille contemplated Braun's words. Then she said, "He could even show you a vision."

Braun nodded with raised eyebrows. "Sure. If that's what he wants to do, but he could just as well tell us. I don't need a vision."

"I know you don't, but a vision would be easier to figure out."

"Not necessarily."

"But still, prayer might work," said Chenille with a spark of hope in her eyes. "I know he'd talk to you."

"He'd talk to you, too."

"Not like he talks to you," said Chenille.

Braun shook his head. "You doubt your ability to receive revelation?"[18]

"No."

"Then what's the problem?"

"I don't know. I guess I'm just afraid."

"Afraid of what?"

Chenille shrugged. "I'm not sure. I think it's that God might just let us die here. What's death to him?"

"Well, we'll never know what he wants unless we ask."

Chenille nodded. "I know."

"So let's kneel."

"Right here?" asked Chenille.

"Sure, why not? There's no one around. It's perfect."

"OK," said Chenille kneeling on the snow. "But you say the prayer."

"OK," said Braun as he closed his eyes. After thinking about what he wanted to say to the Lord, he set his heart out to find him. After centering his mind, he started.

"Dear Father. Chenille and I come to you in solemn prayer. …We're lost, Father. …We're out of food. …We don't know which direction to go. …We are anxious to continue to live on this earth and do thy will in bringing souls to thee through our examples and through children that will come into our home if thou wills for us to live longer upon this earth…. Please, Father, fill our minds with an idea of which way to go, or better yet, please send someone to show us the way…"

"Brother—Rogers," said a soft tenor voice, with obviously difficult English.

Braun opened his eyes in surprise. Above him stood a man with a tan face, black hair, and a wide bright smile. He was wearing a white animal skin coat with fur around the hood. In complete surprise Braun asked, "Where did you come from?" Then he looked around as if he would see more people.

The man pointed to four large reindeer and one other man who looked similar to the first in dress and appearance. The man and the reindeer were standing only about twenty feet away.

Braun looked at Chenille with a confused stare and she returned it.

"How come we didn't see you before?" asked Chenille, her face filled with wonder. "We were alone!"

The man just continued to smile and with broken English he said, "Come to us. You lost. We have food and warmth."

"Were you sent by Mr. Daimler?" asked Chenille.

The man looked at Chenille with a blank stare. It was obvious he didn't understand her.

"Come," he said, and pointed to the wooden sled pulled by the four reindeer. "Get on. You ride."

Chenille stood up and brushed the snow from her coat. Then looking at Braun with wonder she approached the team of reindeer and makeshift sled. "So the rumors are true? Reindeer really do pull sleds in the north pole?"

The man nodded, but Braun and Chenille knew he didn't know what she was referring to and they cast a humorous glance at each other.

The stranger held out a hand to invite Chenille onto the sled.

Chenille nodded and said, "Thank you," and stepped carefully onto it.

Braun mounted behind Chenille and held onto the rail around the edge of the sled and put another gently on Chenille's waist to assure her balance.

"Ahhhyaka!" called the second man with a flick of the reins and a long wooden pole.

The reindeer bolted forward and Braun and Chenille had to hang on tight so they didn't fall off.

After a time of riding in the silence, Braun turned to the man who had talked to them first and asked, "What's your name, and how come you knew mine?"

The man nodded with a smile to Braun but then turned to his companion and started speaking in a strange foreign language.

Braun repeated his question, "Excuse me, who are you?"

The second man had an incessant smile, just like the first, said, "Good, good!" nodding, then returned his attention to the first man.

"Maybe these people can't speak English," said Chenille behind her hand.

"Yes, they can. You heard him speak to me."

"Yes, but he didn't say much. Maybe they only know a few words."

Braun studied the men and said, "Maybe."

Then Chenille nudged Braun with her elbow. In a quiet voice she said, "See? I told you the Lord would answer you."

Braun smiled reflectively and looked at his beautiful Chenille. "I guess we can get married and have a family of little Brauns and Chenilles after all."

Chenille blushed with a smile and put her head on Braun's shoulder. "Won't that be cute?"

"I think so," said Braun, feeling thankful his deepest desires were finally coming true.

"I'm looking forward to it," she whispered in his ear.

A shiver ran down Braun's back and he had to shrug to stop it. Now all he could do was smile.

Notes to "Urgent Needs"

Jax's Burden

[1] "And I will give unto thee the keys of the kingdom of heaven: and whatsoever thou shalt bind on earth shall be bound in heaven: and whatsoever thou shalt loose on earth shall be loosed in heaven" (Matthew 16:19).

"In this latter day the promise of eternal families was restored in 1829 when the powers of the Melchizedek Priesthood were restored to the earth. Seven years later, in the Kirtland Temple, the keys to perform the sealing ordinances were restored, as recorded in the Doctrine and Covenants....With the restoration of these keys and priesthood authority comes the opportunity for all who are worthy to receive the blessings of eternal families....An eternal bond doesn't just happen as a result of sealing covenants we make in the temple. How we conduct ourselves in this life will determine what we will be in all the eternities to come. To receive the blessings of the sealing that our Heavenly Father has given to us, we have to keep the commandments and conduct ourselves in such a way that our families will want to live with us in the eternities" (Robert D. Hales. "The Eternal Family," *Ensign*, Nov 1996, p. 64).

[2] "...Deal justly, judge righteously, and do good continually; and if ye do all these things then shall ye receive your reward; yea, ye shall have mercy restored unto you again; ye shall have justice restored unto you again; ye shall have a righteous judgment restored unto you again; and ye shall have good rewarded unto you again" (Alma 41:14).

"O the greatness and the justice of our God! For he executeth all his words, and they have gone forth out of his mouth, and his law must be fulfilled" (2 Nephi 9:17).

[3] "I say unto thee, my son, that the plan of restoration is requisite with the justice of God; for it is requisite that all things should be restored to their proper order. Behold, it is requisite and just, according to the power and resurrection of Christ, that the soul of man should be restored to its body, and that every part of the body should be restored to itself. And it is requisite with the justice of God that men should be judged according to their works; and if their works were good in this life, and the desires of their hearts were good, that they should also, at the last day, be restored unto that which is good" (Alma 41:2–3).

[4] "The plan of the Father is that family love and companionship will continue into the eternities. Being one in a family carries a great responsibility of caring, loving, lifting, and strengthening each member of the family so that all can righteously endure to the end in mortality and dwell together throughout eternity. It is not enough just to save ourselves. It is equally important that parents, brothers, and sisters are saved in our families. If we return home alone to our Heavenly Father, we will be asked, 'Where is the rest of the family?' This is why we teach that families are forever. The eternal nature of an individual becomes the eternal nature of the family" (Robert D. Hales, "The Eternal Family," *Ensign*, Nov 1996, p. 64).

[5] "The Lord has declared, 'He that feareth me shall be looking forth for the great day of the Lord to come, even for the signs of the coming of the Son of Man,' signs that will be shown 'in the heavens above, and in the earth beneath' (D&C 45:39–40). The Savior taught this in the parable of the fig tree whose tender new branches give a sign of the coming of summer. 'So likewise,' when the elect shall see the signs of His coming 'they shall know that He is near, even at the doors' (JS—M 1:38–39; see also Matt. 24:32–33; D&C 45:37–38)" (Dallin H. Oaks, "Preparation for the Second Coming," *Liahona*, May 2004, pgs. 7–10).

[6] "These signs of the Second Coming are all around us and seem to be increasing in frequency and intensity. For example, the list of major earthquakes in The World Almanac and Book of Facts 2004 shows twice as many earthquakes in the decades of the 1980s and 1990s as in the

two preceding decades (p. 189–90). It also shows further sharp increases in the first several years of this century. The list of notable floods and tidal waves and the list of hurricanes, typhoons, and blizzards worldwide show similar increases in recent years (p. 188–89). Increases by comparison with 50 years ago can be dismissed as changes in reporting criteria, but the accelerating pattern of natural disasters in the last few decades is ominous" (Dallin H. Oaks, "Preparation for the Second Coming," *Liahona*, May 2004, pgs.7–10).

[7] "It isn't until you come to a spiritual understanding of who you are that you can begin to take control of yourself. As you learn to control yourself, you will get control of your life. If you want to move the world, you first have to move yourself. President Spencer W. Kimball (1895–1985) often quoted an unknown author: 'The greatest battle of life is fought out within the silent chambers of the soul. A victory on the inside of a man's heart is worth a hundred conquests on the battlefields of life. To be master of yourself is the best guarantee that you will be master of the situation. Know thyself. The crown of character is self-control.' Be responsive to the counsel of the prophets, seers, and revelators, who will help you to reach true self-mastery. Be responsive to the promptings of the Spirit. The Spirit will influence your conscience and help you to refine yourself by working on the little tasks of self-control—like controlling your thoughts, words, and actions—which leads to self-control of your whole self, of mind, body, and spirit" (Dieter F. Uchtdorf, "On the Wings of Eagles," *Ensign*, Jul 2006, pgs. 10–15).

[8] "Many things are required to make an airplane fly and fly safely, but the most important thing, as I used to call it, is the 'wind beneath your wings.' Without it, there is no lift, no climb, no flight into the wild blue yonder or to faraway, beautiful destinations. The Holy Ghost will be the wind beneath your wings, placing in your heart the firm conviction of the divinity of the Lord Jesus Christ and His place in the eternal plan of God your Eternal Father. Through the Holy Ghost you will know your place in this plan and your divine eternal destination. You will be converted to the Lord, His gospel, and His Church, and you will never fall away" (Dieter F. Uchtdorf, "On the Wings of Eagles," *Ensign*, Jul 2006, pgs. 10–15).

[9] Faith is belief in something that cannot be seen but is true. Hope is the desire to believe in the unseen. After we have taught our children appropriately, we can have faith in those teachings, and hope they touch our children's hearts at moments of great need. In this way, we can have confidence of eternal blessings of families.

"...If a man have faith he must needs have hope; for without faith there cannot be any hope" (Moroni 7:42).

[10] Every parent wishes the best for his or her children. However, after the teaching moments of the home are past, it is our responsibility to stand back and allow our children to make their own decisions without interference or leverage.

"The Prophet Joseph said that man, if taught correct principles, would govern himself. (See JD, 10:57–58.) ...The Doctrine and Covenants...noted that power or influence should be maintained 'by persuasion, by long-suffering, by gentleness and meekness, and by love unfeigned; by kindness, and pure knowledge' (D&C 121:41–42)....If otherwise impermissible force cannot be made legitimate by its use in accomplishing a good end....Latter-day Saint theology spells out the permissible means one person can use in influencing another's beliefs—and they are peaceful persuasion, tolerance or long-suffering, appreciating diversity, and 'love unfeigned.' These means guarantee and are in turn guaranteed by freedom of conscience. Brigham Young stated: 'Our religion will not permit us to command or force any man or woman to obey the Gospel we have embraced. And we are under no obligation to do this, for every creature has as good a right, according to his organization, to choose for himself as the Gods' (JD, 14:94.)" (Edwin Brown Firmage, "Eternal Principles of Government: A Theological Approach," *Ensign*, Jun 1976, p. 11).

[11] "And behold I say unto you all that this was a snare of the adversary, which he has laid to catch this people, that he might bring you into subjection unto him, that he might encircle you about with his chains, that he might chain you down to everlasting destruction, according to the power of his captivity" (Alma 12:6).

[12] "Because of the importance of the family to the eternal plan of happiness, Satan makes a major effort to destroy the sanctity of the family, demean the importance of the role of men and women, encourage moral uncleanliness and violations of the sacred law of chastity, and to discourage parents from placing the bearing and rearing of children as one of their highest priorities. So fundamental is the family unit to the plan of salvation that God has declared a warning that those 'individuals who violate covenants of chastity, who abuse spouse or offspring, or who fail to fulfill family responsibilities will one day stand accountable before God [their maker]....The disintegration of the family will bring upon individuals, communities, and nations the calamities foretold by ancient and modern prophets'" (Robert D. Hales, "The Eternal Family," *Ensign*, Nov 1996, p. 64).

[13] "And because of the righteousness of his people, Satan has no power" (1 Nephi 22:26).

[14] "...Let us consider what we should teach. Scriptures direct parents to teach faith in Jesus Christ, repentance, baptism, and the gift of the Holy Ghost. Parents are to teach the plan of salvation and the importance of living in complete accord with the commandments of God. Otherwise, their children will surely suffer in ignorance of God's redeeming and liberating law. Parents should also teach by example how to consecrate their lives—using their time, talents, tithing, and substance to establish the Church and kingdom of God upon the earth. Living in that manner will literally bless their posterity. A scripture states, 'Thy duty is unto the church forever, and this because of thy family'" (Russell M. Nelson, "'Set in Order Thy House'," *Liahona*, Jan 2002, pgs. 80–83).

[15] "The Prophet Joseph Smith declared—and he never taught more comforting doctrine—that the eternal sealings of faithful parents and the divine promises made to them for valiant service in the Cause of Truth, would save not only themselves, but likewise their posterity. 'Though some of the sheep may wander, the eye of the Shepherd is upon them, and sooner or later they will feel the tentacles of Divine Providence reaching out after them and drawing them back to the fold. Either in this life or the life to come, they will return. They will have to pay their debt to justice; they will suffer for their sins; and may tread a thorny path; but if it leads them at last, like the penitent Prodigal, to a loving and forgiving father's heart and home, the painful experience will not have been in vain. Pray for your careless and disobedient children; hold on to them with your faith. Hope on, trust on, till you see the salvation of God'" (Joseph Smith, as quoted by James E. Faust, "Dear Are the Sheep That Have Wandered," *Ensign*, May 2003, p. 61).

[16] "In the churn of crises and the sinister swirl of global events, true disciples will maintain faith in a revealing, loving God and in His plan for redeeming His children, which plan is the why of all that God does! (See Moses 1:39.) ...True disciples will also maintain faith in His atoning Son, Jesus Christ, and, by being 'converted unto the Lord' (3 Ne. 1:22), will be steadily undergoing a happy and 'mighty change' (see Mosiah 5:2; Alma 5:12–14). Actually, brothers and sisters, Jesus is already victorious in the greatest battle anyway: 'In the world ye shall have tribulation: but be of good cheer; I have overcome the world' (John 16:33). '...True believers' (4 Ne. 1:36) will maintain faith in the latter-day Restoration with its empowering visitations, its prophets and apostles, and its 'plain and precious' scriptures (1 Ne. 13:29). ...With scriptures to anchor and reassure us, we, too, can 'look unto God...and he will console [us] in [our] afflictions' (Jacob 3:1). We, too, can be 'supported under trials and troubles of every kind, yea, ... he will still deliver [us]' (see Alma 36:3, 27). For the Lord has said: 'I will be in your midst' (D&C 49:27). 'I will lead you along' (D&C 78:18). Furthermore, God will give us priceless, personal assurances through the Holy Ghost (see John 14:26; D&C 36:2).

Whether in tranquil or turbulent times, our best source of comfort is the Comforter" (Neal A. Maxwell, "Encircled in the Arms of His Love," *Liahona*, Nov 2002, pgs. 16–18).

[17] "Verily, verily, I say unto you, ye must watch and pray always, lest ye be tempted by the devil, and ye be led away captive by him" (3 Nephi 18:15).

Men in White

[18] "We succeed in the Church, by and large, in teaching our members to pray. Even our little ones are taught to fold their arms and bow their heads, and with whispered coaching from their parents and from brothers and sisters, they soon learn to pray. There is one part of prayer—the answer part—that perhaps, by comparison, we neglect....It is difficult to separate from the confusion of life that quiet voice of inspiration. Unless you attune yourself, you will miss it. Answers to prayers come in a quiet way. The scriptures describe that voice of inspiration as a still, small voice. If you really try, you can learn to respond to that voice....There are so many of us who go through life and seldom, if ever, hear that voice of inspiration, because 'the natural man receiveth not the things of the Spirit of God: for they are foolishness unto him: neither can he know them, because they are spiritually discerned' (1 Cor. 2:14). The scriptures have many lessons on this subject. Lehi told his sons of a vision, but Laman and Lemuel resisted his teachings: 'For he truly spake many great things unto them, which were hard to be understood, save a man should inquire of the Lord; and they being hard in their hearts, therefore they did not look unto the Lord as they ought' (1 Ne. 15:3). They complained to their younger brother, Nephi, that they could not understand their father, and Nephi asked this question: 'Have ye inquired of the Lord?' 'And they said unto [him]: We have not; for the Lord maketh no such thing known unto us' (1 Ne. 15:8–9). Later they intended to do Nephi harm and he said to them: 'Ye are swift to do iniquity but slow to remember the Lord your God. Ye have seen an angel, and he spake unto you; yea, ye have heard his voice from time to time; and he hath spoken unto you in a still small voice, but ye were past *feeling,* that ye could not *feel* his words' (1 Ne. 17:45; italics added)" (Boyd K. Packer, "Prayers and Answers," *Ensign*, Nov 1979, p. 19).

CHAPTER NINE

THE LORD PRESERVES

"The LORD is nigh unto all them that call upon him, to all that call upon him in truth. He will fulfill the desire of them that fear him: he also will hear their cry, and will save them. The LORD preserveth all them that love him: but all the wicked will he destroy" (Psalms 145:18–20).

00:03:10, 20:55:02, Zulu
Friday, September 19th

Missed Messages

Provo, Utah
8:05 p.m.

A busy signal rang loudly in Corrynne's ear after she dialed the police chief for the umpteenth time. His phone didn't even allow her to leave a message. Nothing was working right. She put her phone on automatic redial as she walked down the hall to her bedroom.

Passing Carea's room, she peeked in. The bed was untouched and her things weren't strewn on her bed. No. Carea hadn't been home yet.

Suddenly Corrynne's phone jingled, indicating that her call had been successful. Corrynne looked down at it in amazement. She honestly expected it not to work, judging from the way the radio had been acting earlier.

Ducking into Carea's bedroom for privacy, she answered, "Hello?"

"Chief Morgan," said a voice on the other end. The connection was incredibly clear.

"Chief! Hi, this is Corrynne Rogers," she said with urgency, holding the phone with both hands.

"Corrynne. I've been trying to get ahold of you but, as you probably know, all the phones have been out of order due to another round of solar flare emissions."

"Were you calling me about Carea?" asked Corrynne feeling her heart thump in her chest.

"Yes. How did you know?"

Corrynne's heart fell. Jax was right. Feeling the start of a strange numbness swirl around her she said, "One benefit of having many children—many eyes and ears—but you didn't give me the answer I wanted."

"I know. I'm sorry…"

Corrynne shook her head as she listened to the chief's words. It took everything inside her to be calm and listen.

"…Then you know."

"I know what my son told me. He said Carea was taken to jail."

There was a pause and then the chief said, "Yes, she was."

Corrynne took a deep breath and put a shaking hand to her forehead. "How can this be happening, Chief?"

"I'll cut to the chase."

"Please," said Corrynne sitting on the bed so her legs didn't buckle.

"She was arrested, Corrynne, because she's a *Bat*. Tell me how she became involved with the Bats."

Corrynne pressed hard on her forehead. "I—I…" The chief's question caused her head to start pounding. "Chief, I'm sorry. We've been living through a nightmare."

"Considering what I know about you, I'm sure you have been. Fill me in."

Corrynne took a breath and leaned forward with one folded arm across her chest. "I don't know if I can."

"Take a deep breath and try. Remember, I'm your friend," said the chief.

"Alright. What I'm going to tell you, you'll probably have a hard time believing…"

"It's OK. I'll believe you. You know that I will."

"Carea was kidnapped by the Bats six months ago. She was marked and a chip was implanted under the skin of her forehead against her will."

"What? That's the strangest…"

"Hey, you said you'd believe whatever I said," said Corrynne not wanting to defend her statements. She didn't have enough energy.

"Oh, yes, I did, didn't I?"

"Yes, you did," said Corrynne emphatically.

"OK, go ahead," said the chief, sounding resigned.

"Do you remember Elizabeth Smart?" asked Corrynne, looking for an angle the chief would relate to.

"Of course I do."

"Well, I don't know if it was a copycat situation or what, but Imam Mahdi, the religious leader for the Bats, stole her out of her bedroom."

"What?"

"It's true, and for the same reason."

"What? Because he was a fanatical madman?"

"Well, that too—but I was referring to the wife part," said Corrynne, her hand gesturing to help her explain things.

"He stole her to become his *wife*?"

"Yes. I know it sounds so strange, but I swear that's what happened."

"And I didn't know about this?" asked the chief.

"You did. Bo and I filed a missing person's report and you came to our door the next day."

"I did? I don't remember that."

There was a pause. "It doesn't matter now," said Corrynne.

"I'm sorry. I'll have to look that one up…"

"Chief. It's fine."

"I'm glad she came home though. That was good, right?"

"It was good and bad," Corrynne cringed, knowing how insane the next part of the story was going to sound.

"How can Carea coming home, be bad?" asked the chief.

"Having her home was wonderful, but we found out that the chip that she carried was different from everyone else's. It had mind controlling capabilities," said Corrynne.

"Mind controlling capabilities? Am I hearing you right?"

"I know. I know. I'm sorry, but you wanted the story."

"No, Corrynne, don't get me wrong. I'm listening. This just sounds so unusual."

"I know."

"There's something I don't understand."

"What's that?"

"If Carea was kidnapped to become Imam Mahdi's wife, why was she allowed to come home? That's very unusual."

"I don't know," said Corrynne thoughtfully, pulling at her lip and remembering the whole ordeal. "Few things make sense. I'm still unraveling all the details, but I see what you're getting at. You're asking why he didn't just keep her."

"Right," said the chief.

"To be honest, I don't know that answer. Maybe it was to try out his chip on her? To see if he could control her mind to the degree of changing her will? I'm not sure."

"Hmmmm," said the chief. "OK, tell me more about her behavior that made you think the chip was affecting her mind. What did she do that was unusual?"

"She had terrible headaches and wouldn't sleep or eat. Her emotions were very erratic. I just thought she was getting sick, but later I learned that the chip she had in her head was made from a new technology that enabled it to auto-generate little tendril-like projections that wove through her brain. Those tendrils would send electrical pulses to the parts of her mind that controlled the basic functions of her body."

"That's terrible!"

"I agree."

"What would be the purpose of such an elaborate device?" asked Chief Morgan.

"I believe it was to condition her, through negative and positive feedback, toward a desired behavior. The theory is as old as the hills, but using it in conjunction with brain control is new."

"So what particular things did you notice? Give me an example of what you're referring to by 'positive and negative feedback.'"

Corrynne made a heavy sigh. "Chief. This is very hard for me."

"I know Corrynne, but I need to understand this in case it happens again. These things have a way of repeating themselves. I'm taking notes."

Corrynne nodded and pushed forward. "Carea was mercilessly punished by starvation and emotional upheaval for undesirable actions and rewarded by a sense of happiness for desirable ones."

"Whose desirable actions?"

"Imam Mahdi's."

"Was he tracking her? Watching her?"

"Yes. We didn't know it till later, but yes. He knew everything about her. He knew where she was, what she was doing, how she was responding, everything!"

"How?"

"Honestly, that part I don't understand completely either. I'm assuming he filled our house with surveillance devices, although I've never found one, and since our house has been demolished and re-built since then, I'm sure they're all gone."

The police chief groaned and said, "Corrynne, all of this sounds very dangerous."

"I know," said Corrynne, deep in thought, as she reviewed again the things that had happened to Carea. Suddenly, a long sought-after understanding hit her square in the face. *She understood!* In a moment all became clear!

"Now that I think about it, you know what?" Corrynne asked with urgency in her voice.

"What?" asked Chief Morgan.

"It just dawned on me. I know *exactly* why all this happened!"

The chief sounded surprised. "Why?"

"Carea was a guinea pig!"

"What?"

"Yes, think about it, like you said, why *did* they let her return home? Elizabeth Smart wasn't allowed to come home."

"No she wasn't."

"That's why! Imam Mahdi was trying his technology out on her! He kidnapped her, implanted his chip, and let her go to see if she would come back! That's the only thing that makes sense to me. I think the new bride was just a cover for what was really going on."

"Hmmmm," said the chief. "That sounds plausible. But why Carea?"

"Ahhh," Corrynne thought more. Connections were solidifying in her mind. Again, she knew! "Because she was headstrong, but I'm convinced the main reason was—*because she was my daughter*."

"What does that have anything to do with anything?" asked the chief.

"Don't you remember Dr. Page?"

"Yes, the doctor you worked with who..."

"Who created the original chip!" said Corrynne, finishing for the chief. "Meant to do what?" Corrynne waited for the chief, but no answer came. "To control the followers of *Imam Mahdi*, Chief Morgan, remember? A disease was unleashed in their blood stream if they didn't obey? Dr. Page used chemical triggers to cause the chip to punish the followers but they ended up to be less than accurate so there were unintentional victims, remember?"

"Ahhh, I see where you're going with this, yes I remember. The Streptococcus A would eat their flesh."

"Right! So, I bet you Dr. Page tagged Carea for Imam Mahdi as a test subject for a new chip with new abilities, if not for any reason but to torture me."

"Before he died?"

"Sure. I knew his secrets. What better way to control me and who I told, than threaten my children," said Corrynne. "He didn't know then that he wouldn't be around later."

"I see what you're saying," said the chief.

"And wouldn't it make sense that Imam Mahdi would continue Dr. Page's plans, even if he died? I mean, if he already had Carea's information and the plan to use her as a test, why wouldn't he follow through with them?"

There was silence on the line.

"Chief Morgan?"

"I'm here. I'm just thinking about what you've been saying. This is heavy stuff. Did that chip work? Was he able to change her normal behavior? Did he control her mind?"

"Yes, it worked! I didn't recognize Carea when she was home. If Imam Mahdi hadn't been killed, I would worry about what would've become of her."

"Killed? Imam Mahdi isn't dead," said the chief.

Corrynne frowned. "Yes, he is."

"No. I don't watch international news with too much interest but I thought I heard somewhere that he converted to Catholicism."

"Converted?" asked Corrynne. She almost laughed. "Are you talking about the imposter that became the pope?"

"*Imam Mahdi—is the pope?* How did he manage that?"

"I don't know, Chief, but rumor has it a miracle occurred and Imam Mahdi rose from the dead and has assumed his position as leader of the religious world. He's still saying he's all the predicted saviors of the world.

His persona includes Imam Mahdi, the pope, as well as Jesus Christ and Buddha. Don't you watch TV? He's gaining popularity over in Europe and the Eastern world."

"So…Imam Mahdi ended up to be a pretty tricky guy, didn't he?" asked the chief, sounding a little disoriented, as if he was doing two things at the same time.

"No, Imam Mahdi is *dead*, Chief Morgan. The man who claims his name is an *imposter*."

"How do you know?"

"Because I saw a support beam go through his head with my own two eyes, and so did Carea. She was being presented as Imam Mahdi's wife to the people when the earthquake hit."

"The earthquake that caused the dam breach and leveled the riverbottoms?"

"Yes."

"How come I didn't know about this incident either?" asked the chief.

"It happened in Skull Valley on an Indian reservation. You wouldn't be notified. It was out of your jurisdiction."

"Ahhh, that makes sense."

"Also, you were busy pulling people out of the muck after the dam ruptured."

"Good point. I wasn't available for anything else but rescues for a long time after that." Chief Morgan sighed and then said, "OK, I have another question that's slightly off the topic."

"What?" asked Corrynne looking at her watch. Time was growing short. The kids would be finding her soon.

"Since we're talking about Imam Mahdi and his local organization, did Carea ever share with you what role Steve Shale had in Imam Mahdi's organization."

"Why?" asked Corrynne.

"Because I'm getting pressure by the Congressman to release his son from prison. He was carted away just like Carea."

Corrynne felt her breath catch in her throat. "Are you going to do that?" she asked, feeling reality return in the form of stomach pains. She wanted Carea returned, too.

"I can't. I don't have the power they think I do, but he and his political buddies don't believe me."

Corrynne was disappointed, almost to the point of tears. "Then why are you asking?"

"I just want to know if he's as innocent as his father proclaims."

"He's not innocent. He's one person who loved to be a Bat just because it represented rebellion against everything he'd been taught," said Corrynne.

"That's too bad."

"In fact, Steve was the one who delivered Carea to Imam Mahdi."

"Steve kidnapped Carea?"

"No. We still don't know who did that, but we know that Steve picked Carea up for a Rave at the precise moment she left our house in one of her angry fits caused by the chip."

"I see."

"In other words, he was sent for her."

"Hmmmm," said the chief. "It still bothers me that I wasn't told about any of this. For the third time, level with me and tell me the real reason you didn't call me. I deserve that much respect, Corrynne."

The chief's question tore at Corrynne's heart. She was silent for a while as she thought about what to say. A tear fell down her cheek and quickly she brushed it away. "Because it wouldn't have done any good," she said bluntly.

"Why not?"

"Because, she's a teen and she's a girl. If I notified you that she had a chip, you would have just recorded her and deduced she had joined the Bats, despite what I told you. I didn't know all the things I do now."

"I see."

"And at that time, I didn't think she deserved any more stress. She needed to recover from her experiences. As it is, she was just barely getting back to normal before this happened."

"I'm sorry about that," said the chief. "And…I can see your point. You pegged what I would have done very accurately."

"I've seen you in action," said Corrynne with a sigh.

"Yes, I know you have."

"I just thought that I could keep her safe by hiding her chip and use my good relationship with you in combination with the benefit of the doubt in hopes she'd fly under the radar if she was ever discovered."

"I see…and your plan was well thought out, but Corrynne, the one thing you didn't plan on was a Presidential Executive Order."

Corrynne was startled. What was the chief talking about? "Wait. *Executive Order? From the President?*"

"Yes. Of course."

"What Executive Order?" asked Corrynne, frowning.

"I'm sorry, I thought you knew."

"No, I knew about jail, I didn't know about anything else. Why was the President writing an Executive Order committing Carea?" asked Corrynne. Her body was shaking.

"It wasn't just for Carea. Her arrest was part of the State of Emergency precautions."

"Wait!" said Corrynne putting her hand up automatically. "My radio wasn't working today and my television only gets a couple of channels. I've been in the OR, away from everything. What did I miss?"

"Today, orders were given to round up all known violent groups to try and keep the peace during the banking crises."

"What banking crisis?" asked Corrynne putting her hand to her forehead. "Oh my goodness, did the world fall apart in a day?"

"In a way…yes," said the chief.

Corrynne felt a river of tears begin to fall as helplessness engulfed her. "I can't believe this. What happened?"

"The money in the banks has been drained by the International Monetary Fund."

"What? How?"

"I don't understand it all, all I know is that the United States is in full-fledged chaos, the President is nowhere to be found, and every known high-risk violent person, from the Crypts to the Bats, are being taken to secured camps to protect the rest of the people in America."

"And *that's* why the Bats were arrested?" clarified Corrynne.

"Yes. I'm sorry. Carea had a chip in her forehead associated with the Bats. The SWAT team automatically took her in. She's in federal custody."

"And that's why you can't do anything for me or the Congressman's son," said Corrynne, now understanding the chief's powerlessness.

"Right."

Corrynne nodded and folded her arms in emotional surrender as she sat down again on the bed. "So, what's next, Chief?"

"I don't know. I say, just hang tight. There's not much anyone can do at this point but wait and watch where things shake out. I wish I could tell you something different."

Corrynne shook her head as she let herself cry hard, holding the phone out from her face.

"…Corrynne?" called the chief.

Corrynne couldn't answer. She was too upset.

"Corrynne? …Do I need to call back later?"

Corrynne took a deep breath, wiped her face, and shook her hands. Returning the phone to her ear she asked, "Where did they take Carea?"

"Alaska."

Corrynne blinked hard. Was she hearing right? *"Alaska?"* she asked as her voice cracked.

"Yes, they're taking all the Bats from this area to the prison camp in Alaska."

"Until when?" Corrynne felt like she was going to faint as the room began to spin.

"To be honest, I don't know. Nothing in my communication said anything about a release date."

"Can we see her?" she managed to ask.

"No. I'm sorry. I don't believe so."

"We can't even see her?" asked Corrynne, now not hiding her tears anymore.

"No, Corrynne. She's considered a threat. She's being treated the same as a terrorist. She's under the highest security. No one can see her until things cool down. America is under security alert. Everything is locked down."

Corrynne looked up at the ceiling. *"I can't believe this is happening!"*

"I can't believe it either. I'm sorry about it though. I wish there was something I could do. I feel terrible."

Corrynne took another deep breath. With a broken heart, she asked, "If you think of something will you call me?"

"Absolutely."

"The *minute* you hear something."

"Yes."

"OK, thanks," said Corrynne, feeling completely defeated and tired. "I've got to get off the phone, Chief."

"OK. Sorry, Corrynne."

"I know."

"Good-bye."

"Good-bye."

Corrynne closed her phone. She couldn't even think. She had cried hard and now she was numb again. *This is insane!* Those were the only words she could think. They repeated over and over in her head.

Corrynne turned and knelt by the bed. As she did, Carea's perfume filled her nose. A pain of loneliness for her daughter ripped at her heart. "Carea," she said wistfully as she began to cry again.

Shaking her head, she started praying. She needed help. She needed comfort. She needed to know how to go on, how to be a mother, how to be a wife.

After a while Corrynne heard, "Mooooom!" followed by many footsteps.

Corrynne opened her eyes. Her time alone was over. She needed to get back to her family. With a big sigh she stood, brushed Carea's bedspread with a slow, loving touch and then left the room.

Water Travel

Atlantic Ocean
1:30 a.m.

Dane and Nebraska had traveled for over eight hours. Nebraska slept soundly on the floor of the boat under layers of sleeping bags—of the four they'd found, Nebraska had three—and the night continued as smoothly as before.

Dane wore a jacket over his vest to keep warm as he searched the boat thoroughly. It was obvious the man who owned this boat had been well off. It was supplied with the best equipment. But there was one thing he was missing: a map! He wondered if there was a map in one of the compartments and he had just missed it. Now that Nebraska was asleep and there was nothing but open water in front of them, he needed a map to know how to get to Washington, D.C., where they were, and how far they had traveled.

Rummaging once again in a nearby compartment, Dane was rewarded by a fold-out map of the Eastern United States coastline. He laughed with satisfaction as he unfolded it. Then he set to work studying it by the light of the dashboard. What harbor was Washington, D.C., close to? "Let's see, Washington, D.C.... where's Washington, D.C.," he said to himself. "There it is," he said, locating it with his finger. "Wow, it's almost right on the water—no it *is* right on the water, and the White House is located only a mile east of the riverbank!" Dane hadn't realized how close the White House was to the river, but then again, he had never looked. "So I can just drive this boat right to where I need to go," he said, tracing the Potomac River out to the part of the East Coast where he thought he was. "This trip isn't going to be bad at all!"

He let out another satisfied chuckle as he returned his attention to the map. So, how exactly would he get to the White House? With his finger he continued to trace. He saw that the Potomac River was the fourth river off the Chesapeake Bay. He would just follow the river straight to the White House. Then, after he moored the boat, he and Nebraska could just walk a mile.... Dane looked up from his map. "Snap!" he said happily, looking up into the darkness. Something inside clicked. It dawned on him who was at the White House. *Braun was at the White House!* All he would have to do was get to the White House and then Braun could help him do the rest. There'd be food and water and he was sure Braun would help him find Nebraska's grandmother, probably by limo! Dane was ecstatic. All problems solved! Then he could find the nearest base camp and go back to work. This was perfect!

Dane smiled and looked up into heaven. This couldn't have worked out any better if he had tried to plan it! He whispered a thanks.

Dane, basking in the imminent success of his plans, looked over to the land. The electricity was out. It was pitch black except for fires here and there. Every so often he would hear an explosion. He wondered what was happening. Who was attacking who? Who was the enemy and who was the ally? How was the military responding? What would he be doing if he were back on land?

Dane shook his head. He was glad he wasn't on land, although he did feel a little guilty since he wasn't doing his part to protect America from itself. But what choice did he have? If he had been at base camp, he would have been dead. If he hadn't realized he was being poisoned, he would have been dead. If he had landed on his head instead of on his back on that car after the explosion, he would have been dead. So considering all of those things, he thought he was doing pretty well. No one would be looking for him for a while, that was for sure, and if they did, chances are, they would just assume he was—*dead*. So, for the time being, he felt free to help Nebraska get home safely. In his mind, everything was working out for the best.

A stray thought touched his mind. One from earlier, but he hadn't had time to contemplate fully. Now it returned like a boomerang. Who could have gassed a whole city? The great New York, the jewel of America, the United States' symbol of success and freedom? It was such a tragedy! So many people gone in just seconds![1] And did the gassing have anything to do with the banks losing all their money? Dane thought about that for a moment. ...It did seem coincidental that they both happened at the same time, too much of a coincidence—but if there was a connection, what could it have been?[2] The most obvious choice would be to blame it on the Middle Eastern radicals,[3] but was that too easy? It seemed too obvious to him, but then again...he didn't know enough about politics and the international environment to make any judgments. He'd give anything to see the news. He bet it was brimming full of information. He imagined news channels in every store, in every home in America tuned into New York, just like it had been on 9-11.

Then it hit him. If the news was focused on New York, what would his parents think? Would they think he was dead too? Oh, that would be painful for them. Dane frowned. He couldn't cause them that much pain. He had to call them as soon as possible to stop them from worrying. He wished he had a cell phone, but he didn't. He had washed it in his clothes a few weeks ago. That was probably the most stupid thing he'd ever done in his life, but it happened. Dane shook his head. OK, that was enough. He couldn't think about his parents any more. It wouldn't do any good. He'd call them when he could.

"Next," said Dane in a sigh. He didn't want to think of anything depressing any more. "What about this boat...." Again, Dane rummaged in the storage compartments in the bow of the ship. He found an owner's manual. "Bingo!" he said happily.

Dane started flipping the pages. "OK, this is a Kachina Drone 34 Sport Boat. It was built in 2009—a few years ago, but working fine," he said as he patted the dashboard. "Now let's see how many gallons of gas this baby holds." Dane flipped more pages until he saw what he was looking for. "Whoa!" exclaimed Dane in whispered astonishment. He couldn't believe what he was reading. This boat's fuel capacity was 200 gallons![4] But the bad news was it tended to only get six miles to the gallon. "Ooooh, that's not good," Dane said to himself, shaking his head. Then he read that the boat ran the best when it was run at about 4,000 RPMs. Anything higher or lower than that reduced the boat's efficiency. Dane looked down at his gages. He was running the boat about 4,500 RPMs. He hadn't been running it that high the whole time, but lately he thought he would turn it up a notch. With a bump of his fist, he slowed the throttle down, taking it down to 36 miles per hour.

Dane looked back at his map. So how many miles over the water was he going to have to travel to get to the Capital, after traveling down the East Coast, up the bay, and into the Potomac River? He looked at the key of the map. Every inch and a half was a hundred miles. With his fingers he estimated how far it would be. It took him four inch-and-a-half lengths to travel along his planned route. That meant it was about 400 miles! That was twice what he expected! A feeling of doom grew in his gut. What if the boat didn't make it? That would be horrible! What would he do? He didn't have enough food to walk any length of distance with Nebraska.

Quickly Dane did the math. If this boat achieved six miles to the gallon, that would mean he would need approximately 66 gallons to go 400 miles. He looked down at the gage that now demonstrated the boat was half empty. If he had been traveling approximately eight hours, that meant he had traveled 288 miles already. OK, that part sounded good. If his estimations were right, he had only used 48 gallons, and that would make sense, because when he found the boat, it had three-quarters of a tank left, and that would be 150 gallons. Half of 200 was 100, and 100 plus 48 was approximately 150! Dane felt good. Again, things were working in his favor. So, how much would he need to get to Washington, D.C., from here? Well, 400 minus 288 was…112 miles remaining of their trip. And 112 miles divided by 36 was…3 hours! They were almost there! Dane felt like jumping for joy! They'd have more than enough gas! That was a relief!

Then Dane had a thought. If they had already traveled 288 miles, when would he turn up Chesapeake Bay? Dane searched the coast line. He realized he couldn't see buildings any longer. In fact, he couldn't see the land either. Where was he? *Had he accidentally gone out to sea?* Fear started to grow inside him. It wouldn't matter how much gas he had if he had been going the wrong direction!

Dane looked down at the compass that moved erratically on the dashboard of the boat. He knew from being in the military that the compass wasn't as dependable a tool to identify direction as it was once thought to be.[5] He had been taught that the magnetic north pole was wandering, moving 40 km per year,[6] but not only that, new magnetic poles were appearing all over the world.[7] There were even places in the Atlantic Ocean where the magnetic strength of the earth had almost disappeared,[8] and since he was driving the boat in the Atlantic Ocean, he didn't trust anything the compass said.

Dane looked up in the sky. There was more than one way to figure out direction! "Let's see…where's the North Star?" he asked out loud. He located the Big Dipper. It was behind him in the sky. Next, he traced an imaginary line from the two stars that made the broader side of the bowl to the brightest star just beyond it. "There you are," he said. There was the North Star. It was behind him and to the east. Good. That meant he was going south west; just where he wanted to go.

Despite his assurances, Dane turned the steering wheel to the right. He watched the North Star approach the starboard side of his boat. This would confirm that he was going west in the dark, towards land. It was time to go ashore to figure out just where he was. Calculations aside, there was nothing like assurances. And it was time for one.

Nenets

Yamal Peninsula, Russia
11:00 a.m.

Braun and Chenille rode swiftly across the tundra on a fresh coat of snow. They were sitting bundled with furs, in a sleigh led by strong, galloping reindeer. Silently, they listened to the drivers shouting commands and watched as they poked and tapped the reindeer's sides with wooden poles that looked like lances knights might use.

"How do these men know where to go?" Chenille whispered into Braun's ear.

Braun looked out at the flat land. The open tundra seemed to never end and the air was bitterly cold. Braun breathed hot air into his mask to warm his nose and mouth. Then he shook his head. "I have no idea, but I'm glad they do.'

"I see some tee-pees," exclaimed Chenille, as she pointed.

Braun looked carefully across the snow. Then he saw them too. There were about five specks on the snow in front of them. "Do you think that's where we're going?" he asked.

Chenille looked at Braun and said, "I think five homes would make a town out here."

"You think?" asked Braun looking back at the cone-shaped tents. Then he shrugged, "I don't care what it is, as long as they have food."

"I hope they have *edible* food," said Chenille with a grimace.

Braun had to laugh. "That's right. You didn't serve a mission, did you?"

Chenille looked at Braun with a question in her eyes.

Braun continued, "Food is food."

"I don't know about that."

"When in Rome, eat as the Romans eat," said Braun. "Anything is better than nothing."

"Oh," said Chenille, nodding. "I agree. I'm starved. I'm just anticipating a culture shock."

Braun laughed and hugged Chenille. "I love you," he said, almost automatically. He was grateful that if he had to be lost in a land of nothing, Chenille was with him.

Chenille smiled wistfully. Whatever she was thinking, she kept it to herself.

The reindeer slowed as they approached a tee-pee with wood piled high outside and smoke billowing generously out the top. Braun looked around. Where would these people get wood? He hadn't seen a tree for miles. Despite that, there it was, piled high in neat rows.

"Choom," said the first man to Braun and Chenille.

"Choom?" asked Chenille.

The man nodded and pointed to the tee-pee and repeated himself. "Choom."

"Is that the people's name or the tent's name?" Chenille asked Braun quietly.

Braun shook his head. "Got me."

A young man, a woman, and three children gathered excitedly around the sled as if Braun and Chenille were long-lost relatives. The mother and children gave Braun and Chenille generous hugs while the young man waited his turn.

Braun's eyes met the young stranger's, but they didn't feel strange. They felt familiar, almost as if Braun was having a powerful déjà-vu. For an instant he remembered not only this man's looks, but he knew this man's person, his being—but how could that be? He was in the Arctic. He had never met this man in his life—ever! Or had he...there was a feeling that...maybe he had? Braun dismissed his thoughts. They were impossible.

"Welcome to the Yamal Peninsula," the stranger said in perfect English, extending a friendly, firm handshake. "Yamal is translated to mean the 'end of the earth.' I hope you'll enjoy it here at the Arctic Circle."

"Thank you. Are you responsible for bringing us here?" asked Braun.

The man nodded.

"We are so grateful for your kindness!" said Chenille wrapping her arms around herself to diminish the effects of the cold. "We had run out of food and didn't know the way to safety."

"I'm glad we helped," said the man.

"How did our rescuer know my name?" asked Braun, casting a brief look back towards the driver.

"I told him your name."

"How did *you* know?" asked Braun.

"Shamen know many things of the Spirit."

"Would the spirit happen to be named Matthew Daimler?" asked Braun with a smile.

"No, the Spirit has no name other than what describes what he is."

Braun and Chenille looked at each other with a puzzled stare. "So you don't know Matt?" asked Chenille. "He didn't tell you to save us?"

"I don't know a man with that name. Let's go into the tent," said the man ducking into the skin-covered structure. "Take off your outer boots right inside the door," he said pointing down before he entered.

Chenille followed the stranger.

Braun moved too, but then stopped to thank his rescuers—however—they were gone. ...*Gone?* he wondered. How did that happen? When did they leave? Braun didn't hear them go!

In confusion Braun back tracked to study the marks of the sled and reindeer in the snow. He located the tracks leading up to the tent, but none leaving. Perfect snow lay in every other direction. That was very strange. Braun took a couple more moments to look around, making sure he wasn't missing something. He wasn't. The landscape was completely empty. "That's bizarre," he said to himself. "Appear out of nowhere and disappear into thin air." Braun shivered a little as his question remained unanswered. The men were real, weren't they? He pinched himself. Yes, he was awake. Shaking his head he decided to join the others and ducked into the entrance of the tent.

Braun took off his boots and stood in his stocking feet on a dark reindeer skin as the young man, the family, and Chenille were talking in the middle of the tent. It looked to Braun as if the young man was explaining to Chenille the tribal décor of this home.

"Ah, Braun," said the young man. "Let's all have a seat around the stove," he said with his hand out. "I'm sure you're cold."

Braun did as he was told as he continued to process all his thoughts. He sat in front of the family's only black, flat-topped wood stove. It had a chimney that reached out of the top of the tee-pee.

"Aren't those other men going to come in and eat with us?" asked Chenille gesturing to the door of the tee-pee.

"No," said the young man. "They need to go back to the village where they live, out among the Chukchi."

"They're already gone," interjected Braun with a pointed stare.

Chenille looked at him questioningly and then turned back to their host as she too found a place to sit. "So is the Chuckchi a group of people?"

"It is," said the young man, sitting also.

"Do they live close by?" asked Braun, beyond suspicious.

"No, it's a ways off, but it won't take them more than a moment to get there."

Braun thought about this man's answer. It wouldn't take more than a moment to get there? Considering how the tracks of a sleigh, reindeer, and two men just disappeared, he decided to probe. "So when you say a 'moment,' does that mean a day, a couple hours, a minute…"

The man considered his answer and then said, "No, I mean a moment."

"A moment," said Braun thinking deep, as unusual possibilities began to play out in his mind.

"Is this your family?" asked Chenille.

The man looked at the children lovingly, who were also taking seats around the stove. With a hand he patted the oldest boy's hat that was closest to him and said, "Yes, they are *of* my family, but no, they are not *my* family."

Chenille looked at Braun in confusion.

Braun missed the statement all together. He was too caught up in his thoughts. He shrugged helplessly in response to Chenille's stare.

"What do you mean?" asked Chenille turning back to the shaman.

"These people are distantly related to me. I'm their spiritual leader. I lead them to truth. This particular family is just learning of that truth."

"Do you have a name we can call you?" asked Chenille.

"My given name is John Zebedee."

"John Zebedee..." said Braun slowly, frowning. That name rang a bell. Where had he heard it before? "John Zebedee," he whispered quietly, trying to remember.

"It's wonderful to meet you," said Chenille in her public relations voice.

"It's good to meet you, too," said John.

"John, huh?" asked Braun again, still processing, but not wanting to make outlandish assumptions and be thought of as rude. "That's a strong English name. How did you get that name way out here?" he asked looking for more clues.

"Actually, the name is Hebrew meaning 'God is gracious.'"

"Hebrew?" asked Chenille sitting up. "You know about the Hebrews?"

"Yes," said John. "I teach the gospel."

Braun raised an eyebrow. "The gospel?" he asked. That was a strange word for a tribal man to use. This whole situation was becoming stranger and stranger.

"You're a Christian preacher?" asked Chenille, as the woman handed her a piece of bread. Chenille smiled and nodded to thank the woman who continued to hand more bread out to the rest of the group.

John looked at Braun and Chenille and nodded. "Yes, if you mean, 'do I preach of Christ?' then the answer is 'yes'. I'm a Christian preacher."

"Is that your job?" asked Chenille.

"Job?" asked John.

"Your employment," clarified Chenille. "The way you make money."

John shook his head. "No, I have no use for money. There was a time that I used to be a fisherman, but I've long since given that up."

"So how did you come to learn English?" asked Braun, continuing to probe. "I hope you don't mind me asking so many questions."

John shook his head. "No, please ask as many questions as you like." Then he took a deep breath and said, "I speak many languages. If you speak it, I speak it."

Chenille looked like she was waiting for the punch line, but there wasn't any. "If we speak it, you speak it?"

"I mean, I have a gift for languages."

"So does Braun," offered Chenille with a smile.

John looked at Braun. "You do?"

Braun's eyebrows arched. "Well, I spoke Spanish on my mission. Other than that, I don't speak any other languages."

"Spanish," said John thoughtfully. "That will be useful. There are many of our relations that we haven't met yet, who speak that language."

Braun nodded. "People speak Spanish up here?" he asked, thinking that was odd.

John shook his head. "No, not here. We will go to those that speak Spanish."

"How?" asked Braun.

"We'll walk."

"Oh," he said, feeling dumbfounded. "Ah, Chenille, may I speak with you outside?"

Chenille smiled apologetically. "Why?" she asked under her breath.

"I just need to talk to you," he said motioning to the door to the tent with intensity.

"We'll be right back," she said as she stood with an apologetic smile.

Both Braun and Chenille put on their boots and exited the tent.

Notes to "The Lord Preserves"

Water Travel

[1] The way this storyline is designed is directly from the statements of the prophets and the scriptures. New York is identified as one city that will be hit by the calamities of the last days.

"Their great and magnificent cities are to be cut off. New York, Boston, Albany and numerous other cities will be left desolate..." (Orson Pratt, *Millennial Star*, October 6 1866, Vol. 28, pgs. 633–634).

Another quote from a dream that John Taylor experienced and was recorded in Wilford Woodruff's journal describes something in the air in New York that seems to cause men to die after a very short period of exposure. Considering the modern day chemical warfare capacities, the "disease" described in this quote could very well have been a deadly gas, a substance that wasn't in existence when John Taylor recorded his dream in 1877. The effects of Sarin, Tabun, or Soman would cause the body to die quickly (1–10 minutes), and since its chemical makeup is denser than air, it would hover over the ground level of any city exposed to it. See the following:

"I next found myself in Broadway, New York and there it seemed the people had done their best to overcome the disease. But in wandering down Broadway I saw the bodies of beautiful women lying stone dead and others in a dying condition on the sidewalk. I saw men crawl out of the cellars and rob the dead bodies of the valuables they had on and before they could return to their coverts in the cellars they themselves would roll over a time or two and die in agony..." (*Journal of Wilford Woodruff*, p. 180).

[2] In researching the last days, it seems that the devastation that occurs in America comes from within. Almost every prophecy concerning American troubles discusses the fighting as state comes up against state, city comes up against city, and so forth. However, there are statements of prophets that allude to the involvement of other nations in our destruction. See the following:

"You have scarcely yet read the preface of your national troubles. Many nations will be drawn into the American maelstrom [violent whirlpool] that now whirls through the land; [note: aren't most of our political troubles involving other nations today?] and after many days, when the demon of war [internal strife, as stated in other prophecies and scriptures, and/or, Satan, and/or secret combinations] shall have exhausted his strength and madness upon the American soil, by the destruction of all that can court or provoke opposition, excite cupidity, inspire revenge, or feed ambition, he will remove his headquarters to the banks of the Rhine [Rhine river, located in West Germany, one of the founding nations of the European Union, and member of the G-8 today]" (Orson Hyde, *Millennial Star*, May 3, 1862, Vol. 24, p. 274).

Could it be that just as in the text of this book, and as stated clearly in the scriptures quoted other places in this book, that other nations passively and secretly sow America's internal destruction while giving the impression of world peace? Review the following scripture discussing the strength of a secret entity that takes ultimate control of the nations.

"And through his policy also he shall cause craft to prosper in his hand; and he shall magnify himself in his heart, and by peace shall destroy many: he shall also stand up against the Prince of princes; but he shall be broken without hand" (Daniel 8:25).

[3] It is common knowledge that the Islamic nation is anti-American. Often they are looked to for the source of future attacks. Whether or not they will be is unknown. However the question may be asked why? Why do the Middle Eastern people hate Americans so much? The situation is described in a nutshell below:

"To Muslims generally, and to militant Middle Eastern Muslims particularly, the United States has done too many things to be qualified as an enemy subject to the Islamic law of war. The United States, for example, has bombed Libya, the Sudan and Afghanistan. The attacks on Iraq continue. American bombers have 'terrorized' major Arab cities: Baghdad, Tripoli and Khartoum. Several Muslim States, including Syria and Iran, are on the US list of terrorist states. The United States politicians demonize Islamic leaders but embrace undemocratic rulers, such as the ones in Algeria. To add to this all, the US troops are stationed not too far away from Mecca and Medina, the holiest cities of Islam.

"The militants see more than the US bombing of Muslim countries. They see that the United States has imposed economic sanctions against almost the entire Islamic world. Even Islamic states, such as Pakistan, which have supported the United States in its wars, are not immune from economic sanctions. Perhaps, the most serious case is Iraq where the economic sanctions have resulted in the death of thousands of children, for want of medical facilities. The rest of the international community is willing to lift these sanctions. But the United States continues to exercise its veto.

"For Muslims who hate the United States, the most dramatic scenes come from the Israeli siege of Palestinians. There is a general perception among Muslims that the United States has failed to be a neutral peacemaker in this conflict. In fact, they conclude that Israel will be much more willing to end its occupation if the United States withdrew its money and weapons. Thus, the militants see the United States as the ultimate enemy against the liberation of Israeli occupied territories. This perception is further reinforced when the United States openly supports Israel in its public statements and blocks Security Council resolutions that might benefit the Palestinians, resolutions such as stationing international observers around the occupied territories" (Professor Ali Khan, Washburn University School of Law, "Attack on America: An Islamic perspective," *Jurist, Legal Intelligence*, http://jurist.law.pitt.edu/forum/forumnew29.htm).

[4] This boat can be researched at http://www.travelizmo.com/archives/000621.html.

[5] "At most places on the Earth's surface, the compass doesn't point exactly toward geographic north. The deviation of the compass from true north is an angle called 'declination'. It is a quantity that has been a nuisance to navigators for centuries, especially since it varies with both geographic location and time. It might surprise you to know that at very high latitudes the compass can even point south! Declination is simply a manifestation of the complexity of the geomagnetic field. The field is not perfectly symmetrical, it has non-dipolar 'ingredients', and the dipole itself is not perfectly aligned with the rotational axis of the Earth" (*National Geomagnetism Program*, "What is declination?" http://geomag.usgs.gov/faqs.php#qone).

[6] "During the last century the Pole has moved a remarkable 1100 km. What is more, since about 1970 the NMP [North Magnetic Pole] has accelerated and is now moving at more than 40 km per year. If the NMP maintains its present speed and direction it will reach Siberia in about 50 years" (*Geological Survey of Canada*, "Geomagnetism: Long Term Movement of the North Magnetic Pole," http://gsc.nrcan.gc.ca/geomag/nmp/long_mvt_nmp_e.php).

[7] "The magnetic field is created by a complex interaction involving a churning, electrically conducting liquid metal outer core, the release of heat at the surface of the solid inner core,

and the spinning motion of the Earth.. .The Earth's magnetic field is not uniform. The intensity and direction of the field changes not only from one location to another, but over time as well....Additional north and south poles appear at the core. These additional poles may not appear at the Earth's surface—at least not initially—though these islands of reversed polarity can weaken the overall magnetic field strength" (*Nova*, "Magnetic Storm," http://www.pbs.org/wgbh/nova/magnetic/reve-04n.html).

[8] Beneath the South Atlantic, science has found a region of magnetic anomalies, places where the magnetic field is already beginning to reverse, and these anomalies are growing:

"We've seen very abrupt changes in the Earth's magnetic field beneath the South Atlantic Ocean....As we get into the beginning of the 20th century, we see the emergence of a new patch of reverse flux, a region where the field lines, instead of coming out of the core, are looping back into the core. And that patch then drifts towards the west, hooking up with [another] patch of reverse flux to create a large region of what we call the 'South Atlantic anomaly' where the field is about 30 percent weaker. And that patch has grown substantially during the last hundred years in particular" (*Nova*, "Magnetic Storm Transcripts," http://www.pbs.org/wgbh/nova/transcripts/3016_magnetic.html).

CHAPTER TEN

WITNESS

"The same came for a witness to bear witness of the Light, that all men through him might believe. He was not that Light, but was sent to bear witness of that Light" (John 1:7–8).

00:03:10, 16:46:52, Zulu
Saturday, September 20th

News Update

Chesapeake Bay, Maryland
2:14 a.m.

Dane slowed the motor as he let the boat coast. He was looking for someone, *anyone*, to ask directions. Now, except for which way he was headed, he was lost. The night had been so black he was unsure of which bay of the four along the Chesapeake he had turned into. He couldn't afford to waste any gas so asking someone, he thought, was the best idea.

Aside from occasional fires burning on the land, sending their flickering light up into the sky, Dane noticed a single, consistent dim glow. It was very low to the water and he could see someone moving within it. As he approached, he noticed that the light was shining from the underside of a dock. That was strange. Could someone be repairing the dock at this hour? It seemed improbable, but maybe. More likely, considering all the fighting that was going on, someone was probably *hiding* under the dock rather than working on it.

Dane turned off the motor and let the boat coast slowly into the docking area. He didn't want to frighten away whoever was under there. He needed directions and it seemed like this person was the only one out tonight.

As the boat quietly approached, Dane could see an old man covered in rubber fishing gear. He was leaning over the water and studying it as he sat on a wooden ledge under the dock. In the man's hand was a string, or a line of some sort. He was carefully pulling it hand over hand, out of the depths of the bay.

"Hello there," Dane said quietly, when he was within talking distance. He didn't want to wake Nebraska.

The old man looked up with a start. Then with an angry face he shoved his hand into a pocket and pointed a finger, as if he had a gun. *"Go away! These are my crabs! You git! Ya hear? You git or I'll shoot ya."*

Dane held up his hands and said, "I don't want your crabs. I just want to ask you for directions."

The old man looked around for other boats, and then said, "I pay my taxes. I live the laws. I keep to myself. Don't harass me!"

Dane looked down. This man thought he was acting in an official duty because of his military uniform. "No, no, no, I'm off duty. I'm not here for any other reason but to ask directions. You're the only person around it seems, so if you don't mind, I have to get a little girl to her grandmother. Just point me in the right direction."

With a grimace and profuse mumbling, the old man wrapped his line around a nail sticking out of the wooden seat he was perched on. After taking off his fishing hat, scratching his head, then replacing his hat he asked, "Where's this little girl?"

Dane pointed to the floor. "She's asleep. Keep your voice low."

The man got to his feet, stooped low so he didn't hit his head on the dock, and limped out on a thin wide plank that was secured to the bottom of his seat. The plank bowed with his weight, but the old man didn't seem to be bothered. He took a hand and steadied himself with the support beam of the dock that grazed his head. Then, finally close to the boat, he bent over so he could see into the hull. "Where is she?"

"Right here, by me," said Dane. "There's her blonde hair sticking out of her sleeping bag."

The old man nodded. "How do I know she ain't dead and this is all a ploy?"

Dane pulled back the covers. "See? She's breathing. She's just sleeping."

After studying the little girl, the old man stood up and said, "OK, I believe ya. How old is she?"

"She's about five," said Dane. "I rescued her out of a sewer. Her brother thought it was a funny joke to leave her there. He had told her he wanted to play hide-and-go-seek."

"Where's her parents?"

"I couldn't locate them. It's possible that they're dead."

"Hmmm," said the old man, then he looked at Dane. "So where're you going?"

"I'm going to Washington, D.C. This little girl has a grandmother that lives there."

The man shook his head. "I wouldn't take her there. Tarnation! The whole city's one big mob. She's likely to be killed. It's no place for children."

"The whole city's a mob? What do you mean?"

"Where've you been, son?"

"I've been on this boat in the dark for nine or so hours. I don't know what's going on. Tell me."

"The banks have all closed. The media says there's no money in 'em."

"Yeah, the same thing happened in New York," said Dane.

"They did heres too. It was like the Depression all over, people bawling about their life savings." The man put up a hand and said, as if in confidence, "I never trusted banks since the first time they took my Pa's money back in 1929, so I took *precautions*." The man smiled, showing his rotten teeth, with a wink. "If you know what I mean."

"You stashed your money?" asked Dane.

"Shhh," said the man as he looked around. "Don't say that too loud."

"OK," said Dane looking around, too.

Then the fisherman came very close and said, "I stashed my money somewheres no one would be able to find it."

"Good for you. So you still have your money?"

"Every last dime of it."

"That's great."

"I have to take care of myself," said the old man.

"Of course you do. So tell me about D.C.," suggested Dane. "What's going on there?" The old man was getting off the topic.

"Well, I hears the President's miss'n."

"She is?"

"Yep. Rumors are that she's been killed."

"Where's the Vice President?"

"In some bunker like a little coward. He's hiding. I say if you ruin the country, you should stand up and take responsibility for it. I know I'd like a swing at him."

"I see," said Dane. "So why is it so dark? Where's all the lights?"

"Oh, that's part of a curfew the government's tryin'."

"Curfew?" asked Dane. "That must be a new thing."

The old man continued, "Yep. Supposed to keep the people in their houses."

"I see," said Dane.

"Anyways, the power goes out around 6 p.m. and doesn't come back on until 6 a.m. If there aren't any lights, the politicians think we can't see." Then the old man started laughing and pointed to his head. "But I's outsmarted them. I got a generator! I can see any time I want to."

Dane nodded. "That's smart. So is the darkness to discourage mobs?"

"Yep and it has, except for around the White House. Demonstrators built bonfires with furniture from houses. Then someone blew the place up with something like C-4, I imagine. You can read about that stuff on the Internet, at least you could when it was working. Ain't that stupid?"

"Yes, that's stupid. So you're saying the White House has been destroyed?" asked Dane with a gulp.

"Yep. You should see it. The roof is nearly clean blown off."

Dane was shocked. What had happened to Braun? "Did you hear if anyone was hurt inside?"

The old man shook his head. "Nah, all them rich folk had long gone underground. The building was empty."

Dane nodded as relief flowed through him. He was sure Braun would have left the building when it came under attack. Maybe he was with the Vice President.

"So I wouldn't go to D.C.," continued the old man.

Dane looked down at Nebraska's sleeping form. "I have to. I have to do something. It'd be best if I found the grandmother. This little girl needs to be with her family."

"Do you know where her family is?" asked the old man.

"Not a clue. That's why I have to find her grandmother."

"I've got a phone book of D.C. Let's look the woman up."

"That would be great," said Dane as he tied his boat around the mooring hook on the dock. It looked like he was going to stay for a few more minutes.

The old man limped back along the plank then climbed up the pole on the far side. There must have been a hole in the dock because within minutes, the old fisherman was on top. With a wobble, the man disappeared behind a building.

While the man was gone, Dane tried to figure out what he was doing under the dock in the middle of the night. He had said something about crabs.

Dane studied the set-up under the dock. There were empty wire mesh boxes that sat haphazardly on the wood ledge that obviously the man had made for himself. There was a bucket with something pink and slimy in it, then a string-like line that disappeared into the water. Dane concluded that he was probably trying to catch crab, since he told Dane he couldn't have any.

"Hmmm," said Dane quietly. "Crab is good," he said as his stomach grumbled. Wouldn't it be great to have some right about now?

After a few minutes the old man hobbled back. He climbed down the hole in the dock, and then approached the boat with a beat-up book that was fat and wrinkled. The first few pages were covered with stinky, fish-smelling stains.

"Here's the book. I've used the yellow pages to wrap bait in, but the white pages still are readable."

Dane took the book and thumbed through it. "What year was this printed?"

"Ahh," said the old man, taking it back and looking for the answer. Obviously not finding it he said, "It's in the two-thousands, I'm sure."

Dane smiled at the man. He was trying to be helpful. "Thank you very much."

"What's the tyke's grandma's name?"

"Jenkins," said Dane. "That's all I know.

The man nodded. "That shouldn't be too hard to find," he said as he started flipping through the pages.

"So tell me," said Dane. "You're fishing for crab, right? You're crabbing?"

The man smiled. "Yes, sir—ee. Blue crab. The best crab you've ever tasted on the Chesapeake!" as he thumbed through the pages.

"So, how do you do that?" asked Dane.

The old man handed the book back to Dane. "My eyes are bad. You'll have to look. While you look, I'll show you how to crab."

"Great!" said Dane feeling like he had hit the jackpot.

The man turned back and hobbled to his wooden seat. Picking up a wire mesh box he hobbled back. "This here's how you catch those buggers."

Dane looked at the box. It looked like it had compartments and levels.

"It's a crab pot," said the man. "You see, the crab crawls in one of these four funnel shaped holes to get the bait. It squeezes through the large end but then once in, it can't get back out," he said as he pointed to four long openings in the box that narrowed as they lead into the center. "It's made with chicken wire."

"I see," said Dane nodding.

"You put the bait in the small square in the center. The mesh is too fine to let the crabs get to the bait so it's never eaten."

"Ahh, smart," said Dane.

"Saves on cost!" said the man, again tapping his head.

"Right," said Dane.

"Then the crabs try to get away but they can't so they go to the only place they can. They go upstairs in this box through another funnel, but because the opening narrows at the end, they can't get out again."

"Why do you want them to do that?" asked Dane.

"So you can catch more crabs as they enter the pot for their try at the bait."

"I see, so you can catch more than one crab with one pot."

"Sure, you can catch four or five," said the fisherman.

"What do you use for bait?"

"I use chicken parts that the restaurants throw away, but you can use almost any kind of meat. The chicken neck is the best."

"I see. This is a pretty slick set up."

"Ya don't always have to have a pot to catch crab though."

"You don't?"

"No. You can tie bait to a line that reaches the bottom of the bay with a weight attached and slowly lower it into the water. When ya feel a nibble, slowly raise the line to the surface. You've got to go slowly and try not to scare the crab. Then when the crab is close to the top of the water, use something to scoop 'em out of the water. They'll be clinging to the end of your line when you bring it up."

"Are there a lot of crabs around here?" asked Dane.

"Yes. That's the secret of our bay. They're everywhere."

"May I buy one of your traps?"

The old man looked at Dane sideways. "Do you have money?"

Dane fished for his wallet and then opened it. "I have twenty bucks."

"I'll take it," said the old man snatching the bill from Dane's hand and shoving it deep in his pocket. Then he hobbled back to his ledge, stirred around in a cardboard box, and then brought Dane a pot, a line, and a chicken neck. "This should get you started."

"That's great! Where should I lower this crab pot first?"

"Crabs live in places where the tide meets the river."

"How do I know when that happens?"

"In bays, like this one is wheres that happens."

"OK," said Dane nodding.

"There's signs all over this bay that will tell ya, too."

"Oh, that's good to know."

"The signs have red borders with black writing. They have pictures of crabs," said the old man.

"Great. Can I just drop this cage off my boat?"

"Yes, or off a dock. But you have to hide your line if you're going to drop it off a dock and leave it. People steal crab pots."

"Is that why you're out here in the middle of the night under a dock?"

"Yes," said the old man tapping his head again. "I drop my pots at night and come back the next night. I do it under the dock so no one sees me. You have to be sly."

Dane took mental note of everything the man told him. He had a feeling he'd need it. "Well, thank you so much!"

"You're welcome. Good luck in finding that grandmother."

"Oh, I almost forgot to ask. Which way to the Potomac River?"

"It's right over that way," said the old man pointing. "Up northwest for about four miles. At the mouth of that river is a good place to crab."

"Great! Thank you!" said Dane again as he untied his boat and slowly accelerated. "It's been good talking to you."

"You too, son."

With a wave over his head Dane started his motor and accelerated. Boy was he thankful he had stopped!

ξξξξξξξ

Dane drove the boat in silence, just barely turning onto the Potomac River, and was feeling concerned. What should he do? Should he go to Washington, or not? Would it be worth his time and the gas he would use if he couldn't find Braun? What if the grandmother couldn't be found?

Dane gazed at the ripped-up phone book he had tossed onto the seat next to him. Idly, he picked it up again and flipped to the letter J. He would look for the grandmother. How many Jenkins could there be? With the dim light of the console, he skimmed the names in the book with his finger until he came to the name Jenkins.

"What?" he gasped, breathlessly. The name Jenkins went on forever! It was three pages long! Not only that, there were "Jankins," "Jinkins," "Jenkyns," and every other spelling of the name he could imagine. Which spelling would it be? But not only that, what was the grandmother's first name? Was she married? Could the name be under her husband's name instead of hers? In frustration he shook his head as he flipped the pages back and forth. What was he thinking? Now he realized that finding Nebraska's grandmother would be nearly impossible, especially if he couldn't find Braun.

Dane was becoming angry. He slowed the motor down to just an idle. *Where was he going?* He had been so bent on reaching Washington, D.C. that he realized he hadn't thought things through completely. He didn't want to waste another ounce of gas until he figured things out.

Dane imagined mooring the boat in D.C. What next? His original plan was to get out of the boat with Nebraska and go to the White House, but now, there was nothing left for him at the White House. What should he do? He didn't have a car. If the city really was in as much turmoil as the old man had said, there wouldn't be any buses. He couldn't just carry Nebraska through the streets of a mobbing, warring city, and with all those Jenkins in the phone book he wouldn't even know where to go!

Then there would be police and barricades surrounding the White House if it had been attacked as the old man had said. He knew the disaster protocol. Dane knew he could get through the barricades just by showing his ID to other soldiers, but then what? And what about this boat? If he moored it, it wouldn't be there when he got back. He was sure it wouldn't be. It would be poor planning to leave a boat like this just out in the open. The boat was his key to safety for Nebraska, plus, he still had a third of a gas tank left. That was approximately 70 gallons. He could go 400 plus more miles on that! No. Dane shook his head as he made a swift turn. "No go. Won't work," he said to himself. "Got to cut my losses."

After turning the boat around he set about finding a crabbing place along the bank. He was hungry. He'd drop his crab pot off the side of the boat while he caught some winks. Then he'd be doing two things at the same time. Yes. That was good. He had to hurry. Nebraska would be waking up soon.

He'd worry about the next step later. He was too tired to think any more.

John

Yamal Peninsula, Russia
11:46 a.m.

"Tell me what's so important that we have to come out here in the freezing cold?" asked Chenille, shivering, once she and Braun were out of the tent and beyond earshot.

"Chenille! I'm getting strange feelings from the people inside that tent," said Braun pointing with energy.

"Why? That's ridiculous! These people saved our lives! They're good people!"

"I know, I know!" said Braun with a hand now to his brow. "They aren't *bad* feelings, they're just…"

"What?"

"Bear with me here," he said looking into Chenille's eyes. "I have to run something by you."

"What is it?"

"Strange things are happening around here, don't you see them?"

Chenille shook her head. "No."

"What about those men that just appeared when we prayed."

"That was a miracle, plain and simple!" said Chenille.

"No, we didn't hear them approach, we didn't see them in any direction before we prayed, and our prayer wasn't long enough for them to walk across the tundra to get to us."

"What are you getting at?" asked Chenille.

"I don't know, but I do know this. Our rescuers…" started Braun, but then he stalled.

"Yes?"

"When you went into the tent and I was still outside…" said Braun grabbing his coat.

"Yes?" coaxed Chenille. "Finish your thoughts."

"Those men *disappeared*."

"What do you mean, 'disappeared'?"

"I mean vanished. Gone. Poof! Not there any more!"

"Whaaat?" asked Chenille with disbelief in her eyes. "Why are you saying this?"

"Because I looked! I wanted to thank them for saving us, but they were gone. One minute they were standing beside us and then, right after you went into the tent, poof! They were gone!"

"So what do you want me to say?"

"I don't know," said Braun beginning to pace. "All I know is that I want someone else to know what I know."

"Or what you *think*," said Chenille.

Braun shook his head. "No. Come on Chenille, work with me here."

"OK," said Chenille nodding. "I have to admit, things don't quite make sense to us now. I didn't hear the men approach either. But I'm sure there's a logical explanation. That's why I'm not bothered." Chenille turned to go. "Now let's go back in..."

Braun caught Chenille's arm and said, "That's it?"

"Sure," said Chenille.

Braun held out his hands and said, "No. Wait. There's more."

"What Braun?" asked Chenille impatiently.

With a thumb over his shoulder he said, "How about this John guy? I'm thinking something unusual about him, too."

"Like what?"

"Like he's *John*."

Chenille studied Braun and nodded slowly, "Yes, his name is John—so what?"

"No, I mean *the* John; John the Beloved, from the New Testament."

"What?" said Chenille completely surprised and almost choking on her question.

"Think about it!" said Braun counting on his fingers. "We know that John didn't die, right?"[2]

"Sure—but..."

"We also know that he had a mission in the last days to teach and prepare the Lost Tribes, right?"[3]

"Right," said Chenille nodding.

"What if these people *are the Lost Tribes*!"[4]

"Braun," said Chenille with a worried look.

"No! Just consider that thought. What if they are? He said he was their spiritual leader, leading them to truth. Doesn't that sound like someone preparing them?"

Chenille looked down at the snow with her hands on her hips.

"And, think about it, what did he say his profession was?"

"A preacher?" she asked, looking up.

"No! *A fisherman!!*"[5]

"People fish out here! Everyone's a fisherman!" said Chenille.

"OK, how about this? What's his last name?"

Chenille thought for a moment and then shook her head as if she was losing patience. "I don't remember."

"Zebedee! Chenille! He said his name was John Zebedee!"

"So?"

"So? Don't you remember what John's father's name was in the New Testament?"

"No, I remember his brother's name was James and they were called the Sons of Thunder. That's all I remember."

"Then I'll tell you. His name was—*Zebedee*.[6] That name is not a usual name."

"Maybe he's a copycat. There have been many preachers in the world that imagined themselves some great person and took on their name."

Braun looked at Chenille and considered her words. It was true, anyone could take the facts out of the scriptures and mimic them, taking on the persona of ancient people. "So you don't think this could be John?" asked Braun.

Chenille shook her head. "He's too young. He's like our age."

"What age do you think he should be?"

Chenille shrugged and looked around. "Not in his twenties."

"Why not?"

"I don't know. I guess I've just imagined him being old with a beard."

"Why?" asked Braun. "If he's ageless, why wouldn't he look like us? Why wouldn't his body be young and not old?"[7]

"I just don't think this is John, OK?" said Chenille. "I mean, what are the chances of meeting John the apostle in the *North Pole*?"[8] she said sarcastically.

Braun smiled and shook his head. "OK. Fine. I'm not going to try and convince you any more. Let's go back in. Just keep in mind everything we've talked about. Maybe it will all make sense later."

"OK," said Chenille with a patronizing smile. "I can do that."

Both Braun and Chenille ducked back into the tent.

As they took off their boots, Chenille looked back. "I'm so sorry."

John nodded and held out a hand to the places next to him. A small, low table had been placed in the center of the group. "Please sit, Talia has the mid-day meal ready for us."

Braun and Chenille sat down readily.

"Eat some fish," said John as the hostess sat a single plate on the table. The plate was filled with a complete fish: head, tail, and all.

Chenille looked at the fish, trying to keep a happy face.

John unsheathed a knife from somewhere under his coat and cut into the belly of the fish, slicing it up the front. Then generously, he cut the fish into three portions. Pointing at it with the end of the knife he said, "This is fresh. Do you eat fish where you're from?"

Braun looked up at John. Even though he was starving, he wasn't hungry. There was too much on his mind.

Chenille answered for Braun. "Yes, we eat fish, as long as it's cooked. Is this fish cooked?"

"No, we eat it straight from the ocean," said John. "It's the sweetest when it's slightly frozen."

"Ooohh," said Chenille, obviously disappointed but trying to maintain a smile.

"Try it. Do you have a knife?" John asked.

Chenille shook her head.

"We eat fish with our own knives like this," he said as he cut off a slice, speared it and popped it into his mouth. After chewing a couple of times and swallowing he said, "This fish was caught today, which is getting difficult because the seas are not as healthy as they used to be. We were blessed today. This fish in particular has a great flavor."

"Well, hmmm," said Chenille looking at Braun. Then as if she figured out what he was thinking she smiled, and said, "I think I would like to eat this fish. If the Japanese can eat raw fish, I'm sure I can too. Can I borrow a knife?"

Quickly John spoke to the family in their own language and then the mother and the oldest son produced knives for Braun and Chenille from under their coats.

Braun nodded and said, "Thank you."

Chenille stared at her knife. "Braun!" she whispered. "This knife is rusty and dirty."

Braun looked at the knife in her hand. It was very old and had leftover food from a previous meal. *"Use it,"* said Braun with emphasis. "Don't offend them," he said simply.

"I'll need a tetanus shot," said Chenille in a whisper.

"I'm sure you've already had one," said Braun. "You'll be fine. Take a bite."

"You go first," she said.

Braun thoughtfully cut off a piece of fish and popped it into his mouth. He chewed a couple of times, and then swallowed. Interestingly, the fish did taste sweet. In fact, it wasn't bad at all.

"Is it good?" asked Chenille.

Braun nodded to her. "It is. Go ahead, take a bite. I think you'll like it."

Chenille cut a slice and cautiously put it in her mouth too. After chewing a bit, she swallowed. "It is very good," she said smiling at Braun. "Not at all 'fishy.'"

John translated and the mother of the home nodded, smiling wider than Braun ever thought a human could. Then she said something back, pointing to her son.

Braun and Chenille looked to John for the translation.

"Talia says her son caught it himself."

"Wow," said Chenille to the shy boy who couldn't have been older than twelve. "Good job!"

"Talia?" asked Braun. "Talia is the name of our hostess?"

"Yes, and this is Alexander," said John of the boy to his left. "He's ten."

"Ten?" asked Braun. "I can't believe a ten year old can catch fish like this."

"These are a very blessed people," said John.

"Tell us the names of the other children," said Chenille smiling at the little ones who were following their mother around and hiding behind her coat.

"The little girl is Valia, she's seven. Artur is two but almost three."

"They are adorable children. Obviously they love their mom."

"Yes, they do," said John.

"Where's the father?"

"He is out herding the reindeer not far from here."

"What language does this family speak?" asked Chenille.

"Russian and Nenets," said John.

"Nenets?" asked Braun, still thinking and reviewing everything he was learning. "I've never heard of that language."

"It was an unwritten, lost language till just a hundred years ago. It's written with the Cyrillic alphabet today."

"This is so interesting," said Chenille leaning forward with interest.

"There's only about 26,000 people that speak this language today but the clans speak it so differently that often they can't understand each other. That's one of the side effects of being a nomadic and isolated people," said John.

"You know what this situation reminds me of?" asked Braun obviously to Chenille.

"What?"

"The people in the Book of Mormon."

"Which ones?"

"The people of Mulek. They forgot their language because it wasn't written down."[9] Looking at John he said, "They were sort of a *lost tribe*."

John looked between Braun and Chenille and smiled as if thinking private thoughts. Then he took another bite.

"The Mulekites weren't lost, Braun. They knew exactly where they were," she said, chiding him.

John slowly pulled something out of his pocket and held it so all could see.

"What do you have in your hand?" asked Chenille politely after cutting another piece of fish.

In John's palm was a device that looked like a large rock but it was clear like glass. He put it down in the middle of the table.

Braun looked at the stone in amazement and then looked at Chenille. He had to pinch himself again. Yep, he was still awake.

"This is a translator," said John.

Braun coughed and whispered behind his hand, *"Urim and Thummim."*[10]

"Stop it Braun," said Chenille. Then apologetically she said, "You'll have to excuse him, he's a little delirious from being out in the cold too long. How does it work?"

"You speak and the translator will spell out what you say so these people can understand you," said John.

"Let me try it out," said Chenille, turning to her hostess. "Talia, thank you for your hospitality."

The stone produced the words, almost before Chenille was finished talking, in the Nenets language. It was quite impressive.

John motioned to Talia and she approached the table. After reading what the stone said, she smiled broadly. Then she pushed the remaining fish closer to the three at the table.

John let out an appreciative belch and patted his stomach.

Chenille looked at Braun with a stifled smile, but he was still staring at the stone. "Stop staring!" she whispered.

"I can't," he said.

Looking back at Talia, John said in Nenets, "Talia, тянуть вытягивать. протягивать растягивать."

Slowly, Braun leaned forward to read the writing in the stone. It said, "Talia, we are finished. Num is very pleased with you and your sacrifice this day. Thank you. He will bless you beyond your capacity to embrace."

Braun smiled and nearly laughed. Num must be the Nenet's name for God. He couldn't believe what he was witnessing. Could it be true? Could this be John the Beloved?

Suddenly, a beautiful baritone voice echoed in his memory. Braun remembered it was the Lord's voice. "John, my beloved, what desirest thou?"

"...Lord, give unto me power over death, that I may live and bring souls unto thee..." said John in return.

Braun was surprised. Where did that memory come from? From that thought his mind began a waking vision. He saw himself and Chenille and thousands and thousands of people walking across a frozen landscape beside John. It was cold and the winds blew mercilessly. People suffered except for John and three others who lead the pack with inhuman endurance. Then the vision closed quickly.

Braun nodded as a smile began to creep on his face. Yes, now he was sure. *This was John!* And yes, these were his lost people. What a miracle to meet him! Braun's smile continued as he reveled in the realization that he knew a secret that had been kept hidden for thousands of years. He knew what very few knew.

Amazing....

Hot Anguish

Provo, Utah
3:10 a.m.

Bo woke up in the middle of the night. He looked at Corrynne. She was asleep by his side. She must have snuck in without him knowing.

What time was it?

Bo looked at the clock. He had already slept seven hours. He hadn't meant to go to sleep for the night. Now what was he going to do? Would he be able to go back to sleep? He doubted it.

Bo pushed the covers back carefully and got out of bed. He didn't want to disturb Corrynne.

As he stood there, Bo's previous thoughts came rushing back. They weren't so poignant, but they still bothered him.

Bo moved to the dresser drawers and pulled out some jeans. As he put them on, Corrynne's phone on the dresser caught his eye. He remembered something. She had been on the phone last night. He had wakened slightly and heard her talking about Carea being gone. Who was she talking to? He flipped open her phone and looked at the history. "Chief Morgan," he whispered. Why would she call the chief?

Quietly he put the phone back where he had found it and left the room. On his way down the hall, Bo stopped at Carea's room. The door was ajar. He pushed it open with his foot. Carea's room was empty and her bed was made. Bo frowned. Where was his daughter? She *was* gone. Next he walked to his boys' rooms. He opened their doors. All three were sleeping soundly in their beds. Then he moved to the twins' room. They too were sleeping. "So Carea is the only one that's missing…" he whispered, still trying to figure things out.

Bo squinted his eyes as he stood in the hall. He tried to remember. He had heard parts of Corrynne's conversation when she was on the phone with the chief. She had sounded upset at first and it alarmed him, but then he must have been very tired, because he had dozed back to sleep.

"Alaska," Bo said, rubbing the back of his neck. "Corrynne said something about Alaska and school…" Finally he gave up. He couldn't remember.

With anxiety beginning to fill his chest again, he went back into his bedroom and stood next to Corrynne's side of the bed. "Corrynne!" he whispered. "Corrynne! Where's Carea?"

"What?" asked Corrynne bouncing out of bed, with a gasp. "Oh, Bo! It's you!" she said, taking deep breaths. "I didn't know who was standing over me."

"Where's Carea?" he asked, as Corrynne sat up and pulled her legs out of the covers. She sat on the side of the bed and looked down on the floor, seeming to think for a moment.

Bo waited patiently but then decided to cue his wife to speed up her thought processes. "Corrynne, you were on the phone with the police chief. Was it about Carea?"

Corrynne looked up at Bo and slowly nodded her head.

"Why didn't you wake me up?"

Corrynne looked pained. She rubbed her neck and said, "I'm sorry, Bo. I was very upset. I didn't want to get you upset too. Since there was nothing we could do, I figured it would be better that we both got some sleep before tackling this one."

"What's so wrong that it got you *that* upset?"

Corrynne looked at Bo for a moment and then said, "Carea has been taken to an internment camp in Alaska because the police thought she was a Bat."

Bo was startled. *"An internment camp?"*

Corrynne nodded.

"In Alaska?"

Again Corrynne nodded.

"How could this be?" asked Bo feeling numbness flow through his arms and legs.

"I don't know. I asked the chief the same thing," said Corrynne.

"When did this happen?" asked Bo feeling his anger returning.

"Yesterday morning at school."

"Why weren't we called?"

"I guess the phones were out most of the day yesterday."

Bo remembered that they had been. "Where is she now?"

"Enroute to Alaska," said Corrynne.

"Did the chief tell you how to get her out?"

"He said we couldn't. She's considered a terrorist and her lockdown is final until things cool down."

"We can't get her out?" asked Bo, feeling like now he was losing control of his anger. He was going to blow.

Corrynne shook her head. "No. He said we can't even talk to her on the phone."

"How is that legal?" asked Bo with increasing volume, feeling his face turn red.

"Bo, shhh, the kids don't need to wake up right now," coaxed Corrynne. "Maybe we should go downstairs to talk."

"Fine," said Bo, gritting his teeth as Corrynne retrieved her bathrobe out of the closet.

"Did the chief say why she was taken?" asked Bo when they were halfway down the stairs.

"Yes," Corrynne said in a hushed tone. "He said it was because there was mass rioting in America and all the high risk, violent populations were put in camps so they couldn't add to the trouble," she finished as they entered the living room.

"Corrynne! Did you tell the chief that Carea isn't a Bat?"

"Bo! Of course I did," said Corrynne looking back at him with a finger to her lips. "It didn't make any difference. She was already gone."

Bo cringed as he tried hard to regain control as he paced. He opened and closed his fists angrily. Breathing hard he said, *"We can't just sit by and let this happen!"*

"We're not letting it happen. It's happening whether we sit by or not. Bo, we have no control over this situation. I've explored every option. There's nothing we can do."

"There has to be ***something*** *we can do!"*

Corrynne shook her head. "There's nothing, Bo, I promise you."

"Let's call…" Bo searched his mind for who they could call. "Call the Mayor, the Congressman, the President—I don't know, call them all!"

"The Congressman's son is one of the boys they took away. He can't even get his own son out. It's a federal operation."

"I don't care! Call the rest of them then!"

Corrynne paused and just looked at Bo. Bo felt her stare. *"What?"* he exclaimed.

"Bo, anger isn't going to help this situation. We have to be calm and think productively."

Bo laughed angrily, feeling fury enter every particle of his body. "Oh, I'm thinking productively. I'm thinking—*I want to get my Smith and Wesson…"* Bo turned and headed for the closet where the gun safe was kept.

Corrynne rushed in front of Bo. "Bo, you aren't thinking clearly! There's nothing you can do with a gun!"

"I can do many things with a gun!" said Bo as he pushed by his wife. Furiously he ripped open the closet door and began pressing the buttons for the combination.

"Bo! Listen to me! I don't know what's wrong, but we need to talk about things."

"Talk?" asked Bo. Stopping for a moment, he stared at Corrynne pointedly. "Talk is the last thing I want to do. I want action! I want people to listen to me when I tell them to let my daughter go!"

"Who, Bo? Who are you going to talk to? She's not here! *She's almost in Alaska!* There's nothing you can do with that thing but get yourself killed. It's not worth whatever you're thinking!"

"You don't know what I'm thinking," said Bo, pulling open the safe and selecting a shotgun.

"Bo *THINK* about this! Think who you're trying to bully! You're thinking about going up against the police! They have bigger and better guns than that one. You can't do anything with that!"

"I can if I catch them off guard," said Bo as he looked for ammunition on one of the shelves.

"Now you are sounding insane! Bo! ***Stop!***" said Corrynne grabbing the end of the gun.

"What, Corrynne?" asked Bo feeling stifled.

"You aren't like this! You're a man of peace! You're the Lord's bishop for our ward! Please, remember who you are and what you stand for! Don't do this!"

Bo took a step back and looked at his wife. She was pleading with him. He ground his teeth and felt his chest empty and fill with oxygen. His muscles were ready for war. How could he stay? He had to do something. "I don't know what to do, Corrynne, but I know I can't just say, 'Oh, they took my daughter? OK,' and then roll over and go back to sleep like you can."

Corrynne looked at Bo as if he had slapped her across the face. Then she said, "OK, that was a mean and dirty thing to say. I didn't just roll over and go to sleep after finding out my daughter was in a prison camp! I have thought over this, prayed over this, called who I could when the phones were working, I..."

"You didn't tell me," said Bo defiantly.

"No, Bo! I didn't tell you! I didn't tell you because I didn't know what kind of day you had had already, and my coming home to flour everywhere, the kids running around like wild Indians, and you in bed, told me you were in no condition to hear this bad news."

"That would have been my call."

"Maybe, but I made it for you."

Bo stared at Corrynne. Then with rough movements, he threw the gun back into the safe, slamming the door. "So what are you thinking we should do?"

Corrynne shook her head. "I don't know, Bo. I really don't know."

"Should we drive to Alaska?" asked Bo.

Corrynne shook her head. "With what gas? We're out of gas, remember?"

"I'll go to the bank and get some money."

"There isn't money in the banks."

"Yes, there is, I just made a deposit."

"No, Bo, there isn't. The rioting started because there isn't any money in the banks."

"What?" asked Bo with both hands to his head. He felt like ripping out his hair. *"What is going on around here?"* Dropping his hands to his sides he asked, "Where is the money?"

"Gone. It was taken to pay American debts."

"That can't happen! How are we supposed to survive? What are we going to do?"

Corrynne looked at Bo for a moment and then said, "I don't know, Bishop. Maybe you need to ask the Lord."

Bo felt like he had been punched in the stomach. Shaking his head he said, *"The Lord? The Lord? Where is the Lord? Where is he, Corrynne?!"*

"He's as close as you let him be. You taught me that. You decide how close he is."

"No," said Bo. "No! He's not! *He's not here!* He's off somewhere away from where there are no banks, or crooked police, or riots, and I don't know how he can look down from where he's at and just allow all this to happen! How can he do that, Corrynne?"

Corrynne moved to Bo and put her arms around him. "I think you're panicking. I think you're feeling helpless and you don't know how to deal with that."

Bo pushed Corrynne away. *"Yes, I'm panicking! Why aren't you? What's wrong with **you**?"*

Corrynne looked at Bo with sad eyes. "Bo, nothing's wrong with me. I just understand…"

"What, Corrynne? What do you, in your *infinite* wisdom, understand that I'm not getting?"

Corrynne opened her mouth but Bo interrupted.

"Do you understand how Braun is in Siberia? Do you understand why someone evil is adopting our first grandson? Do you understand how our son Dane is caught in violence on the other side of the continent and why our daughter isn't home asleep in her bed? Do you understand how everyone in America is going to be kicked out of their houses because they don't have jobs or money and allowed to starve? Because if you understand all that, then you are a saint and you shouldn't be here!"

"Bo!"

"No!" exclaimed Bo with his hands up. He felt like he was going to explode. "I can't stay here any more. I have to leave." Then he turned and walked out of the front door.

Notes to "Witness"

John

[1] Because John and the three Nephites have translated bodies, they have capabilities that normal mortals do not have. One, as indicated by the scripture below, is the ability to "appear" to whomever he wishes just as angels can. It's a literary extrapolation to assume that they can move matter, or physical objects with them. "And they are as the angels of God, and if they shall pray unto the Father in the name of Jesus they can show themselves unto whatsoever man it seemeth them good" (3 Nephi 28:30).

[2] "And the Lord said unto me: John, my beloved, what desirest thou? For if you shall ask what you will, it shall be granted unto you. And I said unto him: Lord, give unto me power over death, that I may live and bring souls unto thee. And the Lord said unto me: Verily, verily, I say unto thee, because thou desirest this thou shalt tarry until I come in my glory, and shalt prophesy before nations, kindreds, tongues and people" (D&C 7:1–3).

[3] In the following scripture, we see definitions of John's missions: "Q. What are we to understand by the little book which was eaten by John, as mentioned in the 10th chapter of Revelation? A. We are to understand that it was a mission, and an ordinance, for him to gather the tribes of Israel; behold, this is Elias, who, as it is written, must come and restore all things" (D&C 77:14).

In June of 1831, Joseph Smith stated, "John the Revelator was then among the ten tribes of Israel…to prepare them for their return from their long dispersion to again possess the land of their fathers" (History of the Church, 1:176). Because of the relative "modern" date of the statement and the language, stating that he was in a process to "prepare them", this author has chosen to also place John with the ten tribes as he continues to "prepare them" for their imminent return.

[4] We do not know who the lost tribes are. The people in the text represent extrapolations of what we do know: 1. There is a remnant of the original 10 tribes that exist today and will return together as a body (D&C 133:26–33). 2. They are unaware of their identity today, but will "come in remembrance before the Lord" (D&C 133:26). 3. They will be a strong people, skilled in combat (D&C 133:28). 4. They will have fallen into apostasy but will be converted before they return (Jacob 5:45, 52). 5. They will bring their scriptures to join with the stick of

Ephraim and Judah (D&C 133:30). 6. They will be led by their prophets (D&C 133:26). 7. They will receive their temple blessings at the hands of Ephraim (D&C 133:34).

[5] "Jesus came into Galilee, preaching the gospel of the kingdom of God, And saying, The time is fulfilled, and the kingdom of God is at hand: repent ye, and believe the gospel. Now as he walked by the sea of Galilee, he saw Simon and Andrew his brother casting a net into the sea: for they were fishers. And Jesus said unto them, Come ye after me, and I will make you to become fishers of men. And straightway they forsook their nets, and followed him. And when he had gone a little further thence, he saw James the *son* of Zebedee, and John his brother, who also were in the ship mending their nets. And straightway he called them: and they left their father Zebedee in the ship with the hired servants, and went after him" (Mark 1:14–20).

[6] And James and John, the sons of Zebedee…" (Mark 10:35).

[7] A translated body does not have the seeds of death, thus cannot age nor die. A translated person theoretically could live forever in this state unless acted upon by celestial powers to end such probation. In 3 Nephi 28:8 it says that all translated beings will be changed from the translated state to a celestialized state in a "twinkling of an eye" at the time of Christ's coming. We also learn that these beings can interact with mortals as normally as any man.

[8] The true location of the lost tribes is unknown to the world at this time, although the scriptures are clear that the Lord is aware of them and knows where they can be found (see 3 Nephi 17:4). The area bordering the Arctic Circle, mainly in the country of Russia, was chosen to be the fictional place of residence for the lost ten tribes. This was done not to try and identify the actual place, but to create a plausible storyline that includes all the clues given to us in the scriptures and from the prophets. Geographical characteristics of the world were also considered: 1. They were lead by the Lord to the north (D&C 110:11). 2. They will come from a place of ice, where the land will rise up out of the deep and serve as a highway for them to cross (D&C 133:26–27). 3. They will come from a harsh land (Jacob 5:14).

[9] "And at the time that Mosiah discovered them, they had become exceedingly numerous. Nevertheless, they had had many wars and serious contentions, and had fallen by the sword from time to time; and their language had become corrupted; and they had brought no records with them; and they denied the being of their Creator; and Mosiah, nor the people of Mosiah, could understand them" (Omni 1:17).

[10] "Instruments prepared by God to assist man in obtaining revelation and in translating languages. In the Hebrew language the words mean 'lights and perfections'" (*Guide to the Scriptures*, "Urim and Tummim," www.lds.org). In the scriptures, we see that prophets through the ages were given access to these tools when the necessity demanded (D&C 17:1; D&C 10:1; Abraham 3:1,4; Exodus 28:30; Ether 4:5).

CHAPTER ELEVEN

GOING HOME

"O Lord, wilt thou give me strength, that I may bear with mine infirmities" (Alma 31:30).

00:03:10, 13:45:52, Zulu
Saturday, September 20th

Num Is Calling to His People

Yamal Peninsula, Russia
12:15 p.m.

The door flap opened to the choom and a cheerful Nenet man entered. The children jumped up from their corner and rallied around him. The mother welcomed him too with a modest kiss. The father hugged each one and then greeted the rest of the company. Upon seeing John, he immediately knelt on one knee and bowed his head.

John stood and placed his hands on the man's head as if giving a blessing. "Мир коренных народов живая арктика."[1]

Braun looked into the rock to see the translation. It read, "You are just in time, friend. Come and commune with us."

The man stood and with tears in his eyes, embraced John heartily, speaking other words quietly.

Braun gave the man his privacy. They were probably words of confession or of admiration.

Looking away from the stone, Braun smiled confidently. Nodding he said to Chenille, "This is John."

Chenille looked at Braun with a question. "You really think so, don't you?"

Braun nodded. "I *know* so. There's no question in my mind."

Chenille returned her gaze to John with childlike awe, as if she was considering the truth for the first time.

The father took his place across from Braun and Chenille, making a circle on the thick animal skins.

John moved to the table. "This is Braun and Chenille. They were lost in the snow, but then my companions brought them here," he said in English to the father. "They are very grateful for the great warmth of your choom."

The man eagerly picked up the stone, read the words and then nodded. "ненёця," he said with a generous smile as he handed the rock to Braun.

"My eternal welcome," surfaced in the rock that Braun held so both he and Chenille could see it.

Braun nodded and smiled in acknowledgement.

"Thank you," said Chenille with a slight nod.

"I assume this is the father of the family?" asked Braun with a hand extended. "It's nice to meet you."

The man smiled and shook Braun's hand.

"Yes, this is Anton," said John.

"Anton," said the man with a hand on his chest.

"Anton," Braun repeated. "Great."

"Now that everyone is here," said John taking his place in the circle around the table too, "it is time to discuss ancient teachings and how they affect us today. You're welcome to join in on the conversation," John said to Braun and Chenille.

"Thank you," said Braun, feeling enthralled. To listen to John the Beloved teach the gospel? *In real life?* What a concept! He secretly pinched himself again. Yep, he was still awake. "We're pleased to."

"Good," said John. "I'll be looking forward to your enlightening interpretations you bring to us through your experience of your own teaching. I'll be speaking in Nenets, so both of you follow along with the stone for timely translation."

"Thank you," said Chenille.

John quietly bowed his head and meditated for a few moments. As he did, an electrical feeling entered the tent. The walls vibrated slightly.

Braun noted that his flesh seemed to warm up, as if a heater was blowing on him. It was incredible! "Did you feel that change?" Braun asked Chenille in a whisper.

Chenille's eyes were wide. "Yes, I felt it. The hairs on my arms are standing up!"

"Yeah, mine too," said Braun contentedly. He was watching a miracle.

After the quiet, John lifted his head and said in Nenets, "As you know, our God, Num, through his son, created our world. He gave spirits to all living things including the plants, animals, and even the world."[2] Then John paused and looked to Braun and Chenille. "Go ahead," he said in English. "Expound."

Braun looked at Chenille. "What does he want us to do?"

Chenille shrugged. "Not us, *you*. He wants you to bear your testimony, or comment."

"Yes, please say what comes to your mind," said John. "We'll all be edified together."

"OK," said Braun as he studied the rock and the writing in it, feeling intimidated to add anything to this great man's words. Finally, glancing at John for final approval and receiving an encouraging nod, he started. "Ahhh, God the Father created this world through Jehovah, his son.[3] We are his children,[4] born of him in the spirit.[5] We have the potential to become like him.[6] This world and all that's in it has spirits created by him also."[7]

John smiled. "Good," he said in English.

Braun nodded feeling relieved. Secretly he wanted to live up to John's expectations. He didn't know what John wanted, or how it would help, but his answer seemed to suffice.

"We believe this already," said Anton, looking between John and Braun and Chenille. He took his quiet 2-year-old on his lap as his shy seven-year-old daughter leaned against him with her hand in his hair. "It's the Nenets way."

John continued. "I'm here to tell you that Nga, the evil son of Num, and all his evil spirits, wish for this world to be consumed with a curse and you along with it," again John looked at Braun expectedly. "Expound."

Braun swallowed. He looked at John with surprise. *Expound?* Expound was more than "comment." Was he being tested? Maybe he was being taught. Or maybe he was being prepared. After a moment of contemplation he decided it didn't matter. He wanted to be of service to John and this was the process.

Braun concentrated, opening his mind. He desired direction from the Spirit to say the right things and inspire Anton and his family in the right way. He took a breath and started, "Lucifer, the most powerful fallen spirit son of God who wished to rule in heaven,[8] and all the spirits that followed him,[9] wishes to…" Braun searched for words.

"Deceive everyone," suggested Chenille.

"No, the curse he's talking about is much more than that," he said quickly to Chenille. "It's Satan's desire that *no* son or daughter of Heavenly Father be saved through the power of the atonement and resurrection of Jesus Christ,[10] including Anton and those he loves."

Turning to speak to the family, Braun continued, "To save your family from the power of Satan, or Nga, you have to be strong as well as brave to do what needs to be done. You have a choice in front of you. What you do with that choice[11] will dictate your eternal future…"

Anton nodded in understanding.

"This family and each person who has ever lived on the earth must be given the chance to be baptized[12] and receive their blessings in the temple,"[13] continued Braun. "It's Satan's desire to stop the work of John or anyone good, at all costs. He doesn't want you entering heaven. He wants you to be lost and confused like he is.[14] If he can stop you and your wife and children from seeing the truth, receiving your keys to heaven and being righteous, through distractions, anger, suffering, or any other obstacle he can throw into your path, then he has won and the plan of salvation has been foiled."

Anton looked at his wife and children briefly with concern, then back. With a nod, Braun continued.

"You must not let this happen. No one can let this happen. We must fight Nga and teach everyone we can how to identify his lies. You, being a son of Num, deserve the right to progress. All people on the earth deserve the right to know the truth and progress. If we can't teach of Num, or God, and lead people to baptism, repentance, and the temple[15] then the earth will fail to serve its purpose in bringing about the eternal potential of man to become like our Eternal Father,[16] and be smitten with a curse and utterly wasted at Christ's Second Coming."[17]

Chenille looked at Braun. "Wow," she whispered, obviously impressed.

Braun smiled slightly. He didn't want to be distracted from his thoughts. He continued. "Since saving ordinances can be performed for both the living and the dead in the temple, the great plan of God allows the curse to be avoided, and all the righteous exalted as God's sons and daughters in their rightful place at his side.[18] Because of the temple, God's plan *will* be fulfilled. He *will* be successful and Satan, or Nga, will *fail*. However, if Anton doesn't accept the gospel, become baptized, choose to be righteous and receive the sealing power of the temple, he could suffer a curse personally, still giving Satan partial victory at least over him."[19]

Anton read the words as Braun explained them. "We make the proper sacrifices to protect ourselves from Nga," said Anton. "We sacrifice a reindeer, a dog, and a fish to appease the evil spirits every third full moon."

John shook his head. With a kind touch he said, "You understand the desires of evil improperly. They do not care for the blood of your animals. They care for the blood of people. Evil spirits wish to imprison you and your family. They wish to destroy your happiness." John stopped and waited.

"Your turn," whispered Chenille to Braun as Anton looked to Braun.

Braun's mind was moving faster now. The answer came quickly. "Satan and his servants will tell you anything to lead you in any direction but the truth.[20] He's happy when you think sacrifices protect you from him. In fact, he laughs as you search blindly for safety, not knowing where to find it.[21] There is only one faith, one baptism, one Godhead,[22] and one angel prophesied to fly through the heavens to bring the gospel to the earth.[23] That gospel has been restored in its fullness and it now paves the way for all mankind to find eternal life.[24] Once set on that very narrow path, you and your family must be continually strong and walk that path the rest of your life.[25] If you do, it will be a path that will take you to a strange land and a new people,[26] but you will be happy and will inherit joy beyond all your understanding in the eternal heavens of Num."[27]

When Braun finished, the tent felt like it was expanding with energy. Fire filled every heart. The truth was being spoken powerfully and everyone knew it.

Chenille, unblinkingly, leaned over to Braun and whispered, "What do you mean, 'a strange land and new people'?"

Braun leaned into her and said, "I saw a waking vision today."

"You did?" asked Chenille. "You didn't tell me."

"I haven't had time."

Anton looked at his wife and his children and then back. "I want to walk this path. I want protection from Nga. I want real joy that lasts forever."

"Then follow my words, which are the words of Num," said John. "If you take upon yourself covenants of obedience to Num, give up your weaknesses, and love him with all your heart,[28] you will be given power over Nga just by asking for it."[29]

Braun didn't offer any more other than a confirming nod. John had said it perfectly.

"I want that power," said Anton. "I power to protect my family."

"Then you shall have it," said John with a smile.

Anton closed his eyes and hugged his wife as both of them broke down in tears.

"I can promise you," continued John, "that the day is coming that your family will be lifted up and enveloped in protection[30] as Nga is conquered and bound."[31]

It took a few moments for Anton to control his emotions. Finally, after wiping his tears he asked, "What can we do to prove our desires and receive these blessings now?"

John placed a gentle arm around Anton's shoulder. "You need to prepare. You need to learn of Num," said John. "You need to read his words from your ancestors as well as from his other books written by spiritual men who have come before this people.[32] Once the truth stirs your soul, make them a part of you[33] and take upon you the look of Num."[34]

"Where do we get these books?"

John turned to Braun and Chenille and said, "Give me your book."

Braun opened his hands with confusion and said, "What book?"

"The book in Chenille's bag."

Braun looked at Chenille inquisitively. "Do you have a book in your bag?"

A light came on in Chenille's face. "I have my quad…"

"Quad," repeated John thoughtfully. "Does that have the words of the sticks of Jews, and of Joseph?"[35] asked John.

Chenille nodded. "It does. It's four books of scripture, written by the tribes of Judah and Joseph, unified in one book for convenience. The Bible, The Book of Mormon, The Doctrine and Covenants, and the Pearl of Great Price."[36]

"Good. That's what I want. Give it to Anton. He needs to read them to his family."

Chenille stood and went to the door of the tent where her bag sat. She unzipped it and reached in, pulling out her scriptures. "Here. They're a little beat up but you can still read them," said Chenille.

John nodded and held out both of his hands. "This will do. I will obtain scriptures for this family, but until then, this will do. Do you mind?" he asked.

Chenille shook her head. "It's the least I can do," she said as she handed her scriptures to John.

A reflective look came across John's face as he touched the book, as if he was touching a long sought-after object. Slowly he opened the first few pages and with his index finger touched the table of contents gently. He hesitated over a couple of the titles of the books and then he proceeded to open the fine pages of scriptures, slowly flipping from section to section. Finally, he began reading in Nenets, translating from English. His words flowed evenly and easily without difficulty as the stone filled with his words.

"Blessed is he that readeth, and they that hear the words of this prophecy, and keep those things which are written therein: for the time is at hand." John looked up and smiled and then he closed his eyes and continued, quoting from memory. "Behold, he cometh with clouds; and every eye shall see him, and they *also* which pierced him: and all kindreds of the earth shall wail because of him. Even so, Amen."[37]

"Amen," said Anton humbly.

"Amen," Braun said, as he realized John was quoting words he had written himself over two millennia ago from his book of Revelation in the New Testament. He smiled as he realized they had been written for them and all the others that searched for God in the last days. It didn't matter that they were in a little tent in the farthest reaches of the earth in front of one family. By small means were great means brought to pass.[38]

John closed the book and handed it to Anton. "Read these words with the stone. Live by its precepts, and when you feel ready, be immersed in living water in the name of Num's son, who has died for you. In this ordinance, as I have promised, you will be blessed with eternal protection and the opportunity to enter a place where Nga and all his evil spirits can never follow."

"I'll do it," said Anton as his wife nodded in agreement. "I and my family want to be immersed now. I can chip away the ice so we can be immersed in water," said Anton. "We need protection now."

John shook his head. "No, Anton. You need to learn. Read and learn. Pray to Num, find his truth in his words. Break the traditions of your fathers and cling to what you discover in the words of your ancient ancestors. Then when you are ready, when your sweet wife and children are ready, we'll progress and give you the blessings you desire."

"Who will protect us from Nga until then?"

John motioned to Braun. "These strangers have been brought here from a far land for that purpose. Braun has power and he will protect you."

Chenille smiled at Braun and put her arm in his.

With a shaking hand, Anton laid the stone on a page.

Braun saw the stone translate the English into Nenets. To see the seer stone work in person was life-changing.

In the next moment, Anton began to read out loud to his family. The sound of his voice pulled Braun's attention from his thoughts as he became mesmerized by the lyrical language of the Nenets.

Bartering

Lexington Park, Maryland
8:55 a.m.

"Ohhh, those are ugly!" said Nebraska, her nose turned up. "They look like spiders."

"They aren't spiders, they're crabs. Blue crabs and the most beautiful sight I've ever seen."

Nebraska watched Dane unhook the crab pot and pull the crabs out one by one, and then she said, "Why do you like those things so much?"

"Because we can eat them."

Nebraska shook her head. "I'm not going to eat them."

Dane looked at Nebraska, "Sure you are. Aren't you hungry?"

Nebraska nodded. "I want Captain Crunch cereal."

"Well, I don't have Captain Crunch cereal. All I have is crabs and whatever is left in my pockets."

"I'm thirsty."

"I know. I'm thirsty too," said Dane. "Let me tie these crab pinchers together and then we'll take these and go find some water."

"Why are we going to take them? Do they need water too?"

"Yes, they do need water, but we're going to try and sell them. People might want to buy them. We can get other food with the money."

"OK," said Nebraska watching Dane carefully wrestle the crabs, ten in all, wriggling from a string tied between their bound pinchers.

Tying the long end of the string into a loop, Dane lifted it over his head and arm, allowing the wriggling things to hang down his side freeing his hands.

The low tide allowed enough room for Dane to hide the thin sport boat under a dock on the Chesapeake Bay. The old crabbing man had given him valuable insight. He planned to hide everything he didn't want taken. They had a couple of hours yet of low tide, and if they were back in three, that would be enough.

Climbing carefully out of the boat Dane stepped on a thick stake sticking out of a piling and swung around to the other side of it. He held out his hand for Nebraska. "Come on. I'll carry you up to the dock."

"OK," said Nebraska and she launched herself into Dane's open arm. "But don't let those craps touch me."

"They're *crabs*," said Dane as he scaled the pylon with a chuckle. He quickly jumped up to the dock when he reached the top.

"Let's go this way," said Dane. He could see some storefronts ahead, skirting the beach. Taking hold of Nebraska's hand, he suggested, "Now don't let go of my hand, OK?"

"OK," said Nebraska with the characteristic compliance of a child.

At the little market place, people were standing in line and complaining loudly at the storekeepers. *"What do you mean you're all out? It's just nine in the morning. You just barely received your catch today!"*

Dane saw his opportunity. With a loud voice he pulled the string of crab off his shoulder and held it up. "I've got fresh crab here! I just pulled them out of the water minutes ago! They're still alive and kicking!"

An angry, red faced man turned abruptly. "How much do you want for 'em?"

Dane didn't know how much to charge. "Ummm, ten dollars?"

"Ten dollars each?" asked the man fishing desperately in his pocket.

"Ahhh, yes!" said Dane smiling. The man had set his own price; much more than Dane had thought he could ask for.

"I'll take all of them," said the man as he fumbled with his money.

Dane was surprised. "All of them?" Dane's excitement deflated. Obviously the price was too low, but it was too late.

The man pushed a hundred dollars at him and shook it. "Yes, yes, take it! Take it!"

"Fine," Dane said as he made the exchange. "Crabs that bad in the stores, huh?"

"No, there aren't any crabs. The stores are empty, there's no water and no gas and none coming."

"Already?" asked Dane.

"Yes, already, and I promise you that no government will ever feed me, and I suggest you don't let them feed you either!" said the man, looking up and down at Dane's military fatigues. "If they feed you, they own you. Do they own you?"

"No. The government isn't feeding me. I'm feeding me," said Dane defensively.

"Good. *Keep it that way*."

"Alright," said Dane with a confused stare.

The man turned abruptly and walked quickly down the sidewalk still mumbling, "I'm not *down* until I'm *out*! And I'm not *out* till I'm *dead*!"

Dane watched the large man for a little longer as he walked away from him with the crabs wriggling by his side. Then he looked down at his money and shrugged. Oh well, he had sold his crabs and that was all he cared about right now. He put the money in his pocket.

"OK," said Dane, looking down at Nebraska.

"Did you get some money?" she asked.

"Yes," said Dane, "now we can buy some food you might like."

"Yea!" said Nebraska doing a little skip in place. "I want some pop!"

"How about something good for you first?" asked Dane thinking he sounded like his mother.

"OK," said Nebraska, looking around. "I want a hot dog!"

Dane made a face. "A hot dog?" Then he looked at the little stores. "I don't know if that's good enough for you. Let's see what we can find at these little kiosks."

"OK," said Nebraska. "I really want some water," she said. "I'm thirstier than *death*!"

"Thirstier than death?" asked Dane smiling at Nebraska's cute little phrases.

"Uh-huh," said Nebraska with a nod, stroking her throat.

"That's pretty thirsty! Well, I think I can get you some water," said Dane, feeling like a good provider now that he could say those words to his little companion. He moved to a nearby counter and said, "I would like two bottles of water please."

The Hispanic woman, who was busily wiping her counters, ignored him.

"Excuse me, we'd like some water," Dane repeated.

"No water," said the woman in accented English as she put out a closed sign.

"No water?" asked Dane.

"No, no water anywhere. All sold out," she said waving her hand.

"All sold out?"

"Yes," said the woman with a firm nod.

"Where's a drinking fountain then?"

The woman looked at Dane with almost an angry look. With a finger in the air she said, "Don't let that little girl drink the water out of the fountain. It's poison!"

"OK..." said Dane, not knowing quite what to make of this woman. "Why is it poison?"

"Not purified. Ahhh," the woman flung her hands in circles, looking for the right words. "Machines not working anymore."

"What machines?"

"To clean it! Go to Lexington Park Center," said the woman pointing behind her. "The people from the UN are there. They have water."

"The UN?" asked Dane, making sure he was understanding correctly.

"Yes, they're helping us. They are angels," she said clasping her hands together and looking up to the sky as if in prayer.

"How far is the center?" asked Dane.

"That way," said the woman pointing again behind her. "Go to the park. Go now, the line is getting long and they might run out of water."

"Thank you," said Dane turning to Nebraska. "Come on! We've got to run fast!" he said as he swung her up onto his back. "And you have to hold on tight!"

"OK!" said Nebraska. Her voice was already vibrating from the pounding of his feet, since Dane was already jogging past the stores into an area filled with people.

Winding in and out of obstacles and people by the hundreds, Dane came to a sign. It read:

CLEAN WATER

UN
Disaster Relief

"Relief for the suffering."

"So, this is where I can buy some water?" Dane asked a hunched-over old man, leaning on his cane as he stood in a line.

"No, the water is free."

"Free?" asked Dane as he put Nebraska down.

"Yep. They didn't waste any time did they? Pretty quick, huh? Our water purification systems went down and *bam*!" said the man banging his cane on the ground. "These guys are here with fresh water."

"Wait—I thought the banks closed and that's why they were here," said Dane. "Did something else happen?"

"Well, yes, we lost our water."

"Why?"

"Dunno. Don't care. I just care that there's sweet, fresh water up ahead of me."

"Hmmm," said Dane trying to figure things out.

"Losing money's pretty bad," continued the man, "but losing water at the same time. That's deadly. I say, having our purification systems go down was a blessing in disguise."

"What do you mean?" asked Dane.

"Because, if the purification systems hadn't gone on the blink and we had clean water, we would be waiting in line for assistance like every other city in America. But because we lost our water, we've jumped to the head of the line. Now we have food, water, and any other care we need. No waiting! No suffering. I say that's a pretty good deal."

An older woman with grey shoulder length hair, dressed in a dirty, tattered business suit approached Dane and asked, "Do you have any gas?"

Dane shook his head. "None that I can spare, I'm sorry."

"But you *do* have gas," said the woman eagerly. "I need gas to get to Nevada."

"I'm sorry," said Dane, shaking his head.

"Dane! I'm thirsty!" said Nebraska with her face turned upward.

"I know. I'm working on it," said Dane. Turning back to the old man he asked, "Does the UN give out gas?"

"It's rationed but they do."

Dane turned to the woman. "Get in one of these lines. I'm sure the UN will give you some gas to go to Nevada. You might not get enough right now, but in time you might. That's better than nothing."

The woman looked at Dane with obvious irritation but then she changed her expression. "No, thank you. I'll try someone else."

Dane turned his attention back to the old man. "Are we standing in the water line?"

"Nope, the water line is over there. This is the food line. I got my water today already."

Dane nodded and put up a finger to thank the man. "Thanks and good luck."

Dane, with Nebraska's hand firmly in his, walked over to the line that the old man had pointed to. It wound around poles like a ride in Disneyland.

"A new water line is forming on the north side, near the large oak tree," said a woman with a megaphone. "Proceed in an orderly fashion."

Dane looked at his watch. Too much time had passed. He had to hurry. "Where's the north end?" he asked a passer-by holding a bottle of water.

"It's over there," said the woman pointing in the direction Dane was headed. "You're going in the right direction."

Dane pulled Nebraska up into his arms and began to jog. Straight ahead he saw a table where a woman with a white veil and robes was handing out water. The line was short but people were joining it quickly.

"I see a line for water," said Dane.

"Where?" asked Nebraska.

"Right—here," said Dane as he took his last steps into the line and dropped Nebraska to the ground.

Dane could feel Nebraska moving around and he looked down. She was standing on her tip-toes to see the woman behind the table. "What are you doing?" asked Dane.

"Is that lady an angel?"

"No, she's just wearing white clothes. I think she might be a nun," said Dane.

"Didn't that lady back by the ocean say that she was an angel?" asked Nebraska, looking up at Dane with the most serious expression he had ever seen her have.

Dane stopped and thought for a moment. Then he remembered what Nebraska was talking about. The Hispanic woman had said the UN were angels for handing out water. "Oh, right!" he said laughing, "she did say they were angels but she didn't mean real angels. That woman meant that these people were kind, *like* angels."

"No. I think she's an angel," said Nebraska with a nod. "Angels wear white."

"OK," said Dane, not wanting to argue. "All I know is that there's water for you here."

The line moved up and Dane and Nebraska took a few steps.

"A series of unanswered tragedies have rocked the United States," said an announcer's voice from far off.

Dane looked around. Where was that voice coming from? It sounded like a news broadcast.

"Large explosions have been reported in Missouri, New York, and Washington, D.C., all seem unrelated...."

The sound drew Dane's eyes up until he saw a television screen set on a tall pedestal.

"In New York, true tragedy hit the city. Toxic fire from the explosion of a chemical plant created fumes that were deadly to the whole city. Because of the brisk wind, millions were overcome by the fumes, causing unnumbered deaths..."

"Hey, that's not what happened in New York," said Dane aloud. "Atropine wouldn't counteract fumes from a chemical plant..."

"Severe solar storms are being blamed for the water purification system malfunctions in Maryland, Texas, and Missouri. High-tech purification systems were installed just last year that were meant to handle triple the capacity of traditional purification systems. Now that they are down, the UN has set up relief stations in many cities in the affected states."

"Are you in the military?" asked the man who stood in front of Dane.

"I was, I mean, yes, I am."

"Do you serve around here?"

Dane shook his head, "No, I'm on special assignment. I have to find this little girl's family. She was lost in New York."

"New York?"

"We were visiting the mu-se-um," said Nebraska.

"Were you caught in the fire?" asked a woman.

"How did you get out?" asked the man.

"Did everyone really die?" asked the woman.

"Ah, yes," said Dane looking down, but beginning to feel uneasy. "But we didn't."

"Die?" Nebraska asked Dane. "Who died?"

"But I'd rather not talk about this right now," Dane said to the couple, motioning at Nebraska with his eyes.

"Oh, OK," said the woman nodding. Then she put her arm on her husband's arm and then he nodded. Both of them turned back to face the tables.

"Who died?" Nebraska asked again, her eyes wide.

Dane considered what he should say. Then carefully he said, "Do you remember all those sick people in New York? The ones that were lying on the ground?"

Nebraska shook her head.

"You don't?"

She shook her head again.

Dane considered this situation. It wasn't unusual for people to forget near-death events. If Nebraska wasn't aware of the trauma that occurred, should he tell her all about it? What good would it do to tell her? Maybe he shouldn't, at least not here in line.

"Never mind, Nebraska. It doesn't matter," he said. "Don't worry, things are good." Then he wanted to change the subject. "So, how are you doing now?"

"I'm thirsty," Nebraska said with sad, worried eyes. "I've been getting thirstier and thirstier. My stomach says it needs water," she said pushing in on her abdomen.

"I know," said Dane, smiling, trying to comfort Nebraska. "We'll get some water soon," he said as he took off his military vest and unbuttoned the top buttons of his shirt. He needed to look less like a soldier so people wouldn't ask him questions that might cause problems.

"You've been very patient. I'll get you the first drink they hand us, just because you've been so brave," said Dane.

Nebraska looked down at the ground and nodded.

The line moved. "See? We're moving again. It's almost our turn."

"Here, fill out this information," said the older woman standing in front of them as she handed Dane a clipboard. "You'll get your water faster if it's already filled out."

Dane looked at the clipboard. There were many questions about identity: name, social security number, address, phone number, but then the sheet went into health history and occupation, among other things.

"What's this for?" Dane asked, not willing to divulge any information about himself that might impede his ability to help Nebraska.

"I'm not sure," said the woman. "I just know everyone has to fill them out to get the water."

Dane looked at the woman in white who was processing the clipboards and handing out water. Something strange was going on here. Why would anyone need information about who needed food and water? "Excuse me," said Dane as he leaned forward to talk to the woman. "Why do we have to fill out this form? Can't we get water without it?"

The woman smiled kindly. "It is possible to have water without filling out the form."

"Good," said Dane as he tossed the clipboard back on the table and the people in front of him progressed to another table.

"Nebraska! It's our turn!" said Dane, animated.

Nebraska clapped her hands and held them out eagerly.

The woman looked at Nebraska and instead of reaching for the water she crooned, "Oh, she is so cute. Is she yours?"

Dane looked at the woman. She was being cruel. Nebraska was really thirsty! "Can we just have the water?" he asked pointedly, pounding the table.

The woman looked at Dane without flinching as she folded her hands. "Yes, I'll give you the water, but you must know what you are doing by refusing to fill out the information sheet."

Dane looked at Nebraska; it looked like she was going to cry. "Please, just give her the water now and I'll listen to whatever you have to say."

The woman nodded and reached into a bin behind the table. "Here, honey," she said, her tone obviously superficial.

Dane grabbed the water bottle and opened it with a single twist and handed it to Nebraska.

Nebraska drank thirstily.

Dane watched her and was feeling very thirsty himself, but just to see Nebraska be satisfied made him feel happy. Looking back at the woman he said, "Thank you."

The woman nodded.

"So, give me your pitch," said Dane, trying not to be sarcastic, but feeling that this whole situation, with women dressed as nuns handing out water and television screens high in the trees, felt more like a show than a relief organization. He was losing his patience.

The woman picked out another water bottle and set it aside, as if to tantalize Dane so he would listen to her.

Despite Dane's desire not to be influenced by the woman's tactics, he saw the water and it was torturing him. He was beyond any level of thirst he had ever felt before in his life. He refused to look at the bottle and focused on the woman.

"Have you heard the story, if you give a man a fish, you feed him for a day, but if you teach him to fish you feed him for his whole life?"

Dane nodded. "Yes. I've heard that. What of it?"

"Today we give you a bottle of water, but what are you going to do tomorrow?"

Dane looked at the UN woman. What was she getting at? "I'm sorry?"

"We'll cure your thirst for the moment, but to have enough for another day, something different has to happen. We need to give you the mechanism for renewal. We need to show you how to fish."

"OK, please get to it," said Dane now extremely impatient for the water. "What are you suggesting? If you're trying to get me to fill out that form, you're out of luck."

The woman smiled and nodded. Then she said, "I understand your hesitance, but let me continue."

"Hand me the water and I'll let you finish," said Dane.

The woman put her hand on the bottle but didn't give it to him.

Dane watched her hesitate and then said, "Come on, Nebraska, let's go." Secretly, leaving without a drink was torture to Dane, but the woman toying with him was worse. He wasn't going to stand for it. He'd find another source of water.

"Here," she said, holding the water out. "Here's your water."

Dane turned back and slowly he took the bottle. With a quick twist, he had the cap off and drank deeply. He drained the entire bottle with one breath.

"Now, you said you'd listen. Please give me that courtesy," said the nun-like woman.

Dane breathed heavily and wiped his face with his forearm. He nodded and said, "Yes, I said I'd listen. So go ahead."

The woman folded her hands, so that she looked like a Catholic image of Madonna, then said, "The facts are clear. All anyone has to do is look at the television and one can see that America is in trouble."

Dane looked up at the televisions that continued to show devastation everywhere around the nation, but it was a moot point. No one needed to tell him about the chaos in America. He had been fighting against it for months now.

The woman continued, "Money is gone, and people are suffering. They aren't just suffering in places, but all over. We are here to help the suffering, but we need your cooperation to do that. We need you to help us help you."

Dane looked at the woman and tried to keep contempt out of his stare, but was not very successful. "How can *I* help you?"

"What if I can guarantee you not one more day of hunger, not one more day of thirst, not one more day of suffering? In these times, how would that sound?"

"How can you guarantee that? How can anyone guarantee that?" asked Dane.

The woman put her hands out. "It's the miracle of the day," then she put her hands back together again. "Through God, all things are possible."

"Since when did the UN speak of God?" asked Dane, his eyes narrowed. Who were these people?

"Since we've become enlightened and selfless. Humanity is our business. It's the way of the future. God is with us always."

Dane looked at the woman. She seemed serious. Was she for real? "OK, what if I said I was interested in what you have to offer, what would you say next?"

"I would say that was good. It's the right choice."

Dane thought this conversation was very interesting. This woman was using insinuations of good verses bad. There was morality in her messages, for what purpose? She wasn't talking about things of heaven or hell, she was talking about compliance verses non-compliance.

"So what do I need to do?" asked Dane getting a funny feeling. Somehow he knew what was coming next.

The woman took Dane's hand gently and looked at the back of it.

Dane's stomach began to crawl. He had been *here* before.

"We have a way of always making sure you have what you need. You will always be accounted for. Your food will never be given to another." The woman pulled from behind the desk a strange looking syringe. "All you have to do is…"

Dane ripped his hand away from the woman and took steps back in terror. She *was* talking about what he thought! *She wanted to put another chip in his hand!*

"No way! You aren't touching my hand!" said Dane stepping backwards and tripping over the feet of a woman behind him. Catching himself before he fell he said, *"I'd rather die than have you track me!"*

"What's wrong?" asked Nebraska with a frightened look on her face.

"Nothing," said Dane taking her hand. "We have to get out of here."

"But I want more water," whined Nebraska as she began to cry.

Dane picked up Nebraska and hugged her as he ran out of the park. When he was far enough away from the UN woman that he was feeling like he could slow down, he slowed to a jog. With a comforting voice he said, "Don't cry, Nebraska. We'll find more water. I know how to find water. We don't need that lady. We're going to be fine."

At the pier where their boat lay under the dock, Dane set Nebraska down. "Do you want to go for another boat ride?" asked Dane, trying to help her forget what they had been through.

"No, I'm hungry," said Nebraska.

"OK," said Dane putting his hands in his pockets and feeling the money. Turning around and walking backwards, he scanned the little bay kiosks. They were all closed down. "I'll figure something out for you."

As Dane turned back around, he ran right into someone. It was the woman who needed gas. She tripped and would have fallen, but Dane held out a hand and caught her.

"Oh! I'm sorry!" Dane said automatically. "I wasn't looking where I was going."

The business woman nodded and looked down. Her heel had caught in the slats between the wood and broken off. She bent down and picked it up. "Well that's that."

"Have you found any gas yet?" he asked politely, not knowing what else to say.

The woman continued to look at her heel and shook her head. "These were very expensive shoes."

"I'm sorry," said Dane. "I'm sure we can figure out how to fix them…"

The woman shook her head. "No. Expensive shoes are a waste. A good pair of athletic shoes would do me better."

Dane put his hands out at his sides and said, "Plum out of women's shoes."

Dane was trying to be funny, but the woman didn't laugh; instead, she put her head down in her hands and began to weep.

"Oh, great!" he said to himself as he rolled his eyes. Had he caused this woman to cry? What should he do?

"Lady," said Nebraska as she pulled on the woman's ripped skirt. "Lady, you look like my grandma. Do you live in washing machine C.C.?"

The woman stopped crying and looked down at Nebraska. Then she looked at Dane for clarification.

"She means Washington, D.C. Her grandmother lives there."

The woman smiled through her tears and touched Nebraska's head. "Oh, no, I used to live there, but I don't anymore."

"Why?" asked Nebraska.

The woman hesitated.

"You don't have to answer that," said Dane smiling and shaking his head apologetically.

"But I love that I look like your grandma. That's the nicest thing anyone has said to me all day. Thank you, sweetheart!"

Suddenly, Dane remembered the time! He was late! Looking down the pier he saw that the water was too high! It was licking the bottom of the dock! His boat! It was probably under the water and on the bottom of the bay! "Oh, freak!" he said grabbing his head.

"What?" asked the woman surprised as she too looked down the pier.

"My boat!" exclaimed Dane.

"Where?" said the woman. "I don't see a boat!"

Dane shook his head. He couldn't think what to do! All his things were in the boat. Everything to help him survive, his gun, his backpack…what was he going to do? He began to pace to try and figure things out.

"What's wrong? Can I help you with something? Did someone steal your boat?" asked the woman.

Dane looked at Nebraska and then at the woman. *What do I do?* he asked heaven. His mind was blank. *Help me! Please!*

Quietly, an answer came to him. It fell on him like dew on the meadow. He was to give this woman the gas from the boat.

He stopped and wondered at that impression. If the boat was under the water, would he be able to do that? Maybe it wasn't under the water yet. Maybe he could save it! He rushed out immediately to look at the boat. When he got to the end of the pier, he lay down on his stomach and looked under it. There it was! It was fine! The tide wasn't too high. He had just panicked and thought it was too high. His mind played a cruel joke on him. Getting up and feeling relieved, he walked contently back to the woman, taking Nebraska's hand in his.

Looking at the poor business woman, Dane said, "Never mind. Everything's fine."

"Oh, good!" said the woman looking relieved.

"What's your name?" asked Dane holding out a hand in greeting.

The woman's eyes were drawn in worry but she managed a smile. Clasping Dane's hand she said, "My name is Louise Anderson. Mrs. Louise Anderson."

"Well Mrs. Louise Anderson, I have gas," said Dane out of the blue.

The woman looked at Dane in a strange way, as if she didn't know what to say.

"I have gas for your car so you can go to Nevada."

The woman's look changed from confusion to joy. "Oh! I'm sorry! I thought you were telling me your stomach hurt."

Dane shook his head slowly and said, "No. I am to give you my gas and you are to drive me and Nebraska to Utah on your way to Nevada."

Mrs. Anderson's face changed to amazement as she brought both hands to her mouth. Then with happy tears she said, *"I can do that! I drive right through Utah to get to Nevada! It's a deal,"* she said as she shook Dane's hand for the second time.

Dane smiled as he quietly thanked Heavenly Father. His blessings were so amazing. God was leading him. He was teaching him. The way wasn't easy, but it was possible. Dane nodded and accepted the handshake. It was a deal.

Notes to "Witness"

Num Is Calling to His People

[1] The written language in the text is genuine Nenets.

[2] The gospel lesson is discussed with the words and concepts that the Nenets might understand to encourage understanding.

"The Nentsy religion is a type of Siberian shamanism in which the natural environment, animals, and plants are all thought to have their own spirits. The earth and all living things were created by the god Num, whose son, Nga, was the god of evil. Num would protect people against Nga only if they asked for help and made the appropriate sacrifices and gestures. These rituals were sent either directly to the spirits or to wooden idols that gave the animal-gods human forms" (World Cultures, "Nentsy,"http://www.everyculture.com/wc/Norway-to-Russia/Nentsy.html).

[3] "And I, God, said unto mine Only Begotten, which was with me from the beginning: Let us make man in our image, after our likeness; and it was so" (Moses 2:26).

[4] "I have said, Ye *are* gods; and all of you *are* children of the most High" (Psalms 82:6).

"Jesus answered them, Is it not written in your law, I said, Ye are gods?" (John 10:34).

[5] "…We have had fathers of our flesh which corrected *us,* and we gave *them* reverence: shall we not much rather be in subjection unto the Father of spirits, and live?" (Hebrews 12:9).

[6] "The Spirit itself beareth witness with our spirit, that we are the children of God: And if children, then heirs; heirs of God, and joint-heirs with Christ; if so be that we suffer with him, that we may be also glorified together" (Romans 8:16–17).

[7] "And every plant of the field before it was in the earth, and every herb of the field before it grew. For I, the Lord God, created all things, of which I have spoken, spiritually, before they were naturally upon the face of the earth" (Moses 3:5).

[8] "How art thou fallen from heaven, O Lucifer, son of the morning! How art thou cut down to the ground, which didst weaken the nations! For thou hast said in thine heart, I will ascend into heaven, I will exalt my throne above the stars of God: I will sit also upon the mount of the congregation, in the sides of the north" (Isaiah 14: 12–13).

[9] "And there was war in heaven: Michael and his angels fought against the dragon; and the dragon fought and his angels, And prevailed not; neither was their place found any more in heaven. And the great dragon was cast out, that old serpent, called the Devil, and Satan, which deceiveth the whole world: he was cast out into the earth, and his angels were cast out with him" (Revelation 12:7–9).

"Behold, the devil was before Adam, for he rebelled against me, saying, Give me thine honor, which is my power; and also a third part of the hosts of heaven turned he away from me because of their agency" (D&C 29:36).

[10] "Satan stirreth them up, that he may lead their souls to destruction" (D&C 10:22).

"Behold, verily, verily, I say unto you, ye must watch and pray always lest ye enter into temptation; for Satan desireth to have you, that he may sift you as wheat" (3 Nephi 3:18).

[11] "Wherefore, men are free according to the flesh; and all things are given them which are expedient unto man. And they are free to choose liberty and eternal life, through the great Mediator of all men, or to choose captivity and death, according to the captivity and power of the devil; for he seeketh that all men might be miserable like unto himself" (2 Nephi 2:27).

[12] "And he commandeth all men that they must repent, and be baptized in his name, having perfect faith in the Holy One of Israel, or they cannot be saved in the kingdom of God. And if they will not repent and believe in his name, and be baptized in his name, and endure to the end, they must be damned; for the Lord God, the Holy One of Israel, has spoken it" (2 Nephi 9:23–24).

[13] "Christian theologians have long wrestled with the question, What is the destiny of the countless billions who have lived and died with no knowledge of Jesus? With the Restoration of the gospel of Jesus Christ has come the understanding of how the unbaptized dead are redeemed and how God can be 'a perfect, just God, and a merciful God also' (Alma 42:15). While yet in life, Jesus prophesied that He would also preach to the dead (John 5:25). Peter tells us this happened in the interval between the Savior's Crucifixion and Resurrection (1 Peter 3:18–19). President Joseph F. Smith witnessed in vision that the Savior visited the spirit world and 'from among the righteous [spirits]...organized his forces and appointed messengers, clothed with power and authority, and commissioned them to go forth and carry the light of the gospel to them that were in darkness.' 'These were taught faith in God, repentance from sin, vicarious baptism for the remission of sins, [and] the gift of the Holy Ghost by the laying on of hands' (D&C 138:30,33). The doctrine that the living can provide baptism and other essential ordinances to the dead, vicariously, was revealed anew to the Prophet Joseph Smith. (See D&C 124, 128, 132.) He learned that the spirits awaiting resurrection are not only offered individual salvation but that they can be bound in heaven as husband and wife and be sealed to their fathers and mothers of all generations past and have sealed to them their children of all generations future. The Lord instructed the Prophet that these sacred rites are appropriately performed only in a house built to His name, a temple (D&C 124:29–36)" (D. Todd Christofferson, "The Redemption of the Dead and the Testimony of Jesus," *Ensign*, Nov 2000, p. 9).

[14] "And because he had fallen from heaven, and had become miserable forever, he sought also the misery of all mankind" (2 Nephi 2:18).

[15] "The vicarious ordinances we perform in temples, beginning with baptism, make possible an eternal welding link between generations that fulfills the purpose of the earth's creation. Without this, 'the whole earth would be utterly wasted at [Christ's] coming' (D&C 2:3). Elijah

has, in fact, come as promised to confer the priesthood power that turns hearts and establishes the welding links between the fathers and the children so that once again what is bound on earth 'shall be bound in heaven' (Matthew 16:19). When he came, Elijah declared, 'The keys of this dispensation are committed into your hands; and by this ye may know that the great and dreadful day of the Lord is near, even at the doors' (D&C 110:16)" (D. Todd Christofferson, "The Redemption of the Dead and the Testimony of Jesus," *Ensign*, Nov 2000, p. 9).

[16] "For behold, this is my work and my glory—to bring to pass the immortality and eternal life of man" (Moses 1:39).

[17] "The Prophet Elijah was to plant in the hearts of the children the promises made to their fathers, Foreshadowing the great work to be done in the temples of the Lord in the dispensation of the fulness of times, for the redemption of the dead, and the sealing of the children to their parents, lest the whole earth be smitten with a curse and utterly wasted at his coming" (D&C 138:47–48).

[18] "Of transcendent significance is that within the sacred walls of the temple, husbands and wives make eternal covenants. These covenants are sealed by priesthood authority. Children of that union, if they are worthy, may enjoy an eternal relationship as part of a family and as children of God. As the Apostle John wrote: 'What are these which are arrayed in white robes? ...Therefore are they before the throne of God, and serve him day and night in his temple' (Revelation 7:13,15). The Lord has said that His work is 'to bring to pass the immortality and eternal life of man' (Moses 1:39). It follows then that all mankind, living and dead, should have the opportunity of hearing the gospel either in this life or in the spirit world. As Paul said to the Corinthians, 'Else what shall they do which are baptized for the dead, if the dead rise not at all? why are they then baptized for the dead?' (1 Corinthians 15:29) This is the reason we do ordinance work in temples for our deceased ancestors. No person's choice or agency is taken away. Those for whom the work is done may accept it or not, as they choose" James E. Faust, "The Restoration of All Things," *Ensign*, May 2006, pgs. 61–62, 67–68).

[19] "...I would that ye should look to the great Mediator, and hearken unto his great commandments; and be faithful unto his words, and choose eternal life, according to the will of his Holy Spirit; And not choose eternal death, according to the will of the flesh and the evil which is therein, which giveth the spirit of the devil power to captivate, to bring you down to hell, that he may reign over you in his own kingdom" (2 Nephi 2:28–29).

[20] "And there shall also be many which shall say: Eat, drink, and be merry; nevertheless, fear God—he will justify in committing a little sin; yea, lie a little, take the advantage of one because of his words, dig a pit for thy neighbor; there is no harm in this; and do all these things, for tomorrow we die; and if it so be that we are guilty, God will beat us with a few stripes, and at last we shall be saved in the kingdom of God. Yea, and there shall be many which shall teach after this manner, false and vain and foolish doctrines, and shall be puffed up in their hearts, and shall seek deep to hide their counsels from the Lord; and their works shall be in the dark....Because of pride, and because of false teachers, and false doctrine, their churches have become corrupted, and their churches are lifted up; because of pride they are puffed up....And behold, others he flattereth away, and telleth them there is no hell; and he saith unto them: I am no devil, for there is none—and thus he whispereth in their ears, until he grasps them with his awful chains, from whence there is no deliverance" (2 Nephi 28:8–9, 12, 22).

[21] "And they shall wander from sea to sea, and from the north even to the east, they shall run to and fro to seek the word of the LORD, and shall not find it" (Amos 8:12).

"And he beheld Satan; and he had a great chain in his hand, and it veiled the whole face of the earth with darkness; and he looked up and laughed, and his angels rejoiced" (Moses 7:26).

[22] "One Lord, one faith, one baptism, One God and Father of all, who is above all, and through all, and in you all" (Ephesians 4:5–6).

[23] "And I saw another angel fly in the midst of heaven, having the everlasting gospel to preach unto them that dwell on the earth, and to every nation, and kindred, and tongue, and people" (Revelation 14:6).

"The Apostle John saw in vision the time when an angel would come to the earth as part of the Restoration of the gospel. That angel was Moroni, who appeared to the Prophet Joseph Smith. He directed Joseph to the place where golden plates containing ancient writings were deposited. Joseph Smith then translated these plates by the gift and power of God, and the Book of Mormon was published. This is a record of two groups of people who lived centuries ago on the American continent. Little was known about them before the coming forth of the Book of Mormon. But more importantly, the Book of Mormon is another testament of Christ. It restored precious truths concerning the Fall, the Atonement, the Resurrection, and life after death" (James E. Faust, "The Restoration of All Things," *Ensign*, May 2006, pgs. 61–62, 67–68).

"And the book is delivered to him that is not learned, saying, Read this, I pray thee: and he saith, I am not learned.…Therefore, behold, I will proceed to do a marvelous work among this people, even a marvelous work and a wonder: for the wisdom of their wise men shall perish, and the understanding of their prudent men shall be hid" (Isaiah 29:12, 14).

[24] "And then are ye in this straight and narrow path which leads to eternal life; yea, ye have entered in by the gate; ye have done according to the commandments of the Father and the Son; and ye have received the Holy Ghost, which witnesses of the Father and the Son, unto the fulfilling of the promise which he hath made, that if ye entered in by the way ye should receive" (2 Nephi 31:18).

[25] "And now, my beloved brethren, after ye have gotten into this strait and narrow path, I would ask if all is done? Behold, I say unto you, Nay; for ye have not come thus far save it were by the word of Christ with unshaken faith in him, relying wholly upon the merits of him who is mighty to save. Wherefore, ye must press forward with a steadfastness in Christ, having a perfect brightness of hope, and a love of God and of all men. Wherefore, if ye shall press forward, feasting upon the word of Christ, and endure to the end, behold, thus saith the Father: Ye shall have eternal life" (2 Nephi 31:19–20).

[26] "And they who are in the north countries shall come in remembrance before the Lord; and their prophets shall hear his voice, and shall no longer stay themselves; and they shall smite the rocks, and the ice shall flow down at their presence. And an highway shall be cast up in the midst of the great deep.…And the boundaries of the everlasting hills shall tremble at their presence. And there shall they fall down and be crowned with glory, even in Zion, by the hands of the servants of the Lord, even the children of Ephraim" (D&C 133:26–27, 31–32).

[27] "Therefore the redeemed of the LORD shall return, and come with singing unto Zion; and everlasting joy *shall be* upon their head: they shall obtain gladness and joy; *and* sorrow and mourning shall flee away" (Isaiah 51:11).

[28] "But take diligent heed to do the commandment and the law, which Moses the servant of the Lord charged you, to love the Lord your God, and to walk in all his ways, and to keep his commandments, and to cleave unto him, and to serve him with all your heart and with all your soul" (Joshua 22:5).

[29] "Now this change was not equal to that which shall take place at the last day; but there was a change wrought upon them, insomuch that Satan could have no power over them, that he could not tempt them; and they were sanctified in the flesh, that they were holy, and that the powers of the earth could not hold them" (3 Nephi 28:39).

[30] "Then we which are alive and remain shall be caught up together with them in the clouds, to meet the Lord in the air: and so shall we ever be with the Lord" (Thessalonians 4:17).

[31] "And he laid hold on the dragon, that old serpent, which is the Devil, and Satan, and bound him a thousand years" (Revelation 20:2).

[32] "Search the scriptures; for in them ye think ye have eternal life: and they are they which testify of me" (John 5:39).

[33] "And because of your diligence and your faith and your patience with the word in nourishing it, that it may take root in you, behold, by and by ye shall pluck the fruit thereof, which is most precious, which is sweet above all that is sweet, and which is white above all that is white, yea, and pure above all that is pure; and ye shall feast upon this fruit even until ye are filled, that ye hunger not, neither shall ye thirst" (Alma 32:42).

[34] "And now behold, I ask of you, my brethren of the church, have ye spiritually been born of God? Have ye received his image in your countenances? Have ye experienced this mighty change in your hearts?" (Alma 5:14)

[35] "Moreover, thou son of man, take thee one stick, and write upon it, For Judah, and for the children of Israel his companions: then take another stick, and write upon it, For Joseph, the stick of Ephraim, and for all the house of Israel his companions" (Ezekiel 37:16).

[36] A Quad, or the standard works is "A recognized, authoritative collection of sacred books. In The Church of Jesus Christ of Latter-day Saints, the canonical books are called the standard works and include the Old and New Testaments, the Book of Mormon, the Doctrine and Covenants, and the Pearl of Great Price" ("Cannon," *Guide to the Scriptures*, www.lds.org).

"The stick of Judah: This refers to the Bible as a record of the house of Judah (Ezek. 37: 15-19). In the last days, when the various branches of the house of Israel are gathered, their sacred records will also be gathered together" ("Stick of Judah," *Guide to the Scriptures*, www.lds.org).

"A branch of Ephraim will be broken off and will write another testament of Christ, (JST, Gen. 50: 24-26, 30-31). The stick of Judah and the stick of Joseph will become one, (Ezek. 37: 15-19). The writings of Judah and of Joseph shall grow together, (2 Ne. 3: 12). The Lord speaks to many nations, (2 Ne. 29). The keys of the record of the stick of Ephraim were committed to Moroni, (D&C 27: 5). The stick of Ephraim or Joseph: A record of one group from the tribe of Ephraim that was led from Jerusalem to America about 600 B.C. This group's record is called the stick of Ephraim or Joseph, or the Book of Mormon. It and the stick of Judah (the Bible) form a unified testimony of the Lord Jesus Christ, his resurrection, and his divine work among these two segments of the house of Israel" ("Stick of Ephraim," *Guide to the Scriptures*, www.lds.org).

[37] Revelation 1:3,7

[38] "...By small and simple things are great things brought to pass..." (Alma 37:6).

CHAPTER TWELVE

LIFE IN THE FAST LANE

"Behold, I am the law, and the light. Look unto me, and endure to the end, and ye shall live; for unto him that endureth to the end will I give eternal life" (3 Nephi 15:9).

00:03:10, 09:30:52, Zulu
Saturday, September 20th

Choice

Provo, Utah
7:30 a.m.

Bo sat defeated on the wooden porch steps of his house. With one knee up he rested his elbow and propped up his head with his hand.

The sun was shining. It was a bright new day. The air was crisp, cool, and clean. Breathing it, smelling it, tempted him to give up his anger, but no, he wasn't ready, so he grumbled inside instead. It was ironic that in the darkest moments of his life, the sun was shining so brightly. It mocked his anger, which made him feel like he wanted to get even angrier. It was not making things better.

The door opened behind him. He turned to see Corrynne look out at him from the doorway but he didn't say anything, he just turned back to his previous position. He didn't feel like talking.

"Bo, can I talk to you?"

Inside Bo said "no," but he refrained from verbalizing it. Instead he just sat without responding.

"Where've you been?" asked Corrynne as she took a seat next to him.

"I've been out walking."

"For over six hours?"

"Yep."

"Where did you go?"

Bo looked at Corrynne, took a breath, then put his leg down so he was sitting upright. "I went to the bus stop and back."

"Which one?"

"The one that would take me to Alaska."

Corrynne stifled a laugh.

"What?" asked Bo looking at Corrynne.

"A bus to take you to Alaska?"

Bo stared out at the mountains that surrounded the city on every side. "It was my last option. Obviously it didn't work."

"You're serious?" asked Corrynne. "You really tried?"

Bo nodded.

"With what money?"

"My silver coins."

"From your collection? How did you get it? You didn't come back into the house."

"I had the collection in my truck. I was going to cash it in yesterday for some extra money, but the coin store was out of business already."

Corrynne took Bo's hand in hers and laid her head on his shoulder. "I'm sorry, Bo."

Bo shrugged. "For what? It's par for the course."

"I'm sorry that you felt you had to cash in your collection. I know how much you love it."

"I don't love it," said Bo. "I was just saving it for a rainy day. Today's a rainy day and now I can't even cash it in."

"I see," said Corrynne looking out at the view too. "Silver is good though. I'm sure we can still use the coins to buy things we need from people in general, even if the stores are closed."

Bo nodded. "I paid $35.00 per dollar coin, so I guess, as long as we are buying something for that value, it might be worth it."

"Sure…." said Corrynne, but didn't offer anything else.

They sat together in silence on the porch, both deep in their own thoughts.

After a few minutes Corrynne said, "Bo, I want to talk to you about something else. Do you mind listening for a few minutes?"

Bo cocked his head and looked at Corrynne briefly. "I'm here."

Corrynne nodded and took a breath. "This morning when you left, I didn't know what I should do. I'm at a loss too. All the things that are bothering you are bothering me too. So I went to the Lord and prayed. I prayed a long time, and during my prayer I was inspired to look up some talks from the First Presidency."

"About what?" asked Bo.

"About adversity, suffering, loss, and choices."

"Those are broad subjects."

"I know. But through my reading, I found a story I think you should hear. It really applies to this situation."

Bo thought a moment. Did he want to hear these things? He knew on one hand he should listen, but on the other, he was still stinging inside. He felt abandoned by the Lord, and to listen to some trite words that were so general that it was even questionable if they applied, just didn't appeal to him. He wanted to work things out on his own. He didn't need his wife following him around, quoting things to him. "You know, Corrynne, I'm really not in the mood."

"Bo, please. I think this will help. Please listen," begged Corrynne.

Bo closed his eyes. He didn't want to listen. He wanted to refuse to listen. He wanted to punish God for what he was doing to his life.

With a heavy sigh, Bo looked at Corrynne. There was longing mixed with pain in her eyes. He had seen that look before. He realized that she needed to talk about things, almost as much as he didn't want to talk. He knew from being a bishop that if he did not make an effort to be aware of his wife's thoughts and efforts, it could eventually lead to the destruction of their relationship. Was that something he was willing to lose? After everything else?

Bo nodded. "OK. I'll listen."

Corrynne smiled. Wrapping her arms around Bo she asked, "Do you know I love you?"

Bo put his arms around his wife and nodded. "I do know that."

"Do you know that even though this world seems to be spinning out of control, that we still have all the blessings of eternity through the blessings of the temple and our righteousness?"

Bo looked into Corrynne's warm brown eyes. Her look was intense. "Of course I know those things."

"OK, then why are you letting the circumstances of our life, things that can change from moment to moment, things that of course we can't control, things that don't matter eternally, affect you so much?"

"I thought you were going to talk to me about what you read."

"I am. I just want you to think about that question as I tell you a story."

"OK, I will," said Bo with a hint of a smile.

Corrynne pulled Bo to stand and then she lead him to their porch swing. With her hand in his, they sat together and began to swing slightly.

"Now, I want to tell you a story," said Corrynne.

"You said that," said Bo, beginning to soften inside.

"Oh, good, you were listening," she said with a smile.

Bo nodded but didn't comment.

Corrynne started. "There once was a perfectly upright—and very good looking—man who feared God."

Bo smiled and shook his head. "Flattery will get you everywhere—I mean," he pretended to cough, "nowhere."

Corrynne smiled and continued. "This man fought against evil on every front. Because he was such a great man, he was given the blessings of heaven, a beautiful wife, seven sons, and three daughters. They lived in a quaint little cottage down in a valley surrounded by majestic mountains."

"Let me guess," said Bo. "Everything was destroyed and then it was given back again."

"Bo!" said Corrynne. "Let me tell my story!"

"I'm sorry. Go ahead," said Bo laughing a little. He liked teasing Corrynne.

"Anyway, to make a long story short, Satan was unimpressed with this man. So what if he had lived uprightly before the Lord his whole life? He was blessed! It was easy to live righteously when it paid off. Satan believed that if this man had some tragedies in his life, he could cause this righteous man to curse God and turn away from him."

"Hmmm," said Bo nodding. He didn't want to admit it, but he *was* having those temptations. That was shocking! Could it be true that he was being tempted to curse God and turn from him? Bo continued to listen.

"Then one day tragedy did strike. His two eldest sons were taken to a far land. His two eldest daughters were locked up in prisons. His third eldest son left the home to fight in a war, and at the same time, all the money in his counting house was stolen from him so he could not rescue any of them."

Bo nodded. "I can relate to this man."

"But even though all these things happened to him, his love for God did not waver. Do you know what he said at the deepest, darkest moment of despair?"

Bo knew what came next. Corrynne was telling a variation of the story of Job, using him as Job,[2] but to be funny he asked, "No, did he ask 'Where's the beef?' Because I know I'd wonder what 'beef' God had with me."

Corrynne shook her head, enduring Bo's humor. "No, Bo, he said, 'I came into this world naked and without anything. I know that the Lord gives blessings—and in his infinite wisdom, he can take blessings away. Blessed be the name of the Lord.'"

Bo nodded. "I get the hint. You want me to be patient in my afflictions."

"No, *I* don't," said Corrynne with a shocked look in her eyes and a hand to her chest.

"You don't?"

"No. Let me continue."

"Fine," said Bo.

"Satan still wasn't impressed with the man's integrity. So, he had not turned from God when things were taken away? That didn't prove anything. He had had a life of luxury and ease! It would take a lot more sadness to turn him from God."

"Oh, no. Now I see where you're going with this..."

Corrynne continued. "He was afflicted with sickness and wounds that wouldn't heal."

"Wouldn't his wife use her talents to heal him?" asked Bo, again trying to be funny.

Corrynne shook her head. "There wasn't any medicine. There wasn't anything she could do."

"I think you're changing the story," said Bo.

"But still, the righteous man loved God with all his heart. His love wasn't conditional on only having a good life. He would love God through the good times and the bad. After all, God had given him breath and the opportunity to live. Who was he to complain?"

"Wow, this man should be translated," said Bo.

"No, actually, he was human, and being human he went through a really tough time emotionally and psychologically. He began to wonder if he should have ever been born. He began praying for death and for his suffering to end."

"I've had some of those feelings," said Bo, kidding, but a little serious at the same time.

"Then guess what."

"What?"

"This man had a vision. A dream at night."

"Really?" asked Bo, not remembering this part of the story.

"Yes. An angel came and rebuked him for his depressing thoughts."

"He did?"

"*She* did," said Corrynne with a sparkle in her eye.

Bo looked at Corrynne and then laughed. "I guess you are as beautiful as a vision…"

"And guess what?"

"What?" asked Bo.

"The righteous man's whole countenance changed. He realized he was being taught invaluable lessons about the value of life, what makes life good verses bad, the purpose of why we are here, and everything changed.[3] He became a wise teacher. He taught everyone that when men are born, they are born into trouble.[4] Life happens! Our job is to endure it all and come out refined and purified because of the trouble. We are given problems to make us smarter, stronger, and better able to serve each other! In fact, we should be humble and thank Heavenly Father for our afflictions because in them we become like him! And when we become like him, we are able to have everything he has!"[5]

Bo looked at Corrynne. She had light in her face. She was right. He knew she was right. He hung his head in self disgust. What was his problem? He knew better than to act like a spoiled child who wasn't getting his way. When he was angry with God, all he was doing was being self-destructive. He had been choosing a path that didn't lead to the tree of life and why? Because he was angry? Because he wanted God to suffer? That was *stupid*. What would being angry do except to make him depressed? It wouldn't make his life better! It wouldn't bring his children back. It wouldn't make Corrynne happy.[6]

Bo looked at Corrynne and kissed her. "Thank you," he said. "You *are* my angel."

Corrynne smiled. "You're a good guy, Bo. The Lord loves you. We might lose things for a while, but someday they'll all be returned. You are not like Job yet."

Bo nodded. "You're right." Then he stood up. "I am blessed. Now if you'll forgive me, I need to go repent and become what God is preparing me to be."

Bo walked down the stairs and down the sidewalk. He would go on another walk. Not to Alaska, but back to God. He hoped through his prayers he could find a shortcut back.[7]

Nursery Rhymes

Frankfort, Germany
8:00 p.m.

Matt leaned against the door jam of the soon-to-be-nursery in the massive mansion in Germany. He watched his father hang pictures and mobiles with sausage-like, ring clad fingers. MD seemed to be brimming with an almost a giddy excitement over something. He had an unlit cigar hanging half out of the right side of his mouth and he was singing. To Matt it was a strange sound. He didn't think he had ever heard his father sing. It sounded strangely morbid. He moved inside the room to hear clearer, and then the familiar tune struck him. His father was singing a nursery rhyme.

"Ring around the rosy—pocket full of posy—ashes, ashes—we all fall down..." The sound lingered in the air eerily. Suddenly, MD looked back with a big clown-like smile.

His father's abrupt movement surprised Matt and he jumped. Swallowing, he calmed himself down. "Hi,." he managed to say. "Just came to look at this place.

MD laughed deep in his throat then said, "Yeah, it's shaping up. Come on in. I want you to see all of it."

A cold chill hit Matt's body, as if an unseen evil had just passed through him. Considering Brea's experiences with evil in the New York house, Matt didn't want to think about what *that* meant so he forced himself to ignore his feeling. "It's looking good in here." He nodded and tried to sound sincere to hide the pain of what the nursery actually meant to him. He prayed for strength.

"Only the best for my *son*!" said MD.

Matt didn't think his father was speaking about him. That meant only one thing.... The thought of handing over his newborn son was so unimaginable. Pain expanded in his chest, making breathing difficult.

"What do you think of this airplane mobile?" asked MD. "Should it go over the crib, or over the changing table?" he asked as he held up a mobile complete with shiny vintage model prop planes, holding it up in both places for Matt to see.

Matt folded his arms and studied the ceiling and the furniture set up. "I think over the changing table would be good," he said.

MD looked at Matt, smiled and said, "Good!" Then he climbed on a ladder, opposite where Matt suggested, and nailed it with difficulty above the crib. "Then I'll hang it here."

Matt understood very clearly what was happening. His father was trying to offend him. He had an agenda. Like always, MD wanted to push his buttons. Maybe he was still testing him. But Matt wouldn't be manipulated. If he got angry, then it would only sabotage his own plans for the future. Matt changed the subject.

"So tell me what's next for America," he said coolly. He wanted to seem unaffected by the devastation occurring in the US as they spoke.

"America?" asked MD looking over at Matt with beady eyes. "America's toast. 'Ashes, ashes, they all fell down.'"

In his mind Matt could hear all evil laughing. He knew his father thought he had won the ultimate victory. "Ashes, ashes?" pretending to not quite make a connection.

"Just like I said. They're toast, gone up in flames, kaput—and now, it's time to cash in our investments," MD said as he stepped back off the ladder, heaving a heavy breath and rubbing his hands together. "Do you have a light?" asked MD now patting his pockets, his unlit cigar still dangling out of his mouth. "I found this great cigar in my stuff in here, but I can't find my lighter."

Matt looked around, secretly bothered by what his father had just said. Why did he have to be so *blasted*—? Matt avoided his thoughts and where they might lead. "Sorry, I don't," he answered, looking around with a blank face. "Are you sure you want to smoke that cigar in the nursery?"

MD took the cigar out of his mouth and said, "Didn't hurt you any."

Matt nodded, anger flickering across his mind, but he squelched it. He had to keep in mind his ultimate end goal. He needed to seem to support his father in everything, even his decadence.

"Hey, I'll find you one," said Matt, heading down the hall to his father's bedroom. He took a lighter and a clip off the nightstand and brought it back to the nursery.

"Good," said MD with delight in his voice. "Light this for me will ya?" he said as he handed the cigar to Matt. "I have a few more things to hang."

Matt looked at the cigar, lighter, and clip. He had seen his father do this a thousand times, but he had never done it himself. He loathed smoking and his father knew that. Again, Matt recognized this as a ploy to get him upset. He wouldn't put the dirty thing in his mouth!

Matt clipped the end into a small garbage can and then applied the lighter to the end for a few minutes. It took a while to light the cigar, but he finally did it. "Here you go," he said as he held it out for his father, the end smoking slightly.

MD looked back at Matt and said, "Thanks, but I hate those kind. You can have it." Then he began hammering a nail into the wall for a picture with a smile on his face.

Matt closed his eyes. He would not get angry.

MD began singing once more. "Humpty Dumpty sat on a wall. Humpty Dumpty had a great fall!" said MD in a sing-song voice. "All the Queen's horses and all the Queen's men couldn't put Humpty together again." He finished and then let out a guttural laugh. "Queen, get it?" he asked Matt.

Matt opened is eyes. What he saw was shocking! The picture MD was hanging was a picture of the White House with its top blown off.

"What's that?" asked Matt, shocked.

"I thought it would be good to have pictures that remind the baby of where he came from," he said with a smile. "Looks good right here, huh? I think it brings the smoky white color out in the dresser. It was hard to get this picture since my satellites were knocked out by those solar flares, but one of my men got a good one. I enlarged the picture today."

Matt swallowed and shook his head. He couldn't resist his next thought and blurted out, *"You're sick!"*

MD looked at Matt with his smile only getting wider. "I'm sorry, I didn't hear what you said. Did you say that I was '*sick*'?"

A feeling of dread settled in Matt's stomach. What had he done? He didn't respond.

MD turned back to his picture and with his handkerchief, he shined the metal frame. "No, son, to respond to your statement, I'm not sick. I'm ruthless and that's why I'm successful. I'm unstoppable and everyone in the world knows it."

Matt watched his father gloat and then all of a sudden he couldn't help himself. With all the anger he had kept bottled up inside him, he exclaimed, *"Who hangs a picture like that in an infant's room?"* He slammed the cigar in the garbage can with a loud bang. Looking back at his father he said, "No, wrong question. *Who hangs a picture like that in **any room**?*"

"This is my work!" said MD with his hand outstretched. "This is my art! Don't you frame your art? This is a miracle of our age! This is war without war! I have conquered a whole nation in one moment, without one nuclear weapon! I've done the impossible! Take note!" he said with emphasis and a finger pointed in Matt's direction. *"You have so much to learn!"*

Matt felt nauseous with the volatile mix of his pent up emotions as he looked at the symbol of freedom destroyed. There was no place he could find peace in his mind. There was pain in every corner. He looked at his father who he knew could see he was melting down inside.

"Come here, son," said MD with his arms out wide. "You look like you need a hug."

Matt stood as still as a statue. Hate was growing inside him.

"Fine," said MD pulling out the rocking chair from the corner of the room. "You don't have to hug me. I know real men don't like to hug their fathers. I can respect that. But come sit." MD patted the highest rung of the stepladder as he squatted and then allowed his round body to fall into the rocking chair. "I want to let you in on a plan that's been in the making for thousands of years and inspired by the works of Mahan."

Matt looked at his father. "Mahan?" What did that mean? Was he referring to the works of—Satan?[9] Because, according to his father, the works *certainly* wouldn't be of God.

MD continued. "After generations of patient planning, finally we are seeing the fruits of that plan. I want you to hear about your rightful heritage." He patted the stepladder again.

Visions of robed men and torches flickered in Matt's head. He didn't want anything to do with his heritage. However, Matt knew it was best to take his father's invitation. With great control and despite his deep-seated revulsion, he forced his legs to move, and then he sat on the small stepladder.

MD pointed at the picture. "I know you, with all your pollyanna-ish morals, see in that picture devastation, tragedy, and human loss, but I see something different and it all has to do with money."

"Money?" asked Matt hardly able to choke out the word.

"Yes, money. Let me ask you. Do you know where money comes from?"

Matt closed his eyes as he considered his father's question. Was he toying with him again? He didn't know. He seemed to have switched into a straight forward mode—Matt thought maybe he was truly trying to teach him something. Maybe his father was using the shock technique to get him to listen. He did that a lot. OK, he was listening. "No, where does money come from?" asked Matt with less than the desired enthusiasm.

"No, really, indulge me," said MD with happiness in his eyes. "Guess where money comes from."

"The government prints it," said Matt. It was a simplistic answer but he was trying to be straight forward so he wouldn't get caught in any more of his father's traps.

"No, you're wrong. The government only prints metal and paper *symbols* of money. That's not the money itself.[10] Would you believe it if I told you that a hundred years ago, your ancestors devised a genius plan that would create money out of thin air?"

Matt studied MD's face. It was obvious he was getting lost in his own story, relishing the information he was about to impart. Matt nodded. "Sounds like a magic trick."

MD's eyes grew intense and he sat forward. "It is. It's a trick that happens a billion, trillion times a day, every day, by private corporations called *banks*."

"I don't follow you," said Matt.

"Most people believe that when they deposit their money in a bank, the bank takes that same money, pays them interest for it and then in turn, loans out that money at a higher rate of interest to make an income, but that's not true."

"What's true then?" asked Matt. He had no idea where his father was going but decided to go along without interfering.

"Banks create the money they loan, not from the depositor's money, not from the interest they earn from the loans they make from the deposits of their patrons, but directly from the promise of people to repay their loans."[11]

"OK, how?"

"When people go into a bank for a loan, they receive money. The bank receives a promise that they will be repaid the money plus the interest or lose the house, or the car for which they obtained the loan."

"Right," said Matt.

"So what does the borrower's signature promising repayment do for the bank?"

"I don't know."

"It allows them to pull the amount of the loan from the air and just enter it into the borrower's account. It's that easy. They create it from the air."

"That can't be true," said Matt. "Banks can't just conjure up money they don't have and make interest on it. That's dishonest and illegal. If I did that, I'd be put in prison."

MD nodded with a satisfied smile. "Yes, you would, unless you were a *bank*."[12]

"What's so different about a bank?"

"The rules that govern them were created for the purpose of making money out of air. Creating money from debt was not only invented by your ancestors, it is now the basis of every progressive economy in the world.[13] It's responsible for bloated and successful economies. People and governments want successful economies.[14] They are addicted to things and the feeling of success,[15] so thus, creation of money from nothing is not only allowed, it's fostered and supported by all governments, as well as by the people."

"So in essence, you're saying something dishonest was invented and supported by my grandfather and great-grandfather and now you, and because it benefits the whole, it's considered honest and legal."

"Now you're seeing the reality of morality. There is no morality,[16] only what benefits the whole verses what destroys the whole. Talk of morality is just mumbo jumbo perceptions, meant to promote cooperation among societies. If we can get people to buy into our view of morality, *it becomes the morality*. Do you see what I'm saying?"

Matt shook his head. "I know what you're trying to do and I'm not going to debate the meaning of morality with you."

MD sat back. "I don't want to discuss or debate anything. I'm stating facts. If you were smart, you'd listen."

Matt sat quietly and looked at his hands. He considered what his father was telling him. Maybe he *should* just be quiet and listen. Anyway, maybe this conversation might lead him to understand the inner workings of his father's mind. He might be able to plan his future better if he could. Looking back up he said, "OK, help me understand."

"Good," said MD with a satisfied smile. "Think about how money came about. At first, money was anything that could be traded for something else that was valuable. Later, goldsmiths made gold in standardized units to make trade easier and eventually, gold or silver coins became the unit of universal trade. But to store all that gold became difficult as well as dangerous. Eventually, the goldsmith built a vault to ensure the protection of his wealth. Others saw this vault and requested that the goldsmith store their gold in the vault to protect their money from robbers and thieves, too. In return, they were charged a fee to store the gold for protection, thus the birth of the first banks."

"I'm following you," said Matt.

"Well, soon the goldsmith realized that rarely did the depositors ever take out all their money, and in addition, they never all came in at once. This was because the claim checks that the goldsmith had given out that represented the depositor's money were being traded as if they were the real gold, thus the birth of paper money, or certificates that claimed a certain value in gold deposited in a bank." MD pointed at Matt. "I'm sure you can guess what happened next."

Matt nodded and said, "Well, knowing you and the men that came before you, I would say that the goldsmith started loaning out the gold in his vault for interest. Even though it wasn't his, he would still loan it out and collect interest on the loans, since everyone was so content with their gold safe in his vault."

"Yes. It was ingenious!" said MD, his hands waving in the air. "The goldsmith made money on other people's money while doing them a service. Everyone was happy, right? Well, yes, until the townspeople figured out what the goldsmith was doing. Then they threatened to pull out their money. So in return, the goldsmith, instead of demanding rent for his vault space, said he would *pay* the depositors a percentage of his gains to use their money, so that, not only would he protect their money for them, but then they could make extra money on the side. It was a win-win situation and once again, everyone was happy. That, my friend, was the birth of the loan business."

Matt nodded. "I can see that."

"What came next was the most amazing part," said MD his eyes lighting up. "Since rarely did people take their money out of the vault and no one knew how much was really in the vault…"

"Let me guess," said Matt, "the goldsmith decided to give out loans on money that wasn't in his vault."

"Right. He would merely write out the loans people demanded, the economy accepted his loan as real money and would give real goods for money that did not exist. Then the people would pay back their loans giving the goldsmith the principal that never existed in the first place, plus the interest. He had just done an amazing magic trick. He had just made money out of thin air."

"Yep, that sounds like the ultimate scam," said Matt.

"Now, come on, Matt. How can you call a single-handed action that led to the economic growth of a whole town, a scam? It was good. It was moral. Everyone benefited. It was the basis of our huge economies today. It was a miracle!"

"Spare me the dramatics, and tell me the downside."

MD nodded. "There was a downside, you're right. If the borrower wanted the real gold instead of the paper representation, and to keep up a good face, the goldsmith paid out the real gold. Then if the depositors decided they wanted real gold for their claim checks also, the gold would quickly run out and the vault would have to close, causing people to lose all their money because the bank was loaning out money that didn't exist. That was the first run on the banks. This was bad for the economy. It caused the opposite of economic growth. The town's government quickly realized that the basis of their economic success was in this practice of loaning out money that didn't exist. So in the spirit of mutual cooperation, the government legalized the practice of loaning out fictitious money if the bank would exercise limits on how much they loaned out. This is the basis for modern banking. Today, banks are allowed to loan out from nine to twenty times the amount deposited in their banks. Central banks were set up with large deposits of gold that would help local banks in the case of a run on the bank so that the system would not fail. It was only in the event of a run on the banks simultaneously that the whole system would collapse."

"Like what's happening in America right now."

"Not exactly," said MD.

"How's it different?"

"Banking today is a bit different from the scenario I just painted for you. It has evolved even further."

"How?"

"Paper money, as we discussed, used to represent a certain amount of gold in the bank, but now, there is no gold that backs the money. You see, gold limited how much money there really was. If a nation wanted more money, they had to find gold in the earth and dig it up to be able to grow the amount they could earn. To eliminate those limits, money today is actually created from debt."

"From debt? How can that be?"

"Every time someone takes out a loan from the bank and promises to pay it back, new money is created from the future expectation of income from that loan. Thus the amount of total real money is in relation to the total amount of debt. A nation must have debt to create money."

"This sounds backwards," said Matt, listening with disgusted awe. "Some banker had to be pretty twisted to come up with this system."

"Maybe, but it works. Not only is money being created out of thin air, it's being supported by money created out of thin air."

"So the banks make money from nothing just because people want to take out loans."

"Absolutely. Money is grown through the general population's desire to obtain things."

"Just how does that work?"

"Through the laws of the government."

"Which laws?"

"Fractional reserve requirement laws. Let's say a person wants to borrow $20,000 and they go to a bank. According to the laws, there must be a 9:1 ratio of money that exists in the central bank in order to give this loan. Therefore $2,222.22 must be deposited by an investment source. Then the loan is given of $20,000, which is roughly 2,222.22 times 9. That person takes that money, which is brand new money, and pays for a new porch for their house. The money is taken by the contractor and deposited in his bank. That bank can now take that money and according to the ratio of 9:1, give out another loan on that money, in other words $18,000 or $20,000 divided by 10, which is $2,000, subtracted from the $20,000, causing $18,000 to be given out as a loan while the remaining $2,000 is deposited in the reserves. That process continues, 90 times, repeating itself until a final return of $200,000 is made which is the return on all the loans that the bank has made on the initial investment of $2,222.22."[17]

Matt stared at his father. Now he could see it. Money was truly made out of nothing.[18] Debt did run the nation. Banks could create as much money as the people could borrow. New money couldn't be created unless people were willing to take out loans and create debt. The theory seemed so impossible yet it was real! Why didn't people know about this?

"I can see those wheels turning in that head of yours. You can see it can't you?" said MD. There was excitement in his eyes. "This is where the real truth lies, my son. Money is power. Because of money, laws are made; because of laws, morality is created; because of morality, justice is maintained and the world continues to revolve, creating success where there wouldn't be otherwise and feeding and clothing nations. Now that is *humanitarianism*! That is true morality. That is the world according to *MD*!"

Matt nodded. "It seems you have a pretty good system."

"Not only that, but I have control. For instance, let's say a certain government offends me. I can bring the whole nation to their knees very quickly. Since I control the money, I also control the governments. Since I control the governments, I control the destiny of the people.[19] I decide if they live or die. I decide if they eat or starve. *I decide*."[20] With his arms out and head back, MD exclaimed in a deep voice, *"I'm the god of this world."*[21]

Matt shivered. Where had he heard that statement before? His father was so evil! "So, how long can debt fund a nation?" he asked quickly, covering his contempt.

"Since money is created out of debt, and debt is needed to grow an economy, a time comes when the economy has grown too big and the debt is too great and people begin to default on all their loans. When that happens, I simply take all the goods that my loans have bought and then I have hard goods for money that never existed, making the ultimate return on an investment that didn't exist. Essentially, because of the laws of the land, I, the loan holder, inherit everything; all the houses, land, businesses. And this, my son, is how one systematically takes over the world."[22]

"I see. Slavery."[23]

"Call it what you want but I look at it as the world is my garden. I plant seeds in giving out loans, I grow it through debt. Then, when the country has the most bounty, when it is at its richest point in history with the greatest amount of goods and largest amount of debt, I call in my loans and collect my fruit. I harvest my garden. It's that simple."

"So that's what you did in America.[24] You called in the international debts and drained the source deposits."

"Yes, that's what I did," said MD looking proud of himself.

"And, not only that, I'm sure you ensured that the National Reserve would not issue new loans, even though it's created out of nothing."

"Of course. I can't give loans to people who have no money, nor any way of making money. To do so would be immoral and unlawful! Even I have to live by *some* rules. Anyway, America is a poor loan risk. It's just prudent business to not allow any more loans to occur now that there is no economy."

"Doesn't it bother you that you're destroying the lives of real people, with real children and real hunger?"

MD shook his head. "No, I gave them the greatest wealth on earth. If it weren't for me, they wouldn't have enjoyed vacations to the Bahamas, suped-up trucks, cruises, mansions, lives of leisure, and square meals every day. And I'm thinking, since I gave them all their blessings, I can take it away if they don't deserve it anymore. The Lord giveth and the Lord taketh away."[25]

Matt hung his head and laughed sarcastically, out of helplessness more than anything else. It was hard to just sit and listen to such blatant blasphemy.

"And the great news—Matt—," MD waited to get his son's attention.

Matt looked back up feeling his face flush with anger.

With a sincere expression, MD said, "The great news is that you, if you choose, can take this knowledge and give success to anyone in the world. You can feed the hungry. You can punish those who offend you. You can keep a balance. You, because you are my heir, can change the world in an idealistic way if you choose to, but that is the key. You must choose to walk with me to get there. There's always a price for your dreams."

Matt considered his father's words. This might be his door in. It would benefit everyone if he complied with his father and was returned to his good graces. Matt humbly bowed his head and said, "I choose that future."

"Ah ha!" said MD slapping his leg loudly and laughing heartily. "Finally, you've come to your senses!"

Matt used all his restraint to keep his humble attitude.

"OK, then! I guess you're going to have to be patient with my ways. Don't judge me. Don't preach to me, just learn from me. Only I hold the keys to your future."

Matt nodded. "I understand."

MD stood back up. "Now, pick up that other picture of New York. It's behind the crib against the wall."

Matt stood and retrieved the picture. It was a gruesome picture from the window of a high building, looking down at thousands of people lying in the streets. Matt closed his eyes. He wouldn't comment.

"Hand me the hammer. I think I see a good spot for it," said MD eyeing the wall.

Matt picked up the hammer and handed both the picture and the hammer to his father.

MD drove a nail into the wall and hung the picture. "Isn't that baby another work of art?" he asked Matt, looking for a response. "Pretty good for an ordinary digital camera, huh?"

Slowly Matt nodded and managed a smile. "Looks great, Dad."

MD nodded satisfied. "That's what I thought."

Somewhere, Matt heard many voices laughing.

Notes to "Life in the Fast Lane"

Choice

[1] "Contention in our families drives the Spirit of the Lord away. It also drives many of our family members away. Contention ranges from a hostile spoken word to worldwide conflicts. The scriptures tell us that 'only by pride cometh contention.' (Prov. 13:10; see also Prov. 28:25.) The scriptures testify that the proud are easily offended and hold grudges. (See 1 Ne. 16:1–3.) They withhold forgiveness to keep another in their debt and to justify their injured feelings. The proud do not receive counsel or correction easily. (See Prov. 15:10; Amos 5:10.) Defensiveness is used by them to justify and rationalize their frailties and failures. (See Matt. 3:9; John 6:30–59.) (Ezra Taft Benson, "Beware of Pride," *Ensign*, May 1989, p. 4).

[2] See Job, chapters 1–5.

[3] "Pride is the great stumbling block to Zion. I repeat: Pride *is* the great stumbling block to Zion. We must cleanse the inner vessel by conquering pride. (See Alma 6:2–4; Matt. 23:25–26.) We must yield 'to the enticings of the Holy Spirit,' put off the prideful 'natural man,' become 'a saint through the atonement of Christ the Lord,' and become 'as a child, submissive, meek, humble.' (Mosiah 3:19; see also Alma 13:28.)" (Ezra Taft Benson, "Beware of Pride," *Ensign*, May 1989, p. 4).

[4] "...Christ's plan of redemption helps put it all into perspective. In our preexistent state our Father in Heaven presented His plan for mortality, which Alma described as the 'plan of happiness' (Alma 42:8). I believe we all understood that by coming to earth, we would be

exposed to all of the experiences of earth life, including the not-so-pleasant trials of pain, suffering, hopelessness, sin, and death. There would be opposition and adversity. And if that was all we knew about the plan, I doubt if any of us would have embraced it, rejoicing, 'That's what I have always wanted—pain, suffering, hopelessness, sin, and death.' But it all came into focus, and it became acceptable, even desirable, when an Elder Brother stepped forward and offered that He would go down and make it all right. Out of pain and suffering He would bring peace. Out of hopelessness He would bring hope. Out of transgression He would bring repentance and forgiveness. Out of death He would bring the resurrection of lives. And with that explanation and most generous offer, each and every one of us concluded, 'I can do that. That is a risk worth taking.' And so we chose…perhaps the challenge is to have the kind of faith during the hard times that we exercised when we first chose. The kind of faith that turns questioning and even anger into acknowledging the power, blessings, and hope that can come only from Him who is the source of all power, blessings, and hope. The kind of faith that brings the knowledge and assurances that all that we experience is part of the gospel plan and that for the righteous, all that appears wrong will eventually be made right. The peace and understanding to endure with dignity and clarity of purpose can be the sweet reward. This kind of faith can help us to see the good, even when life's path seems to be layered only with thorns, thistles, and craggy rocks" (Richard C. Edgley, "For Thy Good," *Liahona*, July 2002, p. 72).

[5] "The revelations, for which we are grateful, show that we should even give thanks for our afflictions because they turn our hearts to God and give us opportunities to prepare for what God would have us become. The Lord taught the prophet Moroni, 'I give unto men weakness that they may be humble,' and then promised that 'if they humble themselves … and have faith in me, then will I make weak things become strong unto them' (Ether 12:27). In the midst of the persecutions the Latter-day Saints were suffering in Missouri, the Lord gave a similar teaching and promise: 'Verily I say unto you my friends, fear not, let your hearts be comforted; yea, rejoice evermore, and in everything give thanks; … and all things wherewith you have been afflicted shall work together for your good' (D&C 98:1, 3). And to Joseph Smith in the afflictions of Liberty Jail, the Lord said, 'Know thou, my son, that all these things shall give thee experience, and shall be for thy good' (D&C 122:7). Brigham Young understood. Said he, 'There is not a single condition of life [or] one hour's experience but what is beneficial to all those who make it their study, and aim to improve upon the experience they gain' (*Teachings of Presidents of the Church: Brigham Young* [1997], 179). As someone has said, there is a big difference between 20 years' experience and 1 year's experience repeated 20 times. If we understand the Lord's teachings and promises, we will learn and grow from our adversities. …President John Taylor on the subject of gratitude for suffering: 'We have learned many things through suffering. We call it suffering. I call it a school of experience. … I have never looked at these things in any other light than trials for the purpose of purifying the Saints of God that they may be, as the scriptures say, as gold that has been seven times purified by the fire' (*Teachings of Presidents of the Church: John Taylor* [2001], 203). Pioneers like President John Taylor, who witnessed the murder of their prophet and experienced prolonged persecution and incredible hardships for their faith, praised God and thanked Him. Through their challenges and the courageous and inspired actions they took to meet them, they grew in faith and in spiritual stature. Through their afflictions they became what God desired them to become, and they laid the foundation of the great work that blesses our lives today" (Dallin H. Oaks, "Give Thanks in All Things," *Liahona*, May 2003, pgs. 95–98).

[6] "The central feature of pride is enmity—enmity toward God and enmity toward our fellowmen. Enmity means 'hatred toward, hostility to, or a state of opposition.' It is the power by which Satan wishes to reign over us. Pride is essentially competitive in nature. We pit our will against God's. When we direct our pride toward God, it is in the spirit of 'my will and not thine be done.' As Paul said, they 'seek their own, not the things which are Jesus Christ's' (Philip. 2:21). Our will in competition to God's will allows desires, appetites, and passions to

go unbridled. (See Alma 38:12; 3 Ne. 12:30.) The proud cannot accept the authority of God giving direction to their lives. (See Hel. 12:6.) They pit their perceptions of truth against God's great knowledge, their abilities versus God's priesthood power, their accomplishments against His mighty works. Our enmity toward God takes on many labels, such as rebellion, hard-heartedness, stiff-neckedness, unrepentant, puffed up, easily offended, and sign seekers. The proud wish God would agree with them. They aren't interested in changing their opinions to agree with God's" (Ezra Taft Benson, "Beware of Pride," *Ensign*, May 1989, p. 4).

[7] "Therefore, blessed are they who will repent and hearken unto the voice of the Lord their God; for these are they that shall be saved" (Helaman 12:23).

Nursery Rhymes

[8] Some of the following quotes do not have complete information about the original publication sources but are generally accepted as factual and can be found easily on the Internet in multiple sites as well as many books about this subject. The incomplete quotes in this text are generally cited as accurate as they are found within this text.

[9] "And Cain said: Truly I am Mahan, the master of this great secret, that I may murder and get gain. Wherefore Cain was called Master Mahan, and he gloried in his wickedness" (Moses 5:31).

"'Mind,' 'destroyer,' and 'great one' are possible meanings of the roots evident in 'Mahan'" (footnote *d* Moses 5:31).

[10] A frightening fact about the topic of money is realizing that our American money does not represent any inherit value; all it is, is an accepted form of exchange for goods and services, backed by the government. One cannot take a dollar and ask for the equal value in gold. This is in direct violation of the Constitution of the United States which states, "No state shall make anything but gold and silver coin a tender in payment of debt...said notes shall be obligations of the United States...they shall be redeemed in lawful money on demand at the Treasury Department of the United States" (See Title 12 US Constitution, Section 411).

From the documentation of the Federal Reserve, they admit that our dollar does not have the value that the Constitution states it must and instead dismisses the subject as insignificant.

"Anything people generally accept in exchange for items of value is money....Currency backing isn't relevant in today's economy. Currency cannot be 'redeemed' or exchanged for Treasury gold or any other asset used as backing. The question of just what assets 'back' Federal Reserve notes has little but bookkeeping significance" (David H. Friedman, "I Bet You Thought," Federal Reserve Bank of New York, Public Information Department, December 1977, pgs. 5, 29).

"In the United States neither paper currency nor deposits have value as commodities. Intrinsically, a dollar bill is just a piece of paper. Deposits are merely book entries. Coins do have some intrinsic value as metal, but generally far less than their face value" ("Modern Money Mechanics workbook," Federal Reserve Bank of Chicago, 1975, p. 3).

[11] "Banks create money by 'monetizing' the private debts of businesses, individuals, and governments. That is, they create amounts of money against the value of those IOUs" (David H. Friedman, "I Bet You Thought," Federal Reserve Bank of New York, Public Information Department, December 1977, p. 27).

"We are completely dependant on the commercial banks. Someone has to borrow every dollar we have in circulation, cash or credit. If the banks create ample synthetic money we are prosperous; if not, we starve. We are absolutely without a permanent money system.... It is the most important subject intelligent persons can investigate and reflect upon. It is so important that our present civilization may collapse unless it becomes widely understood and the defects remedied very soon" (Robert H. Hemphill, Credit Manager Federal Reserve Bank, Atlanta Georgia. In the Foreword to Irving Fisher, "100% Money," 1935, reprinted by Pickering and Chatto Ltd. 1996).

[12] "When you or I write a check there must be sufficient funds in our account to cover the check, but when the Federal Reserve writes a check there is no bank deposit on which that check is drawn. When the Federal Reserve writes a check, it is creating money" ("Putting it simply," Boston Federal Reserve Bank).

[13] Now we see that the international bankers that hold the Federal Reserve in their hands control the economy today of the progressive countries of the world. We see that they can and do create money out of the air. They have made a promise to the people of economic success in return for eventual ownership of all assets and control of the economic freedom of the people. We have seen them at work on our own shores with our own doomed success in America using the fractional banking system and the Federal Reserve. We see that every country wishes to be as economically successful as America and many are buying into the banking system that can do that for them. With that understanding we can also see the future fulfillment of the following scripture as they complete their dominion to encompass all people. The following scripture foretells their complete success.

"I saw a woman [This woman is a whore, the symbol used throughout the scriptures to depict enticement towards evil (See Ezekiel 16:15–16 for an example). She is the package offered by the international bankers of unbridled riches and lasciviousness.] sit upon a scarlet [scarlet is the symbol for the sins of ungodly conduct (Isaiah 1:18; Psalms 51:7)] coloured beast, [the beast is the name used to represent the controlling ruling body in the last days supported by Satan (Revelation 13)] full of names of blasphemy, [the beast claims the powers of God (2 Thessalonians 2:3–4)] having seven heads [seven hills of Rome and representing seven previous kings that ruled with unrighteous power (Revelation 17:10)] and ten horns [ten powers in the last days that help the beast rule the nations (Revelation 17:12)]. And the woman was arrayed in purple and scarlet colour, and decked with gold and precious stones and pearls, [the leaders of the world are enticed by the riches promised (D&C 10:21)] having a golden cup in her hand full of abominations and filthiness of her fornication [the government that arises is without morality as the kings give up the freedom of their kingdoms to the beast in return for riches (See the comment by Richard D. Draper directly below.)]. And upon her forehead was a name written, MYSTERY, [secrecy, combinations of murder, secret works of darkness to fulfill their aims (2 Nephi 9:9, 2 Nephi 26:22, 3 Nephi 5:6)] BABYLON THE GREAT, [example of a godless city of sin, focused on riches (Jeremiah 51:6, 2 Nephi 21:15, D&C 1:16)] THE MOTHER OF HARLOTS [symbolizes inordinate wealth getting that arises through manipulation of money (Ezekiel 16:28–29] AND ABOMINATIONS OF THE EARTH" (Revelation 17:1–5).

"In the Bible the term 'abomination' describes those things so vile that they rouse the instant wrath of God...the Greek form of the word '*bdelugma*' denotes idolatry and harlotry, especially when combined to create a maleficent worship (see Deuteronomy. 29:26; 2 Corinthians 28:3). This worship has its objectives: acquisition of wealth and luxury at the expense of righteousness and decency. The whore represents those forces that move the world to wholesale adoption of the Mahanic principle" (Richard D. Draper, *Opening the Seven Seals,* p. 189).

[14] In Revelation Chapter 17 "John views the period just before the end time when nearly all the world follows after the whore, committing economic, political, and religious immoralities for both pleasure and gain. By promoting her objectives, society purchases her favors and as flatterers and sycophants, they yield to her whims. No class of society is without representation; all have become intoxicated by her lusts. As Isaiah prophesied, 'They are drunken, but not with wine; they stagger, but not with strong drink' (Isaiah 29:9)" (Richard D. Draper, *Opening the Seven Seals*, p. 186).

"...The great whore that sitteth upon many waters: With whom the kings of the earth have committed fornication, and the inhabitants of the earth have been made drunk with the wine of her fornication" (Revelation 17:1).

"When the Federal Reserve System was foisted on an unsuspecting American public, there were absolute guarantees that there would be no more boom and bust economic cycles. The men who, behind the scenes were pushing the central bank concept for the international bankers faithfully promised *that from then on there would be only steady growth and perpetual prosperity*" (Gary Allen, *None Dare Call It Conspiracy*, p. 56, italics added).

[15] "But they that will be rich fall into temptation and a snare, and into many foolish and hurtful lusts, which drown men in destruction and perdition For the love of money is the root of all evil: which while some coveted after, they have erred from the faith, and pierced themselves through with many sorrows" (1 Timothy 6:9–10).

[16] "Wo unto them that call evil good, and good evil, that put darkness for light, and light for darkness, that put bitter for sweet, and sweet for bitter! Wo unto the wise in their own eyes and prudent in their own sight! Who justify the wicked for reward, and take away the righteousness of the righteous from him! (2 Nephi 15:20–21, 23).

[17] A good video that educates simply to the origin of money can be found at http://video.google.com/videoplay?docid=-9050474362583451279&q=%22money+as+de. It's worth the time if one is interested in this topic.

[18] "Banks create money. That is what they are for....The manufacturing process to make money consists of making an entry in a book. That is all....Each and every time a Bank makes a loan...new Bank credit is created—brand new money" (Graham F. Towers, Governor Bank of Canada, 1934–1954. Quoted in "Someone Has to Print the Nation's Money...So Why Not Our Government?" Monetary Reform Online, reprinted from Victoria Times Colonist, October 16, 1996).

"The modern banking system manufactures money out of nothing. The process is perhaps the most astounding piece of sleight of hand that was ever invented" (Sir Josiah Stamp, Director, Bank of England, 1928–1941, reported to be the second richest man in England at the time, address at the University of Texas in 1927).

[19] "I'm afraid that the ordinary citizen will not like to be told that banks can and do create money. And they who control the credit of the nation direct the policy of governments and hold in the hollow of their hands the destiny of the people" (Reginald McKenna, past chairman of the board, Midlands Bank of England. On January 1924, this was a statement he made to the stockholders of the bank, as quoted by W. Cleon Skousen, *The Naked Capitalist,* p. 13).

[20] "History records that the money changers have used every form of abuse, intrigue, deceit, and violent means possible to maintain their control over governments by controlling money and it's issuance" (James Madison, former President of the United States).

[21] "Let no man deceive you by any means: for that day shall not come, except there come a falling away first, and that man of sin be revealed, the son of perdition who opposeth and exalteth himself above all that is called God, or that is worshipped; so that he as God sitteth in the temple of God, shewing himself that he is God" (2 Thessalonians 2:3–4).

[22] "By this means government may secretly and unobserved, confiscate the wealth of the people, and not one man in a million will detect the theft" (John Maynard Keynes, *The End of Laissez-Faire: The Economic Consequences of the Peace*, 1920. Keynes is the father of "Keynesian Economics" which our nation now practices).

[23] "Money is a new form of slavery, and distinguishable from the old simply by the fact that it is impersonal, there is no human relation between master and slave" (Leo Tolstoy, Russian philosopher).

"Banking was conceived in iniquity and born in sin. Bankers own the earth. Take it away from them, but leave them the power to create money and with the flick of the pen they will create enough money to buy it back again...take this great power away from them and all great fortunes like mine will disappear, and they ought to disappear, for this then would be a better and happier world to live in. But if you want to continue to be slaves of the banks and pay the cost of your own slavery then let bankers continue to create money and control credit" (Sir Josiah Stamp, Director, Bank of England, 1928–1941, given at an address at the University of Texas in 1927. Reported to be the second richest man in England at the time).

In Revelations 18:13, slaves and the souls of men are products of Babylon's economy. It is probable that human trafficking will continue then as it does now in many places in the world, but could another interpretation of slavery refer to the power of money in Babylon as the people labor to pay interest as we do today?

"Finally, she [Babylon] offered as slaves the very souls of men. The word translated 'slaves' is literally 'bodies' (Greek, *soma*). Babylon seeks to reduce people to flesh that can be bought and sold for profit. In the conquest, men are dehumanized by the consorts of Babylon. This idea is brought out by the last phrase, 'souls of men.' This is an old Hebrew phrase depicting men as 'little more than human livestock.' This last commodity shows the spiritual depth of Babylon's wickedness; she sold human beings, both old and young, male and female. *Their lives were to be drained away to provide more for those whose fortunes were already so vast that not even the most lavish expenditures should deplete them*" (Richard D. Draper, *Opening the Seven Seals*, p. 200, italics added).

[24] "None are more enslaved than those that falsely believe they are free" (Goethe, German philosopher).

[25] "Whoever controls the volume of money in our country is absolute master of all industry and commerce and when you realize that the entire system is very easily controlled one way or another by a few powerful men at the top you will not have to be told how periods of inflation and depression originate" (James A Garfield, assassinated former President of the United States).

CHAPTER THIRTEEN

FLIGHT OF REALITY

"And if thou wilt inquire, thou shalt know mysteries which are great and marvelous; therefore thou shalt exercise thy gift, that thou mayest find out mysteries, that thou mayest bring many to the knowledge of the truth" (D&C 6:11).

00:03:10, 03:55:11, Zulu
Saturday, September 20th

Plans

Lexington Park, Maryland
3:05 p.m.

Dane leaned back and closed his eyes, allowing the warm sun to bathe his face. He took a deep breath and let it out as cool water washed up on his legs that were dangling over the edge of the pier. It was a perfectly beautiful day and he was taking this moment to purge himself of all the stress of the morning. He refused to be brought down.

It was nearing high tide and right at the end of the dock floated his boat, rising higher and higher. He had been wrong and right at the same time earlier when he thought the boat was in danger. Yes, he had been wrong about the tide coming in. The glare of the sun on the water had made it look like the water was higher than it truly was, but he had been right about the need to give all his gas to Mrs. Anderson. Even though the boat could still take him and Nebraska a ways, it was limited to water travel. It was time for land travel. He would make good on his promise to Mrs. Anderson and abandon the boat after emptying the gas from the tank.

"I see another boat," said Nebraska. "It's bigger than ours. I bet they have food," she said, pointing off in the distance.

Dane opened his eyes and gazed kindly at Nebraska's face, which was full of hopefulness that he would find her something kid-like to eat. Poor girl, she looked famished as she too dangled her feet in the water. She was frail and skinny, with practically no fat on her. Dane guessed she was feeling hunger greater than either he or Mrs. Anderson.

Louise, who was sitting next to Nebraska, smiled discreetly. "I have some high-powered energy pills in my pocket. They taste like candy. Would you like some?"

Nebraska looked like she was considering Mrs. Anderson's offer. "I don't like those kind of things. My mom used to eat them."

"Are you sure?" asked Mrs. Anderson. "They're good for you and they'll make feel better."

Nebraska looked at Dane worriedly.

"Go ahead. I think you'll like them," he urged, knowing that before the money was gone, Mrs. Anderson must have been very well off to have that kind of food for a travel snack. "Those protein pills are very expensive," he told Nebraska. "Only health food fanatics would ever pay for them. They're like a complete meal in a pill."

"Well I wouldn't call myself a fanatic," said Mrs. Anderson, looking at them. "But I do like health foods. I'm not hungry right now. You can have them, Nebraska. I was saving them for a special moment," she said pulling a metal case from her jacket pocket.

"Is this a special moment?" asked Nebraska.

Mrs. Anderson smiled and said, "I think so. So would you like them?"

Nebraska nodded hungrily.

Mrs. Anderson opened the tin and gave about five to Nebraska who immediately popped one into her mouth.

"So, tell me your plan, Officer Rogers," suggested Mrs. Anderson as she watched Nebraska chew happily on an energy pill.

Dane's last name was embossed on his vest. "Call me Dane, please. I'm not on duty."

"Alright then, Dane, tell me the agenda. What's the plan?"

Dane took a deep breath and said, "I'm planning on bringing up my crab pot, cooking whatever crabs have crawled in and eating till I'm sick. You're welcome to join Nebraska and me if you'd like."

"I'm not eating spiders," said Nebraska, shaking her head with her mouth full.

Mrs. Anderson looked at Nebraska and laughed, then returning her focus to Dane she asked, "How do you plan on cooking the crab? Do you have a crab steamer in that boat? Because the only way to eat Blue Crab is to steam them."

Dane felt his vest pockets, not really listening. "I think I still have matches. Let's build a fire right here on the pier and cook them. There should be enough garbage and old twigs on the beach and in that park for tinder and kindling…" started Dane as he searched the shore thinking about how to build a sustaining fire to cook a good meal.

"Cook them in what pot?" asked Mrs. Anderson again. "You need a pot."

Dane was confused. "What do you mean, in what? I don't need a pot. I just need a fire. I'll make a fire right here and throw the crabs on. It will work."

"What? Throw the crabs on the fire? I've never heard of such a thing!" said Louise with a look of distain. "And what about the fire hazard you'll create? You can't start a fire on a half rotten, wooden pier! It'll go up in flames!"

Dane shook his head. "No it won't. Anyway, if the pier caught fire we'd just put it out with the water from the bay. Don't worry, I'll use some sort of metal under my fire to protect the pier. There're garbage can lids everywhere. But to help you feel better, we can build the fire *in* a garbage can," offered Dane.

"A garbage can?" asked Mrs. Anderson with a grimace.

Dane nodded. "Sure. The can will contain the fire. Isn't that what you're worried about?"

"Yes, but a public garbage can is so dirty," said Mrs. Anderson as she shook her hands.

"Yum, yum, this one is a turkey dinner with stuffing," interrupted Nebraska as she looked at another pill up close. "See, Dane?"

Dane nodded. "Yep, I bet it tastes very good."

"Uh-huh!" said Nebraska as she threw it in her mouth and crunched down on it loudly.

Dane turned back to Mrs. Anderson, taking one leg out of the water, planting his foot on the pier with his knee bent, and propped his arm on his knee. "You do know that fire kills all bacteria, don't you?"

"Sure, but…" said Mrs. Anderson.

"Fire makes dirty things clean," Dane continued with a smile.

"That's completely *disgusting*," said Mrs. Anderson with a shiver.

"Your other choice is to eat them raw," suggested Dane with a shrug.

Mrs. Anderson thought a moment and said, "Raw anything from this bay may have diseases because of the pollution."

Dane rolled his eyes. "Don't tell me you're an environmentalist."

Mrs. Anderson frowned. "I respect my environment and I'm educated on the issues. I don't see what's wrong with that."

"Nothing's wrong, as long as you put survival first," said Dane.

"Can I play in the boat?" asked Nebraska with her face turned up again.

Dane nodded. "If you put on the life jacket that's on the captain's chair you can."

"Yea!" said Nebraska jumping up from her seat and climbing carefully into the boat.

Dane watched Nebraska's every move until she was safely protected in the life jacket. Then he turned back to Mrs. Anderson. "Anyway, as I was saying. It's good to be aware of your environment as long as you understand priorities. We have to do certain things to stay alive even if they seem strange and those are my priorities."

"Of course!" said Mrs. Anderson swallowing and blinking. "You have a point. I—I guess it would be OK to cook the crabs over a fire in a garbage can…." Then nervously, she scratched her head and mumbled something.

"What's wrong?" asked Dane.

"Oh—I'm just glad my people can't see me now," she said, smiling superficially. "This would be humiliating."

"*Your* people?" asked Dane. "What does that mean?"

With wide eyes, Mrs. Anderson shook her head and said, "Oh, never mind. Yes, make the fire in the garbage can. I would suggest you just clean it out well."

Dane laughed. "No, it'd be better if we didn't. We want the inside of the can to be dry. We need the garbage and the grease in the garbage to burn. It will be our fuel."

Mrs. Anderson looked at Dane for a few moments as if he was joking but Dane didn't smile. "You're serious aren't you?" she asked.

Dane nodded. "I am."

"You're not going to clean the can."

"Nope."

Mrs. Anderson sighed. "Eating polluted crab cooked in a trash-filled garbage can, on a rotten pier in Maryland—who'd have thought things would turn out this way?" she asked rhetorically as she shook her head in obvious disgust.

Dane was confused. Was the woman complaining? "My crabs will keep you alive," said Dane solemnly. "You have to keep that in mind."

Mrs. Anderson studied Dane and then apologetically nodded. "Oh, I know, and I'm very thankful, I'm just so amazed how my life has changed in the last 24 hours. This all feels like a dream. Frankly, I'm overwhelmed."

"Can I have more energy pills?" asked Nebraska looking healthier already, steering from the boat.

"Sure," said Mrs. Anderson, standing and leaning over the side of the boat to give Nebraska the tin holding the last few. Turning back she asked, "So what happens after we eat crab?"

"Then, I think we need to siphon the gas from my boat."

"We?" asked Mrs. Anderson with a hand to her chest. "I don't know how to do that," she said shaking her head.

"It's easy. I'll show you," said Dane with a sly smile.

Mrs. Anderson shook her head and wagged her finger at Dane. "Oh no. I don't do that kind of thing and I think you already guessed that."

Dane laughed heartily.

"OK, now I think you're teasing me," said Louise.

"Of course. Welcome to the family," he said with a smile.

Mrs. Anderson looked like she was blushing and then laughed politely as she sat back down again on the edge of the pier. "OK, now I'm going to ask you to be serious with me."

"Fine," said Dane.

"Really, how do we siphon gas?"

"Since we don't need the boat any more, I'll just steal a hose from the engine and suck out the gasoline."

"Is that how one siphons gas?" asked Mrs. Anderson. "One *sucks* it out?"

Dane nodded.

"With their *lips*?"

Dane looked at the professional woman and laughed. "Yes. You *were* rich, weren't you?"

Mrs. Anderson blushed. "That is of no consequence." She wrung her hands. "How much gas do you have?"

"Seventy gallons, give or take."

"Seventy gallons?" asked Mrs. Anderson with a look of shock.

Dane nodded. "The boat started out with about a hundred and fifty."

"What?"

"Yep. The tank holds two hundred."

"You've got to be kidding me," said Mrs. Anderson. "How did you afford to fill that tank?"

"I didn't."

"You didn't?"

"No. The boat was originally a dead man's boat. He filled the tank for us. Nebraska and I were just the lucky ones to have found it before anyone else."

Mrs. Anderson looked at Dane for a few moments and asked, "You *stole* this boat?"

Dane shook his head. "No, I didn't steal the boat. The man was dead. How do you steal from a dead man? He didn't need it any more. I needed it to protect Nebraska."

Mrs. Anderson nodded. "I see."

"And now, the gas will help all of us go home."

"Oh..." Mrs. Anderson covered her face with her hands and said, "I'm not very good at survival rules. I've been conditioned all my life to adhere to the controlled world of political correctness. There has always been a right way to do things and a wrong way. Now all my thinking has to be rewired. Forgive me if I seem rude as I question you, but it's my nature."

"What's your profession? Are you a corporate officer or something?"

"No. I'm...a...a...ahhh...*professor*," said Mrs. Anderson with a forced smile.

"A professor?" asked Dane. "Are you sure?" he asked teasing.

"Ahh, yes. I was attending a conference. That's why I'm stranded here."

"Where are you employed?" asked Dane watching the woman squirm. For some reason he didn't believe her. She struck him as a spoiled rich woman. She was probably some heiress, trying to protect her identity so no one would try and take her hidden money. But he didn't care who she was. He didn't want her money. It was just fun to make her uncomfortable.

"I work at UNLV," she said looking a little more comfortable with her answer.

Dane decided to push her further. She needed to get her story straight anyway if she was going to pretend to be someone else. "So what was this conference about?"

Mrs. Anderson looked up in the sky and said, "It was about the sun."

"What about the sun?" asked Dane with narrowing eyes.

"You don't believe me, do you?" asked Mrs. Anderson, looking a little worried.

Dane shook his head. "No, not really."

"Why not?"

"Because you hesitate too much. You look like you're making up your story right as I ask you the questions. Not that I'm an expert in this area, but I think, if you're going to pretend to be someone else, you have to be that person in your head. You have to know the answers before someone asks you the questions, or else no one will believe you."

Mrs. Anderson smiled and shook her head. "You're right again. I am not good at this. Forgive me, but you're right. I do want to keep my personal life private."

"It's all right. You don't have to tell me who you are. I'm sure you have your reasons to keep your identity a secret. I respect that. I'll pretend you're truly a professor and that your name really is Louise Anderson."

"Thank you," said Mrs. Anderson as she twisted a wedding ring on her finger. She looked off in the distance and then back. "Alright, I don't want to talk about me anymore, if that's OK."

Dane shrugged. "Fine."

"I want to talk about what we're going to do tonight and tomorrow. How are we going to get seventy gallons of gas into my car? Seventy gallons is a lot. We'll have to store most of it because my tank only holds twenty."

"I'm sure we can figure things out," said Dane. "The important question to ask is, is seventy gallons enough to drive to Las Vegas?"

"I don't know," said Mrs. Anderson. "My car gets between 30 and 40 miles to the gallon."

"How many miles to Las Vegas from here?" asked Dane.

"Around two thousand, I think," said Mrs. Anderson pulling a piece of paper from her pocket and looking at it. "That's what my Map Quest said at least."

"OK, then, two thousand divided by thirty is what?"

"Sixty six," said Mrs. Anderson after thinking a minute. "We'd need sixty-six gallons."

"Good. We'll have enough then. I'm sure there won't be gas at the pumps on the way, so our gas will have to do."

"I agree," said Mrs. Anderson. "So, what do we store the extra gas in?"

"Let's fill up all those empty water bottles in the trash cans in the park," said Dane. "I bet there's a couple hundred of them."

Mrs. Anderson turned to Dane with a look of surprise. "You're right, there probably are! I didn't think of that."

Dane smiled.

"See, now, that kind of resourceful thinking is brilliant," said Louise with a smile.

"Thanks," said Dane feeling embarrassed by Mrs. Anderson's compliments.

"But how many of those bottles will we need?" asked Mrs. Anderson.

"As many as we can gather," said Dane.

Mrs. Anderson looked out to the water and said, "This is going to take a while isn't it?"

"Yes," said Dane closing his eyes again. "But we're going to live the next few days, no matter whether we sit here or work hard. Might as well work hard and get things done. I bet we can be on the road by morning."

"Alright. I'll be just as optimistic as you," said Mrs. Anderson. "That's something else I have to practice."

"Good," said Dane.

"What about keeping the gas safe from looters?" asked Louise.

"You mean between now and when we leave?"

"Yes. It won't be safe in the back of the car. People will break a window to take it."

"Good question. How do we keep it safe?" asked Dane thinking.

"I think we might have to work at night, so no one sees what we're doing and then just leave as soon as we're done."

"Yes, we could do that," said Dane already feeling tired. He needed a nap so he could work all night. "On that note, I'm going to go sleep under some trees right off the pier. I stayed up all night last night driving here. Would you mind watching Nebraska while I sleep?"

"Not at all."

"Come get me when the sun sets and we'll get to work."

"Alright," said Mrs. Anderson. "Nebraska and I are going to start gathering those water bottles. I think she'll like that."

"Great idea," said Dane.

"OK. Have a good sleep," said Mrs. Anderson waving automatically.

"Thanks, Mrs.—I mean Professor Anderson," said Dane smiling.

"Call me Louise," said the professor.

"Will do," said Dane as he sauntered off. This plan seemed like it was on the right track.

Dane yawned. He was so tired! Sleep would be good.

Truth, Stranger Than Fiction

Yamal Peninsula, Russia
2:28 a.m.

Braun stood under the clear sky. He looked up. There were *billions* of stars. He was in awe. He had never seen so many bright and stunning stars!

One light in particular caught his attention. It seemed larger than the others. Braun studied it for a few moments. ...As he watched, it looked like it was getting larger. Was his imagination playing tricks on him? ...Looking at the other stars in comparison he realized some of them were getting larger too. Was he wrong? He looked again and again. No, he was *right*. They *were* getting larger. How could that be? Could they be—falling? Were his eyes playing tricks on him? He rubbed his eyes and looked again. No, it was clear, the stars were getting larger. Were these meteors, hurdling towards the earth? Would meteors shine bright white, like stars? Could they be comets?

Braun searched for shelter. White tundra lay around him for miles and miles. There was nothing that promised protection. Growing worried he looked back up only to see that the falling stars had turned to balls of—*snow* instead of *stars*, falling lightly and slowly to the ground. Braun shook his head in embarrassment as his heart thumped in his chest. How stupid could he have been? *The stars weren't falling!* The moonlight must have reflected off the snow and made them shine like stars, tricking his mind. But where were the clouds? He could still see the stars through the snow. How could snow fall if there weren't any clouds? Then he understood. He must be dreaming...

One large clump of snow fell lightly on Braun's head and rolled down his back. Despite his realization that he was having a night vision, he thanked Heavenly Father that the ball was snow instead of a meteor. He didn't need anymore stress, even in his dreams.

Another snowball fell on Braun's head and exploded in powder down around his shoulders and some fell into his up-held hands. The snow glittered in the moonlight as it melted into water. His rescue came to mind. Meeting John was a miracle. As Braun watched the snow turn to liquid, he thought of John. He looked so normal—and mortal, but he wasn't.[1] His body, that used to be like Braun's, was different now. Although John had been born of mortal parents like Braun, through Christ's power he was changed to something else. Now he couldn't die, or be injured. He didn't have to eat or sleep[2] and he could move from one place to another just by thought.[3] John's abilities reminded Braun of the different forms water could take. Snow, ice, steam, and water were all the same substance, but because of natural laws, each acted differently. Braun knew that some day his body would be resurrected to a new form[4] through natural laws the world wasn't aware of. The thing that made Braun even more energized was realizing that if the

Lord wanted to, and if there was a reason, he could change Braun's body now to match John's. Wouldn't that be fantastic to experience! He wondered what it would felt like.

Braun had to calm himself down. What was he thinking? The chances of God changing his body was nil to none. He might as well not even tempt himself with the thought. Changing his thinking, he looked up into the sky. "Thank you, Father, for allowing me to participate in thy plans." For a few moments, he basked in his feelings of happiness. The power of God was so amazing to him. It was true that God was in charge. He sustained him from moment to moment, deciding whether or not to allow him to live or die, and right now, he was to live.

Why? Braun asked as his mind searched for his own answers. Although he was grateful to continue on the earth, he wondered why the Lord wanted him to live. He had finished his assignment at the White House; was there more to do? What was it that the Lord wanted for him? A feeling of anticipation grew inside him, as he waited for the answer. Braun looked into the sky. "Father, tell me. What is it that thou wouldst have me do?"

More snow fell, this time on his face, then down on Braun's chest. Abruptly, heavenly communication came to his mind and he understood. Everything he had lived through, all the lessons and trials he had endured had led up to this point. Similarly, the lessons he would learn here would lead him somewhere else. He had been prepared for this moment as he would be prepared for other moments that would come to him! He was clay in God's hands.

Braun nodded, satisfied. He wanted to be clay in God's hands.

Another clump of snow, followed by another, fell upon Braun. The lightly balled snowflakes fell in succession, hitting him and then breaking apart softly, like dust, and falling to his feet. Every time snow touched him it inspired a memory; each layer of snow building on the last, covering Braun in their reality, rolling down his body and piling at his feet, reaching up his legs like snow drifts. He was reminded of all the visions he had experienced up to this point. In his mind, he saw dragons, water, horns, crowns, and Christ with John at his side, visions passing before his eyes, one by one, making layers of memories, the perceptions covering him like the snow.

The memories continued to come, now in multiples, not even giving Braun a chance to finish each. An Antichrist to support the beast…frogs to woo kings…a head of the beast dead, but now alive…explosions of destruction…then the visions stopped—as did the snow…there was stark silence.

A quiet, permeating voice began speaking to him. It was the kind he had felt before; it shook him to his core. *"It is the end of days, teach of Christ to save the souls of men,"* it said. Braun's mind emptied of everything else until it was filled with the single thought that repeated itself in a quiet echo, *"…Teach of Christ…end of days…Teach of Christ…save the souls of men…Teach of Christ…Teach…Teach…Teach…."*

Braun lowered his head. Now he knew what he was being prepared for, led and encouraged to do. "I *will* teach of Christ," whispered Braun, nodding, determined to fulfill the Lord's expectations. "It would be an honor."

Braun waited for more, but it was over. The memories stopped. He looked up into sky, but now only a star-filled sky remained. It was as he had seen it before. It was peaceful. It was quiet.

ξξξξξξξ

Braun sat up with a start as his vision was ripped from him. His breath was heavy in his throat. His eyes darted around the dark. Where was he? Braun was disoriented. Was he in Washington or England? Maybe he was home. ...No, he wasn't home. He was far from home. He was in Siberia.

The flap of the tent opened, startling him.

It was John. He stepped in quietly and closed the door. Again they were in darkness.

Braun's dream came readily to his mind. "John," he said humbly in a whisper. "I am to teach—"

"I know," said John quietly.

"Am I to do it by your side?"

"For a time."

"Will I be serving the lost tribes as you do?"

"Yes," replied John. "Look," said John as he opened the flap momentarily to the tent. "It's snowing, Brother Rogers."

"Is it?"

"The winter is almost here."

"What does that mean?" asked Braun.

"When the world shook a moment ago, a highway rose up from the deep. It's time for this people to go."

"Go where?"

"To your home. It's time to go home, brother. It's time for these people to go home to Ephraim and finally receive their blessings of the temple."

Braun closed his eyes in joy. Could it be that this was really happening? He opened them again to see the outline of John standing by the door. It was real! After England, after Washington, and now in Siberia, finally, he was going home! But...his thoughts stopped.

"What about Chenille?" he asked, looking back at Chenille's sleeping form across from him in the tent.

"She'll be at your side—forever."

Braun smiled. His life had repaired itself. Oh the greatness and mercy and blessings of God to those who served him! He whispered a prayer of deep gratitude. When he looked back up, John was gone.

On the Road

Lexington Park, Maryland
4:00 a.m.

With full stomachs and twenty cooked crab to spare, Dane, Nebraska, and Louise climbed into the professor's uncharacteristically humble, ancient Toyota Corolla station wagon. They had worked through the night filling empty water bottles with the gas from the boat and cooked crab meat.

The gas tank was full and the extra bottled gas was neatly piled all the way to the ceiling in the cargo area of the vehicle, the flip-down seat in the back, and anywhere else they could safely stow it. Plus there were empty bottles set aside for water on the floor. That was their next goal. Find water. The water in the Chesapeake Bay was too salty, and the water in the Potomac River, too polluted. Dane's plan was to go upstream and find some drinkable water, as soon as possible.

Louise had a map in the glove compartment and Dane, who was sitting in the back seat with Nebraska, had unfolded it and was analyzing their route.

Louise stopped at a stop sign as they moved through the city of Lexington.

Bang! The noise came from the right rear of the car.

Everyone jumped.

Dane protectively hugged Nebraska to his side and Louise slammed on the brakes.

"What was that?" asked Louise.

Dane peered out the back window and saw a man running, full speed towards them. When he moved through the light from a street lamp, Dane could see that he had an angry, determined look on his face. There was something he wanted.

"Step on it, Louise!"

Louise hit the gas and the car lunged forward forcing Dane and Nebraska back into the seat.

When they were a safe distance away, Louise looked in the rear view mirror and asked, "What did that man want? He looked insane."

Dane twisted around to look out the back window again. He could see the man standing now in another pool of light yelling at them, motioning for them to stop. "I don't know what he wanted, but we can't afford to pull over to find out."

"Do you think he was trying to stop us?" asked Louise.

"Of course he was."

"Why do you think?"

"Who knows?" said Dane. "Could be a host of reasons. We have gas and no one else does. Or maybe they have an urgent situation and they want a car to get somewhere. Anyway, the bottom line is, we have gas and we have a working car. That makes us a target. If anyone desperate can catch us, you can bet we'll lose everything we've got and who knows what they'll try to do to us after that."

Louise shrugged as she looked both ways and rolled through an intersection. "I just think you have a skewed sense of humanity. People aren't always predators."

"When people get desperate, they get dangerous and some become predators."

"You have a gun, don't you?" asked Louise. "Why are you nervous?"

"Well, I would like to not shoot anyone today," said Dane. "Our best defense is just to keep moving. Then it won't even be an option."

"So, what if that man needed help?"

"Louise, everyone out there needs help right now. We can't help them all. We don't have enough resources. We barely have resources for us and if we aren't wise, they won't last very long."

"No, but maybe we could help one or two," said Louise.

"Which one? Which two?" asked Dane. "Can you distinguish the dangerous ones from the safe ones?"

"Sometimes."

"OK, if we see someone like that, a helpless child or a pregnant woman, I agree, we should do what we can to help, but not crazed men throwing boulders."

A hint of a smile appeared on Louise's face as she listened.

"I'm a proponent for helping your neighbors," said Dane. "I was brought up believing in a united society where everyone helps everyone else, but when there's violence on every side and death is breathing down your neck, you must protect yourself and your loved ones first and get stabilized, so that in turn you might help others later. It's the airplane scenario. Parents must put the oxygen on themselves first before helping their children, because if they put it on their children first and the parents die, who will protect and watch over the child after the plane lands? No one. The end result is that everyone dies. We must be wise in hard times. Sometimes that takes hard decisions."

Louise thought a moment and nodded. "I see your logic. I can tell you're a good man."

"If we want to get to Las Vegas, or Utah, which is over 2,000 miles away, we're going to have to ride like the wind and not stop for anything. We've had so many miracles leading us up to this point, giving us a shot in the dark to get home, that it would be sad if we let our guard down and then ended up dying."

Louise looked at Dane in the mirror and then back at the road. She looked like she was taking in everything he was saying.

"We've got to remember that most people didn't have a large food supply in their homes when the banks went under. This is the third day out so people are beginning to feel gnawing hunger and that will make them angry.

They're getting thirstier by the moment too which will make them even more desperate. I promise, people will try and stop this car, mark my words. We can't let them. The quicker we can get across the nation, the better."

Louise had both hands on the steering wheel. There was a marked silence between them. Finally she said, "OK. I see what you're saying. History does support your conclusions. I just wish it wasn't that way."

"I know. So do I."

"So you're serious when you say we have to keep moving?"

"Yes, and when we're not moving we have to hide. The best idea is to take turns sleeping and driving so we don't have to stop."

"You really think it's going to be that bad?"

"I do," said Dane. "Remember, I'm a National Policeman, I've seen the worst of humanity and I'm here to tell you that people can be animals."

Louise looked around. "So what route did you decide we should go?"

"According to this map, it looks like we should take Interstate 235 North. We have to find some fresh water, so go towards Washington, D.C. I'm thinking, upstream the Potomac, around Great Falls we should fill these water bottles."

"I understand that's a very polluted area," said Louise.

"The pollution is more downstream than upstream," said Dane. "And, in my opinion, it's the best source right now."

"I don't know," said Louise, shaking her head.

"We don't need to find perfect water, just water that's good enough to keep us alive. Since city water is contaminated we'll have to rely on river water. I have bleach drops we can add to kill anything in it."

"I'm not worried about bacteria. I'm worried about toxins from factories," said Louise.

"Hey. A little pollution isn't going to hurt us if it's diluted. It's the *no water* part that will kill us."

"I have an idea," said Louise. "We could go from UN relief distribution station to station…"

"No," said Dane, interrupting Louise. "That's not a good option."

Louise seemed jarred by Dane's abrupt refusal. She glanced back momentarily.

"I'm sorry," said Dane. "I didn't mean to snap. I just had a bad experience back there and I'd like not to repeat it."

"What happened?"

Dane looked out the window and then down at Nebraska. She had fallen asleep in his arms. Returning his eyes to the land moving past the window he said, "It's a long story. You don't want to hear it."

"It's a *long* drive. Tell me."

Dane considered his thoughts and then said, "I just don't trust those guys."

"The UN Relief Organization? They're a tested and tried relief group. No one is as good as they are. I *know*."

"Maybe. Maybe not."

"Why do you say that?" asked Louise glancing at him in the mirror.

"Because they're offering guaranteed relief to *everyone*. How realistic can that be?"

Louise studied Dane briefly with a knowing look. "You bring up a good point."

"No one can do that for America. No one should. It's one thing to get people on their feet, but to offer food, water, housing, and everything people might need would only cripple America further."

Louise nodded. "OK, OK, again, corrected by a mere baby. I remember someone wise telling me once, anyone who has the power to give you everything you need has the power of taking away everything you've got."

"Exactly," said Dane. "And all the other sayings in life…if it sounds too good to be true, it probably is, and…"

"There are no guarantees in life," Louise finished for Dane.

"Right."

"So tell me, what was your bad experience?"

Dane rolled up his sleeve, showing his deformed arm. "See this scar?"

Louise looked in the rearview mirror and grimaced. "How did that happen? Is it a scar from a burn?"

"No. It's a scar from my flesh being eaten away. That chip that the UN is offering is a death device. I had one."

"And it did *that* to you?"

"Yes. It's done worse things to other people. I was lucky. I'm alive."

"I can't believe it!" said Louise in shocked astonishment.

"I had one of the first chips ever made. I was promised food, water, housing, and everything else I needed when it was implanted, but the thing I didn't know was that it had other secret capabilities."

"Like what?"

"Like tracking, compliance control, death."

"Are you sure?"

"Absolutely. Whoever held the button to my chip had the ability to kill me if I didn't do what he or she wanted."

"How?"

"We found out later there was a lethal bacteria that was encapsulated in stasis around the chip. At any time, it could be unleashed with the push of a button. And that's what happened. I was selected to die."

"That's horrible!" said Louise with a gasp, shaking her head.

"It's true. All the flesh on my arm was eaten away. In fact, I actually died, but then by a sheer act of God, I was brought back to life. It was serious stuff."

"Do you still have a chip?" asked Louise.

"No. It's gone," said Dane simply.

"What happened to it?"

"When all the flesh falls away from the bone and there's nothing for the chip to latch on to, it falls out."

"Is that what happened?"

"Yep. Found it in my hospital bed."

"Did you have skin grafts?"

Dane shook his head. "No, my muscles and skin all grew back without any. The doctors were amazed because that never happens."

"Wow," said Louise, looking overwhelmed.

"So that's why I don't trust anyone with a chip, or promises to feed and clothe you in bad times. The trade-off for my freedom is just not worth it. I'd rather crab, farm, raise animals, whatever, than have someone promise to take care of me just so they can control my life, or even *if* I live."

"I agree," said Louise. After a few moments she said, "You're pretty smart for a young kid."

Dane smiled. "I've been taught by the best, and I've changed. That end of life experience made me older than I really am. I'm on my second life now."

"Hmmm," said Louise.

"Something else didn't make sense at the UN relief camp," said Dane looking up at the roof in thought.

"What was that?"

"Just how did that UN organization get to Maryland so quickly? A relief organization normally takes a while to get organized, especially one that's international."

"You're right, it does," said Louise nodding thoughtfully.

"To me, and maybe I'm just as crazy at that man back there, but to me, it appeared as if the UN knew America was going to get hit before it happened. They showed up right at the perfect time to save the day. It takes time to travel across the ocean and then to set up their organization somewhere else. They should have been at least a week out. Doesn't that seem fishy to you?"

"Maybe."

"And why did the UN have television screens set up playing the national news?"

"I don't know," said Louise. "Maybe it's to keep people informed. Most houses on the East Coast don't have television right now."

"Why would keeping people informed about what's happening other places in America be important to those who are parched with thirst and have empty stomachs?"

"I don't know. Why are you asking these questions?"

"Because something isn't right about the whole thing. Don't you agree?"

"I'm beginning to," said Louise looking like there was more on her mind than she was saying.

"I mean, if people are shown pictures of despair everywhere, do you think it gives them relief? I don't. I think it creates heightened panic. I think people become more paranoid than if they didn't see those images."

"I see," said Louise nodding.

"I think the purpose of showing disaster reports is to help encourage people to accept the chip. After all, if a person feels enough threat to themselves or their family won't they eventually decide it's a good idea to find an insurance program to help them stay alive?"

"Maybe."

"Think about it, how did Hitler control a nation? How did he get people to do things they ordinarily didn't want to do? He used propaganda."

"Good point again."

"And that's what I saw back in the park. Propaganda."

"Why?"

"For starters, the news broadcast didn't report the truth."

"How do you know?"

"Because Nebraska and I were in New York when the fire broke out. It started in the old UN building, not a chemical plant. I know because I was right outside. The blast blew me 30 feet into the air and dropped me on top of a car."

"Really? Then how did millions of people die from toxic fumes?"

"They didn't die from toxic fumes. They were *gassed*."

"What are you talking about?" asked Louise, her eyes wide in the rear-view mirror.

"After I rescued Nebraska, she and I were running away from the smoke. It was beginning to get hard to breathe so we put masks on. I put my gas mask on and I wrapped a bandana around Nebraska's face. But then I noticed people were getting sicker and sicker all around us, until people were falling on the ground in seizures."

"You think the city was exposed to a nerve agent."

"I *know* it was. I had an atropine pen and I gave both of us a dose and that's why we're here today," said Dane with energy.

Louise shook her head. She kept shaking her head as if she were too overcome to speak.

"So, now do you understand why I'm skittish of the UN? I think people are being manipulated by fear. By the looks of the long lines yesterday, they're swallowing the propaganda, hook, line, and sinker. Someone is cashing in on the banking tragedy and making things worse than they have to be."

Louise nodded. "I *completely* agree with you," she said with a new resolve in her voice.

Dane looked up and was surprised to see a tear running down her face and a look of anger. It was that moment that he decided to stop talking about this subject. Maybe he had given her too much information. Maybe the reality of the situation was hitting too close to home, he didn't know.

With resolve to try and do the best thing for all of them, he closed his eyes and began to pray. He prayed for Louise. He prayed for himself. He especially prayed for Nebraska. Dane continued to pray for a nation under siege and ended by praying for his family, wherever they were in the world.

Somewhere in the back of his mind, Dane was comforted by a sunlit sky and a soft breeze. Even though he knew the sensation was only in his mind, it was a welcome escape.

Notes to "Flight of Reality"

Truth, Stranger Than Fiction

[1] John's body is "translated." See John 21: 22–23 and D&C 7:1–3.

"Persons who are changed so that they do not experience pain or death until their resurrection to immortality" ("Translated Beings," Guide to the Scriptures, www.lds.org).

[2] "Therefore, that they might not taste of death there was a change wrought upon their bodies, that they might not suffer pain nor sorrow save it were for the sins of the world" (3 Nephi 28:38).

[3] "And they are as the angels of God, and if they shall pray unto the Father in the name of Jesus they can show themselves unto whatsoever man it seemeth them good" (3 Nephi 28:30).

[4] We know by the scriptures and prophetic statements that the mortal body can be transformed to multiple states of being, which include immortality. See the following statements and definitions:

"Our mortal experiences and our finite logic—devoid of divine guidance, and without revelation from on high—would lead us to assume that life has always been as it now is, and that all things will continue everlastingly as they now are. But such is as far from the fact as heaven is from hell. Neither the earth, nor man, nor life of all sorts and kinds, has always been as it now is. Mortality is but a slight and passing phase of existence, a shimmering moonbeam that shines for a moment in the darkness of our earthbound life; it is but a day in an endless eternity; something else came before, and an entirely different way of life will follow after. [Man] has not always been a benighted, corruptible mortal, subject to disease and death, nor will he always so remain" (Bruce R. McConkie, *The Millennial Messiah: The Second Coming of the Son of Man*, 641).

Spiritual/Pre-existent/Immortal: "Man and all forms of life existed as spirit beings and entities before the foundations of this earth were laid. There were spirit men and spirit beasts, spirit fowls and spirit fishes, spirit plants and spirit trees. Every creeping thing, every herb and shrub, every amoeba and tadpole, every elephant and dinosaur—all things—existed as spirits, as spirit beings, before they were placed naturally upon the earth" (Bruce R. McConkie, *The Millennial Messiah: The Second Coming of the Son of Man*, 642).

We also know in this state we could have existed forever and have existed forever. "Spirits…have no beginning; they existed before, they shall have no end, they shall exist after, for they are gnolaum, or eternal" (Abraham 3:18).

Mortality/Earthly/Telestial/Resurrected/Immortal: In the mortal sphere, the one we live in now on earth, there are many states of existence. Telestial is another name for the level of glory we endure now. It's the one we necessarily must live in to learn the difference between good and evil because a telestial law allows both good and evil to exist together.

"In its present telestial state, wickedness prevails on its face and anyone can live here no matter what his life-style. …[After the fall of Adam] sorrow and disease and death entered the world. Man and all created things were able to procreate and reproduce their kind. Blood began to flow in the veins of man and beast. Their bodies underwent a change and they became mortal. Mortality is the state in which procreation abounds and death prevails" (Bruce R. McConkie, *The Millennial Messiah: The Second Coming of the Son of Man,* 643).

There is a fullness of the telestial glory that we do not enjoy now that includes resurrection to immortality for those that live that law. "And also they who are quickened by a portion of the Telestial glory shall then receive of the same, even a fullness" (D&C 88:31).

Terrestrial/Translated/Immortal/Resurrected: After Christ returns to the earth during the Millennium the earth, as well as all that live on it, will return to a state similar to the Garden of Eden and live a higher sphere of existence called the Terrestrial state:

"...Our first parents and the original forms of life of every kind and species were placed on earth in a paradisiacal state. In that state there was no procreation, no death, no mortality (as we know it), and no blood flowing in the veins of man or of the animal kingdom. ...When the earth returns to its terrestrial state, none will be able to live on its surface unless they abide at least a terrestrial law. Hence, every corruptible thing will be consumed when the earth is cleansed at the beginning of the Millennium. That is, all who are worldly, all who are carnal, sensual, and devilish, all who are living a telestial law will be destroyed. ...Some mortals have been translated. In this state they are not subject to sorrow or to disease or to death. No longer does blood (the life-giving element of our present mortality) flow in their veins. Procreation ceases. ...They have power to move and live in both a mortal and an unseen sphere. Millennial man will live in a state akin to translation. His body will be changed so that it is no longer subject to disease or death as we know it...he will, however, have children, and mortal life of a millennial kind will continue" (Bruce R. McConkie, *The Millennial Messiah: The Second Coming of the Son of Man,* 643–644).

Just like the telestial glory, the terrestrial glory has a fullness that will include resurrection to immortality. "And they who are quickened by a portion of the terrestrial glory shall then receive of the same, even a fullness" (D&C 88:30).

Celestial/Immortal/Resurrected: The celestial glory of the body is the highest degree the body can achieve. This state is reserved only for the resurrected immortal who is able to live the highest law like the Father. "For he who is not able to abide the law of a celestial kingdom cannot abide a celestial glory" (D&C 88:22).

"And thus we saw the glory of the celestial, which excels in all things—where God, even the Father, reigns upon his throne forever and ever" (D&C 76:92).

CHAPTER FOURTEEN

METAMORPHOSIS

"I ask of you, my brethren of the church, have ye spiritually been born of God? Have ye received his image in your countenances? Have ye experienced this mighty change in your hearts?" (Mosiah 5:14).

00:03:09, 14:02:09, Zulu
Sunday, September 20th

Stubborn Weaknesses

Provo, Utah
2:58 a.m.

Bo had been awake thinking for a while. His stomach, as well as his spirit, felt hollow. He had wandered downstairs from his bedroom but steered clear of the kitchen since he was fasting. It had been a little over 24 hours since he had last eaten but despite that, he couldn't break his fast just yet. He had more things to think about, more things to pray about. He needed that yearning, hungry feeling. It would drive him closer to the Spirit.[1]

In his mind, Bo traced the timeline, locating the precise moment when all the bad things started happening in his life. He had had a pretty smooth life up to a point and then suddenly, it all fell apart. When was that moment?

Bo remembered the day Corrynne came home from work telling him of a strange killer infection. He remembered being a little amused at her account of the night. The story had seemed so bizarre. Bo smiled at his memory but then his smile stopped. How did things spiral from that moment to this?

Then there was the old woman who had uttered evil prophecies concerning him. He had thought *she* was a joke at first, too. She ended up not to be. ...Bo wondered, had she cursed him? Was that possible? Would the Lord allow that?

Suddenly, in Bo's mind, he was whisked back to the first moment he had met that ugly old woman. She looked like something out of Snow White. She was hunched over, old, and unnaturally ugly. She had long strings of hair that hung like grey wool from her balding head. Some of it dangled over her frightening face, almost hiding her frosty-white blind eye, but exposing the bulging piercingly blue eye that seemed to bore into his soul. He remembered feeling cornered by her gaze. He had wanted to run and hide when she pointed at him with a crooked, knobbed finger and spewed out threatening rhymes. He had thought her ridiculous and mad at first, but then the things she said began to come true....

Bo's memory changed to Carea and Dane's hard trials in the wake of Imam Mahdi. The old woman had predicted suffering for his family and now he understood just how much. But, in his mind, it wasn't the suffering that bothered him as much as the utter helplessness he had felt. Helplessness was more painful to him than any other emotion—causing him great anger. After all, *he was the father* and it grated on him that he was *unable to protect his children.* That was unreasonable! He had been given the job to protect his family before there even *was* a family! Who was *anyone* to say he couldn't?[2]

The memory of his dreams came flooding back. He remembered being told by a heavenly being *not* to interfere with his children's missions and yes, he was also very clearly told that they would be in danger and may even die. So OK, maybe God could and did tell him to back off. But oh, *what a trial*! He wasn't good at this one! He was failing miserably! He supposed that right now, his oldest five were removed from his family, serving exactly where God wanted them to serve. He bet Heavenly Father had bound his hands so he couldn't stop them. Maybe that's what was making him so angry, just the thought that even if he wanted to protect his children, *he couldn't.*[3] Oh, the brutal nature of the ultimate will of God.[4] Would he be faithful enough to lay aside his anger and frustrations and return his trust to his Father in Heaven?

Bo felt hot tears threaten his eyes. He shook his head to get them to leave. He knew all the answers. Yes, the Lord expected him to endure his hardships well. He had been given all the tools to live a happy life. He had been given the *atonement* to take away the pains of suffering as well as sin.[5] He could hear his own voice in his head expounding to him the very things he was lacking. What was his problem?

Bo turned and fell to his knees beside the couch. He had so much anger and hurt welling up inside of him that he needed to let it go. He had to *let it go*. That was the only answer. Instead of indulging his anger, he needed to get rid of it! The only way to do that was to pray and apply faith in the eternal nature of the atonement to bring upon him the miracle of peace after a storm.

Bo began praying fervently.

"Dear Father, help me...I'm so weak. ...I have a dangerous temper...the worst part is that I *know* it. Why can't I change that?[6] *Help me change it! How do I do it?* Teach me how to stop this cycle of hate, anger, and frustration. It's killing me, eating me piece by piece. I have to stop it or I know it will win. If that happens, I'll become an evil and angry man, like that old woman who haunted me on the street. I, like her, will only become interested in serving my anger! I don't want to be like that! Please—help me."

Bo allowed his thoughts to surf his memories as he recovered from his plea. Scriptures and advice he had given to others rehearsed themselves in his mind. He remembered telling people that anger was like a drug. It was addicting and disabling. Satan, the lord of rebellion and anger, didn't become that way overnight. He progressed to his selfish anger bit by bit. We also can do that. We can, if we follow his footsteps, become like Satan, or if we choose, we can go the other way and follow the footsteps of the Savior. It was our life to choose. It was our moment to decide who we would follow. He remembered telling others, saying, "We can't always choose the hardships in our lives, but we can choose how to deal with them."

"Touché," said Bo to himself. "There, Bishop. There's the counsel for you," he said, feeling embarrassed that he was in this situation. Then a thought struck him. That pride, the hot anger against the Lord, that was the same angry pride of Satan that destroyed a god so glorious. The only other being with more glory than Lucifer, besides God himself, was Christ! Now he realized the true root of his problems. It was pride that ate out his insides.[7] It wasn't life! It wasn't hardship! It was his own *pride*! He had been secretly holding on to it, pretending he was over it. When life was easier, when Dane had recovered and Carea returned to her teen interests, Bo had relaxed. It was then his pride returned. It had raised its ugly head once again in his subconscious. He could remember how little by little he had become less patient, less forgiving, less tolerant…less loving…. The understanding of his own path to his weaknesses slapped him in the face. The knowledge was harsh.

"Why, Heavenly Father? Why am I like this? I've learned these lessons already! I know what comes next! I know what will happen if I don't fix this flaw in my personality. Why do I blame others, circumstances, or even thee, for my faults? Why is there a part of me so hungry for anger that I look in every corner for it?"

Bo's question went unanswered. He knew it was rhetorical. He knew all the answers. He needed to continually apply his faith that Heavenly Father knew his heart, his desires, as well as his hopes, and that there was a greater plan, and that all would be made just in the end. Mercy and justice would be applied giving the mourners joy, the hungry food, and the lost a path. His job now was to apply his own knowledge and make it his once again. He had done it before. Now he needed to do it again.

With a full voice, Bo cried out with clasped hands and an upturned face. "Oh, Father! Help me give up my weaknesses! I'm willing to give them up once again. I'm sorry that I've fallen back to my old ways of thinking. I know more is expected of me at this time in my life. I know with thy help I can give up anger. I can quell the hunger for negativity. I know I can find peace in adversity. I know I have the ability to see life from a good perspective. Just give me the vision! Let me see! I promise I'll do better."[8]

Bo lowered his head and began again. "Help me trust in thy plan and allow myself the peace I seek. I know I'm my own worst enemy, but help me change! Help me accept what I can't change. Help me support others. Help me not jump to conclusions just because they fit into my anger… Oh, Father, I'm so sorry.[9] Please bring the Spirit back. I can't live without it. I will fail without it…."

Bo lapsed into silence as he felt the stubborn tears fall down his cheeks. He sat still. Waiting. Waiting. He would wait until the Lord acknowledged him.[10]

Washington, D.C.

Washington, D.C.
5:00 a.m.

"Dane, look!"

Dane woke with a start. "What?"

"I think someone's lying in the middle of the street. What should we do?"

Dane looked out the front window. He saw a figure lying in an abnormal position on the pavement. He couldn't tell if it was a male or a female. He shook his head. "Keep driving, Louise."

"I don't know if I can just drive by a person lying in the street," said Louise with her eyes fastened on the body.

"You'll have to," said Dane. "Think about it. What would you do if you stopped? If that person is dead, there's nothing to be done. If that person's almost dead, what are you going to do? Call 9-1-1? I guarantee you that number long since stopped working around here. If we stop to help that person, I know I don't have the knowledge or the tools to help them. Then, what if this is just a ploy to get us to stop so they can take over the car? If I was starving and thirsty and I saw a car driving by, I just might lay down on the pavement to get them to stop."

"So you just want me to drive away?"

"Yes. I do. I know it's different than what you might've ever done before, but it's the right thing to do right now."

"Dane, this is not good. I can't do this."

"Yes, you can. Stop looking at that person. Just drive. Stay far away from the body."

"OK," said Louise with tears streaming down her face. *"I hate this."*

After the car passed the body, Dane looked back. The body didn't move. Yes, it was far too late to help. He turned back and closed his eyes again.

"…Dane, there's another body!" said Louise becoming even more emotional. "No there's a few more! *Dane what's happening?"*

Dane sat up straight. He looked from body to body. Could the same thing that happened in New York have happened in D.C.?

"Make sure all the windows are rolled up and the vents are closed. Do you have the heat on?"

"No."

"Good. We want as little air as possible to get in from the outside."

"Do you think these people have been poisoned too?"

Dane shook his head. "I don't know, but that seems likely. Do they look hurt?"

Louise shook her head. "I don't know. I'm trying not to look at them."

"Let's assume they have been gassed and just keep driving. How far have we gone?"

"About fifty miles."

Dane unbuckled his seat belt and sat forward. "We only have about thirty miles left. We're almost there. We just have to get above Washington, D.C. where the water wouldn't have been contaminated in case these people have been poisoned. Water downstream of Washington would be very bad."

"OK," said Louise.

As they approached Washington, D.C., they began to see more and more bodies. The streets lay empty of cars and people. Not one soul stirred. It became more and more apparent that something large and terrible had happened.

"I don't understand this," said Louise. "How could anyone wipe out a whole city?"

"I don't know, but it's happened more than one time in history," said Dane feeling overwhelmed too. "But try and keep in mind our objectives. You want to get home. I want to get home. We need to protect Nebraska. Keep focused. We're doing great."

"Right," said Louise as she drove, her arms held stiff. After a few minutes, she asked, "Which way do you want me to go?"

"Just go to 15th Street NW. That's the fastest way through the city and on to the falls. It will take you right by the White House. "

"Alright," said Louise without emotion.

As the car drove along the empty streets, Dane watched the abandoned executive buildings go by. It seemed impossible for such a huge and historic city to be empty of life. His eyes were glued to the window. There were signs everywhere of civil unrest, windows broken, trash thrown everywhere, cars turned upside down, graffiti covering the buildings, but now the whole city lay silent with only empty bodies strewn on every street corner. With all these signs, combined with the story the crabbing man had told him, he was formulating a scenario of what could have occurred.

"Look at all this mayhem!" said Louise, amazed. "I'm so glad Nebraska is sound asleep. I think this might scare her."

Dane looked at the sleeping angel. He was grateful too. "I agree."

Turning back to the city, Dane said, "The crabbing man that I met yesterday told me this city was imploding with civil unrest. He told me that Congress and the White House had been abandoned and then the people went wild, setting everything on fire and looting. He even told me that an explosion had damaged the White House. That was before all these people were gassed, of course."

"Well, we'll see the White House in just a moment," said Louise as she turned onto Constitution Avenue through gates that had been blown open by some explosive.

Dane shook his head. People must have been pretty angry.

As they approached the ruins of the White House, Louise slowed. The sight was painful. The dome had been charred and broken up, just as the crabbing man had said.

"Look—at—that!" said Dane, devastated.

"I can't believe it," gasped Louise. "This is awful!"

"Braun," said Dane under his breath. He had an impulse to jump out of the car and run the halls looking for his oldest brother. His knuckles turned white on his right hand as he gripped the door handle.

"What did you say?" asked Louise looking in the rearview mirror.

Dane shook his head. "Oh, nothing. I used to know someone who worked here."

"In the White House?" asked Louise.

"Yes, but he's long gone. Hopefully, he's safe somewhere far from here."

"Hopefully," said Louise.

"OK, let's get out of here before someone sees us," said Dane.

"Sounds good," said Louise as she accelerated away from the White House.

Fishing for Answers

Provo, Utah
4:38 a.m.

Bo stood in an arid landscape on the edge of either a large lake or a sea. It lay still and smooth as sapphire. The sky was clear and filled with pinks and purples. The air was cool. Bo instantly knew he was in a dream. He was standing on some shore in the early evening hours. Placing a hand over his face to shield the sun that was setting in the horizon to the west, he looked around.

Even as Bo stood on the shore, he felt deep sadness left over from his emotional prayers. He still felt like he had failed the Savior in his selfish anger. He who had sworn his allegiance to Christ's ways, he who had been given so much, he who was a disciple and a steward of his people, he should have handled his hardships better.

"I would love to see the Savior," Bo whispered aloud to himself, recognizing some aspects of this vast body of water to be that of either the Sea of Galilee or the Sea of Tiberius. Since both names referred to the same body of water,[11] he guessed it didn't really matter. What mattered was that Christ came to these shores in the scriptures. Oh, how Bo would welcome the chance to ask forgiveness personally! Of course he had never been able to move dreams to his will before, but his desire to be absolved of his weaknesses was so strong he thought he'd put out his desire and who knew? Maybe the Lord would grant his heartfelt wish. Coming face to face with the Lord might help him burn out his weaknesses from his soul so they might never come back again.

"Come on, Peter!" called a man as he ran past Bo.

Bo looked behind him, was the man talking to him? Could he see him?

"Come on, Peter, *now*! The sun is setting," the man coaxed again turning and running backwards.

Bo hesitated. He pointed to himself with a questioning look.

"Of course! Who doest thou think I'm talking to, the fish?" asked the man with a laugh as he turned back around and kept jogging.

Bo raised his eyebrows. Yes. The man could see him. Bo's name must be Peter in this dream. That was interesting. "Hmmm," he thought, jogging to catch up. "Peter. Tiberius…?" His mind was tantalized with the possibility that, considering this setting, he might meet Christ after all![12]

"What are we doing?" Bo asked, falling into his part and finally catching up to the man.

The fisherman picked up heavy nets but then frowned at Bo. "Thou knowest what we do. Give me a hand!"

Bo quickly set to work and helped lift the nets into the boat.

"We are going to catch our dinner," said the man as he continued to wrestle the nets into the boat until the massive netting lay on the floor. With a heave, he pushed the boat into the water.

Bo and the fisherman went to the deeper areas of the sea and threw the nets overboard. "Tell me your name," Bo asked the man as they sat to wait; he might as well collect information so he could pinpoint his location in time for sure. It would help him to know what to expect.

"Art thou mad?" asked the man with a strange look on his face.

Bo shook his head. What should he say to that question? "No, I'm not mad, I'm….just not myself," said Bo, secretly thinking he was clever in his answer.

"I'm John, your partner of many years. James is my brother, remember?"

Bo nodded. "Oh, yes," he said, wondering if he was Peter of the twelve apostles and John and James his partner fishermen. "Will Jesus of Nazareth be joining us?" asked Bo, thinking he could figure more out by asking leading questions than looking stupid.

Again, John looked at him and said, "Have you a fever? Hast thou become sick?"

Bo shook his head again. "No, I just haven't seen him for a while."

John moved to the side of the boat and pulled up one of the nets. "None of us have. He has died, brother."

Bo was caught by surprise. He should have qualified his statement. He should have realized it was a possibility that Christ had been crucified already, not knowing when this fishing expedition was taking place. But now his heart fell. That would mean he wouldn't see Christ. "Oh, I know that," said Bo, trying to cover his mistake. "But I know he's going to come and visit us again."

John nodded with a knowing smile. "Yes, he will, brother. He will come again to us," he said as he looked at two little fish caught in the net. "I wish he were here already, our nets would break with fish if he just walked onto that beach." John threw back the net and returned to his seat.

Bo considered what John said. He thought Christ appeared to the apostles on the sea of Tiberius after his resurrection. Could this be the time, he wondered? …No, it couldn't be, he decided after considering all the clues. The other apostles were missing from their fishing excursion. That meant everything was all wrong for Christ to visit. In frustration he wondered, if he wasn't going to see Christ, what was the point of this dream?

In silence Bo picked up a twig that lay on the boat floor and began to twist it as he thought. Now he was a hostage, in a boat, in another time. *Greeeaaat.*

ξξξξξξξ

Bo and John fished through the night but time after time, the nets came up empty. After the twenty-something time, he wondered when this dream was going to end? He could sit around and not get anything done at home.

The morning came and a man called to them from the shore, "Have ye any meat?"

Bo laughed to himself. Now they were being mocked because of their poor fishing abilities. With his hands cupped around his mouth, he yelled, "No, we don't. I think I could sit here for a hundred years and still there wouldn't be any fish! I think I'm being punished!" Bo yelled half joking. "Surely this must be hell."

"Throw the net to the right side of the ship and ye shall find what ye are looking for," called the gentleman on the beach with his hand pointing.

Bo and John leaned to the right side of the boat and looked into the water. The water was clear. Not one fish swam below them. They looked at each other, and then John yelled back, "I am sorry, but we have tried that side as well. We've tried every side. There are no fish."

The figure stood silent without reply. There was something authoritative in the way he stood at the edge of the beach. It made Bo ask John, "Who is that man?"

John after thinking a moment abruptly jumped up, causing the boat to nearly capsize.

"What are you doing?" asked Bo as he hung on for dear life. "Slow down!"

John ignored Bo and continued to wrestle the nets as if he was being timed.

"What's going on?" asked Bo now bending down to help.

"I'm doing as I am directed," John said, throwing the mass of nets over the side.

"Why?" asked Bo. "We've fished all night. There aren't any fish. I don't know how many times you've thrown the net in on this side. Why do you keep trying?"

John looked Bo in the eyes and said, *"Simply because I have been asked to."*

Suddenly the boat began to rock violently. It threatened to capsize.

"Grab the nets!" called John. "Pull them up before they break!"

Bo and John fought fiercely with the heavy nets, but no matter what angle, what effort they put into pulling the nets, they couldn't. The nets began to rip.

"We can't hold the nets!" John called to the beach.

"What's going on?" asked Bo, again thinking the boat might capsize as the nets pulled violently out to sea.

"It's the fish, brother. We are being rewarded for our diligence. Blessings don't always come when you want them, but they come!"

"How many are there?" asked Bo feeling abruptly happy and breaking out in laughter. "There must be thousands!"

"Send help!" called John to the beach.

The man still standing and watching them on the shore directed other men who seemed to appear out of thin air. Soon a group of four men were pushing a small boat out into the sea. Within minutes the boat was near.

"Grab our line!" yelled one man from the small boat as he threw a rope to the fishing boat.

Bo caught the rope and tied the two boats together. Were these more apostles, Bo wondered?

The four men began to row their boat aggressively to tow Bo and John's boat and their large catch in to shore.

Bo couldn't help but chuckle in satisfaction as he held on to the nets and looked down into the heap of wriggling fish. He couldn't believe their luck! How did this happen? How could there be no fish one moment and the next, so many that the nets were about to break? Bo looked out to the beach to see if the man who had told them to throw the nets still stood waiting for them, and he was.

With a smile, Bo asked John, "Can you see who that man is yet?"

John smiled wide and said, *"Peter, it is the Lord!"*

Bo jumped up. "The Lord?" he asked, so eager to see the Savior that he nearly tripped and fell overboard Catching himself he looked to the beach. He stood on the bow of the boat while the other men continued to row hard to drag the fish in to shore.

Then something strange happened to Bo, he felt unusually exposed and cold, as if….

Bo looked down. To his horror, he saw that he was naked! He didn't have a single stitch of clothing on! Bo dove for a fisherman's coat that was lying nearby and pulled it around his waist and then dove into the water.

What a nightmare! Right at the most glorious moment of his life, when he was going to see the Lord face to face, he found himself *naked*! What was that *about*?

Bo woke abruptly. His chest was heaving hard and his heart beating so strongly, he thought it might beat through his chest wall. He was still sitting on the family room floor, next to the couch. He had fallen asleep. Thank goodness he wasn't really naked in front of Jesus, the Savior of the world!

Bo got up from his place on the floor. Oh, he had a cramp in his leg! With a limp, Bo unfolded his knees and walked like a long-legged bird as he tried to work the knot out of his muscle.

After circling the room a couple times, he headed for the kitchen. He took a bottle of water from the refrigerator and opened the lid. After several large gulps, he exhaled. Still breathing hard from his dream he whispered, "That was a strange dream," to himself, and then he went to bed. He needed to sleep a little longer before he had to go to his meetings for church.

Knock, Knock

Somewhere in Canada
3:45 a.m.

They had been riding in the prison van—or bus—for what seemed like days. As Carea understood it, they still had more than a day to go. Except for rare stops, the drive was constant.

The tiny bathroom in the back took care of their needs and they had been handed pre-made bologna sandwiches and a bottle of water every six hours during the day. Because it was night, it had now been almost eight hours since she ate last and she was starving!

Carea could eavesdrop and hear news through the barred windows. According to the driver and the guards, food and water were getting low. There was a chance that after their next meal, there would only be enough for half of them to have dinner. Gas was a problem too. As she understood it, they traveled from military base to military base to fill up. Gas was gone in the cities. She also heard that there wouldn't be any more buses bringing prisoners up to Alaska after hers. How lucky was that? *She* had caught the last bus. Wahooooo—*not*!

Big sigh.

Now, they were well into the wilderness of Canada. All she could see as they drove were trees and trees and more trees.

A few girls were asleep right now. Maybe it was because these girls were used to staying up all night, but whatever the reason, most were awake. Carea could see in their eyes that they were just as bored as she was. The morale of the girls was awful. Who'd blame any of them for being in a bad mood? Ripped from their families while the world was self destructing, the stress of the ride was nearly unbearable! People were getting on each other's nerves. Already two girls had been taken out of the bus for causing a riot and practically hog-tied with chains and cuffs. That's *not* what she had planned for herself.

Carea stretched. Her behind was dying from sitting too long. Then she ran her fingers along her forehead. Her skin was oily, she needed a good shower. She could just feel the blackheads getting blacker and the pimples popping out on her face.

Turning to her seatmate she thought she's ask her something, but when the girl turned to look at Carea, a foul cloud of skunk breath came out of her mouth! Yuck! Carea swallowed hard so she wouldn't gag. She had to smile and turn away.

Carea didn't know how long she could just sit there and be quiet. She had to do something or she was going to go ***crazy***! She needed something, anything—a diversion, PLEASE!

Suddenly, Carea had an idea! Since the bus was awake, they might as well do something fun. What the van needed was some comic relief! They all needed to just laugh. Pretend it was a slumber party or something. They were all girls, right? Just because these were gang girls didn't mean they couldn't all have fun together!

Carea looked around and held her breath. Biting on a nail, for a moment she was intimidated. Should she do anything wild? Would these girls respond? How should she start? Looking from person to person she saw that most of the girls were staring out the windows. Others were whispering to each other and pointing to others, as if planning something. The gorilla girl was sleeping and Carea wouldn't try and wake her. She was good sleeping. She'd not bother her—at least not on purpose.

That was it! It was time to do something totally stupid and get this crowd shaken out of depression. So what if it was three or so in the morning? That was the best time to do something strange!

Carea began by humming the stupidest song she could think of, and then she began to sing. "It's the song that never ends, it goes on and on my friends," she began quietly. "Some people, started singing it, not knowing what it was, and they continued singing it forever just because…"

"What're you singing?" asked the girl with stinky breath.

Carea smiled and closing off her nose with the back of her tongue, she said, "I'm singing a song that I remember from when I was a kid. There was this lady and she had a puppet lamb called Lambchops…"

"Yeah, I remember that song," said the girl, light appearing in her eyes. "I used to sing it too. I watched that show!"

"You did?" asked Carea with a broad smile.

Yeah." The girl smiled with her memory.

"What's your name?"

"Octavia," said the girl thickly because of her bucked teeth.

"That's cool! Great name!" said Carea still discreetly not breathing through her nose.

"Thanks."

"I'm Carea."

"Cool," said the girl nodding.

Carea smiled warmly. She liked the change in the girl next to her. She seemed normal in that moment. "OK, sing with me."

"Do you think we should?" asked the girl looking around.

"Sure!" said Carea trying to be as positive as she could be. "What could happen? Other people sing too?"

"I don't know," said the girl still looking worried. "Aren't people sleeping?"

"No. Look around. Hardly anyone's sleeping. Don't worry, nothing will happen," assured Carea. "Come on."

"OK," said the girl, a little sheepishly. "How does it start again?"

Carea nodded and started singing, only louder this time. "It's the song that never ends, it goes on and on my friends." Octavia jumped in, smiling. "Some people, started singing it not knowing what it was, and they'll continue singing it forever just because…"

Someone in the back yelled up to the front where Carea was sitting, "Hey, what-cha doing up there?"

"We're singing the song that never ends!" yelled Carea. "It's quite obnoxious but just what we need."

"I think I know that song," said the girl in the back.

"Sing with us!" said Carea. "It'll be good for you!"

Then two or three more girls began singing the same song. "It's the song that never ends," the volume became louder as more girls joined in, "it goes on and on my friends." Carea got to one knee and began leading everyone in the back, beginning to sing at the top of her lungs. *"Some people started singing it not knowing what it was…"*

Suddenly the gorilla woman woke up and looked at Carea with those foggy blue eyes. "What ya yelling for?" she said with the angriest face Carea had ever seen.

"We're singing," said Carea. "It's a stupid song, but it takes your mind off this bus." The song continued in the back without Carea, gaining momentum as more girls recognized it and joined in.

The gorilla woman stood up and roared to the back of the bus, ***"Shut up! Or I'll kill you!"***

Suddenly the bus went quiet. All the good energy drained out of it. Carea had to act fast if she was going to get it back.

Still up on one knee Carea turned to the scary girl and with a moment of inspiration, she smiled wide and said, "Knock, knock!"

The girl looked at her angrily and said sarcastically, "I'll beat your face in."

"Say 'who's there?'" Carea coaxed happily, bouncing a little on the seat. She knew she was over doing it, but now this was a show for the bus to see: *beauty and the beast.*

"Who's there!" yelled someone from the back.

The gorilla girl looked toward the back of the bus and snarled.

"Jo!" said Carea back with a big smile.

"Jo who?" said another.

"Jo-king!" returned Carea, laughing at her own joke. "Get it? I'm telling a joke?"

"Ah, ha, ha," laughed some of the girls emphatically in the back.

The gorilla girl stepped over her seat mate and stared Carea down. *"I said—shut up."*

"What do you call a fake noodle?" returned Carea, right into the large girl's face, not missing a beat. She wasn't going to back down.

"What?" called some of the girls again.

"An impasta!" said Carea, again laughing hard at her own joke. "Get it? Imposter—impasta?"

More girls began to laugh. Now more than half the van was taking part.

The gorilla girl looked back at the van and then back to Carea, obviously considering her options.

Care knew she didn't want to be handcuffed so she continued, "What do you call cheese that's not your own?"

"What?" called about four other girls, now closer to her.

"Nacho cheese! Get it? Not-your-cheese?"

"Ha, ha, ha, ha!" laughed most of the girls now; it was heartfelt this time.

Carea was feeling good. Things were happening here! She was making a difference! "Hey, the one who laughs last is the slowest thinker!" Carea said, looking at the gorilla woman.

The girl looked back at Carea, but now there was something different in her face. She wasn't frowning anymore.

Carea thought there might be a smile forming somewhere under that rough exterior. "You tell one," Carea whispered. "I've primed the audience."

The gorilla girl turned back at the rest of the girls who were waiting expectantly. Hesitantly she said, "Ahh, knock, knock."

The whole van yelled, *"Who's there!"*

The girl held up a finger and said, "Oh, I forgot something. Everyone hold up their index finger."

The whole bus did.

"Now swirl it in the air."

Everyone followed her directions.

"Knock, knock," said the girl.

"Who's there!" called everyone in unison again, vibrating the metal of vehicle with their voices.

"Woo."

"Woo, who?"

The gorilla girl looked at everyone, expectedly.

There was a pause as everyone processed the joke.

Carea exclaimed, "I got it! *Woohoo!*" she yelled throwing her hands above her head and laughing hysterically.

Laughter broke out all over that matched Carea's and now the gorilla girl was laughing too.

Carea patted the girl on the back and whispered, "Good one."

The scary girl, who suddenly wasn't so scary any more—smiled—like a child and went back to her seat. She kept facing the back and put a knee in the seat like Carea. The jokes went on for a long while and gorilla girl was right in the middle. It felt so good!

As the joking was going on, Carea looked around the van of misfit girls as they all told their own stupid jokes. Finally, they were talking to each other! Blacks were talking to whites, Bloods were talking to Bats, and it didn't matter what gang they were from, what part of town, or the color of their skin. It was the first step of an unlikely friendship of the society rejects. For the first time in their lives they could weave their own lives together to create a unity they couldn't find in society. Now they wouldn't be rejected any more. Carea was happy. She could see a great opportunity. It was a time to help every one of those girls realize they were special and unique. Carea wanted them to know they could change their lives. Maybe she had found her purpose....

"Lovest Thou Me?"

Provo, Utah
6:33 a.m.

Bo tossed restlessly in his sleep. His mind was filled with rapid, rushing visions, whispering voices mixed with his own imaginations and swift currents of complicated music. The rush of information streaming in his mind caused him to remember swimming after his family's inflated raft when the dam broke.

"Hurry, Dad! Swim faster!" he heard a child say. He didn't know which one.

Bo remembered the cold seizing his chest and lungs. He felt the freezing temperature of the water sapping his strength. His arms and legs were stiffening up.

"Bo! Come on! You're almost there!" yelled Corrynne. He'd recognize her voice anywhere.

Bo tried to swim faster in the torrent of images assaulting his mind. He had to survive. He had something to do. What was it? Someone throw him a rope or something! He didn't know how long he could keep swimming!

"You must fulfill your responsibilities," came a comforting voice to him in the night, rising above the churning chaos of images and sound. "You must be a leader in times of trial! Miracles will follow you because of your faith…."

Was that an angel? Was it talking to him again? *"Throw me an innertube!"* yelled Bo in his dream. *"I can make it if I can have something to climb on."*

In the next moment he felt something different. He was being given help, but still, he would reach out to grab a string of understanding only to have it ripped from him, like the slippery innertube had escaped his grasp in the icy rushing water.

Bo was sinking. He was becoming lost in the unknown depths of the complex thoughts and images rushing around him, feeling now more like he was in a vortex rather than a rushing river. He didn't think he could do it any longer. "Help me! It isn't enough!" he pleaded. "How am I to understand my dreams if they threaten to suck me under? Slow the current down!"

Then—there was a moment of darkness. It was like a hesitation, or a pause…as if some unknown powerful being took a breath. The brightness returned, only this time everything had changed. Now, as per his request, he was floating slowly in a raft complete with paddles under a warm sun.

"That's more like it!" he said, feeling the urge to stretch out and relax. Bo was exhausted. He was in severe sensory overload. "I need to rest for a moment, and then we can start again. I'll be better then," he said to whoever was listening. Then within his dream, within his sleep, he went to sleep. After all, it would only be a moment….

With those thoughts, darkness returned to Bo's mind. It wasn't really darkness, but an absence of presence. Whoever was trying to talk to him, whether it be an angel, the Holy Ghost, or Heavenly Father, he didn't know, but whoever it was, he, or they, let him rest. With thankfulness he allowed himself to be bathed in sweet unconsciousness. How long it lasted, he didn't know.

Bo opened his eyes. Not his physical eyes, but the eyes of his mind. Remembering he was in the middle of some sort of dream, he stretched his mind toward heaven. He wanted to try again. "Please send me the dream that I couldn't understand. I'll try to keep up this time." Then he braced himself, concentrating as hard as he could manage.

Suddenly, Christ's kind look fell on Bo.

Bo was at the feet of his master, once again on the beach. His desire had been granted and he was being given an audience!

Bo was surprised! He hadn't prepared for this! He suddenly felt so many emotions all at the same time. He was in awe, yet his thoughts were paralyzed. *What should he do? What should he say?*

As Bo gazed at Jesus, all his thoughts flew from him and instead he found himself wondering, why did he, the Master of all, love the people of the earth? After all, over and over, throughout the ages, they had proven they were a messed up, befuddled, decadent bunch of inconsistent failures.[13] Why would someone so righteous and powerful, such as Christ, care for them? Why would he seek after them? Why would he suffer for them?[14] Then again, why would Christ love *him*? *He* kept messing up! He couldn't keep his heart pure. Even though Bo had studied the gospel his whole life, he was still as weak as water.[15] All these questions burned into his chest as he gazed at the Savior.

Christ held out his hand to Bo and said, "Simon Peter, son of Jonas…lovest me more than these?" Christ motioned to the circle of people sitting around the fire.

Bo, knowing that he was Peter again in this dream, looked around the circle. But instead of the apostles, now Bo saw his family: Corrynne, Braun, Conrad, Brea, Dane, and Carea along with all his little ones. Bo swallowed. He knew what the Lord was asking him. It was a pointed question. He was asking him, knowing that he tried always to be a good steward of his family, why he couldn't also love the Lord enough to trust in his plan for him and his loved ones?[16] Bo wondered the same thing about himself. The real answer to Christ's question was "no" and that understanding pained Bo.

"Simon Peter, son of Jonas…lovest me more than these?" Christ again asked Bo.

Bo hung his head. He couldn't even answer this simple question Christ put to him. The bottom line of the question was, could he give up control? If he turned over his trust to the Savior, then he would have to let go of his anger when things didn't turn out the way he wanted them to. Was he willing to do that? Was he willing to do all that he could in his life, but when that wasn't good enough, stifle his anger and let go of it? Inside, he knew that if he could do that small thing, let go of all of his anger and frustrations and hand them over to Christ, he would be happy. He wanted to.[17]

Christ waited patiently for an answer.

Bo looked down at his hands. He knew what he had to do. He had to turn his face to the Lord and not let anything, not hardships, not his own insecurities, not the life or death of his children get in the way of his love for his Savior. If he could truly put him first in his life, above all else,[18] he knew as he had been taught in another dream, everything he had ever loved would be his forever. *If he let go of everything,[19] he would inherit all.[20]* It was such a hard concept, yet it was the very thing that would give him freedom from anger and slavery to his own weaknesses.[21]

Deciding this was what he wanted to do, Bo looked up at the Lord. As he did, great love filled him. Despite why or how such a glorious being could love someone like him, he did. Bo felt it. Christ loved him, not because of what he could do, or what talents he had, but he loved him because he was his brother. He had suffered for Bo because he was his brother. Christ suffered for Bo and all of mankind for the same reason that Bo wanted so deeply to protect his family, because he loved them and because he had the power to do so.[22]

With that understanding, suddenly, it all made sense. It was good to want to protect and provide for your loved ones, but because we are human and have our limits, the Lord knows we'll fall short of complete protection and provision. We are not to have guilt for that. We are not to be angry because of our limits or our inadequacies. We are to realize that God, who does have power over all, will make up for all our shortcomings and we are to be thankful for that. Through the partnership between man and God, we can achieve our greatest desires, despite our weaknesses.[23] *How glorious that blessing is!* That even though we may labor all our days in the service of our fellow beings and never achieve some of our expectations, in the eternal scheme of things, all will be made whole.

Bo was crying now. He couldn't believe the great love of God! How glorious he was, to care enough for the little things, that he cared enough to assure Bo he would have the desires of his heart.[24] He wished for his family's safety, and through Christ, he would have it. There might be hardships, suffering, and maybe even death, but even despite those events, they all would be safe in the kingdom of heaven.[25] Now he needed to focus on that knowledge. He needed to have it grow in his heart, taking root and becoming a part of him.[26] With this knowledge he would never need to indulge in anger and bitterness again because something didn't work out the way he wished it to. He now could have peace in times of adversity.

Bo looked up at the Lord. He felt he could answer him now. "Yea, Lord; thou knowest that I love thee."

Christ then paused and said, "Feed my lambs."

Bo studied the face of Christ. He was being told to turn away from his anger and in the love he found in Christ, love others.[27] Strive to help others understand the same principles that he now understood. Help them overcome themselves to understand God's great eternal plan of happiness.

Bo bowed his head and nodded. That would be something he could do.

Christ again addressed Bo, "Simon Peter, son of Jonas…lovest thou me?"

Bo looked up, now confused. He had just said that he did. Was there something else? Was he missing another message in Christ's words? "Yea, Lord…thou knowest that I love thee!" said Bo, wondering if this was how Peter felt when Christ asked him so many times in front of his brethren. Then Bo remembered, Christ had asked him this question before in a previous dream. He had promised to put the Lord first then, but then he had failed. Bo shook his head in embarrassment. "I'm sorry Lord. I'll try better this time."

Christ nodded and then once again commanded, "Feed my sheep."

Bo stood before his Savior and nodded, feeling like he needed to defend his loyalty. "Lord, thou knowest all things: thou knowest that I love thee."

"Feed my sheep," Christ said for the third time.

Bo understood. He was being called to serve mankind. He needed to do this above all else. He needed to stand in the stead of Christ as a priesthood holder and feed his sheep as he would.[28] Could he do this? In the hard times to come, could he put aside all his own cares and hardships and become consumed with the work of God?

Then, rapid visual images rushed upon him. His previous dream was played in his head in a moment, only an understanding came with it also.

He saw himself standing on the beach just as at the beginning of the dream. In a moment, in a rush of intelligence, he was given understanding of his dreams.

Bo was standing at the dusk of time, when darkness was about to prevail in its greatest glory. He was standing on the beach, but his call was to get in the boat and fish. He was to use the Lord's guidance to find those souls searching for truth and if he did, his nets would break, but if he didn't, his nets would be empty and he'd be found naked and alone in front of the Lord.

Bo recoiled in horror. To be found unworthy was not the ending he wanted for his life.

Suddenly, he was afraid. Did this vision foretell the ending of his life? Would he be found naked in the sight of the Lord? In sudden power, Bo began praying fervently. "Please don't let that happen to me! Please, don't let me be naked in thy sight."

Suddenly Christ was standing in front of Bo again. With eyes of fire Christ stated clearly, "Thine iniquity is taken away and thy sin purged. Thou art clean every whit."

Bo was astonished. Had he paid a sufficient penance? Had he suffered enough for such complete forgiveness? ...Well, if the Lord said it, he must have! What higher source is there? Now it was time to have faith in the Lord's words and forgive himself.[29] "Thank you, Lord!" Bo exclaimed, feeling full of joy.

Looking inside himself, Bo realized all his pain had left him. He felt light and happy. Yes! He had been forgiven and was indeed clean! He felt like he could jump over a building in a single bound, or stop a bullet with his chest! What a great day!

"Now, go and serve me," said Christ.

"OK, I will," said Bo, nodding excitedly as he felt himself waking. He was emerging from the depth of his mind. It was time to get up and as he realized this, he felt exhausted, but excited. It was time to get things done! Hopefully, everything was going to be better now. It was a brand new day.

Notes to "Metamorphosis"

Stubborn Weakness

[1] "We observe that in the scriptures, fasting almost always is linked with prayer. Without prayer, fasting is not complete fasting; it's simply going hungry. If we want our fasting to be more than just going without eating, we must lift our hearts, our minds, and our voices in communion with our Heavenly Father. Fasting, coupled with mighty prayer, is powerful. It

can fill our minds with the revelations of the Spirit. It can strengthen us against times of temptation. Fasting and prayer can help develop within us courage and confidence. It can strengthen our character and build self-restraint and discipline. Often when we fast, our righteous prayers and petitions have greater power. Testimonies grow. We mature spiritually and emotionally and sanctify our souls. Each time we fast, we gain a little more control over our worldly appetites and passions" (Joseph B. Wirthlin, "The Law of the Fast," *Ensign*, May 2001, p. 73).

[2] "One of the last, subtle strongholds of selfishness is the natural feeling that we 'own' ourselves. Of course we are free to choose and are personally accountable. Yes, we have individuality. But those who have chosen to 'come unto Christ' soon realize that they do not 'own' themselves. Instead, they belong to Him. We are to become consecrated along with our gifts, our appointed days, and our very selves. Hence, there is a stark difference between stubbornly 'owning' oneself and submissively belonging to God. Clinging to the old self is not a mark of independence, but of indulgence!" (Neal A. Maxwell, "Put Off the Natural Man, and Come Off Conqueror," *Ensign*, Nov 1990, p. 14).

[3] "Relying only on your own abilities can lead to the sin of pride. In the opening section of the Doctrine and Covenants, the Lord described the wicked condition of many in the world, and I quote: 'They seek not the Lord to establish his righteousness, but every man walketh in his own way, and after the image of his own god' (D&C 1:16). If we boast in our own strength and 'walk in our own way,' we can slip easily from the straight and narrow path to the broad roadways of the world" (Joseph B. Wirthlin, "Running Your Marathon," *Ensign*, Nov 1989, p. 73).

[4] "The central feature of pride is enmity—enmity toward God and enmity toward our fellowmen. Enmity means 'hatred toward, hostility to, or a state of opposition.' It is the power by which Satan wishes to reign over us. Pride is essentially competitive in nature. We pit our will against God's. When we direct our pride toward God, it is in the spirit of 'my will and not thine be done.' As Paul said, they 'seek their own, not the things which are Jesus Christ's' (Philip. 2:21). ...The proud cannot accept the authority of God giving direction to their lives. (See Hel. 12:6.) They pit their perceptions of truth against God's great knowledge, their abilities versus God's priesthood power, their accomplishments against His mighty works. Our enmity toward God takes on many labels, such as rebellion, hard-heartedness, stiff-neckedness, unrepentant, puffed up, easily offended, and sign seekers. The proud wish God would agree with them. They aren't interested in changing their opinions to agree with God's" (Ezra Taft Benson, "The Faces of Pride," *New Era*, Oct 2003, p. 40).

[5] "At times we may despair that our burdens are too great. When it seems that a tempest is raging in our lives, we may feel abandoned and cry out like the disciples in the storm, 'Master, carest thou not that we perish?' (Mark 4:38). At such times we should remember His reply: 'Why are ye so fearful? How is it that ye have no faith?' (Mark 4:40). The healing power of the Lord Jesus Christ—whether it removes our burdens or strengthens us to endure and live with them like the Apostle Paul—is available for every affliction in mortality. The Atonement also gives us the strength to endure 'pains and afflictions and temptations of every kind,' because our Savior also took upon Him 'the pains and the sicknesses of his people' (Alma 7:11). Brothers and sisters, if your faith and prayers and the power of the priesthood do not heal you from an affliction, the power of the Atonement will surely give you the strength to bear the burden. 'Come unto me, all ye that labour and are heavy laden,' the Savior said, 'and I will give you rest... unto your souls' (Matthew 11:28–29)" (Dallin H. Oaks, "He Heals the Heavy Laden," *Ensign*, Nov 2006, pgs. 6–9).

[6] "Selfishness is often expressed in stubbornness of mind. Having a 'mind hardened in pride' often afflicts the brightest who could also be the best. (Dan. 5:20.) 'One thing' the brightest often lack: meekness! Instead of having 'a willing mind' which seeks to emulate the 'mind of Christ,' a 'mind hardened in pride' is impervious to counsel and often seeks ascendancy. (1

Chr. 28:9; 1 Cor. 2:16; D&C 64:34.)" (Neal A. Maxwell, "Put Off the Natural Man, and Come Off Conqueror," *Ensign*, Nov 1990, p. 14).

[7] "Pride *goeth* before destruction, and an haughty spirit before a fall" (Proverbs 16:18).

[8] "No part of walking by faith is more difficult than walking the road of repentance. However, with 'faith unto repentance,' we can push roadblocks out of the way, moving forward to beg God for mercy. (Alma 34:16.) True contrition brings full capitulation. One simply surrenders, caring only about what God thinks, not what 'they' think, while meekly offering, 'O God, …make thyself known unto me, and I will give away all my sins to know thee.' (Alma 22:18.) Giving away all our sins is the only way we can come to know God" (Neal A. Maxwell, "Repentance," *Ensign*, Nov 1991, p. 30).

[9] "The antidote for pride is humility—meekness, submissiveness. (See Alma 7:23.) It is the broken heart and contrite spirit. (See 3 Ne. 9:20; 3 Ne. 12:19; D&C 20:37; D&C 59:8; Ps. 34:18; Isa. 57:15; Isa. 66:2.) …God will have a humble people. Either we can choose to be humble or we can be compelled to be humble. Alma said, 'Blessed are they who humble themselves without being compelled to be humble' (Alma 32:16). Let us choose to be humble" (Ezra Taft Benson, "The Faces of Pride," *New Era*, Oct 2003, p. 40).

[10] "In the anguishing process of repentance, we may sometimes feel God has deserted us. The reality is that our behavior has isolated us from Him. Thus, while we are turning away from evil but have not yet turned fully to God, we are especially vulnerable. Yet we must not give up, but, instead, reach out to God's awaiting arm of mercy, which is outstretched 'all the day long.' (Jacob 5:47; Jacob 6:4; 2 Ne. 28:32; Morm. 5:11.) Unlike us, God has no restrictive office hours" (Neal A. Maxwell, "Repentance," *Ensign*, Nov 1991, p. 30).

Fishing for Answers

[11] The Sea of Tiberius and the Sea of Galilee are the same body of water. In actuality, it's not a sea at all. It's actually a large freshwater lake but is called a sea by tradition. The names change in the scriptures depending on location of the observer along its banks. Close to Tiberius, it was known as the sea of Tiberius. Close to Galilee, it was the Sea of Galilee.

[12] This storyline is patterned after John 21.

"Lovest Thou Me?"

[13] "Thou art holy and dwellest in the heavens, and that we are unworthy before thee; because of the fall our natures have become evil continually; nevertheless, O Lord, thou hast given us a commandment that we must call upon thee, that from thee we may receive according to our desires" (Ether 3:2).

[14] "And thus God bringeth about his great and eternal purposes, which were prepared from the foundation of the world. And thus cometh about the salvation and the redemption of men" (Alma 42:26).

"And if children, then heirs; heirs of God, and joint-heirs with Christ; if so be that we suffer with him, that we may be also glorified together" (Romans 8:17).

"For behold, this is my work and my glory—to bring to pass the immortality and eternal life of man" (Moses 1:39).

[15] "Wherefore I abhor myself, and repent in dust and ashes" (Job 42:6).

[16] "For the natural man is an enemy to God, and has been from the fall of Adam, and will be, forever and ever, unless he yields to the enticings of the Holy Spirit, and putteth off the natural man and becometh a saint through the atonement of Christ the Lord, and becometh as a child, submissive, meek, humble, patient, full of love, willing to submit to all things which the Lord seeth fit to inflict upon him, even as a child doth submit to his father" (Mosiah 3:19).

[17] "No matter what occurs, no matter how topsy-turvy the world becomes, you can always have the sustaining power of faith. That will never change. The perfect love of your Father in Heaven will never change. His gospel plan gives life meaning and can assure your happiness. His plan is not only to prove yourself here on earth but also that you may receive the growth that comes from correct decisions prompted by faith, enabled by your obedience. Why worry about future calamities or uncertainties over which you have no control? Your righteous character magnifies the probability that you will never have to suffer them. When challenges and testing do come, your faith will lead you to solutions. Your peace of mind, your assurance of answers to vexing problems, your ultimate joy depend upon your trust in Heavenly Father and His Son, Jesus Christ. Right will ultimately prevail. It will yield blessings now as you in faith obey the commandments of God. Remember an unfailing, continual, ever-present source of peace and comfort is available to you. It is the certainty that your Father in Heaven loves you no matter what your circumstance, no matter what winds of trial, turmoil, or tribulation whirl about you. That certainty will never change. Your ability to access that support depends on the strength of your faith in Him and in His certain willingness to bless you" (Richard G. Scott, "The Sustaining Power of Faith in Times of Uncertainty and Testing," *Ensign*, May 2003, p. 75).

[18] "Thou shalt love the Lord thy God with all thy heart, and with all thy soul, and with all thy mind" (Matthew 22:37).

[19] "Behold, I, the Lord, who was crucified for the sins of the world, give unto you a commandment that you shall forsake the world" (D&C 53:2).

[20] "And he that receiveth my Father receiveth my Father's kingdom; therefore all that my Father hath shall be given unto him" (D&C 88:38).

[21] "If thou wilt do good, yea, and hold out faithful to the end, thou shalt be saved in the kingdom of God, which is the greatest of all the gifts of God; for there is no gift greater than the gift of salvation" (D&C 6:13).

[22] "This is the plan of salvation unto all men, through the blood of mine Only Begotten, who shall come in the meridian of time" (Moses 6:62).

[23] "For with God nothing shall be impossible" (Luke 1:37).

[24] "He is despised and rejected of men; a man of sorrows, and acquainted with grief: and we hid as it were our faces from him; he was despised, and we esteemed him not. Surely he hath borne our griefs, and carried our sorrows yet we did esteem him stricken, smitten of God, and afflicted. But he was wounded for our transgressions, he was bruised for our iniquities: the chastisement of our peace was upon him; and with his stripes we are healed" (Isaiah 53:3–5).

[25] "And every one that hath forsaken houses, or brethren, or sisters, or father, or mother, or wife, or children, or lands, for my name's sake, shall receive an hundredfold, and shall inherit everlasting life" (Matthew 19:29).

[26] "And now, my brethren, I desire that ye shall plant this word in your hearts, and as it beginneth to swell even so nourish it by your faith. And behold, it will become a tree, springing up in you unto everlasting life. And then may God grant unto you that your burdens may be light, through the joy of his Son. And even all this can ye do if ye will" (Alma 33:23).

[27] "Thou shalt love thy neighbor as thyself" (D&C 59:6).

[28] "It is a sobering responsibility for those who bear the priesthood to act as agents of the Lord to help those in need. That trust requires faith, worthiness, and a sensitivity to the promptings of the Spirit to communicate the will of the Lord" (Richard G. Scott, "Obtaining Help from the Lord," *Ensign*, Nov 1991, p. 84).

[29] "Behold, he who has repented of his sins, the same is forgiven, and I, the Lord, remember them no more" (D&C 58:42).

CHAPTER FIFTEEN

POWER OF THE SON

"And then shall they see the Son of man coming in a cloud with power and great glory (Luke 21:27).

00:03:09, 08:03:15, Zulu
Sunday, September 21st

Forces of Nature

Outside Indianapolis, Indiana
10:57 a.m.

Dane was driving a long stretch of the lonely, empty I-70. There were miles and miles of quiet farmland stretching out behind and in front. So far, the drive was on track and without event. He hoped it would stay that way.

Nebraska was sitting happily in the back of the car playing an imaginary game with old, hollow shells of some crab legs. Somehow, in her mind, she had transformed the shells that she used to be afraid of and call "spiders" into dolls. She had the pointy ends up, talking to each other and hopping, or "walking," along the seat backs.

Dane watched Nebraska in the rearview mirror.

"Hey, come over here," Nebraska said in a low voice.

"What?" asked the second crab leg in a high voice.

"There's water over here. It's good!"

"Water?" asked the second, who must have been a girl crab leg. "Oh, let me see!" Then it hopped over to where the first one was.

Nebraska put both pointy ends down into an imaginary pool and made slurping sounds.

Dane smiled. He remembered playing with sticks that way when he was little. Who needed toys? Anything could be a toy. The mind was an incredible thing.

He continued to watch Nebraska, alternating his eyes from the straight road back to the mirror. Dane loved how children could be sad one moment and then laughing the next. In a way, he wished he was like that again. Life would be so much simpler. Tragedy would be just a bad day, instead of a life-changing moment. He could feel that he had changed from being a child into an adult, and instead of being carefree and resilient, he had become serious, contemplative, and careful. When did that happen? Did life do that to him? Or was it a maturation thing? Maybe it was a combination of the two.... Dane continued to think about how old he felt. He looked at his hands. They were man hands—not even teen hands. Strange. He had changed. He guessed it was a good thing. He knew that he had become strong in both body and mind and that's what helped him save Nebraska.

Dane's attention returned to the road. New determination filled him. He was going to deliver Nebraska and Louise to safety. Obviously, he had been given wisdom and strength beyond his years and he imagined it was meant to protect them. He continued to play out different scenarios that they might encounter on their journey. Some of them were threatening and ended in his death. But that was OK. He was willing to die to protect his charges. Hopefully he wouldn't, but he was willing to. Every good soldier felt that way. Life was precious and good enough to die for so that others might live.

Dane checked the radio. He pushed the search button over and over. Only static came back. He wondered if cell phones were working yet.

"Louise."

"Yes?" answered Louise and she sat forward in the back seat. She had been quietly looking out the window.

"Do you have a cell phone?"

"It doesn't have battery left," she said, "but it's in the glove compartment. I threw it there because it's a piece of junk."

"You normally buy pieces of junk?" teased Dane as he opened the glove compartment and found the phone.

"No, I didn't buy it."

"You didn't?" asked Dane as he flipped the phone open.

"Ahhh, no—my, ah, employee bought it," said Louise obviously having difficulty explaining her phone.

"Employee?"

"Yes," Louise's eyes widened as she concentrated. "Ahh, he was my driver," she said nodding.

"Oh, that's right. You were a *rich* professor," said Dane as he looked at the battery. There wasn't a lot of energy left, but there was some.

"No really! It was my driver's and he gave it to me when the city went mad. Now that's the *truth*."

Dane nodded. "I believe that statement. I believe you had a driver. I can see it in your eyes."

Louise allowed a resigned smile to peek through her controlled exterior.

"So, what happened to yours?" asked Dane, teasing Louise.

"A bum stole it," said Louise with a shrug and an apologetic smile.

"OK. Whatever. That was a lie. Don't know why, but now you're lying," said Dane as he dialed his home phone number.

Louise covered her face, as if to hide embarrassment. "I'll just stop talking now," she said.

The phone rang. Dane was surprised! It was working! Then the phone gave a beep indicating the battery was about to die.

"Hello?" answered his mother.

"Mom!" he said happily.

The phone beeped again.

"Dane?" she asked, surprised.

"I'm coming home, Mom. I'm on the road!" Dane had to hurry and talk before he lost the connection. "I'm…"

"Where are you?" asked his mother, as they both spoke at the same time.

"Is that your mommy?" asked Nebraska looking at Dane from the back.

"I'm in Indiana, getting ready to enter Illinois. I'm going to lose you, Mom. The battery's dying."

The phone made another beep.

"Dane, I love you!"

Dane was overwhelmed by his mother's voice. Tears came freely to his eyes. "I love—"

The phone went blank and the sound went dead.

"—you, too," he said as he pulled the phone away and looked at its dark face.

"Was that your mommy?" asked Nebraska again with a hopeful expression.

Dane nodded as he wiped his eyes discreetly. "Yep, that was my mommy."

"Can I talk to mine?" asked Nebraska.

Dane showed Nebraska the phone. "The phone lost its energy. My mom is gone now."

"Can I try to call my mom?" she asked.

Dane handed Nebraska the phone. "Sure, you can try, but I think it's dead."

As Dane watched Nebraska and Louise try and make the phone come back to life, he savored the memory of his mother's voice. He hadn't known he missed his family so much. Her voice rang quietly in his mind, reminding him of everything good. He'd be home soon. He could feel it.

"Where's your charger?" asked Dane.

"My driver didn't have time to give it to me, and I didn't think to ask."

"Here," said Nebraska handing the phone back. "It's broken."

Louise looked down and said, "Thank you, honey," as she took the phone and closed it. "I can't believe the phone worked for you." Louise looked at Dane in the mirror from the back. "It didn't do anything for me."

"That's probably because the phone systems aren't jammed anymore," said Dane.

"And the solar flares must have stopped," added Louise.

"That too…." said Dane facetiously, wondering what Louise was talking about.

"I wonder if the satellites have been repaired," said Louise thoughtfully.

"Repaired? From what?" asked Dane.

"The solar storm."

"What does a solar storm have to do with satellites and phones?"

"You're kidding right?" asked Louise.

"No. Should I know what you're talking about?"

Louise laughed a little, but then stopped and composed herself.

"Why is that funny? I've been fighting a war. I don't know what else is going on. Give me a break!"

Louise folded her arms and said, "Now, that's something I know about. Would you like to know about solar storms? They're going to affect your life."

"Sure. I'd like that."

"OK," said Louise as she smiled conservatively. "The sun runs in 11-year cycles. This is the year for a peak in its activity. In fact there was a double peak, making it double the trouble."[1]

"Interesting," said Dane, watching her in the mirror.

"During peaks, which are the storms, the sun emits hot gas in the form of solar flares along with increased radio emissions. During those peaks in activity, bursts of energy interfere with cell phone use as well as the ability of satellites to relay information."[2]

"Really?" said Dane studying Louise. Obviously, this was a *smart*, rich woman. Who was this lady? He wondered if he should know who she was.

"Half the problem occurs when radio waves from the sun hit the towers creating static. It overwhelms the signal at the tower and stops the phones."

"Hmmm," said Dane. "So we've been having a solar storm, huh?"

"Right."

"I just thought the phones became jammed when too many users were accessing the lines." Dane remembered the military telling him something about the recent intermittent unreliability of cell phones but he hadn't made the connection between the phones and the sun.

"Well, that too. In any tragic time cell phones are jammed and can't relay their signals, but this time, it was more than just that."

"So, is this intellectual exposure demonstrating your professor side?" he asked smiling in the mirror.

"Am I exposing myself?" Louise asked with a slight frown.

Dane smiled to see the change in Louise's face. She had been operating on automatic and he had caught her. More moments like this and he might be able to figure out who she really was. "The professor identity suits you well. Keep going. Tell me what else you know."

"You're not interested in what I know," said Louise, subconsciously reaching for Nebraska's blonde curls.

Dane watched Louise. Now she was uncomfortable. He wanted to put her back at ease. "Sure. Tell me more about those solar storms. I like that stuff, and this road in front of us is pretty straight and boring."

"I've been told I'm boring."

Dane laughed. "All real professors are boring, but you've got a captive audience here, so don't worry about it! Go ahead."

Louise looked up at the ceiling as she thought.

"Can I play with your phone?" asked Nebraska, looking up and smiling.

Louise opened her hand and let Nebraska take the phone.

Nebraska opened the phone and started pretending it was a pretty lady.

"OK, I have something that might interest you," said Louise.

"Go ahead," said Dane with a nod.

"Were you aware the magnetic poles of the earth are about to flip?"[3]

"The magnetic poles?"[4] asked Dane. "I know that the magnetics of the earth are changing, but I didn't know they were going to flip. What does 'flip' mean?"

"Change places."

"What?" asked Dane, now thoroughly confused.

"To put it simply, the magnetic north is about to become the magnetic south and south, north."

"How's that possible?" asked Dane. "Are you saying eventually a compass would point south instead of north?"

"That's exactly what I'm saying."[5]

"How?"

"Over twelve thousand years—a gentle rise—and then a rapid fall of the earth's magnetic strength has occurred."

"OK, I know about the weakening magnetic strength of the earth," said Dane.

"The rate of change has been significantly higher in the last three hundred years than it has been for any time in the past five thousand," said Louise.

"So you're saying in the last three hundred years, the magnetic strength has been weakening faster than ever," said Dane, checking his understanding.

"Right. But it's more significant than that."

"What am I missing?"

"Do you know what the magnetic shield does for our world?" asked Louise.

Dane thought about what he knew. He knew a little about a lot of things, but not about that. "I guess I don't. What does it do?"

"It makes a bubble of protection around the earth. It protects us from the harmful energy of the sun. Because of the magnetics of the earth, the harmful rays just skittle across the bubble and off into space."

"That's great. So what you're saying is that our protective magnetic field is going from strong to weak."

"Right and it's gaining speed."[6]

"That's disconcerting," said Dane. "How is this happening?"

"2,000 miles beneath our feet, there is a molten core. A large ocean of liquid iron generates the magnetic force of the earth. When that ocean of liquid agitates it has the ability to flip the magnetic poles of the earth."

"I see. I didn't know that."

"In fact, this is a natural and common occurrence."

"It is?" asked Dane wondering why he hadn't heard about it before.

"Yes, it's happened over and over before on the earth, it's just that it hasn't ever happened while man lived on it."[7]

"So this has happened before and the earth survived, right?" asked Dane.

"Yes, many, many times,"[8] said Louise.

"Then it's not a big deal," said Dane.

"No, it *is* a big deal," said Louise. "It might be normal for the earth, but it's not normal for us."

"To mankind, you're saying."

"Right."

"So what will happen?"

"The magnetic field of the earth protects us from the solar winds and galactic radiation. The problem isn't when the poles flip, it's the weakening of the field before the flip and the instability afterwards.[9] So as the magnetic field increasingly becomes weaker, earth's protection from those deadly forces decreases.[10] Simply put, we're losing the magnetic protection that keeps this planet hospitable for our advanced society."[11]

"This is great!" said Dane sarcastically, sighing. "So explain the effects."

"There are a few," started Louise. "The first being the ozone layer of our earth would weaken and eventually open up. Holes in that layer would allow harmful radiation from the sun to penetrate our atmosphere."

"Isn't that what's happening over the Atlantic Ocean?"

Louise's eyes darted as she thought. "Yes, that's right. And with that weakening, we've been seeing a dramatic increase in skin cancer."[12]

"OK," said Dane nodding. "So, note to self: Stay out of the sun."

"Good," said Louise. "Wear hats and put on more sunscreen."

"What else?" asked Dane.

"Have you noticed the Aurora Borealis in the sky on some nights? It's normally only seen in the farthest north and south, but now, because of the weakening field, the Aurora is seen almost to the equator. And as we lose the shield altogether, it will become a normal occurrence."[13]

Dane shook his head. "I haven't."

"Well, you should look. It's quite beautiful."

"OK, I will. Are there any other effects?"

"Yes. Just as cell phones malfunction, all technology will be affected. On good days, computer chips will exhibit spontaneous changes in stored data due to neutrons colliding with the silicon atom. This might result in phantom commands or lost or corrupted data.[14] On moderate days, electronic power transmission will reset, or malfunction, or fail with static electricity buildup and discharges.[15] On the bad days, whole systems will be fried, just wiped out from too much energy.'"[16]

"Don't we have those problems now?"

"Yes, but not to the degree they will occur as we lose our magnetic shield."

"I see," said Dane.

"Radio communication will deteriorate, making long-range radio communication difficult or impossible. All global-positioning systems, which rely on radio transmission, will be degraded.[17] Electricity will be routinely disrupted, causing blackouts, and will sometimes cause the substations to explode during solar flares."[18]

"Wow."

"Navigation by magnetic compass would be inaccurate…"

"It's already inaccurate now.[19] I should know. I tried to get to Washington, D.C., with a compass and it was hopeless."

Louise nodded. "And like I said, it's going to get worse."

Dane nodded. "OK," he said thinking he could live with those problems. He could adapt. He wasn't worried.

"Migratory animals, which use the magnetic fields for direction, could lose their way. We could be seeing many more beached whales and lost birds."

"I see." Dane wasn't sure if he should worry about those things either. "But I'm sure they'd adapt after a while. Nature has a way of surviving.[20] So far, you haven't said anything that sounds too terrible."

Louise's face took on a serious stare. "That's when the field weakens; when it disappears, it will be a different story."

"What are you holding back?"

"It is possible that as the magnetic shield disappears, our atmosphere could begin to erode and blow away by the cosmic winds, and life on the surface will die from the devastating cosmic rays from the sun. It is possible our earth could become a dead planet like Mars. Because that's exactly what happened to that planet."[21]

"Oh," said Dane. "Now, that's something to be concerned about."

"Absolutely," said Louise.

"But that's the worst case scenario, right?"

"Right."

"Reality is probably somewhere in-between,"[22] offered Dane.

"Most likely," said Louise with a resigned nod.

"OK, so how do we fight this thing, live in a cave?"[23]

"Yes," said Louise with raised eyebrows.

"Yes?" asked Dane, laughing. Was Louise serious?

"Deep in a cave, the harmful rays from the sun and stars will not penetrate the rock and all technology will be safe from electron bombardment."[24]

"Hmmm," said Dane imagining what it would be like to have to live in caves. "How soon should we see some of these manifestations of a weakening magnetic field?"

"We see them now. They have crept upon us so slowly most of us don't notice. As time progresses we'll see more, but as far as the magnetic fields flipping, that's unknown. It could be in a decade or it could be in a thousand years. The earth doesn't disclose its timelines."

Dane looked at his watch. Its digital face had been working off and on for a couple of days. He had hoped it had just gotten wet or something. But now he was wondering if it hadn't been burned out by stray sun rays from the latest solar storm. He tapped it with his finger. "So you're saying the sky is falling."

"In a matter of speaking."

"What do we do about it?"

"What can we do?" asked Louise. "It's bigger than any of us."

"So we just hold on and enjoy the ride?" asked Dane.

Louise looked out the window. "I don't know about the ride, but knowing what we're facing will help us deal with it more productively."

Dane nodded. Louise was right. Understanding and responding appropriately was key in any hard time. We always have a choice. When difficulty comes, do we wallow in self-pity or do we roll up our sleeves and figure things out? That willingness to adapt was central not only to survival but a good life. He would adapt.

"Do you foresee cities that live under manufactured protective bubbles to protect themselves from the sun?" asked Dane.

Louise nodded. "I do."

"I do, too," said Dane.

"Do you have bubbles?" asked Nebraska looking up from her playing suddenly.

Dane laughed. "No, I don't have bubbles, but where we're going, we can make so many bubbles you're going to get sick of them."

Nebraska smiled. "Can I be first to play with them?"

"First behind who?" asked Louise.

"Behind all those other boys," said Nebraska with a scrunched nose.

Dane frowned. What was she talking about? "Where are these boys?"

"At your house," she said, giggling.

Dane looked at Louise in the mirror and Louise shrugged.

"Sure you can be first," said Dane wondering if Nebraska was talking from something she knew, dreamed, or had heard. "You knew we were going to my house?" asked Dane.

Nebraska nodded. "You told your mommy you were."

"Oh," said Dane with a nod. "You're right. I did. How did you know I have brothers at my house?"

"Because."

"Because why?" asked Dane, probing.

Nebraska looked down at her crab legs and the phone, made them kiss, and said, "I don't know."

Dane raised his eyebrows and looked back again at Louise. "From the mouths of babes," she said with a smile and a shrug.

"From the mouths of babes," echoed Dane.

Withering Vine

Provo, Utah
12:25 p.m.

Bo stood at the pulpit and looked out at the ward. "Good afternoon, brothers and sisters." He looked from face to face. He lovingly looked at the families, the widows, the elderly couples hunched over, holding hands. His vision crossed over the youth of the group and then the little children who were busy being busy, not even listening. But that was OK. These were his people. He knew this congregation and he loved them.

"It is so good to be here today." Bo's vision continued to the back of the room. Now, there were people he didn't recognize, and not just one or two. There were groups of three or four. The sight delighted him. Did people from the community decide to come to their Sacrament Meeting? That would be great.

Bo took a breath as he collected his thoughts. "I'd tell a joke, but I've used them all already," he said as the congregation responded.

Bo smiled. He was sure he looked odd, but—he felt happy! Today, he was a new person. Today, he had no weaknesses. He had purged himself of his selfishness and had been forgiven of his sins and now, his only thoughts were for service, being the least of his congregation and those that visited, desiring only to serve his Savior in teaching the truth.

"I assigned myself a talk in light of the sadness and tragedy that has overcome our nation, but I ask, what do you say to people in times like these? I have been praying all morning to know. I'm happy to report that the Spirit is whispering to me right now of the things I need to say to you."

Bo winked at his wife as he folded his hands on the pulpit, having no notes to guide him. He would address the topics that came to his mind as instructed.

"The world is like a vineyard," he started. "It is a miracle, complete in every way to give renewed life to creation. Good plants give us oxygen to breathe and food to eat. The heavens give us water, the main substance of our bodies, and a self-renewing ecosystem to clean our water and our food sources. God made sure the temperature on the earth wasn't too hot or too cold. It was a tricky feat to try and assure the temperature on this globe didn't vary more than a hundred degrees or so, even with the tilt of the axis of the earth. He couldn't allow our blood to boil or freeze since it was made of water.

"For hundreds of thousands of years, or maybe even more, God watched over this planet and cultivated it, prepping it for our arrival. About seven thousand years ago, finally our day began. We appeared on the surface of this planet. It was a beautiful home for sons and daughters of God to flourish, giving life to children, eventually creating whole societies.

"Today we have come to expect these miracles of nature as a given. We expect every day to wake up to a glorious sunrise, to drink pure clean water, and to breathe in fresh air. We expect food to be on the table and water to come from the tap. We complain about our lives, not comprehending that when we complain we forget the great gratitude we owe for our very existence and the very breath we take.[25]

"We are living in a day in which we cannot afford to forget where our blessings come from. We are living in a day where the eyes of the Lord have turned toward this earth. He sees what a mess we've made of it. He sees the wars, evil, and contentions. He also sees that his garden has yielded not the sweet grapes he was hoping for, but wild, bitter grapes and knotted vines.[26] Through our scriptures we hear him ask the question 'What more could I have done?'[27]

"We all know what comes next. When one has a garden that has been overtaken with inedible fruit, the only thing there is to do is to till it under, burn the weeds, and start over.[28] Brothers and Sisters, we are coming to that day. Our earth is on the verge of a burning and a re-birth. A new garden will be planted here under a new heaven and it will flourish and bear sweet fruit of the vine.[29] It is our invitation to be a part of that glorious new world, or be caught in the old, worn out, decadent and unthankful one. Which will we choose? I ask that question because it's our choice. We are 'the who' that decide whether we burn or are protected. *We decide* by our choices, attitudes, and hearts.[30]

"So who are those that will be burned with the garden? According to Isaiah chapter five, it will be those who are chained to their sins like a work horse is chained to the wagon."[31] Bo stopped and looked around at the people who were listening intently. With a hand, pointing to the pulpit, Bo emphasized the allusion. "*Chained to their sins*. What a great phrase. What does it mean? A work horse cannot free itself from the wagon it pulls! A work horse is not its own master. When we sin we give up control of our lives! We become enslaved with chains to the appetites sins create.[32] Sins are heavy burdens to bear with large tolls, for what? *Destruction?* Where is the reward in that? Sins stay with us, follow us, and destroy all that we love.[33] ...I know, because I have sins like these," said Bo, remembering his previous weak and useless rage. Looking back up into the congregation and with both hands out he said, "We all do. *But—we don't have to!* We can free ourselves![34] We must unchain ourselves and run free! Do it now—this very second, before it's too late!"

Bo had to wait a moment to regain his composure; the Spirit today was very strong and it was affecting him. His emotions were becoming unstable. He took a deep breath to gain control. After a few moments he felt strong enough, and then he continued.

"So who are those who will burn with the garden? Those who steal from the poor, taking advantage of the poor's powerlessness in order to become rich.[35] Those who value entertainment above obedience.[36] Those who rise up early in the morning with the sole purpose of increasing their pleasure at any price, obtaining money at any price, or pursuing worldly glory at any price, forgetting or ignoring why they were even born, denying the reality of God and the work of his hands.[37] It will be those who forever pursue knowledge without acknowledging the source of all truth[38] and those who are forever pursuing the riches of this world but never being satisfied.[39] Who are those people? Is it you? Is it me? Do we have these flaws? If we do, we must cast them off because we will be accountable to the Lord. We will be judged according to our thoughts and heart." Bo paused to bring home the point. "*It's an inescapable future.* No matter how rich, powerful, influential, or manipulative we think we are, it won't matter. We can't escape the beat of our own hearts."[40]

Bo changed his stance and leaned on the podium. "So what will happen to the pure in heart? Those who seek the Lord's face? Those who serve him with an eye single to his glory? I'm here to testify to you that *sanctification*[41] will overtake them, being *purified* through the *atonement of Christ* and then being *lifted* up, *changed* to meet the Savior in the clouds.[42] This is not a fairy tale. This is prophecy and it's your future, if you choose it.

"I beg you to choose that future. *There is no other*. Every other road leads to destruction and emptiness. Choose now to seek the Lord's face in everything you do, in all your waking moments and with every breath you take. And if you do, you'll be able to live and love and experience a new day on earth. It will be a miraculous, beautiful, and peaceful day without evil, violence, or fear. *Is this you? Is this me?* I hope so. I pray for it to be true.

"Brothers and Sisters," with that address, Bo choked up. He had to stop. Looking out at his friends and neighbors, he realized his love for them was growing. He shook his head as he grabbed a tissue and dabbed his eyes. Taking a breath, he tried again, "Brothers and my dear, sweet Sisters. Our future is crystal clear. It is up to us; no one but us. We will decide which side we will stand on. Each day will pass whether we choose righteousness or wickedness. Each day will pass and hours will be spent, bringing you closer to that glorious day that you will stand before the Lord. Decide *today* to be on his right hand."

"Excuse me, Bishop Rogers…" said a man wearing a cowboy hat and jeans with his hand raised above his head. "That's what these here people call you, right?"

Bishop Rogers stopped speaking and looked out into the audience. It was odd to have someone raise their hand during a talk in church. "Ah, yes. My friends call me 'Bishop.' I call the title a cursing, but they all swear it's a blessing."

The congregation laughed at Bo's joke and it made him smile. "Do you have a question, sir?" asked Bo.

"OK, no offense, but yes, I have a question."

"Go ahead. This is a friendly crowd," said Bo motioning to the congregation.

The man adjusted his hat and said, "To be honest, I'm pretty tired of hearing the hell, fire, and damnation preaching in every church I go to, saying the sky is falling. Can you tell me, Bishop, is the earth really cycling into destruction to punish the wicked people like me because I like my beer cold and my tamales hot—or are we just looking at a broken political system and natural disasters caused from too much fossil fuel consumption?"

The congregation laughed but then quickly quieted.

Bo smiled warmly at the man who had silver hair that fell down his shoulders and a red, weathered face. He could tell that the stranger's question was real, even though he tried to use humor to cover up his hunger to know the answer. Bo nodded and said, "Yes, my friend, it's really true that the dramatic weather patterns, the increase in earthquakes, the strange diseases and everything else unusual that's occurring around us are all a part of something greater that's about to take place on this earth. They are warnings to encourage people to return to morality, God, family, and integrity."[43]

"Oh, yeah?" challenged the man. "How's going back to God going to stop all those things?"

"Well," said Bo, looking momentarily up at the ceiling, "to be honest, it won't this time. However, since the creation of the world and the writing of scriptures, we have been warned that these things were coming. We know through the scriptures that these cataclysmic events will increase, not decrease, until the earth is empty."[44]

"What do you mean by empty?" asked the man, now obviously interested.

"I mean, that man will not live on the earth as we know it any more."

"You're talking about a mass extinction?"

"Eventually, yes, I am," said Bo nodding.

"But that would include these here good people too since we all share this earth," said the man pointing a finger at the congregation.

"For a while it will include everyone, as you point out, but there will come a time when those who choose to be good will be lifted off the earth and changed."

"Changed how?"

"Their bodies will be changed, being unable to die and will live with heavenly beings until the earth can be restored to its paradisiacal glory."[45]

"Sounds like fairytales to me."

"It's happened before," said Bo.

"To who?" said the man with great skepticism.

Bo held up his hands and started naming people off. "To Moses when he received the Ten Commandments; to Peter, James, and John on the mount of transfiguration; to the whole city of Enoch; to John the Beloved; to the Three Nephites; and it's prophesied to happen again to those whom Jesus Christ identifies as his in the last days of this earth's existence."

"Hmmm," said the man. "I've never heard of most of those people you just named, but then again, I haven't even read the Bible."

Bo smiled patiently as the man continued to consider his situation.

"Isn't it said somewheres that God, or Jesus is supposed to be re-born or something?"

"Not reborn, but return. Christ was crucified, and now he's resurrected and he will return to earth again to purify it."

"Do you think that Jesus is that Muslim pope that lives in the Vatican? He says he's the ressurected Jesus."

Bo had to stop a laugh that threatened to emerge. "No, I don't."

The man shook his head. "Neither do I. There's something strange about him that just ain't right."

Bo just smiled in response.

"Well I say, let the real Jesus come," said the stranger. "This world needs some help and heaven knows we've messed things up pretty bad." The stranger touched his hat and said, "Thank you, Bishop. Continue on with your speech, and I'll promise you I'll try and give up my cold beer for Lent."

Again the congregation laughed.

"Thank you, sir," said Bo smiling from ear to ear. Then to everyone in the crowd he said, "This man brings up a very good point. How do we know that all the things we are seeing today aren't just an exacerbation of global warming? How do we, being just human beings and not all-seeing, all-knowing entities, know *anything*? The answer is we don't." Bo paused for emphasis. "We don't, Brothers and Sisters. It is only through sincere prayer and in reading the scriptures that we will know of a surety of their words. If you turn to the scriptures you will see that all the things foretold by prophets are transpiring just as they said they would. Just as the signs of Christ's first coming were laid out clearly, so are the signs of his Second Coming."

"Excuse me, Bishop?" asked the same man. "What are those signs, if you please?"

Bo nodded. "One sign that is discussed in the scriptures is that the world will believe that evil is good and good is evil. That light is darkness and darkness is light.[46] We see that today all around us, don't we?" asked Bo.

People nodded in the congregation.

"Don't we see how society has decided that marriage, children, fidelity, and morality are outdated concepts? Don't we see that alcohol and recreational drugs are gaining international acceptance as normal forms of entertainment? Don't we see money being the ultimate value? All these things were foretold by prophets who lived a couple thousand years ago! Every one of them is a sign of the day. They are ones that we live every day."

"Amen!" said the man loudly, then when others didn't join him, he stood and said, "Hey you guys, you've got to get into this meeting! Your Bishop worked hard on his speech. Go ahead, Bishop," he said.

"Thank you," said Bo with a nod. "So, I can make you a promise. I promise all of you that the principles that you read in the scriptures, are true whether you want to believe it or not. This world *will* be enveloped in fire. It will burn along with all iniquity. Not one person will be left upon its face until the righteous return. So then, knowing this, what's our responsibility? Our responsibility is to befriend people like this man who is brave enough to come among people he doesn't know to ask questions that everyone is thinking. Our responsibility is to teach the truth to everyone.[47] We need to teach the world the truth so that all who wish to escape the coming anger of the Lord, might. His arm is lengthened still. He calls to his children on earth.[48] *We must listen. We must respond.* And if we do, we will be protected in every sense of the word. That is the truth.

"I say these things in the name of Jesus Christ, amen."

"Amen," said the congregation in unison.

"Amen!" said the stranger with a bright nod.

Notes to "Power of the Son"

Forces of Nature

[1] The last three solar cycles have had two solar maximas rather than the one that had been recorded in all the cycles before it. See http://www.space.com/scienceastronomy/astronomy/solar_max_020123.htm for more information.

[2] For more information about solar flares and dropped cell phone service, see http://www.space.com/scienceastronomy/solarsystem/cell_phone_020306.html.

[3] Everyone has heard of global warming, but has anyone heard of a global pole reversal? Of the two, a magnetic pole reversal is a scientific reality where global warming is still only regarded as a theory in scientific circles since one: the ozone layer has since healed itself from earlier deficits, and two: the world has had a history of varying temperatures even without man upon its surfaces. Because of these two facts, it is this author's opinion that global warming is out of the running for the cause of the apocalyptic occurrences outlined in the New Testament, at least in how it's being portrayed today in mainstream political thinking.

The conversation depicted in this section has been constructed to explore this topic according to scientific sources. Efforts have been made to represent what is actually happening to our earth today. There are striking similarities of potential changes of the earth to some end-of-days scriptural passages. It is this author's opinion that the magnetic pole reversal of our earth could not cause all the symptoms described in Revelation, but it definitely could explain some, in conjunction with other environmental occurrences. See below for some related Internet sites describing what is expected to occur when the magnetic poles of the earth reverse.

Nova, a PBS science-based program, aired an episode on television November 18, 2003, that explored this topic with the help of many scientists from all over the world. Many of the quotes below are taken from that program, the Web site, or other scientific sources linked from that Web page due to its comprehensive nature covering this topic.

[4] Definitions of magnetic poles:

"The North Magnetic Pole – the point on the Earth's surface where the Earth's magnetic field points directly downwards. This pole is constantly wandering; its estimated 2005 position was 82.7° N 114.4° W" (*Wikipedia*, "North Pole," available online: http://en.wikipedia.org/wiki/North_Pole).

"The South Magnetic Pole is the point on the Earth's surface where the geomagnetic field lines are directed vertically upwards. The South Magnetic Pole is constantly wandering due to changes in the Earth's magnetic field; as of 2005 it was calculated to lie at 64.53° S and 137.86° E, just off the coast of Wilkes Land, Antarctica" (*Wikipedia*, "South Magnetic Pole," available online: http://en.wikipedia.org/wiki/South_pole#South_Magnetic_Pole).

[5] "A reversal begins with additional [magnetisms having north and south polarities] appearing at the core [of the earth]. (One such island [of reverse polarity] has appeared beneath the South Atlantic Ocean.) After a short period of instability, the north and south magnetic poles switch polarity" (*Nova,* "See a reversal" available online: http://www.pbs.org/wgbh/nova/magnetic/reve-05.html). When this happens, a compass will then point south instead of north.

"Such reversals in the Earth's magnetic field...are as common as ice ages. That is, they're terrifically infrequent by human standards, but in geologic terms they happen all the time....Hundreds of times in our planet's history the polarity of the magnetic shield ensheathing the globe has gone from 'normal,' our current orientation to the north, to 'reversed,' and back again" (*Nova*, "When the Compass Points North," available online: http://www.pbs.org/wgbh/nova/magnetic/timeline.html).

[6] See *Nova*, "Magnetic Storm," Transcript, available online:

http://www.pbs.org/wgbh/nova/transcripts/3016_magnetic.html for more information dealing with this topic. For a video graphic of the rate of declination of the magnetic pull of the earth, see http://www.pbs.org/wgbh/nova/magnetic/reve-05.html.

[7] See *Nova*, "Magnetic Storm," Transcript, available online: http://www.pbs.org/wgbh/nova/transcripts/3016_magnetic.html for more information dealing with this topic.

[8] "...The Earth's magnetic field reverses is an extraordinary phenomenon, but this reversal process is quite common. The last reversal was...780,000 years ago. Before that, there was one about 200,000 [years previous], before that, again, actually less than 200 [years before that], so in a sense we are a bit overdue for a reversal" (*Nova*, "Magnetic Storm," Transcript, available online: http://www.pbs.org/wgbh/nova/transcripts/3016_magnetic.html).

[9] "Reversals happen...about once every 250,000 years, and they take hundreds if not thousands of years to complete" (*Nova*, "When the Compass Points North," available online: http://www.pbs.org/wgbh/nova/magnetic/timeline.html).

[10] "Space weather is nasty. The winds that blow through the galaxy are winds of radiation, some of the most harmful from distant exploding stars. But there is another source which is much nearer, which is our sun. The sun itself is a thermonuclear furnace, and this flings off huge amounts of dangerous material in very large explosions. In some cases, (the explosion) is about the same mass as Mount Everest actually coming towards us. Every few hours the sun ejects billions of tons of electrically charged particles, the solar wind. Often the Earth lies directly in the path of this onslaught. But magnetism deflects charged particles. This means that the solar wind is unable to penetrate the Earth's magnetic shield, and so flows harmlessly around the planet. The only visible signs of this drama far above our heads are the Northern and Southern Lights, produced when solar particles trapped in the Earth's magnetic field are dragged through the atmosphere towards the poles. Now we're lucky on the Earth, we have the

magnetic field which deflects the particles and protects us. But if we lost the magnetic field, there would be nothing to stop the radiation bathing the whole of the atmosphere, and the effect would be much more dangerous" (*Nova*, "Magnetic Storm," Transcript, available online: http://www.pbs.org/wgbh/nova/transcripts/3016_magnetic.html).

[11] "Although far away, the sun and the other stars are the source of effects which have a considerably stronger influence upon our lives than has been assumed until recently. Many space phenomena have a direct influence upon our earth, not only in the form of life-giving thermal radiation, but also as life-threatening hazards…serious effects have been observed on our increasingly technology-dependent world" (Dr. Frank Jansen, Dr. Risto Pirjola, Dr. Rene Favre, "Space Weather: Hazard to the earth?" 2000, available online: http://thayer.dartmouth.edu/spacescience/wl/res/ae/biblio/swissre00.pdf).

"The intensity of the magnetic field will be weaker, maybe ten, maybe a hundred times weaker than it is today, which means that more cosmic radiation will get through. This basically opens our defenses so that solar and galactic radiation can hit the atmosphere directly. And this means that the radiation at ground level increases as well. One estimate is that our overall exposure to cosmic radiation will double. And in some places it could be even worse. Today, the magnetic field focuses space radiation towards the far north and south where few people live. But as the main field collapses, the weak field that's left will have a more complex structure. Instead of just two magnetic poles, there may be four or even eight, slowly moving across the Earth's surface. The structure of the magnetic field won't be the nice, smooth, simple dipole structure that we have today, which tends to deflect charged particles—cosmic radiation—to the poles of the Earth. Instead there will be several poles all around the Earth, maybe close to the *equator*. And so, not only will the field be weaker, the field will tend to focus cosmic radiation at low latitudes where most people live" (*Nova*, "Magnetic Storm," Transcript, available online: http://www.pbs.org/wgbh/nova/transcripts/3016_magnetic.html).

[12] "'If magnetic shielding is lower [over time], charged particles from the sun would penetrate deeper [into Earth's atmosphere] and create large holes in the ozone,' says John Tarduno, a scientist at the University of Rochester who studies physical forces on Earth. The ozone layer protects you from invisible energy waves called ultraviolet (UV) rays. Without it, radiation would zap your skin, causing increased cancer rates," (Karen Barrow, *Science World*, "Which Way is North? Beware: Earth's Natural Compass May be Turning Upside Down" March 7, 2005, available online:
http://www.findarticles.com/p/articles/mi_m1590/is_11_61/ai_n13248415).

"This unfortunately means more deaths from cancer. It's roughly 15 per million people per year. That is the amount of deaths we're talking about. And if you multiply that over the whole population of the Earth, that becomes a significant number. It's impossible to know for sure, but the best guess is that every year a hundred thousand people would die from the increased levels of space radiation. But of course this would still represent only a relatively small increase in the overall incidence of cancer" (*Nova*, "Magnetic Storm," Transcript, available online: http://www.pbs.org/wgbh/nova/transcripts/3016_magnetic.html).

[13] "Auroras are luminous, deeply mysterious curtains of light that often grace dark skies near the North and South poles. They occur when a space weather event energizes the magnetic force field shielding our planet, churning up electrons and protons and causing them to smash into the mix of gases in the upper atmosphere. The result is a bright glow that can last anywhere from a few seconds to a few hours. During a magnetic field reversal, which can take hundreds or thousands of years to complete, these dazzling natural light shows would be visible every night of the year" (Lexi Krock, *Nova*, "Gallery of Auroras," available online: http://www.pbs.org/wgbh/nova/magnetic/aurora.html).

"The great thing is that it would be possible to see the aurora just about every night all over the Earth...shimmering and moving in the sky as the solar wind hits the atmosphere directly, and it glows like a neon light" (*Nova*, "Magnetic Storm," Transcript, available online: http://www.pbs.org/wgbh/nova/transcripts/3016_magnetic.html).

[14] "We cannot conceive of an industrial society like our own without electronic components. Miniaturization has been progressing for decades, with circuits operating at ever lower voltages and with even smaller flows of electrons. Around 1978, IBM experts started assuming that soft errors in computers also cause electronic noise. Soft errors are non-reproducible, spontaneous errors or changes to stored data...On Earth, soft errors are caused, for example, by particle showers from galactic cosmic rays. The effect of cosmic rays...is that neutrons and pions collide with the substrate (a silicon atom), where fission of the silicon produces an electron storm which may disrupt electronic systems" (Dr. Frank Jansen, Dr. Risto Pirjola, Dr. Rene Favre, "Space Weather: Hazard to the earth?" 2000, available online: http://thayer.dartmouth.edu/spacescience/wl/res/ae/biblio/swissre00.pdf).

[15] "It has recently proved possible to establish a clear link between space weather and its effects on electronic components and satellites.\...Cosmic rays repeatedly caused the entire power transmission to reset, necessitating a system re-start each time. The effects of space weather are many and varied, ranging from...individual instrument failures and static build-ups or discharges on satellites" (Dr. Frank Jansen, Dr. Risto Pirjola, Dr. Rene Favre, "Space Weather: Hazard to the earth?" 2000, available online: http://thayer.dartmouth.edu/spacescience/wl/res/ae/biblio/swissre00.pdf).

[16] The computer is very fragile when it comes to extra energy in the air. Even common static electricity can destroy a computer component. See the following:

"The microprocessor is the component of the personal computer that does the actual processing of data. A microprocessor is a central processing unit (CPU) that fits on one microchip. It is the 'brain' of the computer....The microprocessor integrated circuit package holds a silicon chip that contains millions of transistors and other components fabricated into the silicon. Because the transistors on the chip are very tiny, even a small zap of high voltage current (such as from static electricity) can destroy a chip" (Thomas E. Beach, PH. D., University of New Mexico—Los Alamos, "Computer Concepts and Terminology; Processors," available online: http://www la.unm.edu/~beach/terms/processors.html).

[17] "The ionosphere, ('the part of the atmosphere that is ionized by solar radiation. It plays an important part in atmospheric electricity.... It has practical importance because, among other functions, it influences radio propagation to distant places on the Earth' ['Ionsphere,' available online: http://en.wikipedia.org/wiki/Ionosphere]) is heated and distorted during storms, long-range radio communication, which relies on sub-ionospheric reflection, can be difficult or impossible and global-positioning systems (GPS), which relies on radio transmission through the ionosphere, can be degraded" (U.S. Geological Survey, "What are the hazardous affects of magnetic storms?" available online: http://geomag.usgs.gov/fazs.php#qseven).

[18] "...A lightning strike can still cause, on occasion, a high voltage transmission line to trip. Very high winds, for example, due to a tornado can cause the failure of a line or several lines on a common corridor. However, most of these events generally occur in isolation and power grids are operated at all times to withstand the largest creditable single contingency failure without causing a cascading collapse of the network itself. Space weather differs from ordinary weather in that it has a big footprint and attacks the system across many points simultaneously, causing at times of severe events multi-point failures on the network that can threaten the integrity of the network. Therefore, geomagnetic storms may be one of the most important hazards and is certainly the least understood threat that could be posed to the reliable operation of these (electricity producing) networks...." (John Kappenman, the House

of Representatives, Subcommittee on Environment, Technology and Standards session, "What is Space Weather and who should forecast it?" October 30, 2003, available online: http://gop.science.house.gov/hearings/ets03/oct30/charter.pdf).

[19] "The direction in which a compass needle points is known as magnetic north. In general, this is not exactly the direction of the North Magnetic Pole (or of any other consistent location). Instead, the compass aligns itself to the local geomagnetic field, which varies in a complex manner over the Earth's surface, as well as over time....The North Magnetic Pole is the wandering point on the Earth's surface at which the Earth's magnetic field points vertically downwards...Because the Earth's magnetic field is not exactly symmetrical, the North and South Magnetic Poles are not antipodal: a line drawn from one to the other does not pass through the centre of the Earth (it actually misses by about 530 km)....The Canadian government has made several measurements since, which show that the North Magnetic Pole is continually moving northwest....During the 20th century it has moved 1100 km, and since 1970 its rate of motion has accelerated from 9 km/year to 41 km/year. If it maintains its present speed and direction it will reach Siberia in about 50 years" ("North Magnetic Pole," available online: http://en.wikipedia.org/wiki/North_Pole).

[20] "If whales can run into trouble when the field is reasonably strong, what might happen to them and other creatures that rely on it if the field becomes feeble or even flips? Hans Fromme had found in Frankfurt that when he placed his European robins into a steel chamber and reduced the strength of the ambient magnetic field by a third, the birds' flutterings were no longer directional. This suggested that the birds needed the magnetic field to be a certain intensity to be of use. But Fromme's colleague F. W. Merkel later showed that the birds were able to acclimatize to the new magnetic field within a number of days" (Peter Tyson, *Nova*, "Magnetic Storm, Impact on animals," available online: http://www.pbs.org/wgbh/nova/magnetic/animals.html).

[21] "If we shut down the magnetic field, then the solar wind has direct access to the atmosphere of Mars. Then we have a process which is equivalent to the erosion in the desert. The wind blows and it blows the sand away. In this case, the sands are atmospheric particles. Slowly but surely, the atmospheric gases, which includes water, are carried away and are lost to Mars. The loss of its magnetic shield could well have meant death for the Red Planet. Exposed to the wind of radiation from the sun over millions of years, its atmosphere was gradually blown away, leaving the sterile world we see today. If we were to turn off the Earth's magnetic field, the same process would occur. The atmosphere of Earth would be exposed to the erosional effects of the solar wind, and it would be slowly carried away. The fate of Mars suggests that without the protection of its magnetic shield, the Earth could also become a dead planet, which makes it all the more disturbing to learn that our own magnetic field is fading so rapidly" (*Nova*, "Magnetic Storm," Transcript, available online: http://www.pbs.org/wgbh/nova/transcripts/3016_magnetic.html).

[22] "The field will come back. In the case of Mars we know that the field will not come back, and it has been gone for billions of years, so the effect has been very, very serious on the Mars atmosphere. But on the Earth's atmosphere just a few thousand years of no magnetic field are not expected to result in a very large stripping of the atmosphere" (*Nova*, "Magnetic Storm," Transcript, available online: http://www.pbs.org/wgbh/nova/transcripts/3016_magnetic.html).

[23] Igneous rock would be the best kind of rock to make a protective shelter because of its resistive nature. "Igneous rock—rock that solidified from molten or partly molten material, for example, magma. Igneous rock is high in electrical resistivity and common over large portions of North America" (John G. Kappenman, *Earth in Space*, "Geomagnetic Storms Can Threaten Electric Power Grid," March 1997,Vol. 9, No. 7, pgs. 9–11, available online: http://www.agu.org/sci_soc/eiskappenman.html).

[24] It's interesting to note repeated themes in some quotes of the scriptures concerning the last days, mentioning heat of the sun and people hiding in rocks. Could it be that the sun will scorch the earth and people will be driven into caves? In our society, we do not live in caves. All our homes are built out on the land. Could it be that as the sun becomes more active and the magnetic field of the earth wanes that caves will become places where the more wealthy choose to live to hide from its rays? Could it be as our missionary fervor continues that the wicked hide in those caves not only from the sun, but from the coming of the Son? Another question could be asked why the scriptures mention holes and caves where people hide. How could so many people hide in rocks, unless many holes have been made in the rocks for the people of position to hide in? Look at the scriptures and consider the description of people living in caves, having money or position is mentioned more than one time. See the following scriptures:

"And the fourth angel poured out his vial upon the sun; and power was given unto him to scorch men with fire. And men were scorched with great heat, and blasphemed the name of God, which hath power over these plagues: and they repented not to give him glory" (Revelation 16:8–9).

"And the loftiness of man shall be bowed down, and the haughtiness of men shall be made low: and the LORD alone shall be exalted in that day. And the idols he shall utterly abolish. And they shall go into the holes of the rocks, and into the caves of the earth, for fear of the LORD, and for the glory of his majesty, when he riseth to shake terribly the earth. In that day a man shall cast his idols of silver, and his idols of gold, which they made each one for himself to worship, to the moles and to the bats; To go into the clefts of the rocks, and into the tops of the ragged rocks, for fear of the LORD, and for the glory of his majesty, when he riseth to shake terribly the earth" (Isaiah 2:17–21; 2 Nephi 12:17–21).

"And the kings of the earth, and the great men, and the rich men, and the chief captains, and the mighty men, and every bondman, and every free man, hid themselves in the dens and in the rocks of the mountains; And said to the mountains and rocks, Fall on us, and hide us from the face of him that sitteth on the throne, and from the wrath of the Lamb: For the great day of his wrath is come; and who shall be able to stand?" (Revelation 6:15–17).

"Behold, I will send for many fishers, saith the LORD, and they shall fish them; and after will I send for many hunters, and they shall hunt them from every mountain, and from every hill, and out of the holes of the rocks. For mine eyes are upon all their ways: they are not hid from my face, neither is their iniquity hid from mine eyes" (Jeremiah 16:16–17).

Whithering Vine

[25] "I say unto you, my brethren, that if you should render all the thanks and praise which your whole soul has power to possess, to that God who has created you, and has kept and preserved you, and has caused that ye should rejoice, and has granted that ye should live in peace one with another—I say unto you that if ye should serve him who has created you from the beginning, and is preserving you from day to day, by lending you breath, that ye may live and move and do according to your own will, and even supporting you from one moment to another—I say, if ye should serve him with all your whole souls yet ye would be unprofitable servants" (Mosiah 2:20–21).

[26] "My well beloved hath a vineyard in a very fruitful hill. And he fenced it, and gathered out the stones thereof, and planted it with the choicest vine, and built a tower in the midst of it, and also made a winepress therein: and he looked that it should bring forth grapes, and it brought forth wild grapes" (Isaiah 5:1–2).

[27] "What could have been done more to my vineyard, that I have not done in it? Wherefore, when I looked that it should bring forth grapes, brought it forth wild grapes?" (Isaiah 5:4).

[28] "I will tell you what I will do to my vineyard: I will take away the hedge thereof, and it shall be eaten up; and break down the wall thereof, and it shall be trodden down: And I will lay it waste: it shall not be pruned, nor digged; but there shall come up briers and thorns: I will also command the clouds that they rain no rain upon it. For the vineyard of the LORD of hosts is the house of Israel, and the men of Judah his pleasant plant...Therefore as the fire devoureth the stubble, and the flame consumeth the chaff, so their root shall be as rottenness, and their blossom shall go up as dust: because they have cast away the law of the LORD of hosts, and despised the word of the Holy One of Israel" (Isaiah 5:5–6, 24).

Although this scripture was written to the apostatized Israel and it's people, it is meant as a type and shadow for our day: "Obviously the dark evils that prevailed among the Israelites of the ancient kingdom of Judah help modern readers understand why the judgments of God come upon them...for one need only look to see the same evils prevailing on many sides. The effects of sin today are as devastating as they were anciently" (*Old Testament Student Manual, Religion 302, 1 Kings-Malachi,* p. 142).

[29] "For the LORD shall comfort Zion: he will comfort all her waste places; and he will make her wilderness like Eden, and her desert like the garden of the LORD; joy and gladness shall be found therein, thanksgiving, and the voice of melody" (Isaiah 51:3).

[30] "And it is requisite with the justice of God that men should be judged according to their works; and if their works were good in this life, and the desires of their hearts were good, that they should also, at the last day, be restored unto that which is good" (Alma 41:3).

[31] "Woe unto them that draw iniquity with cords of vanity, and sin as it were with a cart rope" (Isaiah 5:18). In footnote "c" of the scriptures, it clarifies what this statement means: "They are tied to their sins like beasts to their burdens."

[32] "But every man is tempted, when he is drawn away of his own lust, and enticed. Then when lust hath conceived, it bringeth forth sin: and sin, when it is finished, bringeth forth death" (James 1:14–15).

[33] "Then if our hearts have been hardened, yea, if we have hardened our hearts against the word, insomuch that it has not been found in us, then will our state be awful, for then we shall be condemned. For our words will condemn us, yea, all our works will condemn us; we shall not be found spotless; and our thoughts will also condemn us; and in this awful state we shall not dare to look up to our God; and we would fain be glad if we could command the rocks and the mountains to fall upon us to chide us from his presence" (Alma 12:13–14).

[34] "If ye will repent, and harden not your hearts, then will I have mercy upon you, through mine Only Begotten Son; Therefore, whosoever repenteth, and hardeneth not his heart, he shall have claim on mercy through mine Only Begotten Son, unto a remission of his sins; and these shall enter into my rest" (Alma 12:33–34).

[35] "...Wo unto the rich, who are rich as to the things of the world. For because they are rich they despise the poor, and they persecute the meek, and their hearts are upon their treasures; wherefore, their treasure is their god. And behold, their treasure shall perish with them also" (2 Nephi 9:30).

[36] "In Moroni 10:30, we read, 'And again I would exhort you that ye would come unto Christ, and lay hold upon every good gift, and touch not the evil gift, nor the unclean thing.' My thoughts will center on our sometimes innocent involvement in one of the terrible, unclean things referred to by this ancient prophet. Satan, the very devil and the father of all lies, has slyly and slowly lowered the social norms of morality to a tragic and destructive level. In magazines and books, on CDs and tapes, on our television and theater screens is portrayed more and more often a lifestyle that might even rival the excesses of those who lived in Sodom and Gomorrah. The screens, music, and printed materials, etc., are filled with a profusion of sex, nudity, and vulgarity. One of the great tragedies is that too many men and

boys who hold the priesthood of God are watching and listening to this type of so-called entertainment. Some do it only casually at first. They think they are spiritually strong and will be immune to its influence. This trash is nothing more nor less than pornography dressed in one of its many imitation robes of splendor—one of the master counterfeiter's best products. Part of the tragedy I speak of is that many men and boys do not recognize they are trapped or soon will be. Unfortunately, I fear even some within the sound of my voice have an addiction and do not realize it. They see this as a form of entertainment that serves as a relief from the troubles of the day. In point of fact and in reality, it is only relieving them of their spirituality and their capacity to draw on the powers of heaven in times of need" (H. Burke Peterson, "'Touch Not the Evil Gift, nor the Unclean Thing'," *Ensign*, Nov 1993, p. 42).

[37] "The Savior taught with many parables, and they are well known. But he also taught with pertinent and piercing questions. One of them was this: '... what shall a man give in exchange for his soul?' (Matthew 16:26.) This is particularly important when we realize that the Lord defined eternal life as the greatest of all the gifts of God....In other words, he is telling us that salvation is the pearl of great price, salvation is the treasure in the field; and if we only realized its worth, we would give all that we have to obtain it....Shall we not waken to this important lesson? It comes from the lips of God, who cannot lie. Then should we not make every effort to achieve it? But on the other hand, if we do not, what are we exchanging for our souls? ...Who would exchange the privilege of becoming like God for the very questionable and temporary advantages of this world? Who in his right mind would prefer the corruptions of the flesh, the sensual pleasures, and the false excitement of sin, rather than the opportunity of becoming like God; rather than having inspired intelligence, or of some day wielding some of the powers that God uses as he walks in his majesty? ...Whether we realize it or not, we are making this very kind of bargain if we prefer worldly things over our religion. The only way to save our souls is to put God first in our lives" (Mark E. Petersen, "'What Will a Man Give?'" *Ensign*, Jan 1974, p. 110).

[38] "O that cunning plan of the evil one! O the vainness, and the frailties, and the foolishness of men! When they are learned they think they are wise, and they hearken not unto the counsel of God, for they set it aside, supposing they know of themselves, wherefore, their wisdom is foolishness and it profiteth them not. And they shall perish" (2 Nephi 9:28).

[39] "Investment debt should be fully secured so as not to encumber a family's security. Don't invest in speculative ventures. The spirit of speculation can become intoxicating. Many fortunes have been wiped out by the uncontrolled appetite to accumulate more and more. Let us learn from the sorrow of the past and avoid enslaving our time, energy, and general health to a gluttonous appetite to acquire increased material goods" (N. Eldon Tanner, *Ensign*, Nov. 1979, p. 82).

[40] "Prepare your souls for that glorious day when justice shall be administered unto the righteous, even the day of judgment, that ye may not shrink with awful fear; that ye may not remember your awful guilt in perfectness, and be constrained to exclaim: Holy, holy are thy judgments, O Lord God Almighty—but I know my guilt; I transgressed thy law, and my transgressions are mine; and the devil hath obtained me, that I am a prey to his awful misery" (2 Nephi 9:46).

[41] Sanctification: "The process of becoming free from sin, pure, clean, and holy through the atonement of Jesus Christ" (See Moses 6: 59–60). (*Guide to the Scriptures*, "Sanctification," www.lds.org).

"And if your eye be single to my glory, your whole bodies shall be filled with light, and there shall be no darkness in you; and that body which is filled with light comprehendeth all things. Therefore, sanctify yourselves that your minds become single to God, and the days will come that you shall see him; for he will unveil his face unto you, and it shall be in his own time, and in his own way, and according to his own will" (D&C 88:67–68).

[42] "And the saints that are upon the earth, who are alive, shall be quickened and be caught up to meet him. And they who have slept in their graves shall come forth, for their graves shall be opened; and they also shall be caught up to meet him in the midst of the pillar of heaven" (D&C 88:96–97).

"And they shall see his face; and his name shall be in their foreheads" (Revelation 22:4).

[43] "For not many days hence and the earth shall tremble and reel to and fro as a drunken man; and the sun shall hide his face, and shall refuse to give light; and the moon shall be bathed in blood; and the stars shall become exceedingly angry, and shall cast themselves down as a fig that falleth from off a fig-tree...For after your testimony cometh the testimony of earthquakes, that shall cause groanings in the midst of her, and men shall fall upon the ground and shall not be able to stand. And also cometh the testimony of the voice of thunderings, and the voice of lightnings, and the voice of tempests, and the voice of the waves of the sea heaving themselves beyond their bounds. And all things shall be in commotion; and surely, men's hearts shall fail them; for fear shall come upon all people. And angels shall fly through the midst of heaven, crying with a loud voice, sounding the trump of God, saying: Prepare ye, prepare ye, O inhabitants of the earth; for the judgment of our God is come. Behold, and lo, the Bridegroom cometh; go ye out to meet him" (D&C 88:86, 88–92).

[44] "For a desolating scourge shall go forth among the inhabitants of the earth, and shall continue to be poured out from time to time, if they repent not, until the earth is empty, and the inhabitants thereof are consumed away and utterly destroyed by the brightness of my coming" (D&C 5:19).

[45] Transfigured: "The condition of persons who are temporarily changed in appearance and nature—that is, lifted to a higher spiritual level—so that they can endure the presence and glory of heavenly beings" ("Transfigured," *Guide to the Scriptures*, www.lds.org).

[46] "Woe unto them that call evil good, and good evil; that put darkness for light, and light for darkness; that put bitter for sweet, and sweet for bitter!" (Isaiah 5:20).

[47] "And another trump shall sound, which is the fifth trump, which is the fifth angel who committeth the everlasting gospel—flying through the midst of heaven, unto all nations, kindreds, tongues, and people; And this shall be the sound of his trump, saying to all people, both in heaven and in earth, and that are under the earth—for every ear shall hear it, and every knee shall bow, and every tongue shall confess, while they hear the sound of the trump, saying: Fear God, and give glory to him who sitteth upon the throne, forever and ever; for the hour of his judgment is come" (D&C 88:103–104).

[48] "O, ye nations of the earth, how often would I have gathered you together as a hen gathereth her chickens under her wings, but ye would not!" (D&C 43:24).

CHAPTER SIXTEEN

BLOOD BORN OF BLOOD

"Verily, verily, I say unto you, darkness covereth the earth, and gross darkness the minds of the people, and all flesh has become corrupt before my face" (D&C 112:23).

00:03:09, 04:47:54, Zulu
Sunday, September 21st

Strategies to Destroy a Nation

Frankfurt, Germany
8:23 p.m.

MD took a large drag on his cigar and blew it out slowly. With smoke billowing out his nose, he said, "Son, I have to tell you that I'm pleased with your compliance to my requests. I know it must have been hard to divorce Brea, but it's for the best."

"I know," said Matt. They were sitting in high-back leather reclining chairs in the library. There was a fire going in the fireplace. "You are wise, it's just hard to admit it," said Matt, trying to play up to his father.

"Are you angry with me?" asked MD, hiding an amused smile.

Matt knew his father couldn't care less if he had hurt him or not, but his job was to go along with everything. His heart had to be stone cold. Matt thought for a moment to consider what to say, and then he shrugged as he lied through his teeth. "Not at all. I'm actually very happy about it. I've never felt freer."

"Good," said MD as he tapped out his cigar in an ashtray. "Exactly what I was hoping for."

"Well, there you go," said Matt forcing a modest smile.

Sitting forward in his chair, MD's belly protruded awkwardly between his thighs. He seemed unaware of his bulk as he bounced his fingers off each other.

Matt could tell by the way his mustache twitched that he was brimming with excitement about something.

"I have something I need to teach you if you're ever going to take my place properly. I want to assure our legacy stays intact long after I've left this world."

"Alright," said Matt, wondering when that would be, since evil was continually renewing his father's life. Maybe he was just trying to torture him again. He didn't know, but it didn't matter. He'd listen anyway.

"But you have to be open to what I say," said MD. He squinted at Matt and gestured as he continued. "I will not tolerate any disrespect. And until my little Matthew is ready to take your place, you're going to have to do. So you'll have to be taught properly. It's time to come into the inner circle."

Matt nodded, keeping perfect control. His father's statements were meant to remind him of his place, but entice him with what he could offer. "No disrespect," said Matt simply, reminding himself this was all just a game.

MD leaned back in his chair and looked up at the ceiling, stretching out his legs and folding his hands over his chest. "I'm going to give you behind-the-scenes information," he said, gesturing with his hands. "I'm going to give you strategies that are tried and true and if you use them, you can steer governments the way you want them to go." MD looked at Matt abruptly, his face growing red. "Are you ready for that?"

Matt nodded. "Always ready."

"Good," said his father, and then he laid his head back on the headrest. "There are many ways to exert power over a nation. And I'll surprise you by telling you that I and my associates have learned that the best ways to do it aren't necessarily through war." MD glanced briefly at Matt and said, "Although war is a great tool and it has its place."

"Of course," said Matt.

"In our complicated society, we have learned it's much better to use mechanisms already in place to drive a nation toward our aims. It's less expensive than war and all assets retain value and function when we assume control. That's something one can't say about a country that's been ravaged by war."

"I understand," said Matt still perplexed. "So, tell me, how would one use mechanisms in place in a country to take power over that country? That almost sounds impossible."

"Tricky, but not impossible," said MD with a smile. "The plan is as follows: Plant people you trust in key positions in whatever nation you wish to take over. Place them in government positions, in communications, in the media, and in mass organizations such as political parties. Have them progressively demand more and more government power as the solution to all problems and persuade the people they represent to agree, using language of freedom, rights, and privileges to win people over."[2]

"OK," said Matt. "Sounds logical."

"Then break down democracy piece by piece and replace it with a socialist government," said MD. "It's a beautiful transition. After such a process, the people aren't angry, no. They're happy! And why are they happy?"

"I don't know," said Matt, allowing his father the joy of telling him.

"Because they're receiving more protection, services, and solutions from the government than ever before and they're blind to what they've allowed to happen to their country. They don't even realize the government has been taken over."

"Aren't you talking about communism?"[3] asked Matt.

"Socialism, communism—sure, sure, either way—but today we don't label it as such. That's an old label. Today, it can have any face," said MD. "Republican," he said putting one hand out. "Democrat," putting the other hand out. "It doesn't matter. What matters is that we're in control of whoever is in power at the time and they lead the country in the direction we want them to go."[4]

"Why communism? You're a capitalist to the nth degree. You believe in ownership."

"Sure, but this plan doesn't reflect me," said MD, wagging his head. "Who cares what I, personally, believe in? What I really care about is my investment. The truth is, the principles of communism allow me, or who's in the driver's seat, to control everything."

"OK," said Matt nodding. "How?"

"Well, our ultimate goal is to create a world system of financial control that will allow us to dominate all the political systems in the world, right?"

Matt raised his eyebrows. That was saying it pretty plainly. "Yes," he said, trying to hide his surprise inspired by his father's candid answer.

"So," continued MD, making a grabbing motion with one hand. "To do that, we need to take the power and money out from the hands of the people, because when the people control their own resources, the growth of the country doesn't behave predictably. It's a bad investment because of the risk. So, to solve that problem, we need a monopoly of power. We need to eliminate any other forces competing for our power. Anything else you want to call it, where the government controls the assets, it gives us what we want."[5]

Matt nodded, "Now I understand. Communism is just the tool to take consistent control of resources, money, labor, the people…"

MD clapped his hands together. "Yes, now you're getting it. And doesn't it make sense that the world's most successful capitalist—me—would want to eliminate all the competition to rake in the best profits?"

Matt nodded. Boy wasn't that a true statement? "That would be the idea."

"Good," said MD as he waved his hand. "And as far as I'm concerned, it's my opinion that only the very naive truly believe that socialism could work, where there is no rich and no poor, yadda, yadda, yadda. No, socialism, or communism if you wish, is just the hammer we use to take control."[6]

"It's ingenious," said Matt, impressed despite his good morals.

"Yes, it is," said MD relishing his instruction. "So, in review, use your political plants to ensure that the government slowly changes through presidential decrees, court orders, and legislation. As the government grows, it grows to serve the people, and politically, it improves the quality of life for all, although we know what's really going on."[7]

"I know President MacEntire was your plant in the Oval Office," said Matt. "But she didn't seem to follow the plan I'm assuming you gave her."

MD nodded once. "True. It wasn't always that way. I groomed her for the White House from college on. I financed her campaigns and ran political defense when she needed it, and at that time she liked the plan and what it stood for well enough. But—what can I say? She went bad. Sometimes that happens." MD shrugged. "Her betrayal didn't change any of my plans. If anything she hurried them to fruition. A true plan works, no matter who jumps ship."

"I see," said Matt.

"Now, to tie in the President with my next subject: what happens when the passive approach to taking over a country doesn't work?"[8]

Matt looked at his father blankly. "I don't know."

"Well, I do." MD tapped his head. "Always have a back-up plan, and here it is."

"Alright," said Matt, crossing his ankle over his knee.

With squinted eyes, MD resumed his relaxed position in his chair, looking like he was debating on where to start. "OK, step one," he said holding up his index finger. "The key to overtaking nations is division. If you can divide a nation, you can conquer it."

"Division," repeated Matt, to assure his father that he was listening carefully.

"Create hatred among the people by using any means to agitate whatever issues are boiling underneath the surface. For example, if nationality or race is a point of contention between the classes, like it was in America or South Africa, incite the Blacks to hate Whites and Whites to hate Blacks. If it's political, make one party hate the other. But don't pick a side. Work both sides of any split."[9]

"How does one do that?" asked Matt.

"When you're trying to come to power, you have to deceive. Produce counterfeits. Teach your people to pretend to be supportive of the enemy and let them publicly fight against what is truly wanted. That will throw anyone off the trail who suspects your plants of insincerity. Don't be afraid to let your cause take one step backward, especially when you need to pacify angry or suspicious people. This will eventually help your cause take two steps forward."

"I see," said Matt, nodding.

MD continued, gaining momentum. "Have key players, your plants, in both camps and exaggerate real grievances of the people. If you can't find grievances, don't hesitate to manufacture false stories and rumors about injustices and brutality between the opposite parties just to get things going. Feed that information to the media and make sure they run it through your plants in that industry. It's even better if you can create martyrs for both sides. People respond to needless death. How well you play upon the mass emotions of the nation, the better the negative emotions will build until both sides smolder with resentment and hatred."

Matt watched his father unflinchingly. His emotions were in check today. "So, cause contention to inspire division," he said, again attempting to let his father know that he was listening.

"You're learning!" said MD sitting forward abruptly. Holding two fingers up, he said, "The next step—step two—is to trigger violence. Drive the emotional masses into the streets in the form of large mobs, the larger the better. They can even be peaceful demonstrations because the groups might think they're 'peacefully' demonstrating, but when the emotionally charged groups are brought into direct confrontation, it will be like mixing oxygen and hydrogen. *Booommmmm!*" said MD gesturing with his hands. "All that's needed is one tiny spark. If the spark isn't spontaneous, create it. Don't let that opportunity escape you."

"OK," said Matt, wondering how many times his father had carried out this plan.

MD continued, "Next, to overthrow an established government once mob violence becomes widespread and commonplace, teach those in leadership in the opposite parties, that violence is the only way to 'settle the score' once and for all."

"Got it."

"Provide leadership and training for guerrilla warfare."

"Was that what you were doing with the Bats?" asked Matt.

MD thought for a moment. Then he said, "The Bats? You mean that piddly little cult group that followed Imam Mahdi?"

"Yes," said Matt.

"That wasn't my idea," said MD shaking his head. "The Bats were a creation of the first power-crazed Imam Mahdi. He had envisioned his own holy war, using the outcasts of society and their rage to break down America." MD shrugged. "It was a good idea for a novice, but when he died, we came into the picture and our plans shifted away from Imam Mahdi's vision. When we made Imam Mahdi the pope, we didn't think the Bats were exactly the right kind of PR, so we left those people alone."

"Ahh, I see," said Matt.

"But, essentially, yes, if we had supported the Bats and given them more formal guerrilla training, they could have been a better disruptive force than they were."

"I understand," said Matt.

"But if you choose to have fighters, which I did in America—they were the disgruntled citizens that performed all my assassinations and bombings..."

"OK," said Matt nodding, hiding his abhorrence to his father's words.

"Have them be trained in terrorism. Fear in the community ensures passive support from the larger inactive segment of the population. Make sure your fighters are trained and familiar with fighting. Stage violence and start battles with police. Finally, at the appointed time, launch an all-out simultaneous offensive in every city."

"I see. This, I assume, is what you did in America."

"Of course. But America was a bugger to break. We had to find the right subject to get everyone really angry."

"So money was the thing to do it?" asked Matt.

"Yes it was. It was the perfect thing to push them over the edge. A war has already been boiling in America. It's called covetousness. Those who have property versus those who don't. Those who don't or cannot obtain property but think it's their right, as an American citizen, grow clamorous. The underclass has long been looking at property as its prey and rightful plunder. That's why it was time for violence and revolution.[10] Out there," said MD, pointing, "the poor are having a heyday taking from the rich. They think it's their right to snatch what they can. And what's even more beautiful is that the people long oppressed from Mexico are pouring across the border to try and stake claims on the land abandoned by those who have died or those who have fled because of fear.[11] To them, this day is the day they've won the lottery!"

Matt shook his head. He could see everything was happening as his father was saying. He was right. "You are very perceptive," he said. Matt wanted to say other things but knew it would destroy all his work up to this point, so he continued to hold his tongue.

"Not only am I perceptive," said MD, his eyes excited, "I am right. I am strategic. We have created psychological desperation in the minds of all the citizens and that will lead the people to accept blindly whatever they are offered. Now, *I* get to take over."

"I see," said Matt. "Congratulations."

"Yes!" said MD, beginning to laugh. "No American ever thought their children would live under a government that was, in every way, communism. No, no, they all foolishly thought it was dead. But as I told you, each nation will eventually bend to cloaked communism with the formula I have outlined. Europe is next and the Middle East after that. If you look carefully, you'll see all these factors to create disharmony coming together so I, in cooperation with the compliant leaders of the world, can come in and create harmony."

Matt considered his father's words. It was true. Each nation was being ripped apart from the inside out. "Interesting..." said Matt.

"It's that easy! World domination is not that difficult. A trained monkey could do it." MD held up his hands and added, "No offense."

Matt shrugged. "None taken."

"But the best thing," continued MD, "is that no one in America will fight their downfall because they are the cause! Our efforts are unseen. But bit by bit the nation just falls and looks outward for help, falling like over-ripe fruit into our hands. Yes! It's time for a take over!"[12] said MD in obvious ecstasy.

Matt nodded. "And that's what you're doing," he said, trying to be as supportive as possible.

"Yes, I am!!!" said MD pounding his fist on the armrest. "Now it's your turn," he said with a fat finger pointing at Matt.

Matt sat up. "What?" he asked as men in black robes poured into the room from an unknown door. "What's this?" he asked again, looking at his father. "Wait!"

MD stood and pulled up his waist band. "It will be easier if you don't fight us."

"What will be easier? *Dad! I did everything you asked! Wait!*" he stood and held out his hands to the masked men. *"What are you doing?"*

"What I should have done a long time ago," said MD as Matt's hands were tied behind his back. "Take him," said MD in a frightening voice that wasn't his own. The evil in the room was overwhelming.

Matt stared at his father in disbelief. Then he understood...playing games with the devil wouldn't be without its price. He closed his eyes in excruciating inner turmoil as he was led away down a winding stone staircase.

Missouri

Independence, Missouri
6:50 p.m.

Dane shook a half full bottle of water from the Potomac Falls. He unscrewed the lid and took a swig. Holding it in his mouth he savored the flavor. ...It tasted just fine! He swallowed. Sure, it was warm, but that couldn't be helped. Louise said it tasted like nuclear waste. He didn't think it did...although he might change his mind once he grew gills or hair on his tongue. That thought made him laugh to himself as he drank down the last bit from the bottle. Yeah, Louise was too paranoid for her own good. Dane bet it was the environmentalist in her that made her overly cautious. Too much knowledge could do that to you.

It was just before sunset and they were nearing their 13th hour of driving. Nebraska was asleep in the back after having a fit and wanting McDonald's food for dinner. She had worn herself out. Louise was in the back with Nebraska, recovering from their wrestling match.

"You OK?" asked Dane looking in the mirror.

"Sure," said Louise. "But I think it's my turn to drive. Nebraska is out so you can rest back here."

Dane pointed with a finger as his hand rested on the steering wheel. "We'll stop at the nearest rest stop."

Louise nodded and stayed silent.

The road continued to be empty before them and behind them. Once in a while Dane saw a car, but not very often. He thought it might be because either people were saving their gas, or they had used it already and couldn't get more. This was the third day, counting Friday, since money practically disappeared from America and the economy had stopped. One sign of that was that almost everything was closed, including gas stations.

"Sure are a lot of fires around here," said Louise.

Dane looked out at the horizon and saw that Louise was right. He could count half a dozen close by and more off in the distance. "I wonder why."

"Maybe they're cooking their food."

"Maybe," agreed Dane.

"Watch out!" yelled Louise.

Dane quickly swerved to avoid two people who had jumped onto the freeway. As he glanced back, he saw that they were engaged in a bloody brawl.

After they had safely passed Dane exclaimed, "What's with them? Why are they fighting on the freeway? Isn't there somewhere better for that?"

"Who knows?" said Louise watching the two out the back window. "But somebody better stop those two or someone's going to get killed."

Up ahead, Dane saw a mob of people off to the right. They were right outside a neighborhood and all of them were swinging bats and sticks, fist fighting, pushing and shoving. He could see some were running from the scene carrying things. "What the...what's..." said Dane, slowing a little to see what was happening. As he surveyed the scene, he saw the origin of the fighting. There was a stalled truck full of grocery store items with its back door peeled open. The people were fighting over the food!

Dane frowned and looked down. The fighting was so brutal, he couldn't watch. Even though he had become used to violence, he wasn't used to seeing normal city people, neighbors and probably friends and family, fight like animals. He shook his head. Was this really happening?[13]

"Dane, watch the road," said Louise.

Dane looked up and had to maneuver around an old tire and some debris. "Sorry," he said. "I was watching those people act like piranhas."

Crack!

Both Louise and Dane ducked as Dane struggled to keep the car straight. Good thing there wasn't anyone else on the road, or there would have been an accident.

"What was that?" asked Dane looking back and seeing a clean hole in the window. "A bullet!" he said, looking back and forth between the road and the hole. "That's what that was. Someone pinged us with a bullet!"

"Let's get out of here, Dane." said Louise from somewhere behind and below. He assumed she was lying low, covering Nebraska with her body.

Dane pushed on the accelerator as he continued to search in the mirrors. "Where did that shot come from?" he said.

"It doesn't matter! Just get out of here!"

Right then, Dane saw a gunman behind them walk out onto the freeway with a rifle. The man spoke into a walkie-talkie as he kept an eye on their car.

"Uh oh," said Dane.

"What?" asked Louise poking her head up.

"Stay down!" he said, pointing firmly at the floor of the car. "We're going to be ambushed."

"How do you know?" asked Louise peeking carefully out the back window.

"Because I just saw the gunman warn someone in his radio that we're coming. Just hang on and stay down."

Dane's senses grew keen as his internal radar turned on. Suddenly, a large fire burst into the sky a ways down the road. Dane could tell it was built on the road and meant to stop them.

"OK. Listen, Louise."

"What?"

"Someone set a fire on the road. We're being forced to stop."

"You're not going to, are you?" asked Louise.

"Not if I can help it," said Dane looking at the map as he drove. "There's a turn-off up here. It's Interstate 435. They've built the fire before that turn-off I'm sure. Somewhere along here I plan on getting off the freeway and going through the neighborhood streets to get to that interstate."

Louise looked along the road. On both sides were guard rails and ravines beyond that. "How are you going to do that?"

"I'm not sure, but we've got to do it. We can't stop!"

"Right," said Louise sounding nervous. "Are you sure the fire is on the road?" asked Louise.

Dane studied the flames and the heat coming off them. It made the road look like liquid. He nodded. "Yes, I'm sure. It's built right on the road." Immediately, Dane started praying for direction.

"Be calm and put your foot on the gas," said a voice in his head. It was the voice that he had come to call his guardian angel.[14] He took a moment to double-check her advice. In a split second, he knew she was right. The Spirit told him to trust this voice. Dane pushed the gas with his foot. The car bolted forward.

"What's going on?" asked Louise who was grabbing the seats with rigid hands.

"I'm accelerating."

"I know that, but why?"

"I don't know why," said Dane tightening his grip on the steering wheel. "I just know that's what I need to do."

"Are you going to get off this road, like you said?" asked Louise looking at the fire growing nearer and Dane not turning to the right or the left.

"I don't know," said Dane waiting for more instruction. *"Hurry! Hurry! Talk to me!"* he said to the voice.

"Go faster and hit the wall of fire. You'll be safe," said the kind but intelligent voice that radiated light in Dane's soul. He felt calmness in her voice and it made him braver.

Still, Dane hesitated as he considered other options. "Is that smart?" he asked in a whisper. "I could go through the guard rail and go another way."

"No. Go faster. Hit the fire!"

"But I don't know what's on the other side!" said Dane quietly, arguing with the voice.

"Safety is on the other side," said the voice.

"OK," said Dane gritting his teeth, searching for another confirming feeling from the Holy Spirit and getting it. Next he shoved his foot to the floor.

"Stop, Dane! Stop!" yelled Louise.

"What's wrong?" asked Nebraska sitting up.

"Get down!" yelled Dane to the two in the back seat. *"Hang on!"* he yelled as he hit one-hundred twenty miles an hour and climbing. *"I'm going through the fire!"*

"What?" yelled Louise. *"Don't do it!"*

Nebraska whimpered.

But the next moment the car hit the wall of fire, taking air. The road had dropped out from underneath them. For a split second the world was in slow motion. The tires were whirring. The engine was revving. Flames licked against the windows as heat flowed inside momentarily. Then came the loud thud, immense jarring, and grating metal as they hit the road on the other side. The car bounced off the ground again but then the spinning wheels caught the road, squealing at first, as they left the fire behind them.

"Wahoo!" yelled Dane ecstatically as he looked in the rearview mirror. "Outsmarted those pirates!" he said as people crawled out of the ditches and watched after them in astonishment. "Yeah!" yelled Dane again as he petted the dashboard of the car. "Good baby."

"That was a tire fire!" said Louise looking out the back. *"They're polluting the environment!"* she said, sounding like she might be going into shock.

"I don't think they care," said Dane laughing happily.

"How did you know you could fly through the fire like that?" asked Louise still watching behind.

"I didn't," said Dane with a great smile.

"The only reason we flew over those tires was because the road is lower on this side," said Louise looking back, sounding like she was explaining things to herself. "They built the fire right in the dip. How did you know that dip was there? Does the map tell you that?"

"Nope," said Dane, thanking his guardian angel and seeing a smiling, glowing face in his mind with a light breeze toying with light brown hair. "But *she* did."

"Who's she?" asked Louise.

"I don't know," said Dane. "She's not always around, but she seems to be there when I need her."[15]

"Who?"

"You could call her a guardian angel."

Louise looked strangely at Dane in the mirror, but he didn't explain. Instead, he rolled down the window and stuck his head out. *"We're coming home!"* he yelled. *"You hear me? Utah! We're coming home!"*

Notes to "Blood Born of Blood"

Strategies to Destroy a Nation

[1] We know through the restored gospel of Jesus Christ that there was a war in heaven where Satan desired the glory of God and to take control of the souls of men (Moses 4:1). When he lost the war, Satan vowed to deceive men and lead them captive to his will (Moses 4:4). We know that Cain was the first to use deception, a secret combination, and oaths of secrecy first to Satan and then to others to gain advantage and control over others (Moses 5:29–31). We know that a satanic plan continued in the Book of Mormon days, as secret combinations such as the Gadianton robbers (Helaman 6:24, 26, 29), not only took control of the government (Helaman 7:4) but was also the downfall of the nation (Mormon 1–6). We also know through the scriptures given to us, the Gentiles, that secret combinations will continue to exist and will seek to obtain power and wealth, and to enslave all men (Ether 8:23). Through the book of Revelation, we see that the Satan-inspired combination will eventually control the world for the same purposes of power and gain (Revelation 13).

What are these secret combinations today? Who is to say for sure? In all probability, the true secret combination has changed faces, parties, and names as often as necessary to throw people becoming aware of them off their track. In fact, today they're probably present in every party, having many political faces and go by many names. So who are they and what is their current real name? From the scriptures, we know what they do, what they hope to do, and what they are doing, but do not know their name. It's up to us to make the connections through the Spirit.

Although the general population is unaware of how powerful these secret combinations are today, because of their strength on a world scale, their works will fulfill prophesy. This segment was written to give you, the reader, a look into their real plans to topple nations. Although the sources used in the endnotes are dated, using terms such as "communism" and "socialism," the principles are consistent with what we see today in our own political system and broadcast through the media. Since the men who penned the words were significant and reliable sources, this author chose to include them, to give us insight into our day.

[2] Some of MD's dialogue was taken from the writings of the warning words of Ezra Taft Benson, then former Secretary of Agriculture and Apostle of the Lord, who eventually to become the Prophet of the Church of Jesus Christ of Latter-day Saints. In the book, *An Enemy*

Hath Done This, an address given during General Conference, September 29th 1967, was used as one of the chapters. In it, he exposes the evil plans, inspired by Satan and carried out by those of the communist powers of the world at that time, to take over countries from the inside. (This plan is drawn from two classic communist manuals published by the communist party and can still be obtained as photographic reprints from American Opinion, Belmont, Mass. 02178.) In the following, Elder Benson gives us a view into the mind of the secret combinations to bring about their goals:

The Communist way to take over a nation from the inside: (Any party in the hands of a secret combination bent on control of the world can be substituted here.)

According to manuals published by the communist party [or any political party], to take over a nation from the inside, one must first employ "...unidentified communist agents and non-communist sympathizers in key positions in government, in communications media, and in mass organization—such as labor unions and civil rights groups—demand more and more government power as the solution to all civil rights problems. Total government is the objective of communism. Without calling it by name, build communism piece by piece through mass pressures for presidential decrees, court orders and legislation which appear to be aimed at improving civil rights and other social reforms. If there is social, economic, or educational discrimination, then advocate more government programs and control...And if riots come? Then more government housing, government welfare, government job training, and finally, federal control over police. Thus the essential economic and political structure of communism is firmly established" (p. 196).

[3] Communism: "A system of government in which the state plans and controls the economy and a single, often authoritarian party holds power, claiming to make progress toward a higher social order in which all goods are equally shared by the people" ("Communism," *The Free Dictionary*, http://www.thefreedictionary.com/communism).

Socialism: "Any of various theories or systems of social organization in which the means of producing and distributing goods is owned collectively or by a centralized government that often plans and controls the economy" ("Socialism," *The Free Dictionary*, http://www.thefreedictionary.com/socialism).

[4] In *None Dare Call It Conspiracy*, a book highly suggested by Elder Benson for every citizen in every free country to read, Gary Allen poses an interesting thought as written below. Even though this was written in 1972, the content is just as relevant today. Keep in mind our own elections today as the following is reviewed:

"Maybe you are one of those persons. Something is bugging you, but you aren't sure what. We keep electing new presidents who seemingly promise faithfully to halt the world-wide communist advance, put the blocks to extravagant government spending, douse the fires of inflation, put the economy on an even keel, reverse the trend which is turning the country into a moral sewer, and toss the criminals into the hoosegow where they belong. Yet, despite high hopes and glittering campaign promises, these problems continue to worsen no matter who is in office. Each new administration, whether it be Republican or Democrat, continues the same basic policies of the previous administration which it had so thoroughly denounced during the election campaign. It is considered poor form to mention this, but it is true nonetheless. Is there a plausible reason to explain why this happens? We are not supposed to think so. We are supposed to think it is all accidental and coincidental and that therefore there is nothing we can do about it. FDR once said, 'In politics, nothing happens by accident. If it happens, you can bet it was planned that way.' He was in a good position to know. We believe that many of the major world events that are shaping our destinies occur because somebody or somebodies have planned them that way. If we were merely dealing with the law of averages, half of the events affecting our nation's well-being should be good for America. If we were dealing with mere incompetence, our leaders should occasionally make a mistake in our favor..." (Gary Allen, *None Dare Call It Conspiracy*, p. 8).

[5] What is the purpose of the secret combinations? As stated above, to obtain gain and power. This sentiment is reflected by Gary Allen, who quotes Dr. Quigley, one of the insiders of the combination: Their desires are "eventually to control all the assets in the world have one aim, 'nothing less than to create a world system of financial control in private hands able to dominate the political system of each country and the economy of the world as a whole'" (Gary Allen, *None Dare Call It Conspiracy*, p.13).

[6] Are those involved in our modern day secret combinations, communist? See the following: "...These men certainly do not believe in the clap-trap pseudo-philosophy of Communism. They have no intention of dividing their wealth. Socialism is a philosophy which conspirators exploit, but in which only the naive believe. Just how finance capitalism is used as the anvil and Communism as the hammer to conquer the world will be explained in this book..." (Gary Allen, *None Dare Call It Conspiracy*, p. 18).

[7] The following statement is taken from a contemporary Communist party Web site to demonstrate their thinking about freedom and the lack of it under socialistic control. Freedom is described as a "privilege" rather than a right:

"People sometimes complain about the freedoms they are giving up for the sake of the party [communism]. But these people fail to question what freedom is under capitalism. Certainly MIM [Maoist Internationalist Movement] does not have the freedom to oppose exploitation and oppression. Black, Latino and First Nation peoples in this country [America] are not free to pursue 'the American dream.' People in America's Third World colonies are not free to eat, have medical care, or go to school. The freedoms that people in this country are afraid of giving up are privileges," (*Maoist internationalist Movement*, "Democratic Centralism" http://www.etext.org/Politics/MIM/wim/democent.html).

[8] "...The Communists are not entirely certain whether force and violence or the use of government or a combination of both would be best for the internal conquest of America....It now seems probable that the communists are determined to use force and violence to its fullest, coupled with a weakening of the economy and military setbacks abroad, in an effort to create as much havoc as possible to weaken America internally and to create the kind of psychological desperation in the minds of all citizens that will lead them to accept blindly government measures which actually help the communists in their takeover. Some wonder if it can happen here. Just take a good look at what has been going on around us for the past few years..." (Ezra Taft Benson, *An Enemy Hath Done This*, p. 196).

[9] If a peaceful attempt to topple a nation is not successful, then according to Ezra Taft Benson, the secret combinations are not beyond planting violence and terrorism to push it more aggressively—look at the violence that is growing in America, in other countries...could this be an outgrowth of that philosophy?

The following is again from a Conference address by Ezra Taft Benson, describing the more violent strategies that may be employed to take over a nation. It is taken from the communist manuals addressed above and is reflected in MD's dialogue:

"1. **Create Hatred**. Use any means to agitate blacks into hating whites and whites into hating blacks. (Or any other political groups hating each other.) Work both sides of the split. Play up and exaggerate real grievances. If necessary, don't hesitate to manufacture false stories and rumors about injustices and brutality. Create martyrs for both sides. Play upon mass emotions until they smolder with resentment and hatred.

"2. **Trigger Violence**. Put the emotional masses into the streets in the form of large mobs, the larger the better. It makes no difference if the mob is told to demonstrate 'peacefully' so long as it is brought into direct confrontation with the antagonist. Merely bringing the two emotionally charged groups together is like mixing oxygen and hydrogen. All that is needed is one tiny spark. If the spark is not forthcoming from purely spontaneous causes, create it.

"3. **Overthrow Established Government**. Once mob violence becomes widespread and commonplace, condition those who are emotionally involved to accept violence as the only way to 'settle the score' once and for all. Provide leadership and training for guerrilla warfare. Institute discipline and terrorism to insure at least passive support from the larger, inactive segment of the population. Train and battle-harden leadership through sporadic riots and battles with police. Finally, at the appointed time, launch an all-out simultaneous offensive in every city.

"Police and national guard units will never be adequate to handle such widespread anarchy—especially if a large part of our men and equipment are drained away in fighting a foreign war...Time the attack to coincide with large-scale sabotage of water supplies, power grids, main railroad and highway arteries, communications centers and government buildings. With fires raging in every conceivable part of town, with wanton police protection, without water to drink, without electrical refrigeration, without transportation or radio or TV, the public will panic, lock its door in trembling fear, and make it much easier for the small but well-led and fully disciplined guerrilla bands to capture the power-centers of each community. Overthrow the government! After complete control is consolidated. Only then allow the people to discover that it was a communist revolution after all" (*An Enemy Hath Done This*, pgs. 192–194).

Now, in light of the above communist plan given by an apostle from communist manuals and that the communist way of governing is supposedly dead, look at the prophecies concerning the breakdown of America and see if the above tactics are not being used today!

"Already combinations are being entered into which are very ominous for the future prosperity, welfare, and happiness of this great republic. The volcanic fires of disordered and anarchical elements are beginning to manifest themselves and exhibit the internal forces that are at work among the turbulent and unthinking masses of the people" (John Taylor, *Journal of Discourses*, April 9 1882, Vol. 23, p. 62).

The next few prophecies have to do with contention and fighting within America during its downfall. Do they not sound like the application of the above communist plan to create so much discord that the government eventually topples?

"Mobs will not decrease but will increase until the whole government becomes a mob, and eventually it will be State against State, city against city, neighborhood against neighborhood, Methodists against Methodists, and so on" (Brigham Young, *Deseret News*, May 1, 1861, Vol. 9, p. 2).

"New York, Boston, Albany, and numerous other cities will be left desolate. Party will be arrayed in deadly strife against party; state against state and the whole nation will be broken up; the sanguinary weapons of the dreadful revolution will devour the land. Then there shall be fleeing from one city to another, from one state to another, from one part of the continent to another, seeking refuge from the devastations of bandits and armies..." (Orson Pratt, *Millennial Star,* October 6, 1866, Vol. 28, p. 633–634).

"It will be a war of neighborhood against neighborhood, city against city, county against county, state against state, and they will go forth destroying and being destroyed, and manufacturing will, in a great measure, cease, for a time, among the American nation. Why? Because in these terrible wars, they will not be privileged to manufacture; there will be too much bloodshed—too much mobocracy—too much going forth in bands and destroying and pillaging the land to suffer people to pursue any local vocation with any degree of safety..." (Orson Pratt, *Journal of Discourses*, March 9, 1879, Vol. 20, p. 151).

[10] "In the nature of things, those who have no property and see their neighbors possess much more than they think them to need, cannot be favorable to laws made for the protection of property. When this class becomes numerous, it grows clamorous. It looks on property as its prey and plunder, and it is naturally ready for violence and revolution" (Daniel Webster, *Great Quotations,* 1820, p. 181).

[11] In light of the present contention over American borders, the many illegal aliens that live in our land against the laws of this land, and the ill feelings of people south of our border towards America because of the treatment of their people, and the prophetic scriptures talking about the Lamanite people [Latinos] and the Gentiles [Americans] take on a new meaning.

"And I say unto you that if the Gentiles do not repent after the blessings which they shall receive after they have scattered my people Then shall ye, who are a remnant of the house of Jacob go forth among them and ye shall be in the midst of them who shall be many; and ye shall be among them as a lion among the beasts of the forests, and as a young lion among the flocks of sheep, who, if he goeth through both treadeth down and teareth in pieces and none can deliver" (3 Nephi 20:15–16).

"And it shall come to pass also that the remnants who are left of the land will marshal themselves, and shall become exceeding angry, and shall vex the Gentiles with a sore vexation" (D&C 87:5).

"To add to the sufferings and great calamities of the American nation, they will be greatly distressed by the aborigines, [Indians were often called aborigines at the time of this statement], who will marshal themselves and become exceeding angry, and vex them with a sore vexation. This event, we believe may not take place in its fullness until the nation has been greatly weakened by the death of millions in their own revolutionary battles. To what extent the Indians will have power over the nation is not stated in this revelation; but from what Jesus informed their forefathers at the time of his personal ministry among them, as recorded in the Book of Mormon, they will have power in a great measure of the whole nation....It appears more improbable, now, to the people of the United States, that the Indians should ever become so powerful an enemy and so dreadful a scourge to them, than it did before the commencement of the rebellion [the civil war] that they would ever engage in so dreadful a civil war as that now raging. Yet this will as surely be fulfilled as have the other portions of the prophecy" (Daniel H. Wells, *Millennial Star*, March 25, 1865, Vol. 27 pgs. 186–7).

[12] "These organizations (the beast, or political entities) were and are grounded on a common philosophy, seek specific objectives, and use a similar methodology. All possess an air of superiority anchored in pride, ambition, vanity, and lust for power. However the fuel that drives their collective engine is derived nether from human ego nor from human spirit but from Lucifer" (Richard D. Draper, *Opening the Seven Seals*, p. 142).

Question: Are we being fed small doses of communism under the guise of politically correct labels? Elder Benson, in his position of Secretary of Agriculture, had a chilling discussion with Nikita Khrushchev about communism. When his comments are considered in light of the political environment today, it makes you wonder about the scripture in Revelation 13:2–3.

"As we talked face-to-face, he [Nikita Khrushchev, First Secretary of the Communist Party of the Soviet Union from 1953 to 1964] indicated that my grandchildren would live under communism. After assuring him that I expected to do all in my power to assure that his and all other grandchildren will live under freedom, he arrogantly declared in substance: You Americans are so gullible. No, you won't accept communism outright, but we'll keep feeding you small doses of socialism until you'll finally wake up and find you already have communism. We won't have to fight you. We'll so weaken your economy until you'll fall like over-ripe fruit into our hands" (Ezra Taft Benson, *An Enemy Hath Done This,* p. 320).

A thought to consider: Could it be that the secret combination in the last days is the beast who was likened to a leopard, bear, and lion (the great ruling powers before him)? This beast received his power and authority from the dragon (meaning the ability to come to power came from Satan). It has seven heads, which indicates it is based out of Europe (Revelation 17:9, Rome was called the city of seven hills") where both powerful banking families as well as strong Antichrist religious powers originate (reflective of powerful rulers in past, present, and future).

"(The beast) seems to be something that under girds and supports governments and leagues in their (antichristian) antireligious movements. Its broad influence and wide domain suggest that this beast should be understood as a philosophical system and political ideology inspired by satanic ideals" (Richard D. Draper, *Opening the Seven Seals*, p. 144).

To continue to analyze Revelation 13:2-3: One head (of the beast) is wounded to death. **Could this be a past power everyone thought was dead?** "And there are seven kings: five are fallen, and one is, and the other is not yet come; and when he cometh, he must continue a short space. And the beast that was, and is not, even he is the eighth, and is of the seven, and goeth into perdition" (Revelation 17:10–11). That head is then miraculously healed, meaning power thought gone and not a threat, comes to ultimate power. This then causes the world to wonder after the beast. Maybe we will ask ourselves when it occurs, "How did this happen?" Might this be the principles of *communism*, or something *like it*, that all people of the world believed was dead...? It's definitely something to think about. Are we sleeping while the enemy is sowing his tares?

"Verily, thus saith the Lord unto you my servants, concerning the parable of the wheat and of the tares: And after they have fallen asleep the great persecutor of the church, the apostate, the whore, even Babylon, that maketh all nations to drink of her cup, in whose hearts the enemy, even Satan, sitteth to reign—behold he soweth the tares; wherefore, the tares choke the wheat and drive the church into the wilderness" (D&C 86:1,3; see also Matthew 13).

Missouri

[13] "...He will speedily fulfill the prophecy in relation to the overthrow of this nation, and their destruction. We shall be obliged to have a government to preserve ourselves in unity and peace; for they, through being wasted away will not have power to govern; for state will be divided against state, city against city, town against town, and the whole country will be in terror and confusion; mobocracy will prevail and there will be no security, through this great Republic, for the lives or property of the people" (Orson Pratt, *Deseret Evening news,* October 2, 1875, Vol. 8, No. 265).

[14] "Without question there are occasions upon which those from the other side of the veil reach out to bless and protect those of us in mortality. Numerous scriptural texts attest to such a thing. Of those who keep their covenant to magnify the priesthood, the Lord said, 'I have given the heavenly hosts and mine angels charge concerning you' (D&C 84:42). Of his missionaries he said: 'Whoso receiveth you, there I will be also, for I will go before your face. I will be on your right hand and on your left, and my Spirit shall be in your hearts, and mine angels round about you, to bear you up' (D&C 84:88). Of those who have been endowed in the temple and have received the promised blessing of protection there, the Lord said they would go forth from his house armed with power and his name would be upon them, his glory round about them, and, he added, 'angels have charge over them' (D&C 109:22)" (Joseph Fielding McConkie, *Answers: Straightforward Answers to Tough Gospel Questions*, p. 113).

[15] According to scriptures and statements by general authorities, guardian angels are real but we are not to suppose that we only have one, or that they follow us around, solving our problems.

"Undoubtedly angels often guard us from accidents and harm, from temptation and sin. They may properly be spoken of as guardian angels. Many people have borne and may bear testimony to the guidance and protection that they have received from sources beyond their natural vision. Without the help that we receive from the constant presence of the Holy Spirit, and from possibly holy angels, the difficulties of life would be greatly multiplied. The common belief, however, that to every person born into the world is assigned a guardian angel to be with that person constantly, is not supported by available evidence. It is a very comforting thought, but at present without proof of its correctness. An angel may be a guardian angel though he come only as assigned to give us special help. In fact, the constant presence of the Holy Spirit would seem to make such a constant, angelic companionship unnecessary" (John A. Widtsoe, as quoted by Daniel H. Ludlow, *A Companion to Your Study of the Doctrine and Covenants*, Vol. 1, p. 558).

CHAPTER SEVENTEEN

INSIDE OUT

"And when we obtain any blessing from God, it is by obedience to that law upon which it is predicated" (D&C 130:21).

00:03:08, 19:20:21, Zulu
Sunday, September 21st

Options Wrought from Obedience

Provo, Utah
9:40 p.m.

Bo flipped the channels of the satellite television programming. On most of the channels, either static or an emergency screen displayed. The international news channels worked, however, and he settled on ITN, a channel out of London. Ironically, it was giving news about America.

"Tragedy continues in the United States as internal strife mounts. A large death toll claims the East Coast in cities such as New York, Baltimore, Washington, D.C., and Miami."

Bo's eyes moved from image to image as they flashed on the screen.

"The dead are left unburied as the nation turns its attention to finding food and water for daily survival. The security systems have been broken down as the military is overwhelmed with looting and fighting. People are flowing into America by the hundreds of thousands on foot from Mexico, adding to the looting, as border patrol and the military have disappeared along Mexico...."

"What are you doing?" asked Corrynne coming into the family room with two cups of hot chocolate. "Did you find a channel that works?"

Bo quickly turned the television off. "The only channel that works is a news channel from England."

"At least the electricity is working. Turn it on," said Corrynne, sitting next to Bo.

Bo looked at Corrynne for a moment and considered the prudence of her request.

"Bo, turn it on. I want to see what's going on," she coaxed again.

"Corrynne, it's all bad news."

"I don't care. I want to know."

Bo turned the power button back on and the TV came back to life. "...UN has set up over one hundred relief stations throughout the more populated areas of the United States to distribute food and water. But it isn't enough for the struggling nation. Travel is limited and if there are needs outside those areas, the people are suffering. In Bangladesh, there's news of..."

Bo turned the TV off. "They're going to report about other nations. I don't want to watch anymore, if that's OK."

"Sure. Now that I know it works, I'll watch it later. I'm sure they'll report that news again," she said as she shrugged and took a sip of her drink.

"I'm sure they will too," said Bo looking idly at his remote, feeling exhausted from a long day of meetings and interviews, let alone the stress of what was happening in his life and his nation.

"Mmmm, Bo, you've got to taste some of your hot chocolate. It's really good."

"Where did you get it?"

"Out of our food supply."

"We had hot chocolate?"

"No, I was in the mood for a treat and saw that we had powdered chocolate, sugar, and milk in our storage, so I blended it all up and heated it in the microwave, and I have to say, it's the best chocolate milk I've ever tasted!"

Bo looked at his steaming cup of chocolate with raised eyebrows. "That really sounds good," he said, thinking he, too, was in the mood for something sweet. He took a drink and the velvety chocolate dripped down his throat giving him instant satisfaction. "Wow, Corrynne, that's really good!"

"Thank you," she said with a smile.

"Did you make more?" he asked looking towards the kitchen.

Corrynne nodded. "Enough for another cup plus."

Bo smiled. "I'm glad the kids are sleeping."

Corrynne laughed. "I'll give them some tomorrow. I think they'll be excited."

Bo took another satisfying sip. It somehow lightened his mood. "Thanks, Corrynne. I needed this."

"No problem," said Corrynne. After a few moments of silence she said, "Wasn't that amazing that Dane called this morning?"

Bo smiled. It was great. It was like a little blessing just for him in return for his repentance. "Yes," he said reflectively. "I figure, if nothing goes wrong and he drives all night, he'll be home tomorrow sometime."

"Tomorrow?" asked Corrynne. "Really? All the way from Illinois?"

Bo nodded. "That's what I'm hoping. If he was smart, he'd drive without stopping anywhere."

Corrynne shook her head and took in a deep breath. "I can't wait to hold him! I'm so happy he's on his way! I just pray the Lord will protect him."

"Ah, he will. Dane didn't die and come back for nothing. He's going to do something here that's important. You just wait and see."

Corrynne adjusted herself on the couch so she could see Bo better and said, "You know, of everything that's happening around us, I can't help but feel we're really blessed. Bo, we have food, water, electricity, the city isn't full of mobs like it is in other places…"

"Because people have things to help them survive."

"Right. Because there's been so many who have listened to the prophet as he has said over and over again to become prepared,[1] pay off debt,[2] and get a food supply."[3]

"There are those that haven't also, Corrynne,"[4] said Bo with a concerned expression.

Corrynne nodded. "I know. You probably know how bad that situation is better than I do since those people go to you for help, but I can guess."

"It's pretty significant,"[5] said Bo taking another sip. "And that fact makes me sad. We have lived in the most prosperous time of our nation, where there was more money per person than any other time, and if you think about it, what food has been the most affordable?"

"Wheat, sugar, salt, the staples of life," said Corrynne.

"Right. So why then are there so many people *not* prepared?"

"Because that's just how it is, Bo. Different people have different priorities. Our place is not to question why, but to answer needs as they are now and be blind to why. Otherwise we'll get angry again."

"You mean I'll get angry again," said Bo looking at Corrynne.

"Maybe," she said with a smile.

"No," said Bo shaking his head. "I won't be getting angry again. It costs me too much."

Corrynne cuddled up to Bo and slipped her arm in his. "I'm glad…Oh, I wanted to tell you, your homemade bread has never tasted so good."

"Really?" asked Bo. "I was worried because the white flour had bugs in it so I didn't use any this time."

"No, it was so good, Bo. You should make it that way every time."

"What do we do with the flour with the bugs in it?" asked Bo.

"We'll just get them out. They aren't dirty bugs. Aren't they just weevils?"

"Well sure, but those are sickening," said Bo with a grimace.

"Maybe, but they're harmless. They're not like flies. You're acting as if you've never seen a weevil before."

"No. I've seen them. It's just that, when I saw them in the flour in the past, I threw it away. Now, with food becoming scarce, I'm realizing I have to get used to them and I'm not feeling good about that."

Corrynne laughed. "You're funny, Bo."

"Why?"

"Because you're such a big man. It's funny to see you're so squeamish with bugs."

"Yeah, yeah, yeah," said Bo with a hint of a smile. "So guess what."

"What?" asked Corrynne.

"In my stake meeting today I learned that the Credit Unions still have money."

"They do?"

"Yes, they aren't backed up by the FDIC or get their money from the Federal Reserve system."

"Who backs them up?"

"The NCUSIF."

"Who's that?"

"The National Credit Union Share Insurance Fund."

"That's a mouthful. What does that mean?"

"It means that our bank has not failed yet. There's reserve that is keeping our system functioning. We still have all our money!"[6]

"That's wonderful! Can you get it out?"

Bo shook his head. "No, we've been urged not to try and get our money out. I have to tell everyone in the ward to just be calm and allow their money to stay in the bank so all the accounts can be serviced. We don't want to force a failure anyway, because that's what's going to happen if everyone tries to get their money out. The only thing that allows a bank to function is the ability to leverage money. That means there's less liquid money in the bank than people have put into it."

"Well that stinks. I want our money," said Corrynne. "I don't want it in a bank anymore."

"I know," said Bo, "but we're really between a rock and a hard place. If we can just keep the public from panicking around here, then we'll be fine. As it is, there's a cap of what we can get out right now, but still, isn't it great it's still there and not sucked up by the IMF?"

"Great. I just feel bad for everyone else."

"I know. I do, too."

Corrynne thought a moment and said, "So you're saying we can go to the bank and get money in the morning and actually go to the store?"

"Well, yes, we can get the money, but no, there's nothing to get at the store. The stores are completely empty again. Nothing left but cardboard boxes and wrappers. Anyway, we don't have to worry. We have enough."

Corrynne nodded. "Oh, I know. I was just hoping we could get some more canned food. We're a little low on those foods from the last time we lived off our food storage, and they seem to make life a little easier. I like just opening a can."

"I have an idea," said Bo.

"What?"

"Don't we still have things to harvest in the garden?"

Corrynne thought for a moment and pulled at her lip, then she said, "Yes. There's five pumpkins. I think there's some carrots still out there and I know there are potatoes and onions still under the ground and tons of tomatoes."

"We could can some of those things—I know it won't make it easier right now, but later, we can just open a can."

Corrynne smiled. "Yes, that's a plan, but I don't want to do it all by myself."

"You won't have to," said Bo. "We'll all help."

"Sold!" said Corrynne.

"And that will beef up our supply until next year when we can harvest more. We'll be just like ma and pa farmer."

"Seeds!" said Corrynne suddenly.

"What's wrong?"

"I don't have any seeds! How are we going to plant another garden without seeds?"

"I thought we had those gardens in a can," said Bo.

"They're gone."

"How?"

"I gave them away as birthday presents to my family."

"Corrynne, why?" asked Bo shaking his head.

"Because we didn't have any money and I wanted to give them a gift. I'm sorry."

Bo shook his head to clear his mind. He wasn't going to let anything bother him. They'd do fine without the seeds. "It's OK. We'll get seeds from the garden we have now."

"How?" asked Corrynne. "I've never successfully harvested seeds for the next year. I've always just bought them."

"How hard can it be?" asked Bo. "It's been done for thousands of years. I'm sure we can figure it out."

"I hope so," said Corrynne looking worried.

"Corrynne, it's simple. We'll take the seeds from the tomatoes and pumpkins and just let them dry. They'll stay, I promise."

"OK, and what about the potatoes and carrots?"

"Those are easy. We'll just leave some potatoes, carrots, and onions in the ground over the winter. They'll come back in the spring."

"Won't they freeze?"

"Not if we insulate them. We can heap up dirt and put grass and leaves around them to make sure that they don't."

"You sure that will work?"

"Yes. I've read some books to tell me how to store them over the winter. We'll be fine."

"OK," said Corrynne. "So what do you think about money? If there's not any food in the stores and there isn't any gas in the stations, do I need to still work at the hospital?"

"I would," said Bo.

"Why?"

"Because there'll be things we'll need money for. Although we don't have much debt because our mortgage is still frozen because of the earthquake, we have some. Bill collectors will want money. We'll have to pay for our electricity and water with money."

"I see what you mean. I'll just have to ride a bike to the hospital. I don't know if I'll like that."

"It's better than walking," said Bo. "Anyway, it's good that we have some way of making something. If the hospital is paying money, we should take it as long as we can."

"Mmmm, I see," said Corrynne nodding. "So what do we do when the hospital can't pay me anymore because they aren't being paid?"

"Then there won't be a reason to go to work, will there?"

"I guess not." Corrynne shook her head. "All this is very strange. I feel like I should wake up any moment."

"I know exactly what you're talking about," said Bo nodding. "But what choices do we have? Survive, or...survive! There are no other choices. We'll simply do what it takes to survive."

"So, here's a question," said Corrynne looking a little uncomfortable.

"What is it?"

"So far, although things have gotten pretty rough, we haven't had anyone in our family die. People are dying all over America, but so far we aren't. How long do you think that's going to last?"[7]

A pain hit Bo's stomach. Corrynne had hit the core of his fears right on the head. "Well," he began and put his arm around Corrynne. "I was told very clearly in a dream that everything we desired—and I mean everything, success, each other, a happy existence, grandchildren, the whole enchilada, everything we care about—would be restored to us in completion and to a degree that we couldn't even imagine."

Corrynne listened intently. "I like how that sounds."

"And because of that, I think we should have confidence that all of this experience is short-term. It will all end and everything will be restored completely."[8]

"Right."

"So when the winds blow, and the rains fall, and when our hearts break because one of us dies, because we all know that all of us will die at some point or another—"

"Right," said Corrynne.

"Then we can find comfort in the words of the prophet and the Savior that whisper peace to us. We can be a happy people if we have faith in their words."[9]

Corrynne sat still for a while. Then she said, "Christ's second coming is soon, isn't it?"

Bo closed his eyes to see if he could feel an answer to his wife's question. The answer he felt was that yes, it was soon, but there was still time left. Accordingly he answered, "Yes, Corrynne, it's soon but not tomorrow and not in a week and probably not for a few years."

"Oh," said Corrynne. "I was kind of hoping it was like in one year, since we only have a year's supply of food."

Bo laughed. "Wouldn't that be perfect?"

"Yes, it would," said Corrynne.

"But don't worry. I have you, you have me, we have our younger children..."

"And our older children," added Corrynne.

Bo nodded, "And our older ones, even though they aren't here and we don't know when we'll see them again, we'll always have them..."

"Right," said Corrynne with a nod.

"I say, thank Heavenly Father for this moment. It's a good one. And this hot chocolate is great," said Bo reaching for his cup and draining the rest of his drink.

"Sounds like a deal," said Corrynne. Then looking up at him she said, "I love you, Bo. You're amazing."

"No, I'm only me, trying to be better."

"Good for me," said Corrynne laying her head on Bo's shoulder.

"And good for me," said Bo feeling very happy and satisfied. Things were going to be OK.

Utah

Orem, Utah
11:15 a.m.

"Dane, wake up. We're in Orem."

Dane opened his eyes and looked out the window, seeing familiar stores go by. He had a mixture of feelings hit him: extreme joy to see things that told him home was very close, but strange awe, to see it so different than how he remembered. Looking around, he had never seen the city so quiet on a Monday afternoon. Usually, at this time, lunch hour was just beginning and the roads were packed with cars. But today, Louise's car was the only one running on the street.

Nebraska was pointing out the window. "Why don't we ever stop at McDonald's?" she complained with longing in her eyes as the arches passed by.

"Because they're closed," explained Louise.

"I hate closed McDonald's!" said Nebraska, angry. "They're stupid!"

"We'll be at my house in a few minutes and I'm sure there'll be a treat for you," said Dane.

"No!!!" she said, beginning to cry. "I hate your house!"

"Dane!" called Louise with a worried voice.

"What?" asked Dane trying to ignore Nebraska's crying that was escalating once again into full shrieking.

"I want McDonald's!" she screamed pounding on the windows.

"There's no one there!" said Dane, wrapping his arms around the little girl. "It's OK. Things will be OK. I'll make you french fries at my house…"

"Dane!" said Louise as the car began to sputter. "This light is on and the temperature gauge indicates the engine is overheating."

Dane abruptly leaned over the front seat to look at the dashboard.

Nebraska stopped crying to see what the emergency was about.

Right then, the car sputtered, jerked, and then stalled in the middle of the street as smoke streamed out from under the hood.

"How long has that light been on?" asked Dane, frustrated to be so close to home and have the car die.

"I'm sorry, but I—I didn't notice it until now," replied Louise, seeming very nervous.

Dane unbuckled his seatbelt and reached back into the now empty back end of the car where his handgun was stored. "I'm going out to see what's going on, you guys stay in here," he said. "Even though Utah has been calmer than other places, we can't be too careful." Then he opened the door and stepped out of the car.

Dane slipped the gun in the waistline at the back of his pants and walked around the car. The hood was so hot, he could barely touch it. He tried once, but his fingers felt like they might burst into flames. He needed to let it cool down a bit. In the meantime he dropped to the ground and wiggled under the car to look at the oil pan. With the oil pan under the car, it was possible that the jump over the fire and the hard landing had cracked it. After wriggling enough to get a good look, Dane realized he was right. There were signs that oil had been leaking for a while.

"Shoot!" said Dane, realizing there was nothing he could do for this one. No stores, no oil, no repairs, meant no transportation. They were stranded.

"Is there a problem?" asked a low voice from somewhere out on the street.

Dane looked to where the voice was coming from and saw shiny black shoes and dark pants from his vantage point. Most likely it was a police officer, or someone parading as one….

Slowly, Dane crawled out from under the car and as he did, there was a sudden scurry of feet.

"He's got a weapon! He's got a weapon!" said a different voice.

Then Dane realized there was more than one police officer.

"Come out with your hands up!" said a commanding voice. "Do *not* reach for your weapon!"

Dane slowly backed out from under the car. As he did, his gun was ripped from his waistband. Slowly, he cleared the car and stood up with his hands in the air.

Immediately his hands were pulled behind his back and he was handcuffed and pushed up against the car, face down on the overheated hood. Dane could hear his skin singeing as his face felt like it was being burned off. *"Ahh!"* yelled Dane squirming and lifting his face off the hood. He could only raise his cheek about an inch above it. The heat was still cooking his face.

"What are you doing, soldier?" asked the first gruff voice who struggled to keep Dane down.

Dane closed his eyes tight, holding his breath in pain.

"Did you defect? Are you a deserter?" asked a second voice.

Dane slightly turned his head to look at the officers. *"No! I'm not a deserter,"* he said trying to find relief for his face and trying to talk, but the officer still had all his weight on his torso, keeping his chest pinned against the car. He couldn't take an adequate breath.

"What military are you from?" asked the first again.

"The National Police," said Dane continuing to gasp for air.

"I found more weapons in the car," said a third officer.

Dane stretched his neck to look up at the windshield to see two more police searching the car with Nebraska sitting in Louise's lap in the driver's seat.

"Hey!" yelled Dane, finally able to stand slightly. "I need my gear. That's federal property."

"Shut up!" said the first officer putting more pressure on Dane's back. "Only speak when we ask you a question."

Dane refused to put his head back onto the hood. His back was getting tired, but he thought he could hang on a little longer.

Dane knew why he was being treated this way, and deep down, he didn't blame them. The police were just as distrustful of him as he was of them. It was hard times and obviously, they had been successful at keeping the peace in this area, something other towns hadn't been able to do. To do that the authorities had to be unyielding until completely sure of the truth.

"Do you see any ID?" the first officer asked one of the others searching the car.

"No," said another.

"Not yet, Sergeant."

"Let's lock this guy up 'til we can get things sorted out," said the Sergeant.

"No!" exclaimed Dane standing up again, *"I have to get..."*

"I told you to speak only when you're spoken to!" said the Sergeant as he put an elbow painfully into Dane's back and yanked up on his arms.

"Ahh!" yelled Dane as his bound arms were pulled high up behind his back, threatening to dislocate his shoulders, and planting his face once again on the hot hood.

"What's that?" asked the second officer with a strange tone to his voice. "I've been bit!" he said batting something out of the air.

Dane looked up in time to see a swarm of bugs attacking the four officers. The Sergeant released his grip on Dane as he too fought off the stinging insects.

Dane ducked down and then wiggled under the car again. There weren't any bugs under the car. It was still too hot.

Dane watched a few minutes of yelling and running from below the car as all four officers eventually passed out onto the pavement. Something strange was going on.

"Dane?" called Louise.

"Dane?" mimicked Nebraska as she looked under the car. "Come out. Louise beat up those bad guys with her glasses," she said.

Dane furrowed his eyebrows as he tried to figure out what had just happened. He wiggled back out from beneath the car and stood up and surveyed the now quiet scene. "What happened out here?" he asked, looking from one unconscious officer to another, then back to Louise. "What's Nebraska talking about?" asked Dane.

Louise had an innocent look and ignored his question. "Let's go. Which way to your house?"

"Now wait!" said Dane. "Tell me what happened!"

"She used her glasses," said Nebraska jumping up and down pointing to Louise's pocket.

Louise walked toward the officers and began going through their pockets. "The keys to those cuffs should be here somewhere."

"They're on the sergeant," said Dane. "Are these men dead?" he asked.

Louise found the keys she was looking for and unlocked Dane's hands. "No, they're not dead," she said calmly.

"What are they then?" asked Dane, getting more and more insistent, turning to look Louise in the eye. "Who are you?"

Louise stared back with cool gray eyes. She looked like she was considering her words carefully. Finally, she said, "You don't want to know. Now just show us which way to go and be thankful you're not in jail."

Dane was so confused. He decided to look at the officers himself. Each one had multiple sting wounds on their neck and face but no signs of even one insect. "So are these guys going to recover?" he asked.

Louise nodded. "We have about fifteen minutes—no, ten now," she said looking at her watch. "They won't remember what they were doing when they passed out, so I think we're pretty safe. Get your gear and let's go," she said to Dane.

Dane reluctantly gathered his things from the various officers and put them back in his pack. After zipping up the pack, he put his vest on and threw his pack and gun over his shoulder. "My house is down about five miles from here. We should go down these neighborhood streets instead of traveling on the main one."

"Sounds good," said Louise with a practical smile. "Let's go." Then with a hand out to Nebraska she said, "Come on, sweetheart. Just a little further."

"Can I do that bug trick?" asked Nebraska jumping up and down.

"No," said Louise.

"Please?" asked Nebraska. "Please?"

"No, honey."

"Please, please, please…"

Dane walked slightly ahead of his companions as he thought about what had just happened. Obviously Louise wasn't as helpless as he had thought, nor was she *anything* he had thought she had been. What was that secret weapon she had used to harness insects? What kind of insects could sting targets with expected outcomes? And what did glasses have to do with it? But the real question was *who was Louise*? Was she some secret agent? A spy of some sort? Was she safe to take to his house? Or was he leading someone undesirable right into the heart of his home?

Dane had five miles to make up his mind.

Snowy Marriage

Yamal Peninsula, Russia
8:30 p.m.

Chenille blinked slowly as she smiled flirtatiously at Braun. She was coming towards him, up a snowy path between rows of kind tribal people.

In the evening light as if noon day, it was perfectly white, as the sun filtered through the thick, white clouds. Heaven was in the air as Braun and Chenille prepared to be joined together in marriage. He couldn't believe the day had finally come to make Chenille his bride! He had waited forever for this day, yet it had snuck up on him in a moment.

Braun couldn't help but gaze at his soon-to-be wife. The snow fell on her perfect complexion, accenting her cheekbones, her eyebrows, and her lips. There was only one word for her: *exquisite*. Everything about her was beautiful. As he watched her walk it was like she was walking in slow motion. She was dressed in the Nenet wedding white furs that flowed down to the ground and trailed behind her. The women of this tribe had selflessly made them from white reindeer hides for this moment. Chenille's blonde hair cascaded down her back and shoulders as the wind gently toyed with it, lifting it and twisting it in patterns, interweaving the snow in its gentle waves.

Braun felt dizzy, caught in a vortex of emotions as Chenille moved closer and closer to him. His dreams were about to come true.

When Chenille had made the final steps towards him, Braun knelt at the marriage altar, made of bone, as Elder John Zebedee stood at the end. Chenille knelt across from Braun and slipped her hand out of her fur glove and under the fur hand-warmer that lay flat on the alter. Braun did the same.

As Chenille's hand touched his, Braun was beside himself in thankfulness. Holding her hand, with her eyes looking into his, was his deepest wish and now it was happening. His marriage, although temporal now because of the lack of a temple, he knew would eventually be sealed up to eternity as soon as they could reach a temple. Oh, how merciful the Lord was!

"Braun and Chenille," said John. "I, having the authority to marry you, pronounce upon your heads every blessing God wishes for you. I promise you children, and joy in your children, forever as you continue in faithfulness to the house of the Lord. I promise you many days and nights of satisfaction as you serve each other and an eternity of happiness. I promise you friendship without end in your companionship and love without measure. I promise you the strength to keep your marriage happy and whole in the coming days of tribulation. I promise you the desires of your hearts as you strive to serve your Savior." Looking to Chenille John continued. "Chenille, do you take this man, Braun Joseph Rogers, to marry, through good times and bad times, to be only his forever?"

"Yes," said Chenille with a smile, looking radiant.

"Braun, do you take this woman, Chenille Kay Chamberlain, to marry, through good times and bad times, eventually to be hers forever, after being sealed at the hands of Ephraim at the holy alter of the temple?"

"Yes," said Braun nodding.

"Then, by the power and authority given to me at the hands of Jesus the Christ, I pronounce you husband and wife. You, Braun, may kiss your sweet Chenille, your bride," said John with a satisfied smile.

Braun leaned over the altar and his lips gently met Chenille's in a soft and lingering kiss.

A wave of clapping ensued as the tribal people watched, not understanding the words but understanding the meaning of the universal gesture.

Braun was lost in Chenille's presence and in that moment, eternity began, the walls fell, and the windows opened. With his wife at his side, he felt their power would be unstoppable. It was a new beginning and nothing else mattered in the world.

Conflict

Denali Federal Prison Camp,
Denali National Park, Alaska
9:40 a.m.

"All out!" yelled the prison guard.

Carea stepped out the back of the bus. Her legs and back were stiff from sitting so long squished into the narrow seats.

The cold air hit her like a punch in the face and it took her breath away. She wrapped her arms around herself to keep warm as she immediately started to shiver. Carea struggled to get her legs to move. She was shaking so bad it was hard to take steps, but she carefully made it down the stairs and stood trembling among the other forlorn-looking girls.

After everyone had unloaded from the bus, blankets and packs were tossed on the ground. The doors slammed with a bang and the engine started.

Carea looked up at the vehicle as it pulled away. She wanted to run after it, but she didn't. Instead she just watched it go, too stunned to move. The bus pulled through the gates and then they too closed with a slam. Carea was stuck.

"Where are they going?" Carea asked Octavia who was standing beside her.

"Away from here, I guess," Octavia said.

"At least they left supplies," said Carea looking at the pile of grey folded blankets lying on the frozen ground as snowflakes floated down upon them.

"I bet they're not very warm ones," said Octavia numbly, shaking uncontrollably.

Carea looked at the blankets with a frown. "They have to be, or we'd die. I don't think they want us to die."

Suddenly, a swarm of people making clicking noises and all clad in masks made out of strips of material, rushed the girls and stole the blankets and packs off the ground.

Quickly, Carea ran after the group. She was very fast and within seconds she had pounced on one person's back, bringing them to the ground. With a powerful thrust, Carea turned the person over and snatched the stolen supplies right from their grasp. "That's my blanket and bag, thank you!" she said with triumph.

Turning she walked back to the group when she felt something sharp and cold at her neck. "Stop right there!" said the voice.

Carea did as she was asked.

In a gritty, angry voice she heard. "Here, those bags and supplies are *ours*." Then a young, but man-sized, hand pulled the bags out of her grasp and threw her to the ground.

Carea looked back behind her to see the man disappear into a thicket of trees. Turning to the girls she realized the scene had caused hopelessness to creep into a group of girls that were already wounded. Suddenly, energy grew within her and she sprung to her feet. No! She would not accept defeat! She would get back those bags! With the speed of lightning, she too disappeared into the woods.

Cloak in the Darkness

Provo, Utah
6:00 p.m.

A ringing noise came from the nightstand in Corrynne's bedroom. She looked over at her cell from the bathtub. From her angle it looked like its face was lit up. That meant she had heard right. *It had rung!* She was intrigued. Now, it had rung twice in two days. That hadn't happened in over a week. She had an impulse to check it. Maybe it was Dane again. He was overdue to be home. But then she looked back at her twins in the water. She'd wait till she got them out of the tub. They were at the age when it was too dangerous to leave them in the tub, even for a second. They were too round and slippery.

"Come on little ones, it's time to get out of the bathtub," she said. The twins were happily wiggling around on their bellies just under the water. They were pretending they were alligators.

"No!" said Striynna who looked up at her mother innocently.

"No?" asked Corrynne with a little grin. "No?" she repeated as she reached down into the water and tickled Striynna. "You can't say 'no' to me."

Striynna let out a lilting giggle that filled the room.

"No!" said Strykker, mimicking his sister with a look of glee. Obviously, he wanted to be tickled, too.

Corrynne tickled Strykker and he too began laughing. Then with a big sweep, she pulled both babies out of the water at the same time.

"Ahhh!" yelled Striynna reaching back for the water. "I a a-igator! I a a-igator!"

Quickly, Corrynne laid her twins on two towels that she had set out on the floor before she had even put the babies in the tub. She had to move quickly before the wiggling started. Slippery bodies meant danger.

Corrynne wrapped both the babies up and then continued to tickle them. She had to distract them from screaming. "I'm an alligator eater!" she said as she pretended to bite Striynna's belly.

Striynna laughed uncontrollably.

"'Ee too!" said Strykker with a big smile on his face as it peeked out from the towel.

Corrynne in turn pretended to bite Strykker's belly too as he melted in laughter.

Again, Corrynne heard another ringing. She looked back at her cell phone again. Was that another text message? She jumped up, "I'll be right back, stay right there, alligators," she coaxed.

Quickly Corrynne rushed over to her phone and opened it up. Yes, she had received two text messages. She selected the first to read. It said, "Hi Mom."

Corrynne was surprised. Who could this be from? Was it Dane again? She selected "view" to look at the details of the message. She didn't recognize the number. Quickly, she went back to the number that Dane had called her from, but it was completely different. Now she was confused.

Corrynne looked up to check on the twins. Striynna had wiggled out of her towel and was attempting to get back in the bathtub with one ankle up on the side. Strykker was still all bundled up and watching his sister.

"No, no, no, Striynna," said Corrynne as she rushed to her daughter. "You're going to slip and hit your head. No more bathtub."

"Ahhhhhhhh!" screamed Striynna as her mother picked her up. And then the wiggling began. Striynna continued screaming and wiggling to try and get free of Corrynne's grasp, but Corrynne was used to this. Immediately she placed her firmly on the floor. Right as Striynna arched her back in a fit, Corrynne slid the diaper under her bum. Then when she began to kick her legs, Corrynne slid the diaper between her legs and fastened it on both sides. She had to be quick, or Striynna would wiggle right off the diaper and it would end up around her thighs.

Next Corrynne pulled a snap tee-shirt out of the pile of clothes and pulled it over Striynna's head and arms. She snapped it between her baby's legs as Striynna continued to scream at the top of her lungs.

Striynna turned over and began to crawl away but Corrynne caught her ankle and pulled her back. "Come back here. I've got to put your pajamas on. You like your pajamas," she said as she flipped her baby on to her back.

"Noooooo!" yelled Striynna. "No jamas! I a a-igator!"

Corrynne tried the tickle trick again. "You're a Striynna Chandelle, you're not an alligator," she said as she tickled with one hand and quickly grabbed the corner of Striynna's floor-length sleeper with the other. After shaking the folds out with a quick whip she attempted to put the neck hole over Striynna's head but she wiggled out.

Corrynne tried again, but obviously she wasn't as good at tickling with one hand because Striynna was not overcome with giggles. Instead she held her breath and her face turned red as she continued to arch her back to get away. "Striynna, stop being a pill," said Corrynne as she pulled her sleeper over her head for the second time.

"I a a-igator!" Striynna demanded as Corrynne finally succeeded in putting the sleeper on her baby. Corrynne pulled the material down around Striynna's ankles.

"Fine, be an alligator," said Corrynne as she released her stubborn little daughter.

Striynna stood up and looked at her mother for a second with her little tongue sticking out at the corner of her mouth; she was obviously planning something.

Corrynne suddenly realized she had left the water in the bathtub. Then she knew the plan! Striynna was going to try and get back into the tub! Quickly Corrynne jumped up and rushed for the bathtub. Striynna screamed a bloodcurdling scream and her face turned a purple-red as the water started to go down the drain.

"No bathtub. We'll take another bath tomorrow—maybe," added Corrynne, wondering if bath time was getting too hazardous.

Striynna fell dramatically to the floor and began to kick and scream.

Corrynne turned back to Strykker who was still wrapped up snug in his towel with wide eyes watching his sister.

"She's silly isn't she?" asked Corrynne as she took her little calm son in her arms.

Strykker looked at Corrynne for a moment but then looked back at his sister.

Corrynne knew that Striynna would entertain Strykker the whole time she would dress him. This was their routine every night.

Slowly Corrynne dressed Strykker who cooperated perfectly. This was her rest period from Striynna. Even though she was screaming, it was a relief to not have to wrestle another baby. Heavenly Father knew she could only handle one wild one this time around.

After Corrynne was finished with Strykker, her mind returned to her phone. There was another text message she hadn't read. She got up from her place on the floor and moved back to her nightstand. Flipping her phone open she looked at the second text message. It was from the same number as the message before it.

Corrynne looked back at her twins. Strykker was sitting close to Striynna, but not close enough to get kicked. He had learned to stay clear during her fits.

Striynna was still crying but she was beginning to lose steam. It still would be a few minutes till this was over. It had only been going on for eight minutes. There were probably at least five more to go.

Corrynne returned to look at her phone and hit the message button quickly. She had to know what it said.

The second message was simple too. It said, "Can I come over tonight?"

Corrynne bit her lip. Obviously this wasn't Dane. He was probably far away still. So, if it wasn't him, who could it be? It couldn't be Braun. He was in hiding on the other side of the world. She knew it wasn't Conrad. There was no way to get out of Israel. The borders had been closed for over a month. It couldn't be Brea. She couldn't leave wherever she was hiding. It was too risky. Matt had emphasized that. Then Carea…the littlest thought of

Carea made Corrynne dissolve into uncontrollable tears. She was the one child she felt the worst about. She felt like she had let her down. Why did she let her go to school? Why didn't she home-school her like she had wanted to a long time ago? She knew there was a risk of more danger. She had felt it. Why hadn't she listened? Why hadn't she taken precautions?

Bo walked into the room and stood at the doorway.

Corrynne looked up and immediately wiped her tears. She didn't want Bo to know how tortured she was feeling inside at that moment. After all his emotions, this would not be good for him.

"What's going on in here?" asked Bo.

Corrynne forced a smile and said, "Oh, the normal routine."

Bo shook his head and reached out for Corrynne. "No, the routine entails Striynna crying—not you."

"I know," said Corrynne. "But I didn't want her to feel left out."

Taking Corrynne in his arms, Bo said, "Are you having a hard day?"

Corrynne shook her head and said, "Only a hard few minutes. I was fine ten minutes ago."

"What's different?"

Corrynne considered whether or not she should show Bo her messages. Would it make him feel sad too?

"Corrynne?" asked Bo. "What's wrong?"

Corrynne looked up at her husband and then couldn't help herself. She began to weep into his chest.

Bo didn't say anything else right then, he just wrapped his arms around his wife. That was nice, because Corrynne knew they had gone through this with him. He could have ignored her because of his own pain, but he didn't and she was thankful. Her own feelings of helplessness and mourning hadn't been addressed, yet they were so pronounced. Right now she just needed to cry and Bo needed to let her.

There was a little tug on Corrynne's jeans.

Looking down, there was Strykker's angel face looking up with concern at his mother. "Hi, baby," she said and managed a smile.

Strykker stiffened his body and made a grunting noise. That always meant he wanted to be picked up. It was sign language that Corrynne understood and she was glad to pick her little son up. His nearness calmed all her mourning. It soothed her soul.

"What's going on?" she asked her son who immediately looked back at Striynna, whose fit had diminished to a whimpering now.

"Do you think she's done having a fit?" asked Bo.

"Maybe, if we ignore her," said Corrynne. "Don't say anything to her right now or she'll start up again."

"OK," said Bo as he turned back to Corrynne. "So, is there anything I can do?"

Corrynne thought a moment as she hugged Strykker and smelled his fresh, clean skin. Rubbing her cheek softly against his she wondered if she gave the phone to Bo, would she hold it together to talk to him about it? Finally, she handed the phone to her husband.

"I received two text messages."

"That's what upset you?"

"Yes," said Corrynne without further explanation. She would let Bo figure things out on his own. The less she said, the better it would be.

Bo read the text messages and looked up at Corrynne. "Did you return this text?"

Corrynne scoffed, "No."

"Why not?"

"Because, this can't be real. The only one who might be thinking of coming over is too far away to do it tonight."

"How do you know if you don't answer it?" asked Bo. "Maybe this isn't a joke, maybe it's an answer to a prayer."

Corrynne looked at Bo considering his comments. Could he be right? Could she even dare to hope? An overwhelming urge to cry again welled up inside her. She took a deep breath and buried her face in Strykker's little chest to hide her emotions.

"Here, I'll do it for you," said Bo as he typed a text and sent it to the sender.

"There, it's done."

Corrynne lifted her head and said, "What'd you write?"

"I asked who it was that wrote the text."

Within seconds, a response came. The phone lit up and the little tune rang. It stunned Corrynne. Whoever was writing the text was waiting and very quick with the typing.

"Do you want to read it?" asked Bo, offering Corrynne's phone back.

Corrynne shook her head. "No, go ahead. I'm good right here, hiding behind Strykker."

Bo smiled and then flipped the phone open. Taking a second, then with a puzzled look he then turned the phone so Corrynne could read the message. "I'm not good at these kinds of puzzles."

"What does it say?"

"It says, 'Third to come, three in one, third to leave, but first in your heart, and last to leave again'."

Corrynne shook her head, "See? It is a joke. Who would answer a text like that?"

Bo studied Corrynne's face as he thought about the riddle. "I don't know, Corrynne. I think we should think about this. Who's third in our family, three in one, and third to leave?"

Corrynne thought for a moment. "I'm assuming the third to come means, third to be born. If that's the case, it would be Brea."

"Yes, and she's three people in one right now."

"And she was the third to leave. She was married right after Conrad went on his mission and Braun was in Europe!"

"Right."

"Do you think it's really her? Matt said there couldn't be any communication."

"Maybe he changed his mind. Or maybe he found a way for Brea to talk to us. He did say that's what he wanted. I bet he's just resourceful enough to figure that one out. Ask her a question only she would know."

Corrynne handed Strykker to Bo and took the phone back. Quickly, she wrote, "If u r u, then tell me what time it is." Then she sent the text.

A second later, there was a ring somewhere outside Corrynne's bedroom door. "What was that?" she asked, alarmed.

Then there was a swishing sound as a person in a floor length hooded brown dress came around the corner.

Corrynne's body went on alert; who was in her house?

"It's bath time, Mom," said a feminine voice as the hood fell down and exposed the beautiful face of Brea.

Corrynne couldn't contain herself. She bolted over to her daughter as she exploded in tears once again. She hugged Brea as Brea, too, began to cry. Both of the women just held each other, shaking and full of emotion.

"Oh, Brea! Are you really here?" asked Corrynne looking at her oldest daughter, studying every part of her sweet face.

"Yes, Mother, I'm here. I've come to be with you."

"Oh, that's wonderful!" said Corrynne hugging Brea once again. "I don't know how this is true, but it's the best thing that could possibly happen right now."

"I know. It is for me too," said Brea with tears running down her face.

Corrynne had to hug Brea again, just to make sure she was really feeling her daughter in her arms.

Corrynne felt a pat on her leg. She knew that was Striynna. She wanted to be picked up now too. Corrynne quickly picked her baby up. "See who's here? It's Brea!"

Striynna immediately leaned over to give Brea a hug.

Corrynne looked back at Bo and he winked. Then it dawned on her. He had known about this. Somehow he had arranged it. She held out an arm to him and he and Strykker joined the group. Together they stood all in each other's arms. The joy was beyond words. They had been blessed.

Notes to "Inside Out"

Options Wrought by Obedience

[1] "I do not know what the future holds. I do not wish to sound negative, but I wish to remind you of the warnings of scripture and the teachings of the prophets which we have had constantly before us. I cannot forget the great lesson of Pharaoh's dream of the fat and lean kine and of the full and withered stalks of corn. I cannot dismiss from my mind the grim warnings of the Lord as set forth in the 24th chapter of Matthew. I am familiar, as are you, with the declarations of modern revelation that the time will come when the earth will be cleansed and there will be indescribable distress, with weeping and mourning and lamentation (see D&C 112:24). Now, I do not wish to be an alarmist. I do not wish to be a prophet of

doom. I am optimistic. I do not believe the time is here when an all-consuming calamity will overtake us. I earnestly pray that it may not. There is so much of the Lord's work yet to be done. We, and our children after us, must do it.…Are these perilous times? They are. But there is no need to fear. We can have peace in our hearts and peace in our homes. We can be an influence for good in this world, every one of us" (Gordon B. Hinckley, "The Times in Which We Live," *Ensign*, Nov 2001, p. 72).

[2] "…I am suggesting that the time has come to get our houses in order. So many of our people are living on the very edge of their incomes. In fact, some are living on borrowings.…There is a portent of stormy weather ahead to which we had better give heed.…I urge you, brethren, to look to the condition of your finances. I urge you to be modest in your expenditures; discipline yourselves in your purchases to avoid debt to the extent possible. Pay off debt as quickly as you can, and free yourselves from bondage. This is a part of the temporal gospel in which we believe. May the Lord bless you, my beloved brethren, to set your houses in order. If you have paid your debts, if you have a reserve, even though it be small, then should storms howl about your head, you will have shelter for your wives and children and peace in your hearts. That's all I have to say about it, but I wish to say it with all the emphasis of which I am capable" (Gordon B. Hinckley, "To the Boys and to the Men," *Ensign*, Nov 1998, p. 51).

[3] "We encourage Church members worldwide to prepare for adversity in life by having a basic supply of food and water and some money in savings. We ask that you be wise as you store food and water and build your savings. Do not go to extremes; it is not prudent, for example, to go into debt to establish your food storage all at once. With careful planning, you can, over time, establish a home storage supply and a financial reserve" (The First Presidency, *All Is Safely Gathered In: Family Home Storage*, Feb. 2007, p. 1).

[4] "Recent surveys of Church members have shown a serious erosion in the number of families who have a *year's supply* of life's necessities. Most members plan to do it. Too few have begun. We must sense again the spirit of the persistent instruction given by Elder Harold B. Lee as he spoke to the members in 1943: Again there came counsel in 1942. '…We renew our counsel, said the leaders of the Church, and repeat our instruction: Let every Latter-day Saint that has land, produce some valuable essential foodstuff thereon and then preserve it' (In Conference Report, April 1943, p. 127.)" (Thomas S. Monson, "Guiding Principles of Personal and Family Welfare," *Ensign*, Sep 1986, p. 3).

"Many more people could ride out the storm-tossed waves in their economic lives if they had their year's supply of food …and were debt-free. Today we find that many have followed this counsel in reverse: *they have at least a year's supply of debt and are food-free*" (Thomas S. Monson, "That Noble Gift—Love at Home," *Church News*, May 12, 2001, p. 7, italics added).

[5] "Then shall the kingdom of heaven be likened unto ten virgins, which took their lamps, and went forth to meet the bridegroom. And five of them were wise, and five were foolish. They that were foolish took their lamps, and took no oil with them: But the wise took oil in their vessels with their lamps…" (See Matthew 25 for the complete parable).

Although this parable is not about temporal, but spiritual preparedness, it is true that those who are spiritually prepared will follow the prophet in becoming prepared for the last days, where those who are not, will not.

"Taking a slightly different view, as is often appropriate in interpreting parables, 'The virgins typify those who profess a belief in Christ, and who, therefore, confidently expect to be included among the blessed participants at the feast. The lighted lamp, which each of the maidens carried, is the outward profession of Christian belief and practice; and in the oil reserves of the wiser ones we may see the spiritual strength and abundance which diligence and devotion in God's service alone can insure.' (Talmage, pgs. 578–579.) This precious parable pertains to the last days; it is now beginning to be fulfilled and will be finally consummated when the Bridegroom comes....All are members of the Church; the contrast is not between the wicked and the worthy. Instead, five are zealous and devoted, while five are inactive and lukewarm; ten have the testimony of Jesus, but only five are valiant therein. Hence, five shall enter into the house where Jesus is and five shall remain without—all of which raises the question: What portion of the Church shall be saved? Surely this parable is not intended to divide half the saints into one group and half into another. But it does teach, pointedly and plainly, that there are foolish saints who shall fail to gain the promised rewards (Bruce R. McConkie, *Doctrinal New Testament Commentary*, Vol. 1, p. 685).

[6] This is a literary extrapolation made on the premise that if the Federal Reserve became crippled, this banking system might remain due to it's independence from the powers that control the Federal Reserve.

[7] Will the Saints be able to escape the days that are coming? It's clear that we will have tragedy among us, but we will control it through the priesthood. See the following dream of John Taylor:

"Some of my brothers present have been asking me what is coming to pass, what is the wind blowing up. I will answer you right here what is coming to pass shortly. I was immediately in Salt Lake City, wandering about the streets. In all parts of the city and on the door of every house I found a badge of mourning, and I cold not find a house but what was in mourning....It seemed strange to me that I saw no person on the street in my wandering about through the city. They seemed to be in their houses with their sick and dead. I saw no funeral processions or anything of the kind, but the city looked very still and quiet. The people were praying and had control of the disease, what ever it was. I then looked in all directions over the territory, east, west, north, and south, and found the same mourning in every place throughout the land" (John Taylor, *Journal of Wilford Woodruff*, Dec 17 1877, p. 179).

[8] "Through centuries of time, men and women, so very, very many, have lived and died. Some may die in the conflict that lies ahead. To us, and we bear solemn testimony of this, death will not be the end. There is life beyond this as surely as there is life here. Through the great plan which became the very essence of the War in Heaven, men shall go on living. Job asked, 'If a man die, shall he live again?' (Job 14:14) He replied: 'For I know that my redeemer liveth, and that he shall stand at the latter day upon the earth: And though after my skin worms destroy this body, yet in my flesh shall I see God: Whom I shall see for myself, and mine eyes shall behold, and not another' (Job 19:25–27). Now, brothers and sisters, we must do our duty, whatever that duty might be. Peace may be denied for a season. Some of our liberties may be curtailed. We may be inconvenienced. We may even be called on to suffer in one way or another. But God our Eternal Father will watch over this nation and all of the civilized world who look to Him. He has declared, 'Blessed is the nation whose God is the Lord' (Ps. 33:12). Our safety lies in repentance. Our strength comes of obedience to the *commandments* of God" (Gordon B. Hinckley, "The Times in Which We Live," *Ensign*, Nov 2001, p. 72).

[9] "Where is peace? Can we ever enjoy this great gift while wars, rumors of wars, discord, evil, and contention swirl all around us? The answer is yes....Certainly peace is the opposite of fear. Peace is a blessing that comes to those who trust in God. It is established through individual righteousness. True personal peace comes about through eternal vigilance and constant righteous efforts. No man can be at peace who is untrue to his better self. No man can have lasting peace who is living a lie. Peace can never come to the transgressor of the law. Commitment to God's laws is the basis for peace. Peace is something we earn. It is not a gift. Rather, it is a possession earned by those who love God and work to achieve the blessings of peace. It is not a written document. It is something that must come from within....True peace must not be dependent upon conditions or happenings. Peace must stem from an inward contentment built upon trust, faith, and goodwill toward God, fellowmen, and self. It must be constantly nurtured by the individual who is soundly anchored to the gospel of Jesus Christ. Only then can a person realize that the trials and tribulations of daily life are less important than God's total goodness. Lasting peace is an eternal personal quest. Peace does come from

obedience to the law. Peace comes to those who develop character and trust" (Marvin J. Ashton, "Peace—A Triumph of Principles," *Ensign*, Nov 1985, p. 69).

A THOUGHT TO PROVOKE THOUGHT...

"We are apt to shut our eyes against a painful truth, and listen to the song of that siren, till she transforms us into beasts. Is this the part of wise men, engaged in a great and arduous struggle for liberty? Are we disposed to be of the number of those who having eyes see not, and having ears, hear not, the thing which so nearly concern their temporal salvation? For my part whatever anguish of spirit it might cost**, I am willing to know the whole truth; to know the worst and to provide for it**" (Patrick Henry, March 23, 1775, *Prophets, Principles, and National Survival,* p. 516, as quoted by Ezra Taft Benson, *An Enemy Hath Done This*, p. 66).

MILLENNIAL GLORY VII

UNITED WE STAND

Look for it 2008!

www.millennialglory.com

AUTHOR
WENDIE L. EDWARDS

Wendie L. Edwards, the author of the "Millennial Glory" series, grew up in Edmonds, Washington. At Brigham Young University she met her husband Ted and they were sealed in the Seattle Temple. She taught early morning Seminary for the Lynnwood Stake in Washington. After five children, Ted and Wendie felt inspired to return to Brigham Young University where Ted received his Master's degree in Tax Accounting and Wendie graduated Cum Laude with a Bachelor's degree in Nursing. Wendie has been an Intensive Care nurse for eleven years and holds a CCRN certification. Ted and Wendie reside in Provo with their seven sons and two daughters.

EDITOR
KATHRYN PACKER

Kathryn Packer, the editor of The Millennial Glory Series, is a BYU-Hawaii graduate with a B.S. in Information Systems and Computer Science. She is a technical writer and trainer by day and uses her memberships in the Society for Technical Communication and the American Society for Training & Development to keep her updated in current trends. Kathryn spent most of her growing up years on a small farm in Idaho raising sheep and other small animals with her 5 siblings. She currently resides in Bothell, Washington. Her true passions include traveling, music, quilting, reading, and fine art, not necessarily in that order.

STUDENT EDITOR
KATE MARYON

Kate Maryon is a soon-to-be graduate of Brigham Young University and is currently getting her degree as an English major with an emphasis in editing. She grew up in Orem, Utah and is the oldest of three kids. Books are the true love of her life, but she also enjoys music, movies, hiking, and theater. She is truly grateful for the opportunity to help in the production of the Millennial Glory books!